OXFORD RESEARCH STUDIES IN GEOGRAPHY

Water and Tribal Settlement in South-East Arabia

A Study of the *Aflāj* of Oman

J. C. Wilkinson

CLARENDON PRESS · OXFORD
1977

Oxford University Press, Walton Street, Oxford OX2 6DP
OXFORD LONDON GLASGOW NEW YORK
TORONTO MELBOURNE WELLINGTON CAPE TOWN
IBADAN NAIROBI DAR ES SALAAM LUSAKA ADDIS ABABA
KUALA LUMPUR SINGAPORE JAKARTA HONG KONG TOKYO
DELHI BOMBAY CALCUTTA MADRAS KARACHI

British Library Cataloguing in Publication Data

Wilkinson, John Craven
Water and tribal settlement in South-east Arabia.—(Oxford research studies in geography).
1. Irrigation canals and flumes 2. Irrigation—Oman
I. Title II. Series
338.1'6 HD1741.0/

ISBN 0-19-823217-9

Printed in Great Britain by Fletcher & Son Ltd, Norwich

EDITORIAL PREFACE

Since at present little is known of the historical and economic geography of Oman, in the southeastern corner of the Arabian peninsula, Dr Wilkinson's study contributes substantially to our knowledge of this marginal area.

Dr Wilkinson has long been interested in the rural society of the interior of Oman, where the survival of agricultural settlements has rested for ages on the *qanāt aflāj*. This term describes the extensive networks of ancient artificial, subterranean channels which drain the meager water resources of the area toward the villages. Complex and fragile irrigation systems of this kind are to be found in various places scattered through the vast afro-asian desert belt from the Western Sahara (where they are called *fuggāra*) to Iran and Central Asia (where the usual name is *qanāt*). In Oman the antiquity, extent, and relatively decayed condition of the *qanāt aflāj* merited investigation.

In relating the successive stages of settlement to the water supply and its management, the author has endeavoured to elucidate the involved and multi-faceted water-man-land relationships which prevailed in Oman before the recent advent of the oil economy. His data is drawn from many sources, including modern Arabic and Western literature on these matters, ancient documents, and careful surveys conducted in the field. Re-tracing where possible the political, social and economic history of Oman, he shows the eventful evolution of its human geography.

The book provides a documented case in a little explored part of the world for the analysis of concordance and conflict between a water dependent community and its social structure. The author suggests a new method of relating the study of water supply, settlement pattern and tribal structure in countries such as Oman. A better understanding of these traditional features of the local society should help its present rapid evolution.

J.G. J.A.S.
F.V.E. C.D.H.

February, 1977

ACKNOWLEDGEMENTS

The chance to acknowledge the help of all those who made the production of this book possible should have proved the one moment of unadulterated pleasure in writing it. In the event the pleasure is attenuated, because the need to select certain individuals to thank specifically may make others think I am unappreciative of their help. This particularly concerns me in the case of those who went out of their way to look after me when I was working in the field. Yet to have to choose certain names from amongst the many who offered me hospitality would be the most invidious task of all, and so I ask them as a group to accept my best thanks and excuse this anonymous fashion of proffering it.

The same applies to the individual members of those corporate institutions which made my research financially possible or allowed me to make use of reports belonging to them; in particular I regret not naming some of my friends and former colleagues in Shell International Petroleum Company without whose understanding and help I should never have been in a position to have pursued my interests in Oman. It is, therefore, as much to them, as to the institutions themselves, that I express my thanks in acknowledging the help offered by Petroleum Development (Oman) Ltd.; by the Iraq Petroleum and Associated Companies; by the Government of Abu Dhabi (in particular its Documentation and Research Department); by the Trucial States Council; by the Ministry of Overseas Development's Middle East Division in Beirut; and at Oxford, by the Committee for Modern Middle Eastern Studies, the School of Geography, St Antony's College, and St Edmund Hall.

Many also helped me with their personal expertise, through lending me manuscripts or their own research material, by commenting on this work, or simply by providing an audience on which to test my ideas: in particular I express my appreciation to Dr R. D. Bathurst, Professor A. F. L. Beeston, Mr J. Carter, Mr R. Candlish, Mr J. R. Colson, Mr. H. Goblot, Dr A. S. Goudie, Dr F. Heard, Mr A. Hourani, Professor T. M. Johnstone, Professor R. B. Serjeant, Mr C. G. Smith, Dr F. Stewart, and Mr M. Watterson. I also acknowledge a particular debt of gratitude to Mr Hugh Massy who, after I left Oman in 1965, went to enormous trouble to collect information for me and find out the answers to the screeds of questions I sent him.

I would also like to mention the efforts of Mrs Jean Barclay who had to compete both with my handwriting and the clock when typing and retyping drafts of this book, of Miss Helen Bromley and Miss Penny Timms in interpreting what I wanted for the maps, and of Mrs Siân Victory for help with editing.

Today it has become something of a convention to thank one's wife for having suffered without complaint the intrusions on private life which writing a book involves; but in expressing gratitude to Anne I thank her not only quite genuinely for her understanding, but also for the technical help she has given me in bibliographical method.

But in the end it is to the people of Oman that I owe the greatest debt of gratitude, for without the character of their country and the personal friendship, hospitality, and courtesy I have encountered there I should never have wanted to carry out this study. And so it is to them that I dedicate this book, and I appeal to them to forgive its shortcomings.

CONTENTS

LIST OF FIGURES

LIST OF TABLES

CONVENTIONS

1. TRANSLITERATION, VOWELLING, AND ORTHOGRAPHY OF ARABIC WORDS

A fairly standard transliteration has been used throughout this work. Initial *hamzas* are omitted. Final long vowels are not indicated except in the case of the long *ā* which distinguishes the *alif maqṣūra* or *alif mamdūda* (these tend to be interchangeable in Omani orthography) from the *tāʾ marbūṭa* (which is transliterated *a* and not *ah*). Names which decline are normally given in the nominative form (e.g. Abu, rather than Abū, Abā, Abī), but an exception is made in the case of the tribal term *Banū* which is given in the colloquial form *Bani*. Very occasionally in quoting a European author his system has been altered (e.g. *š* becomes *sh*) but never in a way to change his basic reading.

A considerable problem arises in transliterating local terms. In general an approximation to the classical spelling is given for words used by the settled peoples, because a systematic framework describing the characteristics of the numerous dialects loosely grouped under the heading 'Omani' is lacking (even though certain aspects have been treated in specialist works: cf. Jayakar 1889; Reinhardt 1894; Rössler 1898 *inter alia*). On the other hand, words and phrases of interest from that group of dialects analysed by Professor T. M. Johnstone in his *Eastern Arabian dialect studies* (Johnstone 1967) are indicated by special transliteration, because this helps indicate which part of the vocabulary derives from the newer Arab settlers and which from the older (cf. Chaps. VIII and IX). The transcription employed is based on one which we used in an article on Qaṭari vocabulary (Johnstone and Wilkinson 1960) and not on the more refined system subsequently employed by Professor Johnstone for linguistic publications. The main features of this are as follows:

Arabic letter	*Transcription*	
jīm (j)	j and ǰ (the latter pronounced y or ī) N.B. In the Omani dialect j tends to be pronounced g or gy	
qāf (q)	g and ǧ (the latter pronounced j)	
kāf (k)	k and č (the latter pronounced ch)	
ḍād (ḍ)	ḍ	these two letters are pronounced as classical ẓā, velarized dh, though they are kept separate in transcription.
ẓā (ẓ)	ẓ	(as above)

The letter *e* is used to denote the neutral vowel *ĕ* which can arise from any of the short vowels. The classical Arabic diphthongs *aw* and *ay* are pure vowels and transcribed *o* or *ō* and *ē* respectively.

Vowelling of proper names that occur in written works has also presented problems. In general the writer has been guided by present-day local forms, but even then the result may be guess-work: for example, ḤMYD could represent either Ḥumayd or Ḥumayyid, though Ḥamīd is excluded. Often too the names of places (which in any case are often 'arabizations') may have a 'correct' orthography, but in such cases the generally accepted local form has been used, e.g. Nizwā rather than Nazwā, Dibā rather than Dabā, (al-)Sumāyil rather than (al-)Sumāʾil: certain well-known names are written with their common European orthography. Difficulties also arise over the use of the definite article in the names of places; here at least the writer has probably been no more inconsistent than the Omani sources themselves. In principle the system employed is to indicate the correct orthography (in so far as it has been possible to ascertain this) in brackets or in a footnote the first time the name occurs. Even so, it must be emphasized that it has often not proved possible to check the form of the name with a reliable local informant (rationalizations by educated Arabs may be highly misleading). Both diacritical marking and the definite article are sometimes omitted on the maps in the interest of cartographic clarity as also in the abbreviated references given in the text.

Throughout this work ʿUmān has been spelt Oman, Imām as Imam, and Sulṭān (when used as a title) Sultan (although as a proper name the diacritical marking is retained), *badw* and *ḥaḍar* as bedu and hadhar respectively. Special attention is drawn to the fact that the spelling 'Baḥrayn' (al-Baḥrayn) has been used for the extensive region of Eastern Arabia so designated in classical Arabic sources, and the spelling Bahrain reserved for the island state which now bears that name. (Cf Glossary)

2. DATES

Normally dates have been given according to the Christian era and AD not added. However, *hijra* dates (AH) have on occasion been used for the early Islamic period, as the writer finds that these give a better point of reference than the Christian equivalent: where this has been done AH is always added. On those occasions when both dates are given they are shown in the form 750/1349-50. If the Christian date has been given more exactly, e.g. as 750/1349, then this shows that the Arabic month, or some other indication, has permitted a more precise dating even though the relevant details may not have been quoted. Conversions have been made from the tables in G. S. P. Freeman-Grenville's *The Muslim and Christian Calendars* (Freeman-Grenville 1963).

3. HISTORICAL PERIODS

Owing to the lack of any standard history of Oman in a European language a problem arises when referring to major periods of importance for this study. The following terms have therefore been adopted (others will be explained in the appropriate place: for the pre-Islamic Persian period, see Chapter VI).

The First Imamate. This specifically designates the first period of full Ibāḍi Imamate rule which followed the final overthrow of tribal **Julandā** (var. Julundā) rule: it roughly coincides with the ninth century. It does not include the earlier, only partially successful, attempt to establish Ibāḍi government in the middle of the eighth century.

The Dark Ages. This represents a much vaguer historical period. At its most extensive it may be considered as covering the whole interregnum between Oman's two 'golden ages', that is from the time of the civil war which followed the deposing of al-Ṣalt b. Mālik al-Kharūṣi in 272/886 to the election of the first Yaʿrabi (or Yaʿrubi) Imam, Nāṣir b. Murshid in 1624. More specifically it covers the period between the final collapse of the early Imamate in the latter part of the twelfth century and the first attempts to restore the Imamate in the fifteenth century: during this more limited period such centralized power as did exist in Oman seems to have been in the hands of the **Nabāhina** *mulūk* (rulers). The title 'Dark Ages' is, of course, subjective and in some measure presumes an identification with the Omani view of history: above all it is a period about which we know very little. The local records are almost a complete blank in the thirteenth and fourteenth centuries, and it is only with the chronicles of the **Late Nabāhina** and the sporadic records concerning the revival of the Imamate movement (fifteenth and sixteenth centuries) that some sort of history can once again be reconstructed.

The Yaʿāriba Imamate. The Yaʿāriba Imamate covers the period from the time of the election of the Imam Nāṣir b. Murshid (1624) to about the middle of the eighteenth century. During the latter part of this period Yaʿāriba rule became increasingly dynastic and its closing stages are marked by civil war and political chaos. Eventually it gives way to the government of the **Āl Bu Saʿīd** Sultans some of whom claimed the title of Imam.

The Twentieth-Century Imamate. Although Āl Bu Saʿīd rule has been maintained until the present day, it was frequently threatened by attempts to re-establish the Imamate. In the nineteenth century these attempts had limited success, but in 1913 Imamate government was set up in the interior of the country under Sālim b. Rāshid al-Kharūṣi (Imam 1913-20). In 1920 the relationship between the Imam and the Sultan was regulated by the so-called Treaty of Sib (al-Sīb), and the understanding was respected until the death of the Imam Muḥammad b. ʿAbdullāh al-Khalīli (Imam 1920-54). With the help of the British the interior was then (1955) brought under the control of the Āl Bu Saʿīd Sultan, but it was not for another seven or eight years that his rule was effectively established there and the pro-Imam (Ghālib b. ʿAli al-Hināʾi) resistance finally broken. In 1970 this Sultan, Saʿīd b. Taymūr was deposed by his son Qābūs.

4. USE OF PRESENT TENSE

Much of the field material used in this book was collected before the full economic impact of oil revenues was to be felt in the Omani region, and society could still justifiably be termed 'traditional'. Since 1966 in Trucial Oman and 1970 in the Sultanate the organization of that society has been undergoing such rapid transformation that it is now somewhat inappropriate to speak of the 'old order' as though still existing. But because much of the research for this book was carried out before these changes occurred, and because this traditional way of life still plays an active role in moulding village social structure and in conditioning the attitudes of the inhabitants of interior Oman, the present tense will be used, even where no longer fully appropriate.

The word 'today' itself may be held to apply to the situation at the beginning of the present decade when the writer started this book. Owing to delays in its appearance the completion date must be considered as 1974: post-1973 literature is therefore not normally cited.

5. REFERENCES

A few of the abbreviated references in the text are given by the title of the book only. These are as follows:

Abbreviation	*Bibliography*
	See under
Kashf	Sirḥān b. Saʿīd
Līsān al-ʿArab	Ibn Manẓūr
Nahḍa	al-Sālimi (Muḥammad b. ʿAbdullāh)
Tāj al-ʿArūs	al-Zabīdi
Tuḥfa	al-Sālimi (ʿAbdullāh b. Ḥumayd)

References from Yāqūt are from the *Muʿjam al-Buldān* unless otherwise specified. As with the *Līsān al-ʿArab* and the *Tāj al-ʿArūs*, the reader is referred to the relevant article rather than to a specific edition of these 'dictionaries'.

EI_1 and EI_2 refer respectively to the old and new editions of the *Encyclopaedia of Islam* (Leiden 1913-38, 1954—).

6. ABBREVIATIONS

The following abbreviations are sometimes used in maps and tables.

A.	= Abu (father)	all followed by a proper name (*Fulān* = so-and-so; *Makān* = such and such a place)
b.	= ibn (son of)	
B.	= Bani (sons of, tribal term)	
H.	= Ḥāra(t) (tribal quarter of)	
J.	= Jabal (mountain)	
W.	= Wādi (valley)	

Muḥd = Muḥammad (proper
name).

7. MAPS

In order to locate the main places and tribal groups mentioned in the text reference should be made to the entry in the Index where the relevant Figure numbers are shown in italics.

8. GLOSSARY

A short glossary of some of the more commonly used foreign words will be found on pp. 266-7.

INTRODUCTION

Although this book is entitled 'Water and Tribal Settlement in South-East Arabia', its sub-title indicates that the subject is more specifically concerned with something called *aflāj* in somewhere called Oman. Neither of these words lends itself satisfactorily to a simple definition. While *falaj* (plural *aflāj*) appears simply to be the local name for the type of tunnelled water galleries which the Persians call *qanāt*, the two words are by no means synonymous. Any water channel is a *falaj* to an Omani, and for him the important thing about it is that it forms part of a system by which a supply of water is distributed amongst the dependent community. The fact that great efforts may have had to be invested to bring the water to that settlement matters little to him, and he does not have any special words to distinguish between different types of irrigation system. This is rather surprising. Anomalies similarly abound in the use of the name Oman, and it most certainly cannot be defined in terms of place alone. This study is therefore something rather more complex than a straightforward account of the way one type of irrigation system works in a particular place.

To understand how man has settled in a particular arid region and what role water has played in determining his traditional life-style requires, in fact, wide-ranging research. Not only is it necessary to examine such factors as how fresh water accumulates, the physical limitations governing its use, its distribution relative to the other potential economic resources of the region, the techniques of exploitation, and the traditional methods of organization, but it is also necessary to look at the attitudes of the people towards the land in which they live, and to examine the social and political structures of the area in order to see what part the land has played in their evolution and how they, in turn, have influenced the pattern of settlement.

This study therefore represents the 'Water, Earth, and Man' approach to Oman, and its objectives are summed up by the editor of that work (Chorley 1969) when he writes: 'the theme of this book is that the study of water provides a logical link between an understanding of physical and social environments. Each chapter develops this theme by proceeding from the many aspects of water occurrence to a deeper understanding of natural environments and their fusion with the activities of man in society.' The treatment here, however, will be quite different, for, if this declared objective of understanding the fusion between the physical and traditional social environment is to be achieved, it is necessary , in the view of the present writer, to try and study both the physical and the social elements with the tools of the respective specialist disciplines. Any explanation based on only one form of analysis will either be incomplete and of limited interest, or else crudely determinist. A true interdisciplinary approach is called for, and in the case of Oman, where the anomalies of land organization require research into the

Persian origins of the settlement pattern, the Ibāḍi concepts of community organization, and the structure of the country's so-called 'tribal' society we must expect to have to enter into the fields of the Arabist, the Islamic historian, and the social anthropologist, as well as those of the hydrologist and geographer.

The writer's task might have been somewhat less hazardous had it been possible to relate his research to a set of authoritative specialist studies in certain of these fields. Unfortunately, because much of inland Oman remained until recently something of a *terra incognita*, such academic studies are rare, while the best government reports on conditions in the interior nearly all date back to the turn of the century. From 1954 onwards a limited number of British military, political, and oil company officials were allowed access to the region (it was in this way that the present writer first visited Oman), but such reports as they made did not become generally available; nor, until the present Sultan came to power in 1970, were any development or scientific studies (except those necessary for oil operations) carried out. No census has ever been taken, and reasonable cartographic coverage only came into existence within the last few years; until the 1/100,000 maps based on a military aerial survey were recently placed on limited release, anyone interested in interior Oman had considerable difficulty in finding out even where a place was, let alone what went on there. Rather more information of a scientific nature is available from Trucial Oman: yet because it was not until the early 1960s that the discovery of oil gave the impetus for carrying out resource and development surveys, most of this material is based on recent short-term observations, started at a time when the traditional way of life was already fast disappearing.

Detailed historical studies of the region really only began when the main India Office reports of the nineteenth century first became available to scholars in the 1950s: not unnaturally, most of these concentrated on the story of British interests in the Gulf, a somewhat more exciting subject for most than that of the region's internal relationships. Some use has been made of local documents by Europeans, but apart from R. D. Bathurst's unpublished D. Phil. thesis (Bathurst 1967) on the Yaʿāriba dynasty (*c.* 1624-1740), most studies have only used the partial translation of some of the chapters of an eighteenth-century compilation called the *Kashf al-Ghumma* made by E. C. Ross under the title 'Annals of Oman' (in the *Journal of the Asiatic Society of Bengal*, 1871), and the Revd. G. P. Badger's translation, under the title *History of the Imāms and Seyyids of 'Omān* (Hakluyt Society 1871), of a work by a prolific nineteenth-century plagiarist called Ibn Ruzayq whose (admitted) partiality to the Āl Bu Saʿīd dynasty has led to more misunderstandings about the country than virtually anything else ever written. Some important articles based on Ibāḍi literature from North Africa have been produced (even though the parallel Omani material has hardly been touched), but most students of Islamic history remain unaware of them and of the significance of these sources; for the most part they dismiss the Ibāḍis as a minor aberration of little interest.

When the present writer first came to study the subject of the evolution of the settlement pattern in Oman he, too, was largely unaware of the existence of most of this Omani written material. His initial work, therefore, was based on the limited field material he had been able to collect while working for oil companies in the area (Qatar and Trucial Oman, 1958-62, Oman 1965), and on a particularly valuable nineteenth-century village document (*The Izki Falaj Book*) which he had been able to see thanks to the considerable efforts made by a former colleague in Oman, Mr Hugh Massy, to obtain a loan of it. Not unsurprisingly his first results did little more than highlight some of the anomalies that exist between the present systems of water organization in Oman and the requirements of an agricultural economy based on *qanāt*; they thus posed rather more questions than they answered. More relevant data began to appear as he started to study the vast mass of written material, sometimes in such unexpected sources as an eleventh-century genealogical work or in a polemic on the difference between the so-called Nizwā and Rustāq parties; but it soon became obvious that no real use could be made of this information until some basic outline of the country's history, social organization, and political ideology had been reconstructed. So the writer deferred pursuit of his original subject and concentrated on trying to do just that: the result was a D.Phil. thesis (Wilkinson 1969) which tried to explain the evolution of the tribal pattern in Oman and its relationship with the Ibāḍi Imamate.

With the present work the writer has reverted to his earlier interests and tried to relate some of the material in his thesis to the broad theme of understanding the relationships that exist between the techniques of water exploitation, social organization, and the evolution of attitudes towards the land. One problem that has naturally arisen is how to present arguments partly based on detailed discussion in his unpublished work without recourse to long parentheses and tedious footnotes. The general solution adopted has been to confine unsupported statements to background information (e.g. the first part of Chapter VII), while giving some indication of sources at points of key interest.

Other shortcomings of approach will doubtless strike the reader, and parts of this study will certainly need re-assessment as others come to work in the field and more data are produced. If, however, it does prove successful in throwing some light on the traditional way of life in a country which is now turning from a great, but difficult, past, to a bright but uncertain future, then the writer will feel that his objectives have been achieved.

CHAPTER I

The Regional Setting

In 1959, when the writer was transferred from Doha to work in Abu Dhabi, he was somewhat surprised when a Qaṭari remarked to him 'Ah, so at last you've got your wish and you're going to Oman'. Shortly after taking up this new appointment, some urgent business arose which required discussion with the Ruler. Inquiries revealed that he was no longer in Abu Dhabi, but had 'gone to Oman'. Here, at last, seemed to be a perfect excuse for visiting this forbidden land. But it was not to be, because 'Oman' turned out simply to be the local name for Shaikh Shakhbūṭ's territory in the so-called 'Buraimi Oasis'![1] Nevertheless the visit did at least provide a welcome change from the endless sand and sea of Abu Dhabi, for here were running water and rich cultivation, and in the distance the shimmer of mountains: here also the writer was able to talk with those who really knew the area, for the group of men with brightly-coloured head-dresses whom he found waiting in the Shaikh's *majlis* were, it appeared, 'visitors from Oman'. Some years later, when the opportunity did at last come to make the journey along the foot of the mountains southwards from Buraimi, the writer called on one of these 'Omanis' at his home at ʿIbri. As he took his leave to carry on towards Nizwa he almost anticipated his host's remark, 'Ah, so you're going on to Oman'!

So perhaps it is not surprising that the special representative sent by the United Nations to investigate the so-called 'Question of Oman' had to open his report (1963) with the warning, 'the name Oman has been used in different ways depending on who is referring to it and in which context it has been used'. Two years later its *Ad Hoc* Committee also came to the conclusion 'In reporting on the question of Oman, not the least of the problems concerns the use of the term "Oman".' Since these two reports (United Nations 1963, 1965) between them take 866 paragraphs and 24 annexes to try and answer the question 'What is Oman?', the present writer will merely content himself by initially defining Oman (correctly ʿUmān) as the region where human organization focuses on the isolated mountain chain which lies in the south-eastern corner of the Arabian Peninsula.

Today this region comprises no less than eight putative states whose size and population vary greatly, as may be seen from Table 1. The details given there, however, reveal only a part of the complex story of territorial fragmentation, for it is obvious from its title alone that some form of further division must exist within the largest territory, the Sultanate of Muscat and Oman,[2] while an examination of the area over which its Sultan claims jurisdiction shows that this includes an exclave of territory in the Musandam Peninsula (the country of the Shiḥūḥ), and the sizeable province on the southern coast of Arabia called Dhofar (correctly Ẓafār): the latter, although contiguous with the main

Table 1 *Populations, Sizes, and Cultivated Areas of the Oman States*

	Present population	*Population at beginning of century*	*Area km²*	*Present cultivated area km²*
Sultanate (excluding Dhofar)	435,000	500,000	200,000	360
Abu Dhabi	46,375	80,000	60-80,000	4
Dubai	59,092		3,900	
Sharja	31,480		2,600	
Ajman	4,275		260	
Umm al-Qaiwain	3,740		780	
Ras al-Khaima	24,482		1,790	
Fujaira	9,724		1,170	
Rough totals	600,000+	600,000–	300,000–	400–

Notes

[1] Population figures.

(a) Sultanate. The present population figures are based on the Whitehead Report (1972). This report discounts recent trends to increase population figures and concludes that the total is certainly well below half a million, a statement with which the present writer fully concurs. The turn-of-the-century figure is based on Lorimer (1908), but this was probably on the high side: Massignan (1908) quotes 400,000, but points out that there had been a notable decrease of population, not enough however to reduce the population from 800,000 in 25 years (cf. Political Agent at Muscat's estimate for 1880 quoted in Kelly 1968, p. 3, fn. 1). In the early nineteenth century the population may have been between 500,000 and 600,000 (Fraser 1825, p. 15).

(b) Trucial States. Present-day figures are 1968 Census figures and already reflect the impact of enormous economic change; in Abu Dhabi, for example, the local population is under 45 per cent of the quoted total. Turn-of-century figures are Lorimer (1908) estimates: for discussion of other nineteenth-century estimates see Kelly 1968, pp. 22–3.

[2] Cultivated areas. Sultanate figures based on Whitehead Report 1972, and Trucial Coast figures on Ministry of Overseas Development 1969.

part of the Sultanate, has few links with it and is not discussed at all in this book. Again, a study of the political divisions in Trucial Oman shows that not only does this tract of formerly largely uninhabited land subdivide into the seven Trucial States (cf Fig. 7),[3] but that each of these, with the exception of Abu Dhabi (correctly Abu Ẓabi), is made up of non-contiguous units of territory: Sharja (correctly al-Shāriqa) is made up of four such pieces; Dubai (Dubayy), Ras al-Khaima (Ra's al-Khayma), and Fujaira (al-Fujayra) of two each, while Ajman (ʿAjmān), whose total areas is not much more than 250 sq. km, subdivides into three. To add further confusion to this political picture, two major states, Persia and Saudi Arabia, have important territorial claims in the region (Wilkinson 1971).

This ludicrous partitioning of territory is of relatively recent origin and stems in large measure from the imposing of European notions of territorialism on a society to which they were foreign. The *ad hoc* process by which this happened started a century and a half ago when Britain initiated a series of treaties with the Sultan of Muscat and the coastal shaikhs of northern Oman, with the purpose of limiting their maritime activities and foreign relationships. Subsequently, as Britain sought to develop an exclusive influence in the Gulf and, later still, to favour the claims of particular companies to act as concessionaires for oil exploration, she was forced first into defending her protégé coastal rulers from attack from the hinterland and then of proclaiming their authority over the population and resources of 'Greater Oman', by dividing it into a number of territories subject to them. This is not to say that the embryonic states she helped create were entirely artificial. Rather it is to imply that from the start the terms of reference by which they came into existence more or less disregarded important aspects of traditional organization within the region, and became increasingly irrelevant in the changing circumstances of the twentieth century. Since it is only with these traditional patterns of organization that this book is concerned, these modern political transformations will be more or less ignored and the term Oman used to designate the region as a whole.

THE MARITIME SETTING

The isolated mountain range that forms the physical core of this region also dominates the Arabian shore of the Gulf of Oman, a northern extension of the Arabian Sea, and sweeps northwards in an arc, some 650 km long, from Rās (Raʾs) al-Ḥadd, the most easterly point of the Arabian Peninsula, to the Ruʾūs al-Jibāl, the gateway to the (Persian/Arabian) Gulf. At this point the range projects 'like a spur into the vitals of Persia' (Lees 1928), so that only the narrow Strait of Hormuz separates the Arabian and Persian mainlands and, like the Bab al-Mandab at the entrance to the Red Sea on the other side of the Peninsula, provides a channel by which the Indian Ocean advances towards the Mediterranean and the Atlantic Ocean through the Afro-Asian land mass. Westward from this constriction the Gulf widens rapidly and the low,

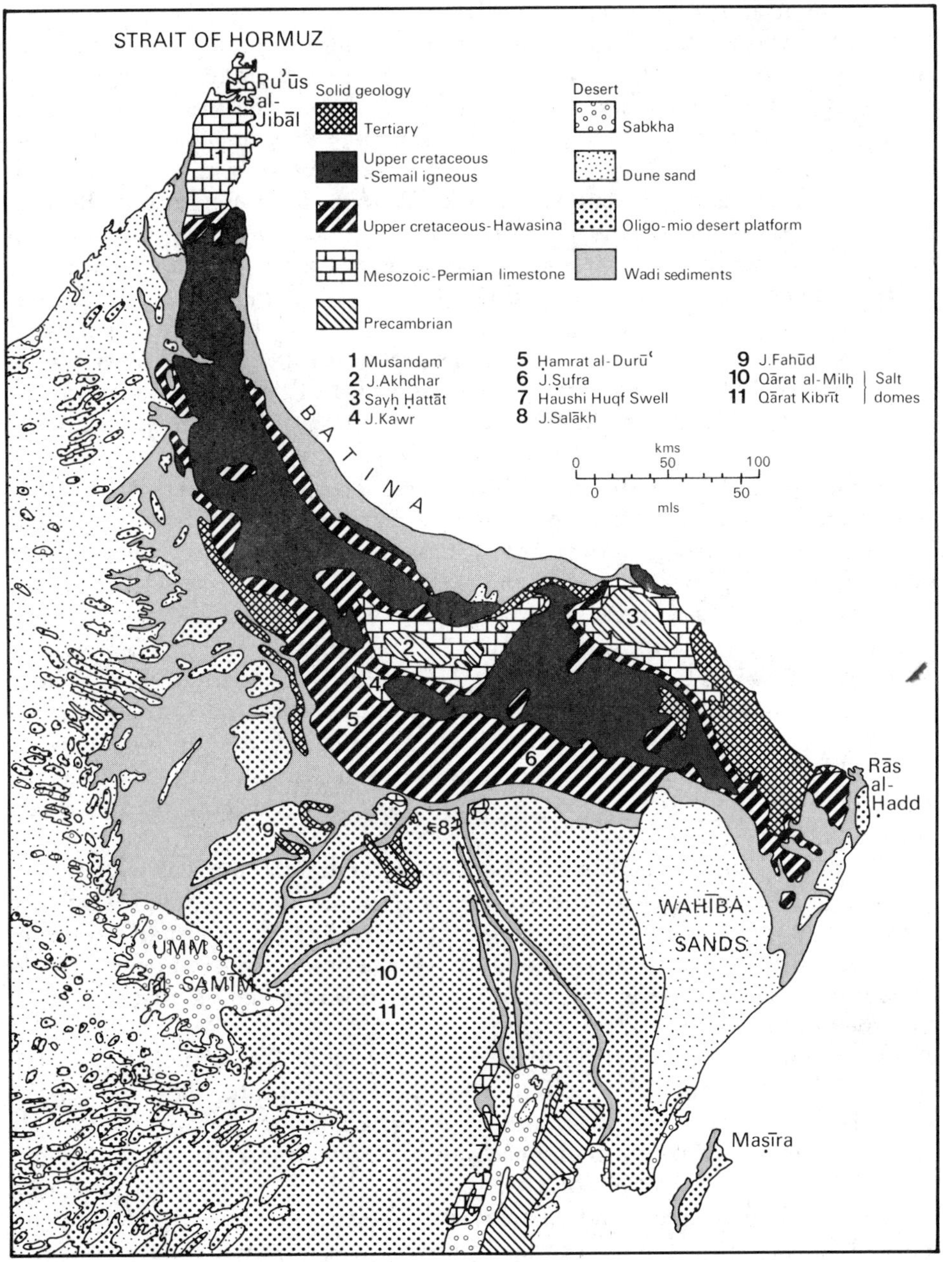

Fig. 1. Oman: main physical features.

prograding shore of Trucial Oman forms a great bay whose shallow waters and shifting banks and channels used strenuously to be avoided by all but local shipping (Pliny VI. xxxii. 149; Idrīsi i. 157).

At either end of this range the mountains plunge straight into the sea and the deep water inlets of a drowned coastline provide small, but splendidly defended, natural harbours. In the centre of the arc the mountains are set back some 20-30 km from the sea, and there the straight coast of the 280-kilometre-long Batina (correctly al-Bāṭina) plain is open to the prevailing wind and offers few good sites for ports. By way of compensation, the rich fresh water and fishing resources of the littoral zone have given rise to a strip of virtually continuous settlement which contrasts markedly with the barrenness of the rest of the plain. At its south-eastern end the Batina terminates fairly abruptly just above Muscat,[4] but in the north it narrows progressively to form a discontinuous belt of coastal lowland known as al-Shimālīya (cf. Fig. 2). This finally peters out around Fujaira and it is only to the west of the Musandam Peninsula, in the vicinity of Shaʿm, that a coastal plain, the Ṣīr,[5] once again develops.

This configuration of the mountain range in its maritime setting gave the inhabitants of Oman certain particular advantages in the traditional sea-borne trade that passed between the lands bordering the Indian Ocean and China Sea on the one hand, and the Mediterranean world and what is now called the Middle East on the other. Most important perhaps is that the way in which the south-west monsoon develops in the Indian Ocean and is modified along the Arabian Coast (Tibbetts 1971, pp. 360-82) resulted in a sailing-pattern which tended to make use of a port somewhere on Oman's eastern seaboard as a major centre for transhipment. Thus in the tenth century we find Ṣuḥār being described by one Arab author as 'the hallway of China, the storehouse of the East [Persia] and al-ʿIrāq, and the stay of al-Yaman' (Muqaddasi, p. 92).

This description applied to a period when the Gulf route was particularly prosperous, but even after the collapse of the Eastern Caliphate and the switching of much international trade to the Red Sea route, Oman's entrepôt role was by no means entirely vitiated, albeit the new commercial network did encourage a shift of the entrepôt port further down the coast, first to Qalhāt and then to Muscat.

As a major international trading centre, the main Omani port has always had a highly cosmopolitan population, with various Hindu, Balūchi, Persian (and later, European) communities living alongside the Arabs, openly observing their own religions and customs and speaking their own languages. In the same way, members of Oman's own trading community have been attracted to live overseas, and particularly close contacts have developed with part of East Africa. These overseas interests have required the support of a considerable navy, and as a result the Oman fleet has frequently been in a position to play a decisive role in the politics of both the Gulf and the Indian

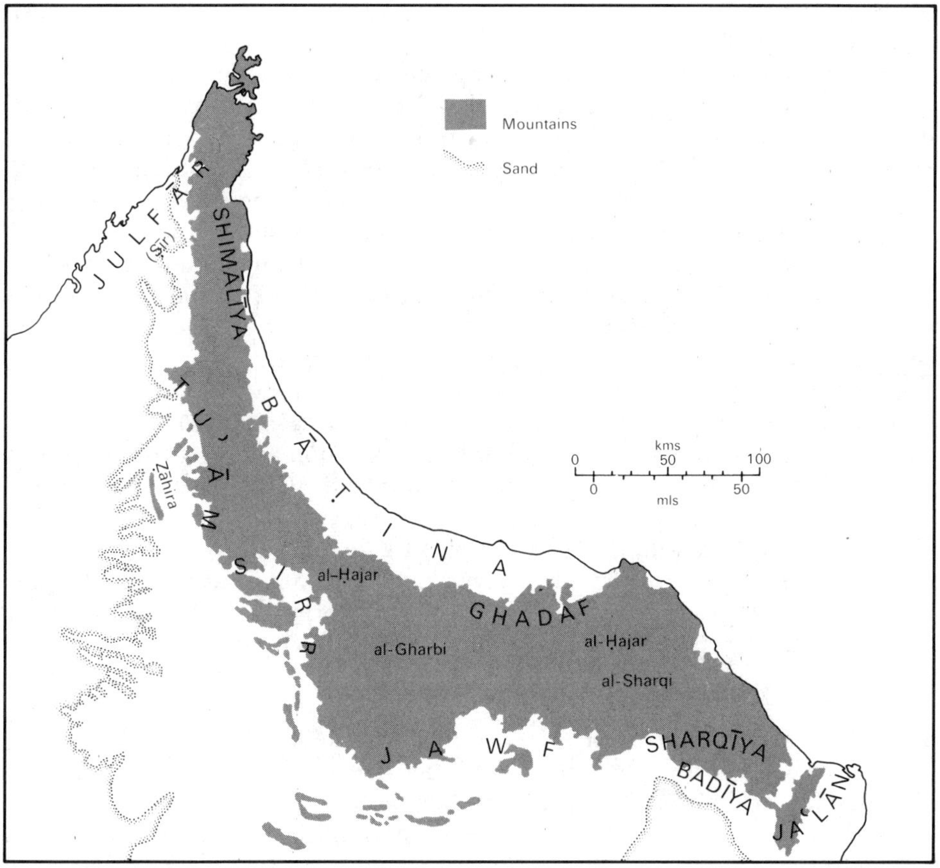

Fig. 2. Oman: The old sub-regional names.

Ocean.

Another major advantage conferred by the region's maritime setting is the strategic one arising from Oman's position relative to the Strait of Hormuz. Yet the obvious power conferred by control of this site has meant that it has frequently been disputed with local dynasties or foreign powers; few of these contented themselves with the 10 per cent levy on goods which seems to have been customarily paid to the Julandā b. Karkar throughout much of the Medieval Islamic period (Yāqūt art. *al-Dīkdān*). Thus in the early twelfth century (Ibn al-Athīr x. 233-4; Idrīsi i. 252; Goitein 1954), the Rulers of Qays exploited their hold of the Strait to force ships to land at their island; in the sixteenth and seventeenth centuries the Portuguese used Great Tunb island as a levy point for enforcing their maritime policy in the Indian Ocean (de Thévenot 1727 edn., iv. 640-1); while in the eighteenth and early nineteenth centuries the activities of the Jowasim (correctly Qawāsim) eventually resulted in the joint British-Muscati expeditions which transformed the 'Pirate Coast' into the 'Trucial Coast'.

From time to time a genuine trading centre did develop within the Strait itself, for Old and New Hormuz as well as Bandar ᶜAbbās (Gombrun) have all enjoyed periods of considerable commercial prosperity. Even so, an examination of the history of these ports reveals that their fortunes tended to depend, not just on hinterland trade and command of the main strategic sites on either coast at the entrance to the Gulf (notably Jashk Island and Julfār), but also on control of the main Omani seaboard with its monsoonal trading centre: Ḣormuz, for example, only flourished so long as it controlled Qalhāt (then the main port of Oman and the centre from which the Hormūzi dynasty itself originated), but rapidly collapsed once the main Omani ports passed into inimical hands (cf. Wilkinson EI_2 art, Ḳalhāt, Williamson 1973a).

So it can be seen that while the Strait of Hormuz has always been a point of strategic importance, and hence a bone of contention amongst the peoples of the area,[6] it is really no more than the doorway to the Gulf; the key is operated from the main Omani coast. It is here, therefore, that the battle for control of Gulf trade is fought, and the story of the struggle for mastery of this seaboard between the inhabitants of the region and outsiders—ᶜAbbāsid Caliphs, Carmathians (Qarāmiṭa), Būyids, Saljūqs, Hormūzis, Portuguese, and British—has formed one of the continuous themes in Omani history.

THE LANDWARD SETTING

In striking contrast to the effects of this maritime location are those arising from Oman's continental setting. Here the theme is not one of contact with the outside world but isolation from it. Surrounded by salt-water sea on three sides, and by a sand sea on the fourth, the Oman mountains are like an appendix to the Arabian Peninsula, an island of settlement that has been colonized by migratory groups filtering into it from the inhospitable Persian mainland opposite, or by waterles tracks along the northern and southern fringes of the so-called 'Empty Quarter'. G. M. Lees (1928) might as well have been speaking of the human as of the physical geography of the region when he wrote:

> From here [Qatar] eastward, however, our preconceived ideas of the behaviour of Arabia completely break down. If Arabia was bounded by a line joining the base of Qatar peninsula and the Kuria Muria Islands it would have almost a geometric rectangular shape and a uniform geological structure . . . The great arc-shaped mountainous belt of 'Oman . . . is the most striking feature of the map of Arabia, in that it is so obviously abnormal.'

THE PHYSICAL CHARACTERISTICS OF THE INTERIOR

The anomalous physical structure which leads to the isolation of our region has only recently begun to be understood: even now its geological history is still debated and much of the relevant evidence remains unpublished.[7] From

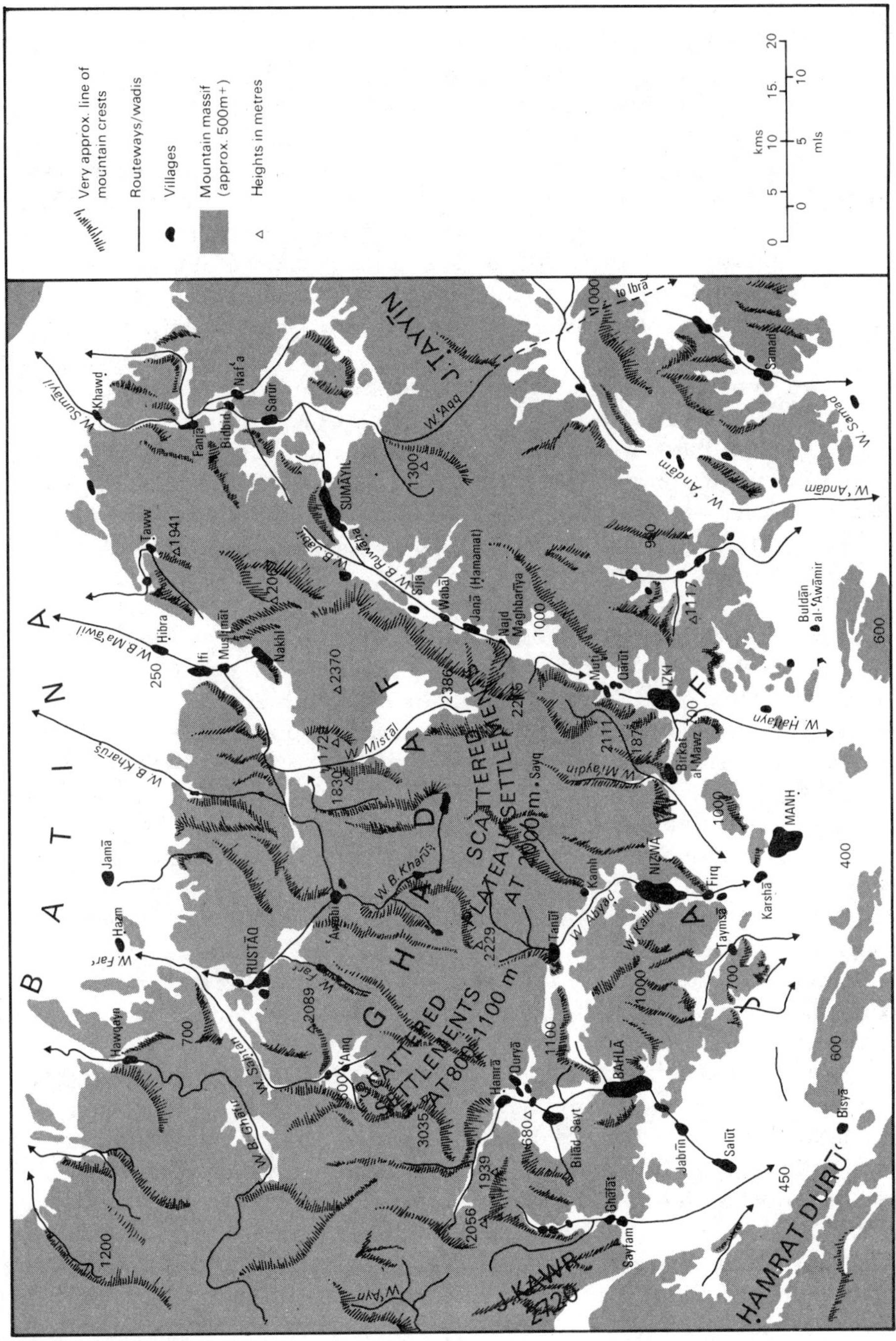

Fig. 3. Central Oman.

the point of view of the physical geography of the region, however, this debate may be ignored and Oman simply divided into two major provinces, the mountainous fold zone and the flat desert foreland (cf. Fig. 1).

The mountainous fold zone may then conveniently be subdivided into four main geological provinces, each with its own characteristic scenery. The most spectacular is that presented by the three limestone-dolomite massifs: the Musandam block in the north, the Jabal Akhdhar (correctly al-Akhḍar) anticline of central Oman, which rises from the piedmont plain at about 400 m to its highest point of 3,035 m, and the somewhat less imposing 'Sayḥ Ḥattāt' uplift behind Muscat. In the last two massifs the core of soft pre-Cambrian metamorphic rocks has been exposed, and in the Jabal Akhdhar the flanking ravines have cut down to it, through a series of limestones and dolomites some 3,000 m thick (ranging in age from Permian to mid-Cretaceous), to leave an isolated central plateau at about 2,000 m, which forms the final bastion in Oman's natural defences (cf. Fig. 3): 'there flows down from this mountain nine wadis each of which has a route leading to it; at their entrances are villages of the Bani Riyām who surround the mountain and protect it like the perianth of a fruit or the halo of the moon' (translation of al-Sharīshi (d. 1222) quoted *Tuḥfa* i. 8-9).

Girdling these limestone massifs are the Ḥawāsina formations, a chaotic mixture of partly metamorphosed clastic deposits, shales, radiolarian cherts, and limestones, which probably represents a nappe of sedimentary rocks deposited in one half of the Tethys ocean and gently emplaced (seemingly by gravity slide and not compression) on the autochthonous series of the Arabian continental margin in late Cretaceous time. The greatest overlap occurs in central Oman, where the Hawasina forms an extensive zone of highly dissected foothills on the desert side of the main mountain range (the Ḥamrat Durūᶜ, Jabal al-Ṣufra, etc.). A characteristic feature in the landscape of this geological series is a capping of 'exotic' limestone blocks (of Permian and late Triassic age) which rise abruptly from the gentler relief provided by the other rocks: one of these, the Jabal Kawr, whose exposed surface alone covers some 600 km^2, forms a mountain massif in its own right, with a stupendous western edge that rises sheer some 1,800 m from the low topography of the underlying radiolarites.

The third main characteristic landscape of the Oman mountains is that of the Semail (al-Sumāʾil/Sumāyil) igneous, a geological formation which probably represents part of the crust of the spreading ocean ridge that bounded the outer flank of the Hawasina basin and which was also emplaced on the autochthonous series. With a thickness of up to 3 km, and extending from Rās al-Ḥadd in the south-east to the base of the Musandam Peninsula in the north, its total outcrop 'amounting to considerably more than 5,000 sq mi, must represent one of the most spectacular exposures of serpentinic rocks in the world' (Wilson 1969). The typical scenery it produces is one of monotonous, barren hills, whose sheen appears to vary between red, brown, purple, and greeny-black, according to the lighting. Even though its relief is less abrupt than that of the limestone massifs, the fact that the Semail forms extensive areas in which the divides of a close dendritic drainage network tend to rise to between 1,000 and 1,500 m ASL means that it forms no less of a serious barrier to movement.

Onlapping these formations are the younger rocks of upper Cretaceous and Tertiary age. In most areas this outer layer has been stripped away, but in places, notably in the Dhahira (correctly al-Ẓāhira), the limestones sometimes frame the range in such a way that the wadis, which have extensively eroded the soft Hawasina rocks upstream, only manage to escape into the desert foreland through narrow gorges (locally known as *lijan* sing. *lijna*). At these points, where both routeways and drainage have been concentrated, villages of considerable strategic and economic importance have sometimes developed (e.g. ʿIbri and Ḍank; cf. Fig. 4).

Two main trends, north to south and north-west to south-east, give this mountain range its arc shape, and it is for this reason that in local toponymy it is divided into two halves, the Ḥajar al-Gharbi and the Ḥajar al-Sharqi. In the centre, where the range is at its widest (130 km), there is an extensive foothill zone, but to the north the relief loses nothing in altitude, even though the

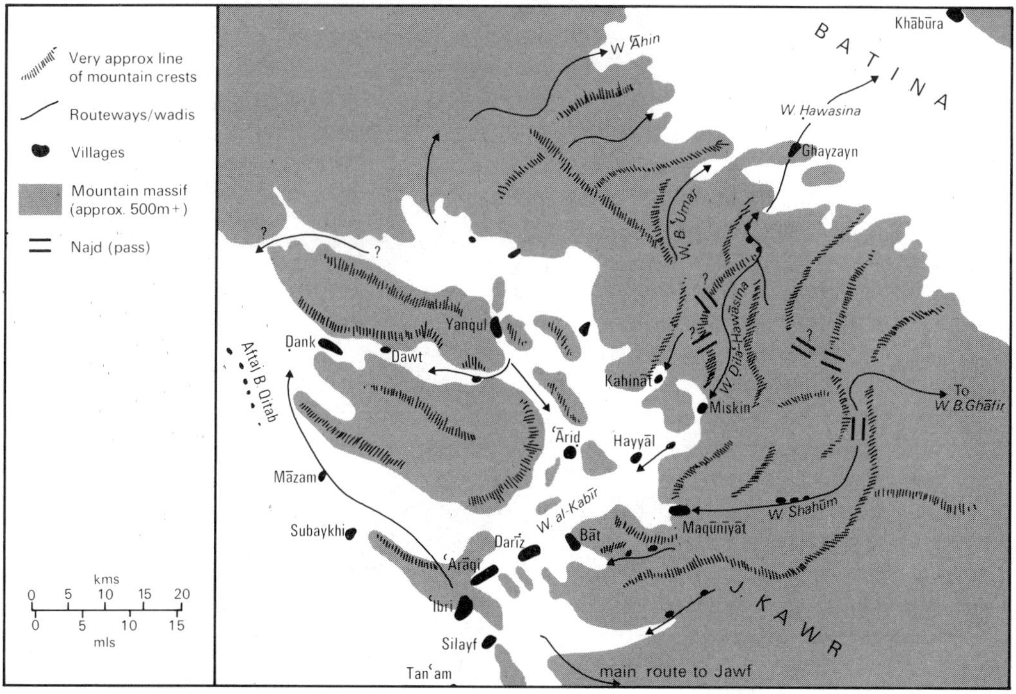

Fig. 4. Sirr to the Batina.

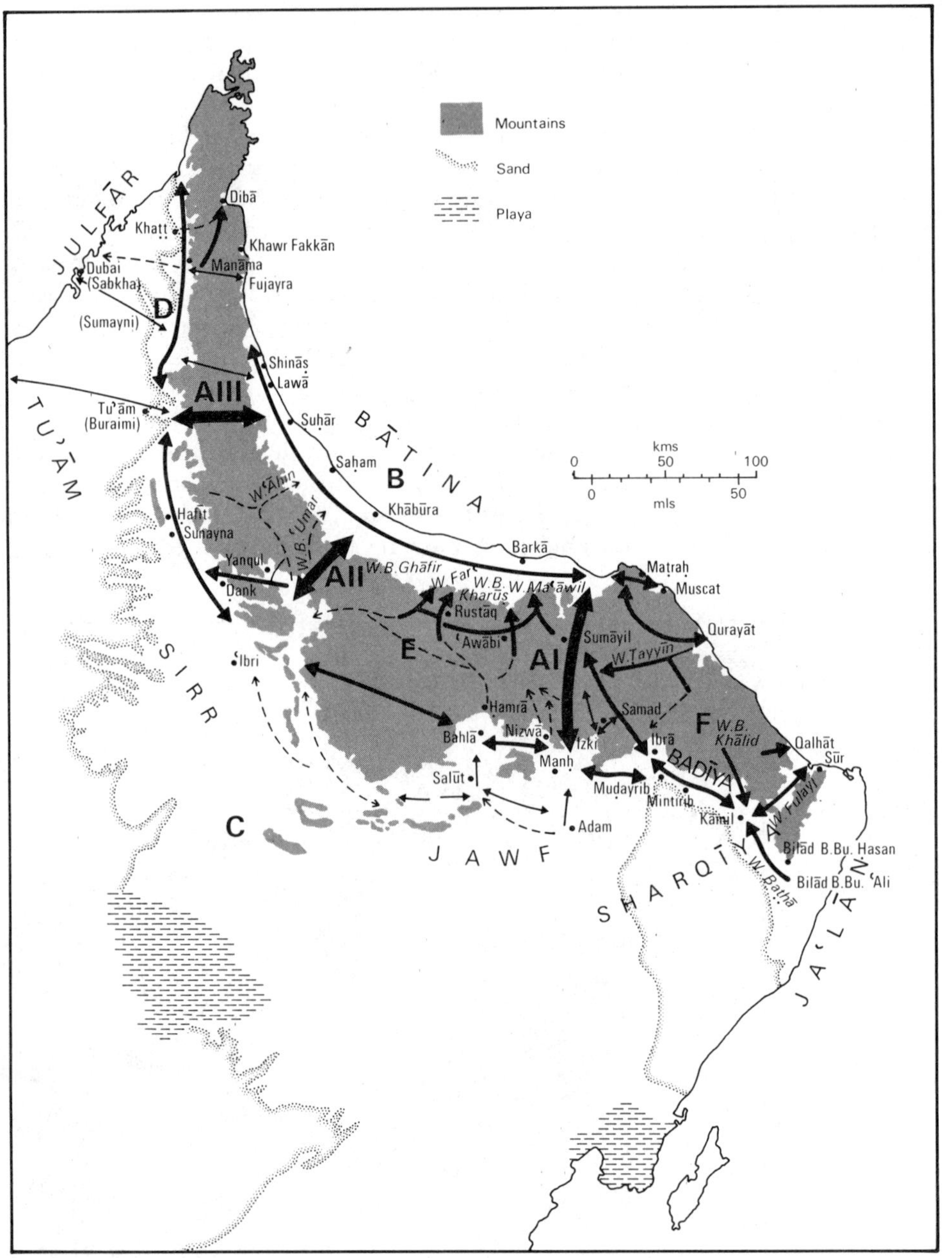
Mountains
Sand
Playa
kms
0
50
100
0
mls
50
JULFĀR
Dibā
Khatt
Khawr Fakkān
Dubai
(Sabkha)
Manāma
Fujayra
D
(Sumayni)
Shināṣ
Lawā
AIII
Tu'ām
(Buraimi)
TU'ĀM
Ṣuḥār
BĀTINA
Saḥam
B
W.'Āhin
W.B.'Umar
Khābūra
Hafīt
Sunayna
Barkā
Yanqul
AII
W.B.Ghāfir
W.Far'
W.B.Kharūṣ
W.Ma'āwil
Maṭraḥ
Muscat
Dank
Rustāq
Qurayāt
'Awābī
E
Sumāyil
W.Ṭayyīn
AI
'Ibri
SIRR
Samad
Hamrā
F
W.B.Khālid
Qalhāt
Sūr
Bahlā
Nizwā
Izki
Ibrā
BADĪYA
Manḥ
Salūt
Muḍayrib
Mintirib
W.Fulayj
Kāmil
Adam
C
JAWF
Bilād B.Bu. Hasan
Bilād B.Bu. 'Ali
SHARQĪYA
W.Baṭḥā
JA'LĀN

Fig. 5. Accessibility Map key

A. TRANSMONTANE (CENTRAL OMAN – BĀṬINA)

AI SUMĀYIL GAP (W. Sumāyil – W. Ḥalfayn systems): JAWF – BĀṬINA
Main subsidiary linkages 1. W. Ṭayyīn (– Qurayāt)
2. W. ʿAqq – SHARQĪYA

AII W. KABĪR/ḤAWĀSINA system: SIRR – BĀṬINA.
Minor linkages W. Ḍank (Dhahira) – W. Kabīr
W. Kabīr – Bāṭina via W. B. ʿUmar
– Bāṭina via W. ʿĀhin
– Ghadaf via W. B. Ghāfir.
(cf. Fig. 4)

AIII W. JIZZI: TUʿĀM – BĀṬINA

B. ALONG COAST BY LAND
Shimālīya – BĀṬINA – Maṭraḥ/Muscat.
– Sayḥ Ḥattāt/W. Mijlāṣ – Qurayāt
N.B. links round Musandam Peninsula and round J. Minqal/B. Jābir bloc (F) to S.E. ports by sea only.

C. ALONG BAJADA ZONE (WEST OF MOUNTAINS)
No particulary important strategic sites but note
1. Access to Gulf Coast (Julfār) passes via Tuʿām area.
2. Sand constricts the passage i Tuʾām – Julfār
ii in Badīya.
3. Useful short-cuts, notably Sirr-Jawf across Ḥamrat al-Durūʿ.

D. NORTHERN OMAN
1. Gulf Coastal Route to 'Baḥrayn'.
2. Gulf Coast – Bajada Zone across desert (via corridors between the W.N.W. E.S.E. sand ridges).
i. Sharja – Manāma area.
ii. Dubai – Sumayni area (Sumayni now ruined).
iii. Abu Dhabi – Tuʾām (Buraimi).
3. Bajada Zone – E. Coast across mountains.
i. Manāma area – W. Sijiy – W. Dibā (Dibā).
– W. Ḥām – Northern Batina (Fujayra).
ii. Sumayni area – W. Ḥattā/Qawr – Northern Batina.

E. J. AKHḌAR/KAWR BLOC
Numerous tracks over the plateau, all difficult of access (by gorges): important for tribal relations (Details on Fig. 3).
Ghadaf Side 1. W. B. Ghāfir
2. W. Saḥtan
3. W. Farʿ
4. W. B. Kharūṣ
5. W. Mistal/Maʿāwil
} all with an internal Ghadaf linkage (Rustaq – ʿAwābi – Nakhl).
Jawf Side. Very steep routes behind most main settlements, notably Ḥamrā, Tanūf, Kamah, Birkat al-Mawz, Muṭi.

F S. E. OMAN (J. Ṭayy/J. Minqāl (now known as J. B. Jābir) bloc)
1. JAʿLĀN.
Main coastal settlements (Qalhāt – Ṣūr area) linked to Kāmil area via W. Fulayj/W. Rafṣa, on which also converge Sharqīya – Badīya linkage, the W. B. Khālid, and the W. Baṭḥā settlements.
2. SHARQĪYA – Badīya – Jaʿlān
– Sumāyil Gap (cf. AI_1)
– Jawf via bajada zone (Cf. C)
} Major linkages (already described)
Minor linkages i. W. Maḥram – W. B. Ruwaḥa.
ii. W. Ṭayyīn
3. There are numerous minor passages through the mountains of SE Oman (Details uncertain).

range narrows and the foothills more or less disappear. In the south-east, by contrast, the range is generally lower but only begins to taper away at the far end in the Jaʿlān, and it presents a final appendix in Maṣīra island.

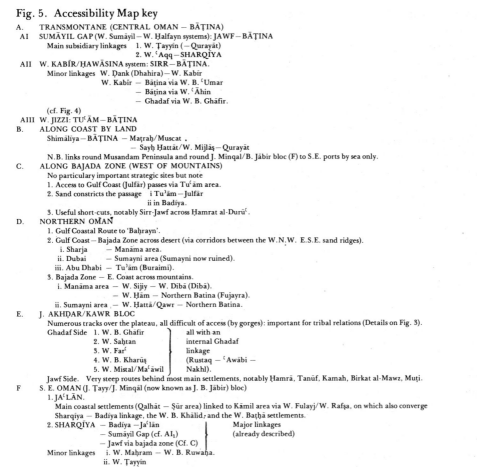

Since there are no major breaks throughout the length of the chain, movement across it is restricted to a few complex weaknesses formed by drainage lines (cf. Fig. 5), and these therefore play an important part in the political relationships of the people of the area. Particularly vital are the three main routes which link the innerside of the mountains to the Batina coastal plain: the Wādi al-Jizzi which connects Tuʾām (the area of the Buraimi oasis) to Ṣuḥār; the Wādi al-Kabīr and Wādi al-Ḥawāsina system, which links the Sirr to its main port at Khābūra; and, most important of all, the so-called Sumāyil (Sumāʾil) Gap, an interconnecting wadi system etched at the junction of the Semail igneous and the Jabal Akhdhar massif. This last route, as well as providing an outlet from the interior onto the lower end of the Batina coast and to the twin port of Muscat-Maṭraḥ, also links the relatively densely populated areas of the Jawf, the Ghadaf, the Sharqīya, and the central part of the Wadi Sumāyil itself.

The contrast between the spectacular scenery of the mountains and the monotonous plain of the desert foreland is remarkable, all the more so as the transition is usually abrupt. Apart from gentle structural relief produced by the block-faulted 'Haushi-Huqf swell' near the south coast and the surface expression of deep-seated salt domes and anticlines (some of which contain oil, notably Fahūd) in central Oman, almost the only features on the Oligo-Miocene desert platform surface are those formed by recent erosional and depositional processes. The most obvious of these are the sand dunes which, under the influence of the dominant *shimāl* (north-west wind), extend from the main part of the Empty Quarter right across to the mountains in the north. In the south-east the isolated dune field of the Wahība sands, whose NNE-SSW ridge alignment is largely controlled by the winds of the monsoon circulation (modified by the mountain barrier), similarly threatens the piedmont settlements of the Badīya and Wādi al-Baṭḥā. In central Oman however, the interplay of the two wind regimes has kept the sand at bay, with the result that a complete classical desert piedmont sequence of mountain, bajada, and playa zones (e.g. the Umm al-Samīm) has developed there without interruption.

The resulting physical layout, of a barren, waterless plain and an outer ring of encircling sand dunes, on the desert side of the mountains completes the natural defences which protect the settlements that nestle under the Jabal Akhdhar massif: on at least two occasions we know of sizeable expeditions which, thinking it easier to strike at the peoples of the Jawf from the desert rather than forcing the mountain passages, simply disappeared without trace in these wastelands (de Goeje 1895; *Tuḥfa* i. 353).

Another feature on the western side of the mountains that has played a determining role in the human geography of the region is the bajada zone, that is the zone of coalescing piedmont outwash fans (*sayḥ* pl. *siyūḥ*) extending up to some 25 km into the desert foreland. Except where interrupted by the encroaching sand and the sprawling foothills, this transitional feature between the mountains proper and the full desert provides a line of relatively easy movement along the foot of the range, and has important grazing and water resources. Its role as a 'frontier of settlement' will be discussed in Chapter III.

DISTRIBUTION OF POPULATION

The twofold physical division of Oman into a desert foreland and a mountain zone is also reflected in the distribution of population, for, in their traditional way of life, some 90 to 95 per cent of the population of Oman probably lived east of the line where the bajada zone finally merges into the full desert. On the other hand, this by no means implies that the settled zone is densely populated, for even in central Oman only $1\frac{1}{2}$ per cent of its land surface is cultivated, while considerable areas of mountain exist which are useless even for grazing. Indeed, it is only in the few favoured spots where run-off is concentrated to provide a regular supply of fresh water adequate for cultivation all the year round that permanent settlement is possible in the interior: and this is the reason why the majority of villages are located in the larger valleys and along the inner edge of the bajada zone. Since, moreover, most of this water is found in underground aquifers, and the *falaj* techniques (see Chapter IV) by which these have traditionally been exploited are only capable of relatively small flows, the villages tend to be small and isolated from each other. Even where the *aflāj* have been grouped, the largest settlement clusters in the mountains (like Sumāyil, Rustāq, and Nizwā) have total populations well under 10,000; for the most part the typical settlement has a population of between 500 and 2,500.

A contrast to this nucleated settlement pattern of interior Oman is presented by the Batina coast, where perhaps a third of the population of Oman live by fishing and agriculture (cf. Fig. 6). Here, there is a virtually continuous cultivated strip, and while the inhabitants do tend to congregate in village units, there is much scattered settlement between, so that the villages merge into each other. Elsewhere along the coast the villages are small and are often cut off from each other by high mountain divides, so that their only means of contact is by sea.

One of the curious features of this traditional settlement pattern is the absence of any urban development. The only exception occurs in the main port, but even here the size of the population varies enormously with the state of the entrepôt trade, and it is to be doubted whether, even at the time of greatest maritime activity, the population of the principal coastal town ever exceeded 50,000.

Before discussing the reasons for this population distribution, we must first obtain some idea of the main economies of the region, and see how these have given rise to two quite different forms of socio-economic organization.

THE REGIONAL ECONOMY

The traditional economy of the region basically depends on the exploitation of its agricultural and maritime resources. While there is some exchange between the coastal, mountain, and desert parts of Oman (cf. Table 7), and pearls, dried fish, dried fruits (dates, some limes, and pomegranates), and livestock (donkeys, camels and, it would appear in earlier times, horses[8]) provide items for export, the settlements are fundamentally self-sufficient and there is little commercial contact between them. The only major centre of exchange is in the main port, but since it is the 'international' merchant class controlling Oman's entrepôt trade that also reaps the largest part of the returns on exports of local produce, the profits are rarely reinvested in the

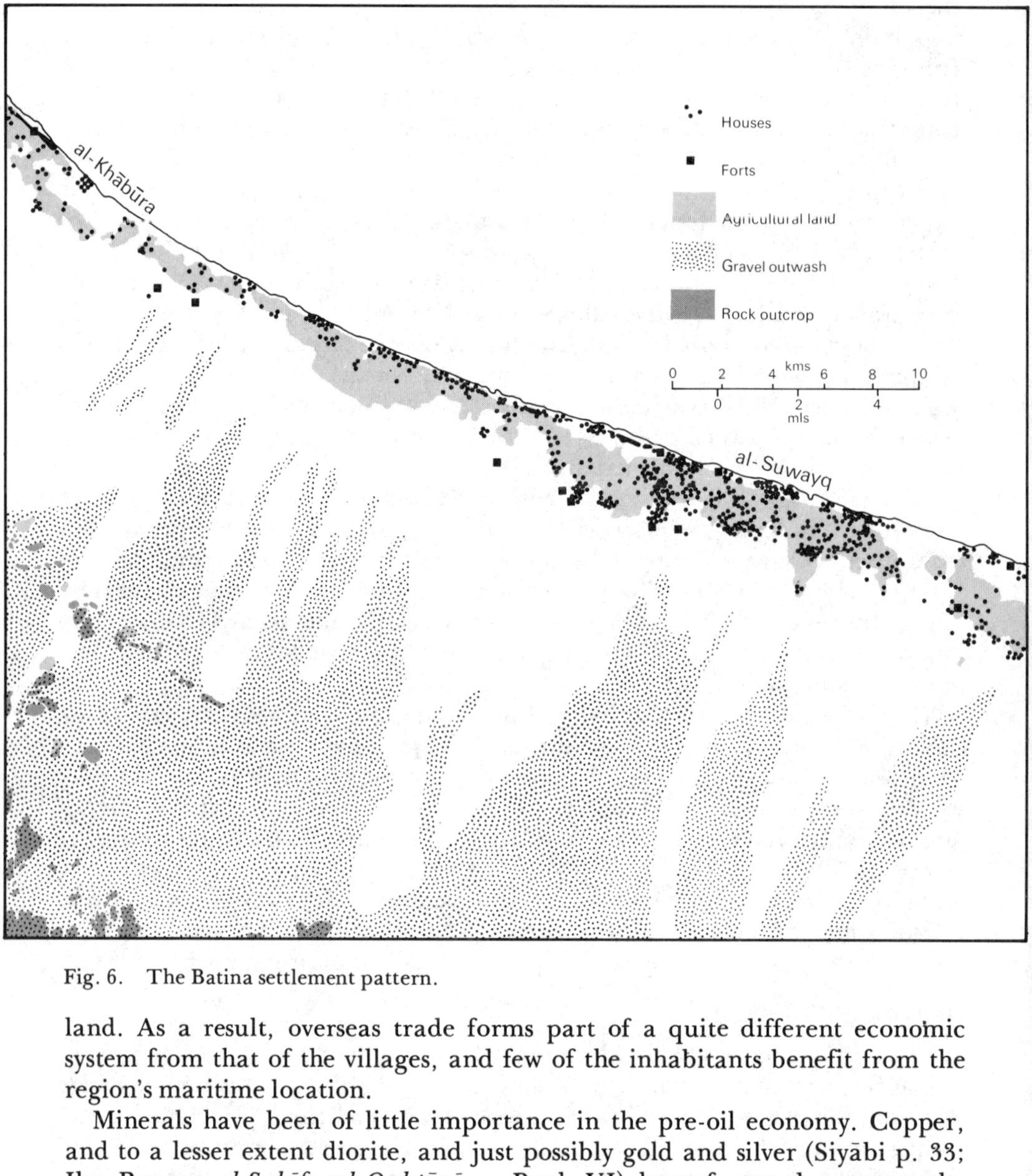

Fig. 6. The Batina settlement pattern.

land. As a result, overseas trade forms part of a quite different economic system from that of the villages, and few of the inhabitants benefit from the region's maritime location.

Minerals have been of little importance in the pre-oil economy. Copper, and to a lesser extent diorite, and just possibly gold and silver (Siyābi p. 33; Ibn Ruzayq *al-Ṣaḥīfa al-Qaḥṭānīya*, Book VI) have featured amongst the products of Oman in the distant past, but their exploitation declined in Islamic times and already appears to have been very much reduced by the tenth century.

Little need be said about the manufacturing and processing industries of the region either. Society is pre-industrial, and the traditional economic occupations gave rise to few secondary activities. On the coast ship-building may once have been of some importance, but it is probable that the larger craft were constructed outside the country and only the smaller pearling- and fishing-boats built locally. In the villages the dyeing and weaving of cloth were formerly important, but this 'home' textile industry collapsed once cheap European woven goods flooded the Afro-Asian market,[9] and by the beginning of this century there were few looms left in Oman (Landen 1967, pp. 144-6; Miles 1910): *sūq* crafts also declined for similar reasons, and only a few skilled copper- and silver-workers now exist.

THE MARITIME ECONOMY

Fresh water and grazing apart, all the other main resources which provide a basic livelihood for the peoples of Oman come from the sea.

Fishing

Each year, from roughly the vicinity of Shiḥr on the south coast of Arabia round to Muscat, cold water, rich in minerals, wells up from depths of over 2,000 fathoms and spreads westwards towards Aden, and northwards along the Omani coast towards the eastern end of the virtually land-locked Gulf. In the strong sunlight of the Arabian summer intense photosynthesis takes place in the euphotic zone and so starts the food chain of phytoplankton, small fish (notably sardine, *ʿawma*, and anchovy, *barīya*), and finally surface-swimming and pelagic predators, which makes the Omani coast rich fishing-ground. Indeed, recent investigations have shown that the general area affected by this upwelling offers one of the few really large underdeveloped fisheries in the world; a rough estimate of its possible exploitation is in the order of a fifth of present world production. The traditional catch, of course, only represents a small proportion of this figure, but even so it provides the local population with a major protein-rich foodstuff, supplementary animal feed, and one of the few sources of fertilizer for an area where soils are highly deficient in organic nutrients. There is also a small export of various types of dried fish, most of which goes to the Indian subcontinent.

In certain parts of Oman fishing is virtually the sole occupation of the inhabitants; a recent study (Ministry of Overseas Development 1969) estimates that even today 30 per cent of the economically active population in the Northern Trucial States (that is excluding Abu Dhabi) living outside the two main towns of Dubai and Sharja are still sea-going fishermen. Generally speaking, however, fishing is confined inshore and is a seasonal occupation of the winter months. Pearling, on the other hand, is a summer occupation. Yet the two do not fully complement each other, partly because the pearl-banks are in different areas from the richest fishing grounds, and partly because pearling is organized on commercial lines, whereas fishing tends to form part of the subsistence economy.

Pearling[10]

The pearl-banks of Ceylon and the Gulf were for long the two main sources of natural pearls for the old world: also associated with this industry was the production of some mother-of-pearl. Just how important the pearl industry was to the traditional economy of the Gulf was brought out by Lorimer (i, 2220) when he wrote at the beginning of this century:

> Were the supply of pearls to fail, the trade of Kuwait would be severely crippled, while that of Bahrain might — it is estimated — be reduced to about one-fifth of its present dimensions and the ports of Trucial 'Omān, which have no other resources, would practically cease to exist; in other words the purchasing power of the inhabitants of the eastern coast of Arabia depends very largely upon the pearl fisheries.

At the beginning of the 1930s, when world trade was already in general recession, the advent of the cultured pearl did produce just such a disaster. For one short period at the end of the Second World War the dying embers of the local pearl trade flickered again, but today they are quite cold. Fortunately for the peoples of the Gulf, this natural resource, hitherto the only indigenous product of major value in international trade, was replaced by a new one, oil. Yet there need be no nostalgia for the passing of the old way of life, for there certainly cannot be many who actually experienced working in the stench of the pearling-boats, with nothing to eat and drink but a few handfuls of fish, dates, and fetid water, and with the prospect of bringing nothing home at the end of the season except debt, who will regret the change.

Unfortunately, the transition from pearls to oil did not take place without economic and social dislocation, for even though oil was discovered in Bahrain in 1932, it was not for another thirty years that production started from the Lower Gulf. As a result the people of Trucial Oman were extremely hard hit, and it is estimated that some 18,000 of them, mostly adult males, had to leave their homes to seek employment further north (Fenelon 1973). In the following discussion of the organization of pearling, the industry will be described as it existed in the pre-cultured-pearl era, and its role in the traditional economy of our area evaluated in that light.

Although there are some fisheries of importance on the Persian coast, notably between Lingeh and Tāhiri, the main concentration of the pearl-banks in the Gulf are in the shallow waters (down to about 20 fathoms) on the Arabian coast. Here the principal pearling-banks are located on either side of the Qaṭar Peninsula; those to the north-west include the famous Bahrain fisheries, while those of the Lower Gulf are enclosed by a line drawn from the tip of the Peninsula to a point just west of Dubai (cf. Fig. 7). Theoretically, the right to seek pearls was open to all the peoples of the Gulf: 'On the Arabian side all the banks, whether near to or far from the coast, are free to the pearl fishers of Arabia and Persia without distinction of race or nationality. The boats from particular ports generally frequent certain localities more than others, but they do this of choice and not necessity' (Lorimer i. 2240-1).

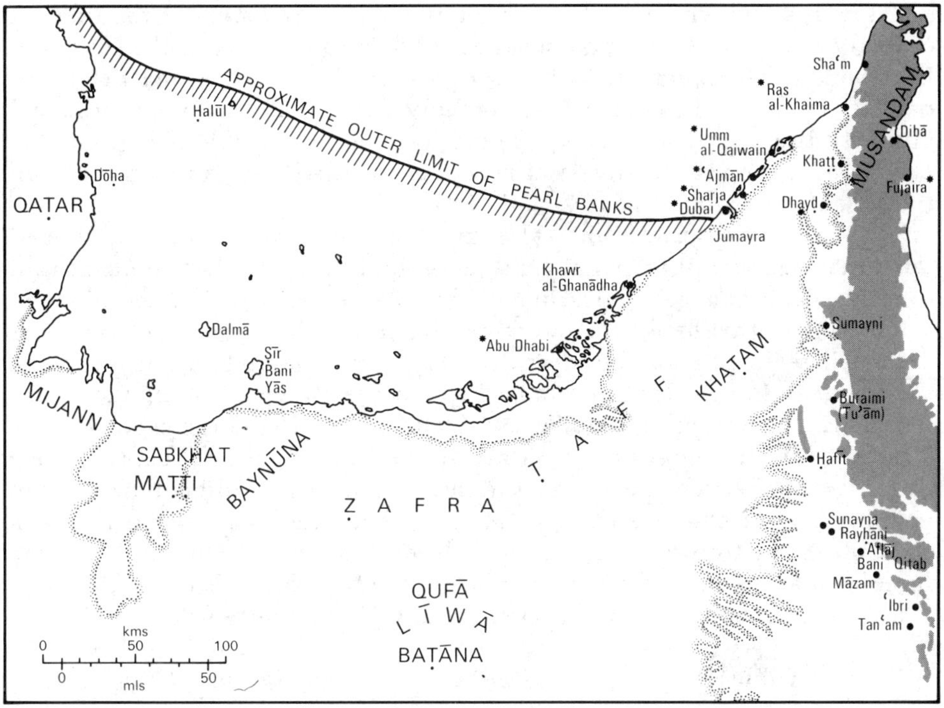

Fig. 7. Northern Oman. The capitals of the Trucial States are starred.

In fact, there was more territorialism involved in fishing the pearl-banks than Lorimer implies. While it is true that there were no overt barriers which prevented the inhabitants of the Gulf from going anywhere they liked to pearl, the fact remains that they could only do so by joining a fleet operating from a particular port. As a result every pearler found himself under the jurisdiction of one of the coastal rules, for each fleet was commanded by an admiral (*sirdāl* in Abu Dhabi terminology) who was appointed by the local shaikh to ensure that the rigid disciplines of the traditional pearling-code were enforced and that all members of his fleet kept to the prescribed timetables; furthermore, any disputes were referred to the local *sālifat al-ghawṣ*, that is the 'divers' court', whose members were also appointed by the shaikh.

The authority of the local shaikh in pearling matters was further reinforced by his right to collect certain taxes from those involved in the industry. While details of exactly what these were have varied at different times in different places, it certainly seems to have been accepted generally that everyone involved in pearling should pay some form of levy to the ruler on whose territory he was based. The producers paid a fixed sum per boat, plus a share of the profit gained by the crew from the sale of pearls of exceptional value, to the ruler of the home port from which the fleet operated; the *ṭawāwīsh* (sing. *ṭawwāsh*) merchants, who supplied the pearling-fleet during the four months it was at sea and who also acted as intermediary purchasers of the finds of ordinary pearls (*qumāsh*), paid a variety of dues to the ruler of the land-base from which they operated;[11] while the merchants who marketed the pearls paid levies to the ruler in whose territory they conducted their principal business (direct taxes were only customarily taken on the sale of high-quality pearls and not on profits made in re-selling the small pearls which make up the bulk of the season's finds).

Thus even though the littoral shaikhs might have no openly defined territorial right over the actual pearling-grounds, they did have some control over the people engaged in pearling, and as a result each of the fleets did tend to go to the pearl-banks that were contiguous to the territory of the ruler under whose jurisdiction they operated. This is why we find that the people of Ḥasā and Bahrain island normally kept to the western side of the Qaṭar Peninsula, the Persians to the Persian side of the Gulf, and the peoples of the Trucial Coast and most of the Qaṭaris to the Lower Gulf: in contrast, those countries which had no pearl-banks in their coastal waters did not take part in pearling and, as can be seen from Table 2, there were no fleets operating in the Gulf either from Ottoman Iraq or from non-Trucial Oman (there may have been a few boats from these places attached to the fleets of the main pearling-ports, but their numbers were relatively unimportant).

Table 2 *Pearl Fishing in the Gulf in 1907*

Sites of Ports	*Number of men employed in pearling*
Trucial Oman	22,045
Qaṭar	12,890
Bahrain	17,633
Ḥasā Sanjāq	3,444
Kuwait	9,200
Persia	8,884
Oman	Nil
Turkish Iraq	Nil
Total approx.	75,000

Source: based on Lorimer i, appendix C.

Commercial Organization of Pearling and Maritime Trade

This system of loose territorial control clearly played a part in stopping a free-for-all on the pearl-banks, and helped prevent the petty squabbles, that easily flared up under the foul conditions in which pearling was conducted, from reaching serious proportions. It does not, however, explain how fleets from hostile states could operate, more or less peacefully, alongside each other, or why the followers of the more powerful littoral shaikhs did not try to appropriate the best pearl-banks in the general area where they fished. The question therefore arises, how could an industry, based on a resource which belonged to no particular group, operate in the highly fragmented political society of the Gulf without some sort of central political authority?[12]

The answer has to be sought in the special mechanisms through which commerce was formerly organized in the Gulf. It is important to understand how these worked, because the explanation is relevant not just to pearling, but also to the entrepôt and carrying trade, so significant to Oman.

The exploitation of the pearl resources of the Gulf demanded a high degree of capital financing. There were two main reasons for this, the shortness of the pearling season and the uncertainties of its profits. Pearling can only take place when the winter *shimāls* have died down and the waters are warm and calm enough for diving. Although in some areas a little pearling did start in spring, when a few of the local inhabitants of the coastal districts fished the very shallow inshore waters on foot (this was known as the *mijanna* — cf. the district Mijann in western Abu Dhabi), the first sorties in boats did not begin until the short *khančīya* season at the end of May, and it was normally not until June that the *ghawṣ al-kabīr* got under way: after this main pearling season had finished in September, a few pearlers might return to the banks (hence the name *al-radda*) for a short period until cold conditions finally drove them back to land. Thus while pearling did take place on a limited scale in some areas for half the year, the effective season only lasted four months. So it can be seen that because the boats were only used for part of the year (fishing and local trade did not absorb the excess capacity in the rest of the year), and because the fleets had to be stocked and equipped, and advances made to the crews so that their families could live during their continuous four months' absence from land, there was a need for greater capital financing than would have been the case had pearling not been a seasonal occupation.

This need was further accentuated by the unpredictability of profits, which varied partly with the fluctuations of the market, and partly with year-to-year changes in the supply of pearls of different qualities. For example, while the accounted average annual value of the pearls exported from the Gulf between 1873 and 1904 was £561,353, the returns for the individual years during that period ranged from £327,968 to £1,493,975. These financial risks were borne by all who took part in pearling, for no one engaged in the industry received a set wage: but they were considerably greater for a crew member dependent on the vagaries of his boat's catch, than they were for the merchant who was in a position to spread his investment. In a series of bad seasons therefore, the ship-owners (*nawkhudhas*) had increasing recourse to the land-based merchants and financiers, while the divers (*ghayṣ* pl. *ghāṣa*), pullers (*sayb* pl. *suyūb*), and other crew-members, unable to repay the advances made to them, grew deeper in debt with their boat captain. Because such debts used automatically to devolve on a man's family so that one of his relatives had to replace him when he died or before he could retire, the resulting system of indebtedness amounted to one of virtual slavery for the poorer people in the old days: their only hope of escape was the miracle of the pearl of great price. To what extent these debtor laws applied outside Bahrain is not clear from the written records, but there the system was so entrenched that when a new pearling-code was introduced in 1926 it had to be enforced in the face of violent opposition from the very men it was meant to help (Belgrave, C. 1960, ch. IV).

The linchpins in this financial system were the *tujjār*, a group of merchants who handled virtually all the external commerce of the Gulf, but who only dealt indirectly with the local *ṭawwāsh* merchants and financiers (*musaqqam*) through an agent (*dallāl*). Their trade was mostly with India, for even though pearls were sold directly in Persia and Baghdad, the major demand came from India which also handled the international market. At the same time the subcontinent consumed, directly or indirectly, most of the other Gulf exports (dates, dried fish, etc.), supplied a large proportion of its imports (notably rice and woven goods), and was the principal entrepôt for goods handled by Gulf shipping.

Since the commerce between the Gulf and India was so intricately linked, and since much of it was made up of high-value goods which had to be handled many times without corresponding transfers of cash, a code of conduct, overruling individual loyalties to race, religion, tribe, or state, developed between the merchants of the two areas. Consequently the *tujjār* formed a quite distinct socio-economic class, and their virtual autonomy was accepted by others precisely because they fulfilled the basic need for economic exchange in a divided society: indeed it might be said of them that, like the international companies of the modern world, 'if they had not existed they would have had to have been invented'. True there were important differences between the Banian (Hindu merchants) and Gulf merchants, and one or other tended to dominate different aspects of commerce at various times:[13] but so long as this was due to economic vagaries, and not to social or political pressures, then the integrity of their commercial organization was unaffected and the economy of the Gulf assured.

On the other hand, whenever a local ruler attempted to impede their commercial relationships or to gain special advantages by other than generally accepted means, he was liable to find his territory boycotted. An example of how the merchants could make or break a place in this way is provided by the story of what happened to the main pearl market of the Lower Gulf.[14] During the nineteenth century this was at Lingeh, but in 1902 the entire international merchant community deserted the port because the demands of the newly reorganized Persian customs service became too exigent; as a result Lingeh became moribund. By contrast, their move to Dubai, then recently opened up by a regular steamer service to India, marked the beginnings of a new era of prosperity for that port, a prosperity which did not decline with the collapse of pearling because the merchants adapted their commercial network to the new ventures of smuggling gold and luxury goods to Persia and India. So the fortunes of ports on the Gulf and Red Sea routes tended to depend far more on attracting the international merchant class through the liberal policies of the rulers and the social attitudes of the inhabitants rather than on any physical advantage of site or location; it was for that reason that the Banians were not only tolerated but were even encouraged to settle in the ports, a fact which frequently called forth surprised comment from European visitors to the area (cf. Hamilton 1727; de la Roque 1715; Niebuhr 1772; de Gobineau 1859).

It was therefore, the existence of this 'international' merchant class which ensured that the Gulf's pearling and carrying trade did not stop, even when individual states themselves might be at war. It was through the merchants, too, that a certain political equilibrium was maintained between the rulers of these states, for should one try to gain control of a source of production or monopolize a sector in the communal industries by other than accepted commercial means, then his port was automatically ostracized. If matters really got out of hand, the merchants tended to desert the Gulf and divert as much of their trade as they could to the alternative ports in southern Arabia and the Red Sea until such time as the right economic climate was restored.

The power of the merchant class was therefore considerable. Traditionally it was they who made the biggest profits from the region's maritime resources and locational advantages, it was they who generated virtually all its foreign exchange (indeed theirs was the only fully monetized part of the economy), and it was they who more or less monopolized the means of contact with the outside world. Yet, precisely because the composition of their society was not determined by country, tribe, race, or religion, they were considered an inferior group by most of the other inhabitants of the region, and were liable to suffer from the caprices of local politics: they also formed an easy target for raiding tribesmen from the interior. Like the Lombards of medieval Europe their position was always precarious: whilst they had tremendous power, they learnt that in order to survive they had to use their influence discreetly and avoid ostentatious display of their wealth.

THE DIVORCE BETWEEN THE ECONOMIC SYSTEMS OF MARITIME AND INTERIOR OMAN

This discussion of the pearling industry and of the general way in which Gulf maritime commerce used to be organized brings out a number of points of direct importance for the region with which we are particularly concerned.

The first of these is the obviously important part played by pearling in the traditional economy of Trucial Oman. Of the total population of this area, estimated at 80,000 (including nomads) at the beginning of this century,

22,000 took part in pearling: in other words every able-bodied male must have been engaged in the industry (women played no part in it). The income of the Trucial Shaikhs (after the suppression of piracy, the collapse of slaving, and the decline of the carrying trade in the nineteenth century) was almost entirely dependent on pearl revenues, and this is clearly brought out by the estimated sources of income of the Ruler of Abu Dhabi at the beginning of this century, shown in Table 3. It should, however, be noted that it was not always the shaikhs of western 'Trucial Oman' who were the main beneficiaries of the taxes arising from pearl-fishing on the Arabian side of the Lower Gulf, in earlier times it was Julfār that appears to have acted as the controlling centre for the industry on this part of the coast. On the other hand, the rest of Oman benefited hardly at all from pearling: there was only one minor area of pearling east of the Musandam Peninsula, and at the beginning of this century the value of pearls handled in Muscat was only 1 per cent of that of pearls handled in the Trucial Oman ports.

Table 3 *Estimated Income of the Ruler of Abu Dhabi at the Beginning of the Twentieth Century*

Source	*Amount in MT dollars*
Pearling dues and taxes	62,000
Agriculture (Līwā 2,500, Buraimi 8,000)	10,500
Cash subsidy for controlling the Bedu of Northern Oman	3,000
Total	75,500

Based on Lorimer ii, 409.

Because pearling in Trucial Oman provided an occupation which was common to all the socio-economic groups living there, the migratory movement to the coast in summer gave rise to a common dimension in the complex pattern of seasonal movements that took place between the summer and winter pastures (in the bajada zone and desert foreland), the cultivated oases (in the mountain zone and the Līwā), and the ports and fishing areas on the coast, and this in turn tended to draw the inhabitants of the different zones of economic production into contact with each other, and at the same time, orientated them towards the Gulf proper and away from the rest of Oman. In contrast, such movements between areas of seasonal economic potential have never been necessary on the Batina coast, where the rich fishing and cultivation in the littoral strip complement each other and compensate for the lack of pearling: there economic links are with the peoples of the hinterland, and the inhabitants look out towards the Indian Ocean rather than towards the Gulf. So the differences in the economic organization of the two parts of coastal Oman have played a contributory role in creating the partial divorce that exists between Trucial and non-Trucial Oman.

The second point of importance for the study of our area arises from the traditional organization of trade, with its concentration of economic power in the hands of a particular class of merchant.

Now Oman, as has already been shown, has certain special locational advantages which have attracted this merchant community to its main ports. So, for example, we find Niebuhr (1780 edn., ii. 124) reporting in the 1760s that in no other Muslim town he visited were the Banians so numerous as in Muscat, and he reckoned them to number more than 1,200 there. He also noted that they received equal treatment with Muslims in disputes, and that they were allowed to live according to their own laws, worship their idols, and burn their dead. Despite this toleration of foreign customs, noted by so many visitors to Muscat, the fact remains that differences in attitudes and interests of these outsiders and the local inhabitants have played a very important part in creating the split implicit in the title of the Sultanate, Muscat and Oman. Muscat represents the outward-looking, cosmopolitan trading society of the main port, frequently under foreign domination; Oman the independent, inward-looking, predominantly tribal society of a subsistence economy. To some degree, of course, the same kind of split existed throughout the rest of the Gulf, but there it rarely manifested itself in the form of territorial dichotomy because the economies of the littoral states were predominantly maritime:[15] in Oman, on the other hand, the agricultural resources and natural defences of the mountain zone allowed an autonomous self-sufficient community to exist more or less independently of Muscat.

This split is sometimes described as a division between the coast and the interior. Such a simplification is acceptable provided it is not taken literally, for what in fact is being labelled is the distinction between the traditional socio-economic organizations of the inward- and the outward-looking parts of the country. Thus even though the inhabitants of the Batina live on the coast and gain part of their living from the sea their attitude and social organization are much more akin to those of the tribal agriculturalists of inland Oman than to the peoples of the large trading ports: this incidentally is one of the reasons why their territory tended to be treated as neutral ground whenever 'coastal' Oman fell under the political control of an outside power.

THE AGRICULTURAL ECONOMY

The basis of the economy in interior Oman is agriculture: cultivation, with some livestock-herding.

The latter is much more a village occupation than is generally supposed. While it is true that the grazing of livestock solely on natural vegetation does provide a livelihood for the bedu (correctly *badw*) in the desert fringes and the *shawāwi* nomads in the mountains (i.e. about 5 per cent of the population), a considerable number of sheep, goats, and donkeys are also kept by the hadhar (correctly *ḥaḍar*, settled peoples) who partly crop-feed the animals: cows, which are entirely stall-fed, are naturally kept in the villages (mostly in those around the Jabal Akhdhar), and it is the camel alone which is the speciality of the nomads.[16]

Thus the cultivation of fodder-crops plays a role in the use of village-land and the animals contribute to the economy of the settled peoples, not only with their produce (milk, meat, wool, and manure), but also by acting as beasts of draught and transport. Significant as this contribution is, however, the fact remains that it is very much of secondary importance when compared with the main economic activity in the village: the growing of crops for direct human consumption.

Cultivation in Oman is entirely dependent on irrigation. There is absolutely no rain-fed land (*baᶜl*), and it is only the excess seasonal flow in the wadis and irrigation systems that is used for the growing of annual crops: these include a variety of grain — wheat, barley, millet, sorghum (the *ṣayf* crops planted in winter and harvested in *ṣayf*, late spring) — and some vegetables (notably onions). Regular base flow is almost entirely appropriated for the irrigation of tree crops, but the less reliable discharge is used for alfalfa and other fodder-crops. Sugar-growing appears once to have been rather more important than it is now, while the cultivation of cotton and various dye plants associated with the now virtually defunct village textile industry has also seriously declined (*Kashf* tr. Ross, p. 170; *Tuḥfa* ii. 122; Ibn Ruzayq *Imams* pp. 106-7: Wellsted 1838; Aucher-Eloy 1843). Rice never seems to have been cultivated at all extensively; however, since it comprised an important element in the diet of all but the very poorest people (Whitelock 1835), it formed far and away the largest item of import destined for local consumption.

Tree crops include a wide variety of fruits, and a number of these have been deiberately introduced into the region. Citrus fruits, of which Oman has a great variety, were first introduced from India and from there spread to other parts of the Middle East and the Mediterranean, according to the tenth-century writer Masᶜūdi (*Murūj*, ii. 438), while the banana was so well established that it was even considered native to Oman by a ninth-century writer (source quoted in ᶜAbd al-Laṭīf al-Baghdādi, p. 61). Under the Yaᶜāriba dynasty a number of new crops were introduced, and local histories report how, among his efforts to broaden the country's agricultural economy, one particular Imam of the seventeenth century introduced dye plants (*wars* and *zaᶜfarān*) and the variety of mango (generically *ᶜimba*) known as *mānghā*, and even started apiculture (Maᶜwali, pp. 371, 379-80; *Nudbhat al-Maᶜāwil*, p. 432; *Nahḍa*, p. 60; *Tuḥfa* i. 164-5). The Jabal Akhdhar plateau, which is above the height at which date-palms normally grow, is a particularly interesting area for exotic fruits; these include pomegranates, whose dried fruit forms quite an important item of export, grapes, from which the local inhabitants (the Bani Riyām) are reputed to make a wine, roses which are grown for making rose-water, peaches, apricots, figs, mulberries, and walnuts. The fact that al-Sharīshi (d. 1222) mentions a number of these fruits in his description of the country confirms that they are no new introductions into the area (*Tuḥfa* i. 7-9).

Despite this variety of fruits nearly three-quarters of the area given over to tree crops is monopolized by *Phoenix dactylifera*, the date-palm, while in the interior this proportion rises to seven-eighths (cf. Whitehead Report 1972).

Oman is famous both for the quantity and quality of its dates, and there are a large number of varieties. V. H. W. Dowson, probably the world's leading authority on this crop, visited Oman in June 1927 (see his report in India Office file R15/3/11/25) and was amazed at the productivity of the palms there, all the more so because his visit came after nine years of drought. In some of the better gardens of the Batina he found trees bearing 12 to 15 bunches, each bunch weighing approximately 15 lb (7 kg), and commented that palms like these would produce more sugar for the same area than the finest sugar-cane grown under optimum conditions.[17] The average yield of the Batina palm he estimated at 75 lb (34 kg), but at Sumāyil his estimate went up to 100 lb (45 kg) per palm, that is twice the yield of the average palm in the Shaṭṭ al-ʿArab (the main source of dates entering international trade). Such estimates were confirmed to the present writer by a local informant who stated that in Buraimi the three commonest varieties (*farḍ, naghāl,* and *khaṣāb*), had about 11 bunches per palm and yielded, on average, 40 kg of dates. Although these figures are well above the world average of 20 kg (44 lb per palm), they need occasion no scepticism, for yields of 328 kg have been recorded, and 400 kg reported for a single palm (Dowson-FAO 1965); in the United States, where date statistics have been kept carefully, the Deglet Noor variety (Algerian origin), that makes up approximately three-quarters of the date-palms grown there, regularly yields between 200 and 300 lb (90-135 kg) per palm (U.S. Dept. of Agriculture 1951). Furthermore, in the Ḥasā province of Saudi Arabia, where yields similar to Oman might be expected, a FAO survey (1952) quotes a modal yield of between 30 and 50 kg per palm, and states that up to 300 kg can be expected from really good palms in the better groves.

Of recent years however, the yield of date-palms in Oman, as elsewhere in the Gulf, has decreased horrifyingly. There are two main reasons for this. First there is a shortage of labour in the villages. In the last twenty years many young Omanis have gone to work in the oil-producing states, while others left because of the oppressive régime of the recently deposed Sultan. While some of these men are today coming back to their homeland, it is not to the villages that they return, but to the rapidly expanding capital area around Muscat where the oil economy is engendering new forms of employment. The impact of these changes on the demographic structure of the settlements in the interior is indicated by a medical survey carried out in a village in the Sharqīya (quoted in Whitehead Report 1972): this shows that males of the over-60 age-group make up 11.7 per cent of the population, against an estimated figure of about 3 per cent for the Sultanate as a whole, while the 15-30 age-group comprises only 13.2 per cent of the village population, as against a norm of about 30 per cent: indeed, the whole population of males of working age (15-60) resident in the village only formed a fifth of its total population. While the reliability of these figures is not very great, they do indicate the way village populations are ageing and the increasing imbalance between the two sexes.

The second reason is that the traditional market for dates is collapsing. Of recent years the all-important Indian trade has virtually ceased, due to currency problems; the East African demand has more or less dried up since the Omanis were driven out of Zanzibar in 1964; while the South Arabian market has similarly shut for political reasons. The United States, which was a significant importer of high-grade dates (mostly of the *farḍ* variety) at the end of the last century, has, as a result of developing its own date cultivation, long since ceased to be an important customer, while the limited European market has been lost to specialist producers like Algeria and Iraq. Even home consumption is decreasing as feeding habits change, and today more and more dates are fed to animals or simply wasted.

The result has been a lamentable decline in the standards of date-farming. While the area under palms has so far changed little (except perhaps that there has been an increase of alfalfa at the cost of the palm), the trees are ageing, they are badly tended, and the female spathes are not properly fertilized: in addition the disease *mataq* (*Omatisous binatosis*) is rife, and in an agricultural survey of 1971 it was estimated that 80 per cent of the palms were infected. It is not surprising, therefore, that the results of the 1971 survey indicate that the average yield of the palm is as low as 22.4 lb (10 kg) on the Batina, and 42.6 lb (19 kg) in the interior. Even allowing for the fact that the Dowson estimates might have been on the high side, these statistics clearly show the measure of the decline in date yields in recent years.

In the traditional economy of Oman, however, the date-palm was all important. Just how vital it was may perhaps best be appreciated by looking at its production in terms of calories per head of population and in terms of its export potential. To take calory yields first: if we work on the basis

1. that the Whitehead survey estimate of 2 million date-palms on the Batina and 1.4 million in the interior of the Sultanate is closer to reality than Dowson's guess of $1\frac{1}{2}$ million and 1 million respectively for the two areas (figures which have subsequently featured in international tables);
2. that a pound of dates (with a moisture content of 20 per cent) yields 1,450 calories (U.S. Dept. of Agriculture 1951);
3. that the *per capita* calory requirement for a population structure typical of Oman is 2,000 calories per day (Clark and Haswell 1970);
4. that the population of Oman is between 400,000 and 500,000, of which half live in the interior (Whitehead Report 1972),

then we can see that even at today's yields dátes provide half the potential calory requirement of the population, while in the interior this figure goes up to five-eighths. In a good year in former times this figure might well have exceeded 100 per cent.

The potential for export is therefore considerable. On the assumption that the *per capita* consumption of dates in the period 1961–3 in Saudi Arabia of 96 lb (43 kg; FAO 1969 commodity notes) was also typical of the traditional pattern in Oman, then it follows that there was a minimal exchangeable surplus in the order of 25,000 metric tons, and this might rise to some three times this figure in a good year. Even at the present very-much-reduced world prices (Dowson 1968) this indicates a minimal export value of close on $U.S. 300,000.

Trade figures from the beginning of this century tend to confirm these estimates. A conservative valuation of Omani date exports from Muscat in the 1890s was $M.T. 750,000 (i.e. in the order of £90,000; it is difficult to work out the exact sterling equivalent, as the silver value of the Maria Theresa dollar fluctuated violently at the time: cf. Landen 1967, pp. 125 and 147; Lorimer i. 2307), while at the beginning of the present century it was £81,000 (Lorimer i, app. D), that is only just under 20 per cent of the value of all date exports from the Gulf (including Iraq). Lorimer adds that the accounted volume may have been as little as a half of what really was exported from the country as a whole. The value of dates relative to other exports is even harder to estimate, but figures for the period 1875-81 as given in the *Muscat Administration Reports* show that they made up about 60 per cent of local produce exports (i.e. excluding re-exports).

The major and steady demand for Omani dates has always been from India. J. Ovington (1696, p. 423) described the situation in the late seventeenth century as follows: 'They have so much plenty of this fruit, for which they have so ready a vent in India, that several ships are sent thither loaded from hence without any other cargo.' India also tended to handle the Omani export to the Far East, but this may not always have been so, for certainly in Sung times China seemes to have received its imports direct (*Chu-fan-chih*: cf. Wheatley 1959).

Dates are exported in two forms, *bisr* and *siḥḥ*, each traditionally having about the same monetary value. *Bisr* are low-quality dates, the majority of which come from the Batina[18] (particularly from the non-irrigated palms which grow just above the shore where the fruit is affected by humidity and salinity); they are boiled (at which stage they are known as *faghūr*) and pressed and are so-called because they are cut at the early *bisr* stage of ripening:[19] in Persia they are known as *khāraq* and in India as *salūq*, according to the author of the *Nahḍa* (p. 60). Such treatment is not for the fine dates of the interior. Most of the very best dates (*khalāṣi, khanēzi, jabari, hilāli*, and most of the *bughūl* varieties) are eaten fresh as *ruṭab* (fully ripe) and are sold on the branch (*ʿadhaq*), and not by weight. Second- and third-class qualities are stored until they turn into *siḥḥ* (the Omani term for *tamar*, this is the state of the date as most Europeans know it), and are then packed and sold in baskets of different size.

THE DUALITY OF THE REGION

With this account of the date-palm, which provides the basic livelihood for so many of the inhabitants of Oman, we may leave this preliminary survey of the region. In doing so, however, the writer would like to emphasize one point that has already begun to emerge, and one that will continue to come out more and more in the course of this study, the duality of the region. When one of the earliest visitors to the interior of Oman, the French botanist Aucher-Eloy, wrote:

> Je ne m'attendais pas à une pareille simplicité à si peu de distance de Mascate, fréquentée par des Européens . . . Du reste, je dois rendre justice à la vérité: si la race mixte de la population de Mascate est fort méchante, il n'en est pas de même de l'intérieur, où j'ai trouvé géneralement beaucoup d'hospitalité, d'honnêteté et parfois de cordialité. Le Cheik de Mascate n'a du reste qu'une autorité fort précaire sur les Cheiks de l'intérieur, qui ont pour lui une certaine déférence, mais ne lui donnent ni argent ni soldats, et si l'Imam [i.e. the ruler of Muscat] voulait être exigeant, ils seraient fort en état de le braver dans leurs forteresses. Je pense que la bonté des gens de l'intérieur tient au gouvernement fort doux et, pour ainsi dire, républicain des Cheiks; le peuple n'y est pas riche, mais on n'y voit aucun pauvre. Il faut si peu de choses à ces Arabes. (*Voyage en Orient de 1830-1838* ii. 566, 575-6)

he was describing the duality which comes out in every aspect of the country that we care to study: Sultanate and Imamate, Muscat and Oman, bedu and hadhar, tribal and non-tribal societies, subsistence and exchange economies, coastal and interior Oman, conservatism and acceptance of change, and so on. But because, like two faces of the same coin, these divisions complement each other, it is not possible to draw clear-cut lines between them, any more than it proved possible (or even necessary) under the terms of the so-called Treaty of Sib (1920), to draw the boundaries between Muscat and Oman, or to define the respective authorities of the Imam and Sultan.

Here in this book it is only with the traditional organization of the inward-looking tribal society living in the villages of the mountainous interior of Oman that we will really be concerned, and little will be said about the obverse of the coin. In other words, when we use the name 'Oman' we shall tend to employ it in the sense of 'Oman' in contradistinction to 'Muscat'. The main theme we shall be pursuing is the way the inter-relationship between social and locational organization has evolved in the region, particularly at the grass-roots level of the village. The next four chapters will thus be concerned with the basic elements which have determined the way man has settled: the where and why of water availability, the techniques by which it has been exploited, and the systems by which irrigation is organized. It will then be possible to consider the peculiarities of this land-use, to find out why it has evolved in certain ways and not in others, and to investigate the respective constraints society and settlement have placed on each other.

Notes to Chapter I

[1] The application of the name of one of the settlements in what is now the Sultanate part of the oasis (cf. Fig. 17) to the whole seems to be a European practice. It may find its origins in ʿAbd al-Wahhāb's *Lamʿ al-Shihāb* which, the writer believes, was specifically compiled at second hand for the Indian Government's Resident in Baghdad in the early nineteenth century (cf. also introduction to sources in Aramco 1952 and Abu Hakima 1965). The old name was Tuʾām or Tawʾam (for argument about spelling see Bakri i. 207), and this still survives in Tayma, the alternative name for al-ʿAyn (or ʿAyn al-Ẓawāhir), which is the main settlement in the Abu Dhabi part of the oasis.

[2] In 1970 the official title was changed to the Sultanate of Oman.

[3] These states are now loosely federated into the United Arab Emirates.

[4] The official Arabic spelling is Masqaṭ. In classical sources it is sometimes spelt with the definite article (e.g. Muqaddasi, p. 93), while Ibn Mujāwir (ii. 284) says its spelling is really Maskat: the form Masqat is used by ʿAbd al-Wahhāb in the *Lamʿ al-Shihāb* (in the original MS. but not the printed edition). The Omani sources frequently write Maskad, and this spelling is supported by the pronunciation in certain local dialects (e.g. Rössler 1898, p. 72). The most extraordinary spelling of Muscat, Maska (with a *tāʾ marbūṭa*) occurs in a letter from the Imam Muḥammad b. ʿAbdullāh al-Khalīli (quoted in *Nahḍa* 80). As with so many other names in Oman (indicated, *inter alia*, by the frequent spelling of a final 'a' with an *alif mamdūda* and an absence or irregular usage of the definite article), the name is clearly an Arabization.

[5] Throughout this work the writer has deliberately revived the use of old regional names (cf. Fig. 2), even though some have dropped out of current use, precisely because they express geographic organization. All of them occur regularly in the written sources, with the exception of 'Ghadaf' which is the local name for the area focusing on Rustāq and contrasts with 'Jawf', the 'Inner' side of the Jabal al-Akhḍar. Sometimes these names were used interchangeably for both the region and its main centre. Thus in some of the older texts, Sirr may refer to ʿIbri alone, and Jāʿlān possibly to the settlements of the Wadi Baṭḥāʾ. By contrast Tuʾām frequently means the region and not just the oasis of Buraimi, which Jul(a)fār (variant Jur(a)fār) may not always refer specifically to the now defunct port near Ras al-Khaima, but to the wider dependent region which extended as far west as Sharja; this region seems to overlap with that known as al-Ṣīr (*Kashf* MS. 503; cf. also Williamson 1973a, fn. 42).

[6] It is worth noting here that central government in Persia has never exercised direct control on both shores of the Strait of Hormuz since the seventh century.

[7] The geological material incorporated in this study is based partly on information and maps kindly supplied by members of the geological departments in Petroleum Development (Oman) Ltd. and the Iraq Petroleum and Associated Companies, and partly on published sources, notably Morton 1959; Tschopp 1967; Wilson 1969; Glennie 1970; Glennie, *et. al.* 1973.

[8] At one time the rearing of horses must have been of considerable importance in Oman, to judge by reports of European visitors to Hormuz. It was probably stimulated in the fourteenth and fifteenth centuries by demand from India, where war-horses were used, but not bred (cf. Williamson 1973a). The decline probably set in in the sixteenth century (Viré, F., EI_2 art. Faras), and by the beginning of the nineteenth century horse-breeding had virtually died out in Oman (Heude 1819, p. 31; Wellsted 1838, i. 303). Today the present writer has found absolutely no traces of any traditions about horse-breeding, and no references in the local sources.

[9] Cf. the account of the impact of European trade on Oman given by the Political Agent in the *Muscat Trade Report for 1919 20:*

Oman is a perfect example, as were Genoa and Venice in former days, of the decay produced by a change of trade routes and methods of transport. And this process of decay has not yet ceased. The opening up of Dubai on the Pirate coast as a steamer port has seriously affected Muscat through which it was formerly supplied, and has more than halved the trade of Sohar which only a few years ago supplied the whole Birami [sic] oases and Hinterland. Manchester piece goods have killed the local industries, wealth has passed almost entirely into alien hands, and it is probable that few people in the world have less cause to bless the advance of European civilization than the Arabs of Oman.

[10] The following account is partly based on original field-work and partly on the following principal references: Lorimer i. app. C *et passim*; British Memorial i. 46 8, 65 7 and app. G; Belgrave, C. 1960, chap. IV; Belgrave, J. 1965; al-Nabhāni *Tuḥfa al-Nabhānīya* pp. 13-22 (cf. also Rentz in ed. Issawi 1966, part V, chap. 3); also on material in EI_2 art. al-Durr (Ruska, J.); Rumaihi 1973; Teixeira pp. 175-81; de Thévenot 1727 edn., iv. 576-9; Whitelock 1835; Wilson 1833.

[11] In the case of the pearl-fisheries of the Lower Gulf, most of these merchants based themselves on Dalmā, an island whose population swelled from a handful of fishermen in winter to 600 in the pearling season; and so it was to the Ruler of Abu Dhabi, regardless of their country of origin or whom they were supplying, that they paid the customary levies.

[12] The fact that there were mechanisms by which the pearling industry could operate without a central political authority did not mean that the latter was redundant. In times of general political instability fighting at sea frequently affected pearling, and it was because of this that Britain arranged and guaranteed a series of annual truces by which in the early nineteenth century the littoral states of the Lower Gulf kept the peace at sea during the pearling season: these truces became permanent after 1858. In other periods of history leading powers in the Gulf have also probably been able to limit conflict on the pearl-banks, and it is worth noting in this connection that the rulers of Bahrain have often been able to exert considerable influence over pearling matters in the Gulf. Nevertheless, even in times of general anarchy, pearling did not stop, and it is principally the reasons behind this that are being investigated here.

[13] For example, Lorimer reported that the Arabs had increasingly come to dominate the pearl trade of recent years, and he reckoned that three-quarters of the entire trade was in Arab hands by the end of the nineteenth century: in the 1820s the situation was the reverse (cf. Whitelock 1835).

[14] For an early tenth century example of boycotting ports as a result of a Jewish member of the merchant fraternity involved in the China trade being seized by the greedy Caliph al-Muqtadir see (attributed Bozorg Ibn Chahrayār), *ʿAjāy ib al-Hind*, pp. 107 et seq.

[15] Conversely one might argue that the split has already taken place, and that is why so many small littoral states have come into existence on the Arabian side of the Gulf. On the Persian coast territorial integrity has been maintained, but in the past the political control of central Government over the coastal areas has all too often been purely hypothetical.

[16] The donkey is the main beast of burden for the settled peoples, and is in no way considered an undignified mount. For the long-distance transport of heavy goods, however, the camel is traditionally used, and so the main carrying trade is in the hands of the nomadic groups. Mechanized transport has rapidly changed this situation and during a recent visit to Oman (1973) the writer did not see a single camel-train in the Sumāyil Gap, whereas when he was previously there (1965) several would have been encountered on this route. The traditional livestock economy of the bedu has also been affected by modern changes (labour shortage, different diets, mechanized transport, etc.) but here the decline has been checked, in some measure, owing to the marked increase in the demand for meat (including camel-meat), particularly on the Trucial Coast.

[17] The dry flesh of the ripe date is made up of 75-80 per cent sugar — normally glucose and fructose, though some varieties have a high proportion of sucrose. As normally eaten, the date has a moisture content of 20 per cent, the rest being made up of 60-5 per cent sugar, 2·5 per cent fibre, 2·5 per cent protein, and somewhat less than 2 per cent each of fat, mineral

matter, and pectic substance (U.S. Dept. of Agriculture 1951).

18 The main palm varieties grown on the Batina are *mubsilli, mulsilli* (correctly Umm al-Silli), and *minōma* (var. *mināma*); *bāṭini* and *khamari* are also important.

19 There is a certain amount of confusion in the terminology used to describe the different stages in the ripening of dates in various areas. In central Oman *bisr* is the green stage and corresponds with what in many other regions, including northern Oman, is called *khalāl*. This is confirmed by the commentary to Ibn al-Naẓar's *Dīwān* (B.M. MS. Or. 2434, fol. 7^{r}), which also gives a number of the other local terms.

CHAPTER II

The Hydrology of the Mountain Zone

The one feature which above all has determined the settlement pattern in Oman is the distribution of fresh water resources. Neither physical difficulties, such as the nature of the terrain and the paucity of the soil, nor human problems, such as cost of investment or the isolation of communities, have impeded the development of the few favoured areas where reliable water supply exists.

These hydrological resources are all located within the mountain and associated bajada zone, for reasons that have more to do with the way run-off concentrates than with orographic influences on climate. Unfortunately, it is difficult to be more precise about this statement because hydrological data are almost non-existent at the time of writing (1973). Sharja (1934-47, and 1950 onwards) is the only station issuing full meteorological reports in the area covered by this study, although two others, Maṣīra Island (1943 onwards) and Salāla (1942 onwards), provide information relevant to the meteorological conditions on the peripheral south coast, while standard long-term observations available from Bahrain and Jashk island help build up the general picture for the Lower Gulf. In addition some simple climatic data are available from intermittent observations taken at Muscat since the end of the last century, and for the last decade by the oil company at its camps nearby (Azaiba and Mina al Fahl). Three years of records also exist from Rās al-Ḥadd (1943-6) in south-east Oman.

All these stations are on the coast. In the interior the only data come from private records kept sporadically at oil-company locations, and some rainfall figures recorded at the agricultural station at Nizwā (1963 onwards). In northern Oman a network for collecting basic hydrological data for development studies has now been started in and around the mountain zone, but the records, published in the Trucial States Council Hydrological Year Books (1965/6 onwards, but at present apparently suspended) do not cover a sufficiently long period for general conclusions to be drawn even about the area directly covered, let alone about conditions in the mountains further south.

RAINFALL

What is quite clear from all sources is that the rainfall everywhere in the country is highly localized and extremely erratic. This may be seen from the annual rainfall statistics of the Trucial Oman stations given in Table 4A, and the distribution of rainfall in what was reputedly the heaviest period of rainfall in the Trucial Coast for 20 years given in Table 4B. The former set of figures illustrate the fact that the unpredictability of rainfall distribution is, as might be expected, most marked in a dry year (cf. in particular hydrological year 1966/7), while the latter shows that even in a good year, rainfall is still

Table 4 *Annual Rainfall (in mm.) by Hydrological Years* (For locations see Fig. 8)

	NORTHERN TRUCIAL STATES (all these stations are within a radius of 45 km)													ABU DHABI		
	East Coast			Mountains		Western bajada zone						Coast				
	Dibā	*Fujaira*	*Kalbā*	*Maṣāfi*	*Masfūt*	*Digdaga*	*al-Muʿallā*	*Manāma*	*Milayḥa*	*Fayya*	*ʿAwīr (18 km inland)*	*Sharja*	*Dubai*	*Buraimi (120 km inland from the Gulf)*	*Abu Dhabi (town)*	*Tarif (West Coast)*
A																
1965 6	50·6	99·1	N.A.	72·3	103·0	61·0	86·9	63·5	N.A.	N.A.	36·2	60·8	61·9	39·5	38·4	59·3
1966 7	21	2	N.A.	75	84	18	30	53	N.A.	N.A.	5	12	15	15	24·5	22·8
1967 8	88·9	121·7	110·0	106·6	109·1	66·6	79·9	107·7	120·0	130·1	85·6	81·8	97·4	77·3	116·4	47·2
1968 9	166·0	206·8	123·7	181·2	130·4	118·6	124·5	163·3	135·6	216·4	96·3	139·8	88·0	47·5	59·1	N.A.
B	*Occurrence of Heavy Rainfall in Period 30 Dec. 1968 to 12 Jan. 1969*															
Dec. 30	Nil	2·5	3·8	4·1	4·6	Nil	Nil	Nil	Nil	Nil	Nil	Tr.	Nil	Nil	1·5	?Nil
31	17·8	Nil	0.5	Nil	Nil	Nil	Tr.	Nil	3·0	Nil	Nil	Nil	0·5	Nil	Tr.	?Nil
Jan. 1	Nil	Nil	Nil	Nil	Nil	Nil	Nil	Nil	Nil	Nil	Nil	Nil	Nil	Nil	Nil	?Nil
2	Nil	Nil	Nil	Nil	17·8	Nil	Nil	Nil	Nil	Nil	Nil	Tr.	Nil	Nil	Nil	?Nil
3	18·8	13·0	24·6	20·3	Nil	4·3	10·2	19·0	32·3	Nil	11·7	2·3	5·3	Nil	Nil	?Nil
4	19·8	26·9	3·3	Nil	Nil	1·8	12·4	Nil	Nil	21·6	Nil	Nil	Nil	Nil	Nil	Nil
5	Nil	7·9	15·5	3·0	2·5	Tr.	5·1	Nil	3·0	5·6	9·7	7·4	5·3	Nil	Tr.	4·0
6	31·7	Nil	Tr.	Nil	Tr.	5·6	0·8	5·8	3·3	Nil	Nil	Nil	12·2	Nil	9·4	2·0
7	26·7	11·4	22·8	8·6	3·8	15·7	31·2	6·3	28·4	68·6	8·1	53·3	5·3	Nil	Tr.	8·0
8	12·7	13·0	70·6	20·3	Nil	11·4	Nil	17·3	Nil	Nil	Nil	1·0	Nil	Nil	2·3	3·0
9	7·4	7·1	4·1	3·8	4·6	0·8	2·5	Nil	3·0	4·3	13·5	0·7	2·8	2·3	12·4	17·0
10	1·5	94·2	67·6	55·9	64·8	0·8	43·2	80·0	80·5	91·7	28·4	16·5	6·9	13·3	1·0	0·5
11	Nil	Nil	Tr.	13·5	2·5	25·4	Nil	Nil	Nil	6·8	Nil	27·9	29·0	17·9	22·4	19·0
12	Nil	Nil	Nil	Nil	Nil	Nil	Nil	Nil	Nil	Nil	Nil	Nil	Nil	Nil	Nil	Nil
Total	136·4	176·0	212·8	129·5	100·6	65·8	105·4	128·4	153·5	198·6	71·4	109·1	67·3	33·5	49·0	53·5

Sources: (a) Hydrological Year Books 1965/6, 1967/8, 1968/9 (1966/7 from Halcrow 1969, drawing 7)
(b) Tarif meteorological records
(c) Abu Dhabi Statistical Abstract 1969

N.B. Hydrological year is from 1 October to 30 September.

highly localized: particular attention is drawn to the main storm of 10 January which seems to have followed a narrow track from the coast at Sharja and Dubai, through ʿAwīr, Falaj al-Muʿallā, Jabal Fayya (correctly Fajja), Milayḥa, across the mountains at Manāma, Masfūt, and Maṣāfi, and so to the east coast at Fujaira and Kalbā (cf. Fig. 8). Buraimi to the south was only just touched by it, while Digdaga and Dibā to the north received virtually no rain at all.

The variations in total annual rainfall are considerable everywhere in Oman, but the most unreliable rainfall, as well as the lowest, occurs naturally enough in the desert foreland. It is perhaps not surprising that amongst the bedu, whose very existence depends on the passing of a shower, rain is simply referred to as *ḥayā* (life), and one of the standard queries in an exchange of greetings takes the form, 'Have you life in your area?'

The order of variability can be illustrated by analysis of the Sharja statistics. These show that while the thirty-one-year mean of the rainfall in the hydrological year (i.e. the beginning of October to the end of September) is 103·4 mm, the range extends from 0·3 mm to 258·2 mm in the sample period, and the probabilities of rainfall occurrence are as follows (Halcrow 1969, vol. i, chap. 1): in three years out of a hundred there is a chance of the extremes of absolute drought or of rainfall greater than 280 mm, while for the rest of the time (94 per cent) the annual rainfall will be 11·5 mm or better; for 75 per cent of the year a rainfall greater than 60·8 mm may be expected.

Further analysis of these statistics shows a tendency towards successions of dry or wet years, rather than a random distribution of dry, average, and wet years: this cyclic pattern appears to be even more marked in south-east Oman, to judge from the observations of travellers and local chronicles.

One of the reasons for the unpredictability of rainfall is that the mountain range of Oman lies at the boundary of two meteorological regions, that of the Saharo-Arabico sub-tropical hot desert and that of the Indian Ocean monsoon regime. At first sight it might be thought that the latter has no influence on the region, because rainfall figures from the south-coast stations show that whereas two-thirds of the 81 mm mean annual rainfall at Salāla (in Dhofar) falls in July and August (accounting for 22 out of the 27 days of rainfall there), the total rainfall at Maṣīra Island, which may be considered as representative of the southern tip of Oman, is only 15 mm, and 10 mm of that falls in the month of December alone.

Such a precipitation pattern seems to fit in with that of the Gulf where rainfall is associated with highly localized cells in the decaying frontal systems that originate in minor winter disturbances of the upper westerlies in the Mediterranean and are partially deflected by the Zagros mountains to peter out finally in the vicinity of the Strait of Hormuz. So it is that at Sharja 99 per cent of the rain falls between November and May (80 per cent by the end of February).

Yet a closer examination of the available statistics shows that even on the

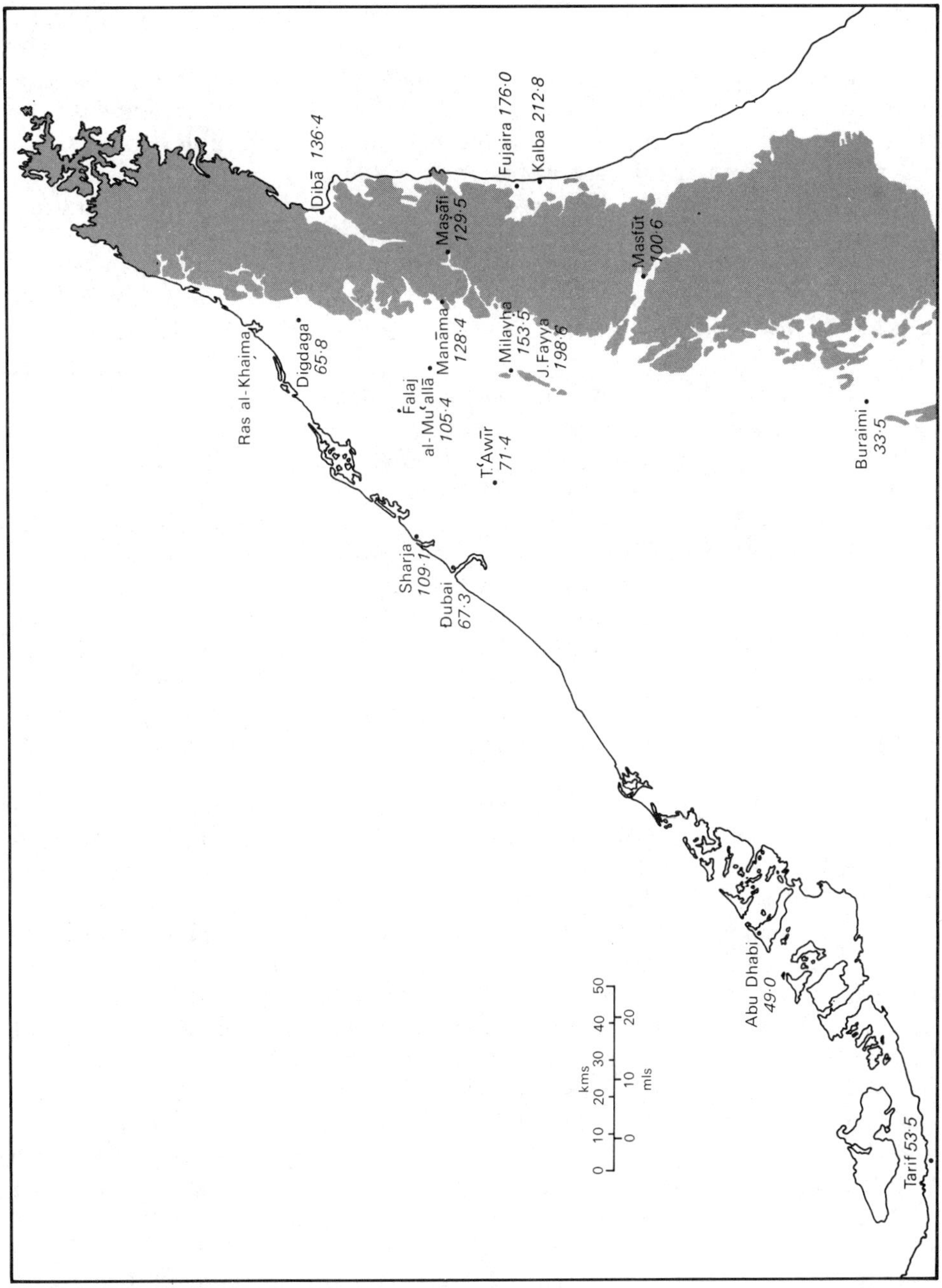

Fig. 8 Rainfall in northern Oman in early January 1969.
Figures, in mm, are the rainfall totals given in Table 4B.

north coast rain can occasionally fall in summer, for while the 1934-68 record at Sharja shows a nil rainfall in June and August, there are three years in which rainfall occurred in July, and in one of these (1955/6) this month accounted for 18 per cent of the annual total of 86 mm. Furthermore, the limited amount of data which has recently become available from Nizwā indicates that summer rainfall makes up over 40 per cent of the total rainfall there (36 mm of about 175 mm falls in July alone), while at the desert station of Fahūd such rainfall as there is (perhaps on average 30 mm p.a.) seems also to be associated with summer storms (e.g. 16 mm in August 1964, 75 mm in July 1967). By contrast, on the other side of the mountains and in the same latitude as these stations, summer rainfall is almost negligible according to the long-term statistics.

Other elements of the climate also indicate that the influence of the summer monsoon in Oman is greater than might appear at first sight. Although the humid air mass brings no rain to Maṣīra Island this is because it is overlain by hot dry air; its influence is still to be felt in lowered summer temperatures and in the high humidity which causes banks of low stratus cloud to form at night (de Gaury 1957). Wind observations from both the coast and the desert interior, again show that it is the south-easterly *kaws* (the modified south-west monsoon wind, which turns anticlockwise into the Gulf of Oman) that prevails over much of Oman, and that the effects of the *shimāl*, the characteristic north-west wind of the Gulf, are largely confined to the Trucial States. Interestingly, the sand-dune pattern indicates that there has been a northward shift of the monsoon belt since late Pleistocene early Holocene times (Glennie 1970).

There is no doubt that the development of the low pressure system in April and May over the Indo-Pakistani landmass has certain repercussions throughout the whole Gulf area (this is the period of the so-called forty day *shimāl*, the *awgāt al-ʿushūr* of the Abu Dhabi fishermen's calendar), but the actual period in which the monsoon first breaks in India also seems occasionally to provoke particularly violent storms in central Oman. For example, even though the thirty-eight-year record at Muscat (Meteorological Office 1958) confirms the general picture of winter rainfall (about 96 mm out of an annual total of 99 mm between October and May), it also shows a fall of 61 mm in a single day in June. And it was in this same season, according to the local histories, that Oman's most disastrous flood occurred. The account of it (*Tuḥfa* i. 163-5, cf. also possibly Yāqūt *Udabāʾ* vi. 492-3), relates how in the year 251/865, after heavy spring rainfall had already swollen the wadis, a night of tremendous storm at the start of June caused flooding, the like of which has never been seen before or since. Destruction was particularly severe at the lower end of the drainage systems where whole villages were washed away, bodies carried down to the sea, the *aflāj* inundated, and trees uprooted. At the northern end of the Batina, Ṣuḥār, then the main port of Oman, was severely damaged by the Wadi Ṣulān, but the most widespread disasters occurred at the other end, in the Wadi al-Sumāyil. There the hitherto important fortress-town of Damā (near modern-day al-Sīb), which guarded access to the southern end of the Batina, was completely destroyed; while further up-stream Bidbid was washed away, and the inhabitants of nearby Qīqā, who had originally developed their settlement because severe drought had forced them to abandon their former home in Manḥ (in the Jawf), now lost all through flood.

In sum, therefore, our knowledge about rainfall in Oman amounts to this. What little there is is highly irregular and comes mostly in winter. The effect of the summer monsoon is, nevertheless, noticeable on the western side of the mountains as far as central Oman, but occasional storms may occur even further to the north in July, and are probably related to unusual travelling disturbances accompanying a deepening of the monsoon and a northward surge of the inter-tropical convergence zone (Pedgley 1970).

Obviously rainfall is higher in the mountains than it is in the lowlands, but because the mountain-chain is relatively narrow and lies on the fringe of two precipitation regimes, its orographic effect is limited; particularly is this true in south-eastern Oman. Outside the mountains the rest of the country is extremely arid desert, and even Trucial Oman has a lower rainfall than other parts of the Gulf because it lies outside the main winter-storm tracks.

From the point of view of drawing up a water balance for the region such data are utterly inadequate. If one did have to attach some figures to the annual average rainfall (in so far as this itself is a meaningful term) the writer would tentatively suggest that where the land is over 450 m high (about 40,000 km*) rainfall is generally between 150 and 200 mm, but on the Jabal Akhdhar block this figure may be slightly higher. In the lowlands the rainfall probably ranges from 30 mm in the main part of the desert foreland, to 100 mm in the bajada zone.

EVAPORATION

Little need be said about the climatic influences affecting the debit side of the area's water balance, for everywhere evaporation rates are extremely high. One obvious set of local variations results from the land-sea distribution. Here, however, it should be remembered that the temperature regime of the Gulf, which is virtually an inland sea whose waters rarely exceed a depth of 100 m, is quite different from that of the main Arabian Sea and the Gulf of Oman, where the oceanic regime is also affected by the summer upwelling of cold water described in Chapter I. While the sea temperature at Bahrain is 65°F. (18·3°C.) in February, it is 70°F. (21·1°C.) off the Trucial Coast and rises to 75°F. (23·9°C.) along the south coast; in August, on the other hand, it reaches 90°F. (32·2°C.) throughout the Lower Persian Gulf, and is generally some 7°F. lower in the Gulf of Oman, while off the south coast the maximum occurs, not at this period at all, but in spring and autumn (May and

November) – and then the temperatures only reach the relatively low figure of 80°F. (26·7°C.).

The corresponding effects on the littoral regions are indicated in Table 5, where the average of the maximum and minimum daily readings for the hottest and coldest months of the year of various coastal stations are given. However, we must also realize in examining this table, that while marine influences may have a strong effect on the diurnal and seasonal temperature ranges, on the direction and intensities of the wind, and on humidity (at Azaiba near Muscat, the average relative humidity at 1300 hrs never drops below 38 per cent (May), and is 57 per cent in August), the effects are confined to a relatively narrow coastal belt; this is clearly illustrated by the set of estimated annual pan evaporation figures for the Trucial States shown in table 6. Further inland still, where summer temperatures are yet higher (Fahūd in 1964 had an average daily maximum from 1 May to 10 September of 42·3°C./108°F.; cf. 38·4°C./101°F. at Azaiba for a corresponding coastal station in the same latitude) and wind velocities may be even greater, it is possible that yet more sensational evaporation rates might obtain.

In the mountains, on the other hand, evaporation rates will be considerably lower, for the influence of relief on evaporation is strong, particularly in the lowest 1,000 m. Although no measurements exist for Oman, the lapse rate of potential evapotranspiration is probably in the order of 700 mm in the first 1,000 m (Thornthwaite, Mather, and Carter 1958, p. 20).

WATER BALANCE

It is clear that while evaporation rates are lower and rainfall is higher in the mountain zone than it is in other parts of Oman, the deficit is everywhere considerable: in Sharja annual evaporation rates are some thirty-two-times greater than precipitation, and it is to be doubted if anywhere in the region this ratio drops below 10:1. The whole area may be classified as very arid, and nowhere is dry farming remotely possible. There is, however, some potential for irrigation, because in the mountains a high percentage of rainfall enters shallow aquifers. It is this potential that has led the range (*Jabal*) to be classed as 'green' (*Akhḍar*), a term which designates the second class in an ancient fourfold colour classification of water resources, (probably adopted from the Chinese by the Sasānids cf. Mazaheri 1973 p. 141).

RUN-OFF

The mountains of Oman are characterized by bold relief and a paucity of soil and vegetation. Run-off is therefore rapid. Almost everywhere the range is intensely dissected, but significant differences do occur due to lithological variations. For example, dendritic drainage densities are particularly high on the impermeable serpentinites and only slightly lower on the gabbros of the Semail ophiolitic series and the metamorphic facies of the Hawasina, but on the limestone there is a widely spaced rectilinear drainage pattern, and there

Table 5 *Selected Temperatures (°F./C.) from Coastal Stations*

Station	*Hottest Month*	*Average daily Max.*	*Average daily Min.*	*Coldest Month*	*Average daily Max.*	*Average daily Min.*
Bahrain	August	100/37.8	85/29.4	January	68/20.0	57/13.9
Sharja	August	103/39.4	82/27.8	January	74/23.3	54/12.2
Muscat	June	100/37.8	88/31.1	January	77/25.0	66/18.9
Maṣīra	May	96/35.6	78/25.6	January	78/25.6	65/18.3
Salāla	May	90/32.2	77/25.0	January	81/27.2	64/17.8
				August	81/27.2	74/23.3

Source: Meteorological Office 1958.

Table 6 *Estimated Pan Evaporation Rates in Northern Trucial Oman*

Station	*Estimated Annual Evaporation (in mm)*	*Mean Wind Movement (km/day)*	*Remarks on station*	
Sharja	3414	154	Gulf coast	western bajada zone
Digdaga	3029	63	12 km inland but lies in the line of a sand-dune belt which protects it from dominant NW wind	western bajada zone
Falaj al-Muʿallā	3705	87	38 km inland	western bajada zone
Milayḥa	4202	104	53 km inland	western bajada zone
Kalbā	3241	100	Gulf of Oman coast	western bajada zone

Source: Halcrow 1969, Vol. i, table 14.
N.B. Estimates based on varying periods of observations.

some of the water enters the rock formations (it should be noted however, that there has been little development of karst features).

These limestone exposures probably provide the only significant recharge into deep aquifers that exist in the mountain area. However, the formations, although sometimes extending as far as the pelagic outer basin of the original 'eugeosyncline' in which they formed (Wilson 1969), are of little value as sources of fresh water.[1] Certainly in central Oman much of the rainwater entering the dolomites and limestones of the Jabal Akhdhar is wasted because the anticline plunges steeply and so the ground water is heavily salinated long before it resurfaces in the desert foreland. In northern Oman the limestone does perhaps offer some hydrological potential in the inner bajada zone, for near al-Khaṭṭ[2] exploratory drilling has had some success in tapping fresh water (with an E.C. of 1,800 μmhos), but in general it may be presumed that the water is rapidly salinated (as shown by studies of the ᶜAyn Bu Sakhna limestone spring near the base of the Jabal Ḥafīt).

Within the mountain belt itself, however, the limestones do locally recharge the main drainage basins. There the occurrence of hot fresh-water springs (e.g. in the Rustāq region, at al-Bawshar and at al-Khaṭṭ) indicates that some of the water re-emerges from considerable depths in a comparatively salt-free state, while villagers from the valleys below the Jabal Akhdhar massif have frequently pointed out to the writer that the performance of their *aflāj* is affected by what happens to the rainfall on limestone hills a considerable distance away.

THE DRAINAGE SYSTEM (cf. Fig. 9)

By far and away the most important concentrations of exploitable fresh water occur in the shallow gravels and conglomerates laid down in the now semi-fossilized drainage system. From the point of view of the hydrology of the region this drainage system may be divided into two parts: an upstream section lying within the mountains proper, and a downstream piedmont section.

The typical valley in the mountains has a fill of gravels and silts (whose texture reflects the recent morphological history of the area) which overlie a base of cemented conglomerates, and it is into these formations that the present wadi channel has cut. Under the climatic conditions now prevailing, flow is largely sub-surface, except after heavy rain, but seepages do sometimes occur along the junctions both of the bedrock and conglomerate and of the conglomerate and gravel, while regular surface flow may take a place where a rock bar forms a constriction in the wadi.

Normally this surface flow, or *ghayl*, is highly localized and more or less ephemeral, but in the lower reaches of the sixty-five-kilometre-long Wadi (al-) Sumāyil there is an increasingly continuous thread of surface flow. Indeed, where the wadi finally breaks through the low-dipping strata of the mountain flanks to debouch onto the Batina plain at al-Khawḍ, running water is

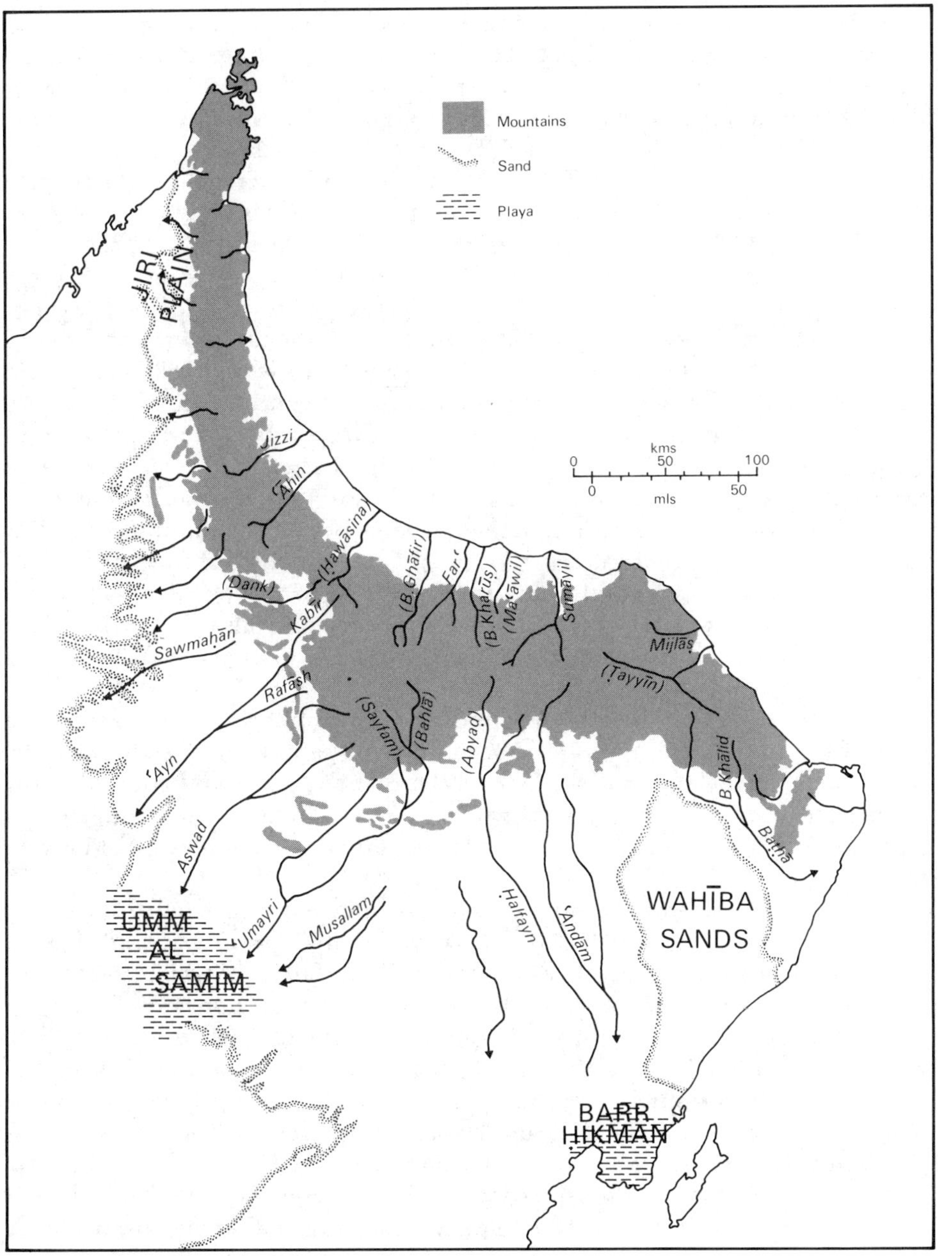

Fig. 9. Oman: the main drainage system.

normally found throughout the year. However, while the series of measurements taken in 1965 which show a mean surface flow of 40,900 m^3 per day (about 450 ls^{-1}) at the end of the dry season (six observations between 12 September and 3 November) may be taken as fairly representative of a good rainfall year, a succession of poor years can lead to the surface flow ceasing altogether in summer, and in the recent droughts it had receded to 2 m below the gravel surface by July (1971). The irregularity of the regime is further demonstrated by the fact that even though the annual average of daily surface flow (taken over roughly monthly intervals for six years) is 45,000 m^3, this has ranged from 9,000 m^3 in 1970 to 104,000 m^3 in 1968 (Shell 1966, 1971).

The discharge of the Wadi Sumāyil is, of course, rather exceptional, for it lies in the highest rainfall region of Oman, has an extensive catchment area of about 1,800 km^2, and could possibly cut into the regional ground-water level of a large syncline whose outer flanks are formed by the relatively permeable limestones and dolomites of the high Jabal al-Nakhl and the Jabal al-Ṭayyīn. Even so, it provides the only proper statistics that exist for a wadi regime in Oman, and these are relevant to other drainage basins in so far as it may be assumed that those have an even more variable flow than the figures quoted.

Once the wadis break through the confines of the mountains their flow rapidly sinks into the coalescing outwash fans of the bajada zone. This happens all the more rapidly because the grade of the detritus which was brought down in the time of the Plio(?)-Pleistocene pluvials is far coarser than would be the case if it was in equilibrium with the discharge of the present floods.

Normally the ground-water fans out and slowly moves desertwards on a broad front so that the contours of both flow and salinity are roughly parallel to the axis of the mountain range. Where, however, it remains laterally constricted by subsurface features, the fresh water may finger out underground for some distance across the piedmont zone following old gravel trains.

On the eastern side of the mountains the drainage lines are towards the sea, whereas on the western side the flow is mainly towards inland basins. However, because at either end of the range the surface flow which created the original wadis did once reach the sea, we find that in northern Oman the contours of subsurface flow still swing towards the Gulf, and in the Jiri Plain area of Ras al-Khaima they are at right-angles to the mountains instead of parallel to them;[3] similarly, in south-east Oman the underground flow of the Wadi al-Baṭḥā is directly towards the sea. Even the flow of the Wadis al-ʿAndām and al-Ḥalfayn, which rise in the northern confines of the Sharqīya, is orientated towards the south coast, so that though their discharge is now largely evaporated in the *sabkhas*[4] behind the Barr al-Ḥikmān, local reports do speak of surface flow still reaching the sea after exceptional floods.

In the central part of Oman, however, the drainage on the western side of the mountains is inland, and so here the classical desert sequence of mountain, bajada, desert platform, and playa zones has developed. Some of these inland *sabkhas*, which form the final evaporation surfaces of endoreic drainage basins, are extensive, and a number of improbable stories (similar to those surrounding the legendary Baḥr al-Ṣāfi), are recounted about the Umm al-Samīm,[5] into which drain the Wadis al-Aswad and al-ʿUmayri.

Little is known at the time of writing about the aquicludes of this drainage system. In the lower courses it is the gypsums and marls of the Fars which may be presumed to form the impermeable layers underlying the water-bearing formations, but in the bajada zone, which is the main area of interest from the point of view of fresh-water storage, the basins have only been investigated in the Trucial States. There, it would seem, the aquicludes are formed by a marl which underlies much of the bajada zone at about 30 m (Halcrow 1969, i. 31), but in central Oman, where the full development of a zone of coalescing outwash fans is interrupted by the western foothills and where the wadis are often laterally confined for considerable distances downstream, the recent sediments are almost certainly underlain by quite different formations. Within the basins themselves, however, variations in flow and infiltration rates are largely to be accounted for by the distribution of the cemented conglomerates and caliches that constitute the principle aquitards in the Quaternary sediments throughout the whole region.

THE BATINA COAST

The hydrology of the drainage basins on the eastern side of the mountains is somewhat different from that on the western because there the flow is direct towards the sea. At either end of the range, where the mountains drop straight into the ocean, the wadis are, of course, confined, and so it is only at their mouths that a little alluvial land and fresh-water storage develop. Thus there is only one settlement (Dibā: in classical sources spelt Dabā) of any significance above the Shimālīya strip on the Gulf of Oman side of the Musandam Peninsula, although in south-eastern Oman, where the drainage basins are somewhat larger, there are a number of such wadi-mouth settlements, some of which have developed into sizeable ports (Maṭraḥ, Muscat, Qurayāt, Qalhāt, etc.).

But in the central area of the range the mountains stand back from the sea, and are separated from it by the great Batina coastal plain. Structurally this is a monocline whose outer flank has been covered to considerable depth by outwash materials that extend right out beyond the present coastline. It is in the development of the interface between the fresh water and the sea water at today's sea-level that the explanation for the extraordinary strip of almost continuous settlement along the littoral is to be found. This may best be illustrated by a study of one particular case, the lower Wadi Sumāyil (based on Shell 1966; cf. Fig. 10A).

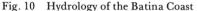

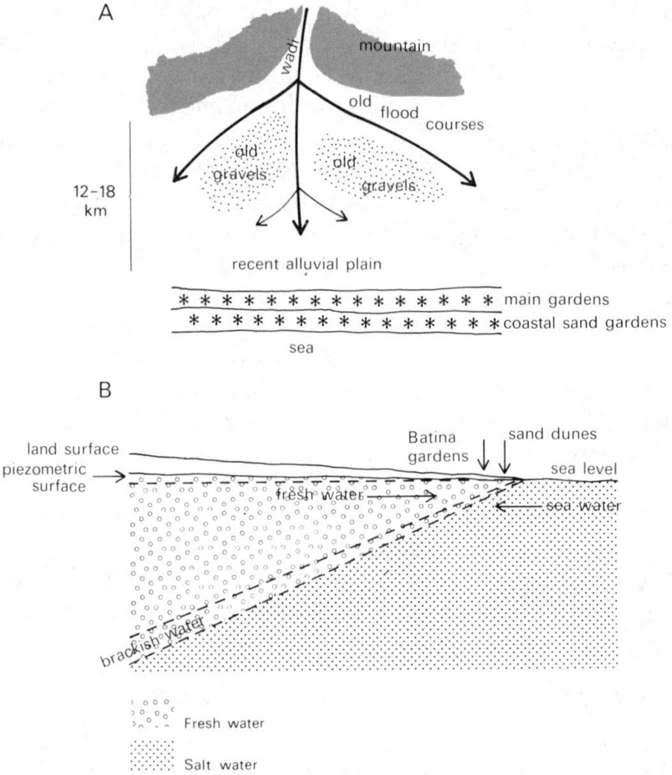

Fig. 10 Hydrology of the Batina Coast

Once the wadi breaks through the mountains all flow in the surface gravels rapidly sinks into the older piedmont deposits of bygone pluvial epochs. So we find that in the dry season the surface flow normally starts to disappear three to four kilometres downstream of al-Khawḍ, and within another four or five kilometres has gone deep underground. At the point where the original main channel starts to fan out, about eight kilometres from the coast, the static water table is now only about 20m A.S.L., but because it is in the order of 30 to 45m below the land surface the fresh water (here approximately 800 ppm T.D.S.) is still too deep for exploitation by traditional techniques.[6] Nearer the coast, however, it starts to come within the range of hand-dug wells, because the land surface slopes more rapidly towards the sea than does the phreatic surface. Unfortunately at the point where settlement begins, the quality of the water also starts to deteriorate (cf. Fig. 10B). This is because the fresh-water wedge, which on theoretical grounds (Ghyben-Herzberg principle) is approximately forty times as thick as the elevation of the fresh-water table above sea-level, has now thinned out so much that it is strongly affected by fluctuations in the hydrostatic balance caused by tidal cycles and seasonal variations in wadi discharge (Cooper 1959).

The result is that the agricultural potential of the settled zone divides into two quite distinct parts. On the dune sands near the shore itself is a strip of palm cultivation where no irrigation is necessary (once the trees are established), because the roots tap the brackish water directly: these are the palms that produce the majority of low-grade Batina dates which are turned into *bisr* (cf. Chapter I). Extending inland for up to three kilometres behind this littoral zone are the gardens which are irrigated from the less saline water which can be reached by wells. Here the quality of the crops is also improved by the marked decrease both in humidity (to which dates are very sensitive) and in the concentrations of wind-blown marine salt particles (partly because the rate of salt deposition falls rapidly in the first 500 m of the wind's travel (cf. Malloch 1972), and partly because the littoral palms act as a wind-break).

WATER POTENTIAL AND UTILIZATION

We have seen that in Oman the concentrations of fresh water are almost entirely related to the surface-drainage pattern. Only in the case of the limestone does any significant volume of water go deep underground, but by the time this re-emerges it is normally far too saline to be of economic value.

Within each drainage basin water is exploitable by traditional techniques at two places on the western side of the drainage divide, and at three on the eastern side. The first area where exploitation is possible is within the mountains themselves. Here the water which is confined in the narrow valleys is at no great depth and is fast-moving. But while it is easily accessible it has limited agricultural value for two reasons, first because it occurs in an area where there is little flat land and soils are poor, and second because there is little groundwater storage and so the supply is unreliable (less so in the area of highest rainfall in central Oman).

The second point of exploitation is where the wadis begin to open out onto the bajada zone. Here the drainage of the whole catchment is concentrated, and as the flow in the upper gravels begins to sink, so the fresh water in ground storage begins to increase. The inconvenience of tapping the water at this point is that the best supplies are at depth, and thus irrigation systems are costly; the advantages are that the settlements are ensured of good, regular base flow. In the case of those wadis where the morphology is such that the aquifers tend to remain laterally confined, a fairly high proportion of this ground water may be used, for there settlement can be extended for some way out into the desert foreland (cf. the Wadis Sayfam and al-Abyaḍ in central Oman). Where, however, the ground water fans out so that the rapid decrease in the transmission rate is matched by a corresponding rise in salinity rates, then the ground water can only be effectively tapped around the head of the fan. In such wadis a considerable amount of underground water goes to waste, while most storm flow is carried out into the desert.

On the eastern side of the mountains this water is not necessarily lost because, unlike the situation on the desert side where the water that goes underground only reappears near the surface in a highly saline state, that on the eastern side is, in effect, dammed by the sea, and so remains comparatively fresh down to the point of the drainage basin's final discharge. As a result any flow that has escaped through the upstream network of exploitation can still be saved with relative ease by constructing a barrage of wells near the coast. This does not mean, of course, that all the water is in fact used, but it does show why the cultivated area on the eastern side of the main drainage divide is some two and a half times greater than that on the western: it should, however, be mentioned in this context that the total cultivated area in the western bajada zone may once have been considerably greater than it is now, notably in the Jawf.

If the writer was forced to be more specific and quantify the potential fresh water available to traditional techniques and how much has in fact been used at various times in Omani history, he would estimate that the total amount of water entering shallow aquifers was in the order of 6 or 7 milliard $(10^9)m^3$, and that something like 1 milliard of this was used today (excluding modern developments). The maximum exploitation probably occurred in the late Sasānid period (end of the sixth century), when the total area of land cultivated was possibly twice what it is now, but this started to decline during the first century and a half of Islamic times. There was something of a recovery during the succeeding period of the First Imamate, which lasted throughout the ninth century, but then came a massive and wanton destruction of the fragile irrigation system (particularly in the Jawf) in the civil war which brought this period to a close. Although a little restoration work to the irrigation systems may have been carried out in the second half of the eleventh and the early twelfth century, the story of the ensuing period is one of general abandonment of land, both in the interior and on the coast, so that it is possible that by the end of the sixteenth century the cultivated area was perhaps a third of what it had been a millenium before. The Yaʿāriba Imamate saw an enormous recovery as money from overseas trade was reinvested in the land and much of the old irrigation system was restored. But this prosperity was to last only a short time, for the civil war in the first half of the eighteenth century saw yet another outburst of massive destruction in the villages of Oman. Fortunately this was not quite on the scale of a thousand years before, and in the succeeding century of Āl Bu Saʿīd rule the agricultural economy began to revive. In the mid-nineteenth century however, decline once again set in, and of recent years has accelerated alarmingly, despite relatively peaceful conditions. Today there is no doubt that Oman is in need of major agricultural reinvestment.

Before discussing how the hydrological resources have been exploited and the reasons for the decline in the cultivated area, sonething must be said about the desert foreland. This forms an integral part of the Oman region, and its peoples have played a far more dynamic role in the evolution of the society of settled Oman than might be suggested by its poor resources and sparse population. The next chapter is therefore devoted to a discussion of the factors limiting land-use there, and will attempt to show that while the economies associated with the two major physical provinces of interior Oman are different, their societies are integrated by a number of features that basically stem from complementary resource specialization.

NOTES TO CHAPTER II

[1] The discontinuous ring of what appear to be anticlines formed by these limestones on the outer edge of the foothill zone in central Oman is, in fact, made up of thrust blocks. The *qanāt* which water the settlements of Adam from the Jabal Salākh are not therefore supplied by deep aquifers, but by run-off from the block itself.

[2] Attempts to drill in the area with greatest potential had to be abandoned owing to a boundary dispute between Ras al-Khaima and Fujaira (*Trucial States Council Newsletter*, Nov. Dec. 1970).

[3] It was perhaps the facts that this drainage is towards the sea, and that the advancing sand dunes tend to pond the flow of flash floods which gave rise to the idea (cf. Idrīsi i. 153) that a river rising at Jabal Sharm flows into the sea at Julfāra (Julfār): such a river is often portrayed on Portuguese maps (cf. Wilkinson 1964).

[4] A *sabkha* (pl. *sibākh*) is a flat equilibrium deflation-sedimentation surface composed of fine sediments, often encrusted with salt and virtually devoid of vegetation. It may be formed in either marine or continental environments, and sabkhas are thus subdivided into coastal or inland (the latter often being referred to as a playa or salina in North America, kavīrs in Persia). Both types have many similar morphological features, notably the high water-table (between 0·03m and 1m below the surface, except in relict sabkhas): in the coastal type the water derives predominantly from the sea, in the inland type from inland drainage. The water in the capillary zone is therefore highly saline, and in coastal sabkhas groundwater salinities range between 70,000 ppm to 356,000 ppm (i.e. between 2 and 10 times normal sea water). On the Trucial Coast, coastal sabkhas occupy an area of 2-3,000 km^2 and may be locally 8-10 km wide, while in the belt extending 100 km inland continental sabkhas occupy an area of 6-7,000 km^2. (Glennie 1970; Evans, Schmidt, Bush, and Nelson 1969; Kinsman and Park 1968.)

[5] While this huge feature could be an infilled deflation hollow, the fact that its surface is only 70 m A.S.L. does suggest that in part, at least, it was a relict arm from a higher sea level during a Pleistocene interglacial; it is not impossible that its morphology was also affected by early Holocene crustal warping (Glennie 1967, 1970).

[6] A conservative estimate of the water in storage in the 20 km^2 alluvial plain is 20 million m^3 (Shell 1966).

CHAPTER III

The Desert Foreland: The Frontier Of Settlement

FRESH WATER ACCUMULATION IN SAND

Beyond the mountain and associated bajada zone the very limited occurrences of fresh water are closely related to the distribution of sand in the desert foreland. Since most of Oman lies outside the great aeolian sand deserts of Arabia, the dune country is largely confined to two areas, the isolated Wahība sand-field in the south-east, and the northern extension of the so-called 'Empty Quarter' in Trucial Oman.

The latter is by far and away the more important, for here the thickness of the sand-cover increases progressively southward from the coast until it reaches an average of more than 100 m in the area around the Līwā. In this huge body of sand two units can be recognized, that in which the dunes are actively being shaped by the dominant north-west *shimāl* and that of a body of slightly indurated sands overlying the desert platform whose morphology, according to Glennie (1967, 1970), has been influenced by a dominant wind with a somewhat more westerly component. But although the actual mineral composition of the two sands is similar and it is only in the degree of consolidation that they are to be differentiated (Gibb 1969, Ch. 9), that in itself affects dune morphology, vegetation cover, and hydrological properties.

From the point of view of water supplies in the desert the importance of sand lies in the fact that it is highly porous and permeable material which accumulates in just such masses as have been described above. The resulting hydrological characteristics of rapid infiltration, low capillary rise, rapid fall-off in evaporation rates below the surface, and a high reservoir potential mean that rain, instead of evaporating in the top layers of the soil or draining to hard-pan depressions as it does in most parts of the desert, quickly works its way down to the base of the dune where it is held in a saturated zone more or less sealed by the relatively impermeable underlying formations of the desert platform (Goudie and Wilkinson, in press). In the northern part of the Empty Quarter, where precipitation is slightly greater than in the central desert, a considerable amount of perched water may accumulate in this way (cf. Fig. 11).

THE EFFECT ON BEDU DISPERSAL

Such concentrations of fresh water in sand country are extremely important for certain bedu groups, and give rise to a rather distinctive pattern of seasonal movements.

Normally in most of the desert border lands of Oman the bedu groups retire in summer into the bajada zone where fresh water and grazing are relatively plentiful. This part of their territory may be considered as the core of their *dār* (tribal territory: cf. *dīra*, and also forms derived from *ḥjr* and *ḥrm* in other regions), and forms the point of return for a pulsatory nomadism which takes them in winter to seasonal wells *(baḥath* pl. *buḥūth* or *baḥāyith*, cf. *mishāsh* in dialects of the western tribes[1]) further down the wadi courses, and to the outer limits of their territory (*ākhar dār*) when the fresh grazing (*ʿishab*) is exceptionally good. By contrast, in much of western Trucial Oman the bedu tend to congregate in winter and disperse towards the core of the desert in summer.

For example, some sections of the Rumaythāt (a clan of the Bani Yās) of eastern Abu Dhabi whom the writer studied inhabited the coastal region called the Ṭaff in winter (cf. Fig. 7), where they clustered around the rather bitter water wells they had excavated in the rock outcrops of the Lower Fars. During this season they supplemented their pastoral occupations with fishing, and some even swam their camels across the shallow creeks to the islands in order to combine the two activities in the same place. But in summer the majority of these groups left the coast and moved some 100 kilometres inland into an area where the topography is characterized by long parallel sand-dune ridges (*ʿargūb* pl. *ʿarāgīb*) overlying desert pavement (*sayḥ/sēḥ* pl. *siyūḥ*). One family-group the writer visited there were found living in a couple of *ʿarīsh* (palm frond) huts by the sweet water well (*ʿugla* pl. *ʿugal*) they had dug in the dune itself. While this supplied their domestic needs the brackish water in the *sayḥ* below was adequate for watering their flocks. It also supported half a dozen palm trees (*ʿayn baqr* variety), which had been irrigated with the fresh water from the dune well when first planted as *ṣarm* (the offshoots cut from the mother palm) but were able once established to survive in the brackish ground water without supplementary irrigation.

This example of the migration-pattern of some of the Rumaythāt also illustrates the role of terrain in dictating the social structure and organization of a tribe living in the desert fringes of Oman. Everywhere, of course, water sources are scarce and unevenly distributed, but in the sand desert a cluster of wells can only support two or three small family units. The result is that when a tribe lives in sand desert all the year round its members are permanently dispersed; in the case of the Murra, whose *dār* just touches on the western edge of Abu Dhabi territory, the sections live on some 162 well-clusters scattered over thousands of square kilometres (Fuad Bey Hamza 1935, in *British Memorial* ii. Annex D, No. 13). Such sand-dwelling bedu form the most independent tribes of Arabia, and it is no coincidence that the most segmented and 'unruly' tribe of Oman are the Wahība, who give their name to the Wahība sands. This 'independence' stems in part from their isolation and in part from the fact that they have no long-term investment in the land. So, whereas in the case of a bedu group living on the fringes of the settled zone government control may be exercised through the threat of rounding up their flocks, filling in their wells and *aflāj* (water channels), and cutting down their palms, the problem of dealing with the sand-dwelling camel-herding bedu are far greater. Even if an expedition can be successfully mounted against them, there is little that can be done to damage their economy, for their livestock are widely scattered and it only takes a few hours to re-excavate a filled-in well. Additionally their sense of tribal cohesiveness (*ʿaṣabīya*) is strongly developed, for even though dispersal may lead to internal segmentation (cf. Chapters VIII and IX), the very vulnerability of the individual groups demands concerted action in the face of outsiders.

AGRICULTURE IN THE LĪWĀ

While the sand-cover of Oman provides limited quantities of fresh water for pastoral groups, it is inadequate to support any significant agriculture except in the area called the Līwā. Here the hollows formed between the south-facing slip faces (*baṭn* pl. *buṭūn*) of the great dune ridges (*qāʿida* pl. *qaʿāyid*) and the hard backs (*ẓahr* pl. *ẓuhūr*) of the succeeding ridge may be deflated right down to the level of the older indurated sands, sabkhas, and desert-platform formations (locally Lower Fars). Since the height difference between the summit of the largest dune in the ridge (*zimma* pl. *zimām*) and the bottom of the hollow (*jaww* pl. *juwwān*, or *bilgaʿ* < *abu'l-qāʿ*) can even exceed 125m, these hollows cut across the perched water in the dune mass, and consequently lateral seepages adequate for cultivating a few palm trees may occur near the bottom of the slip face (cf. Fig. 11).

These Līwā settlements (*maḥḍar* pl. *maḥāḍir*) occur in a crescent that runs west to east for about seventy kilometres, and are located about the same distance inland from the coast, so they form a very distinctive region of settlement (Fig. 7). Estimates of their number vary. *The British Memorial* (i. 18; ii. Annex E) quotes figures of 38, 42, and 48 for various assessments of the number of permanent and temporary settlements, but recent investigations (unpublished) for the 1968 census in Abu Dhabi give figures of 301 families living in 37 hollows. The three largest settlements are Qarmada (32 families), Sabkha and Tharwanīya (30 families each); there are another three with between 20 and 30 families each, ten more with between 10 and 20 families, while the rest have less than 10 families, including eight with only a single family in each.

Although a few people live all the year round in these isolated pockets of settlement, occupation of the Līwā is largely seasonal. In winter the majority of the population is away, grazing their flocks or fishing, and it is only the old and very young who tend to live there all the year round. The main population influx occurs at the time of the date harvest in high summer (*qayẓ*), but even then some members of the occupying family-groups are absent pearling, while others stay with the flocks on wells a little to the north of the hollows because the grazing (mostly halophytes) is usually very poor in the Līwā itself. The main date-palm variety grown in these settlements is *dabbāṣ*, but there are also some *farḍ* and *khaṣṣāb*. Incursion of sand is a continuous risk and each cluster of palms has to be protected by a fence of

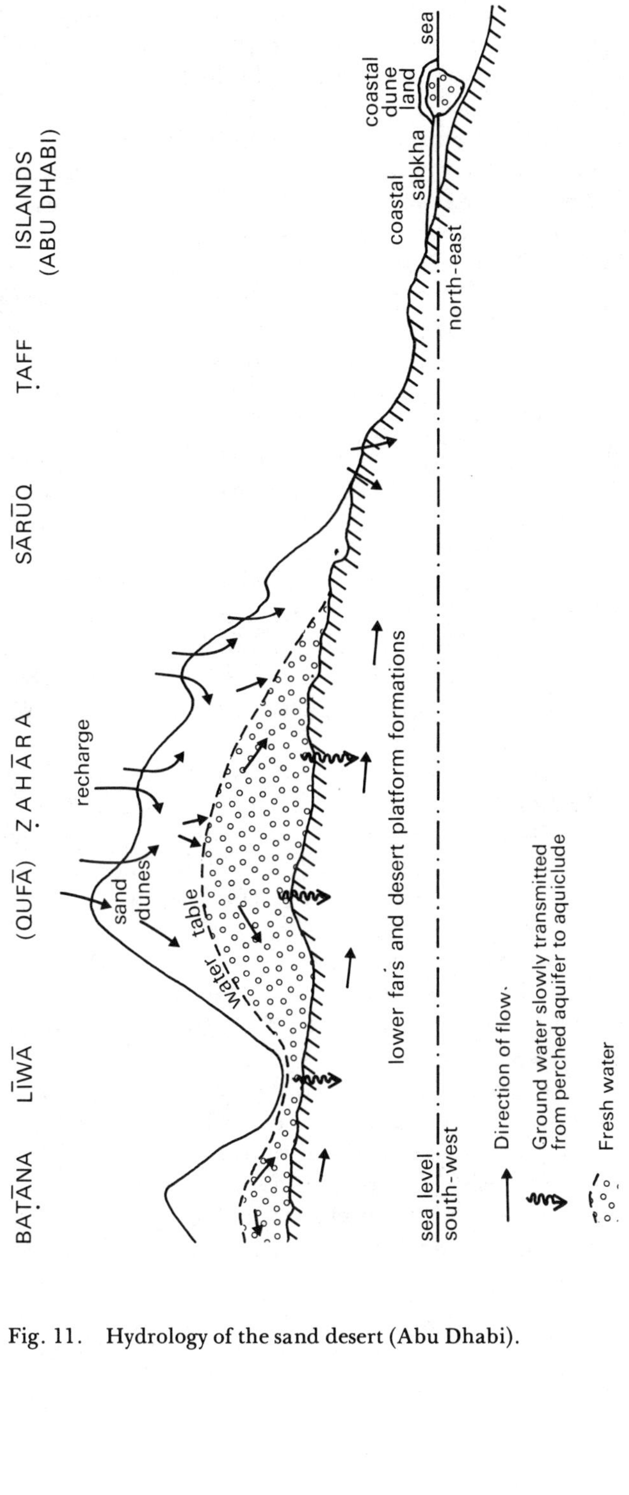

Fig. 11. Hydrology of the sand desert (Abu Dhabi).

palm fronds (*jidār*; cf. Buraimi *ḥaẓār*); even so it is probable that they are eventually overrun by the advance of the sand. This may account for the origin in the surrounding region of vestigial clumps of semi-wild palms (known as *ghayṭ* pl. *ghuyūṭ*) from which the bedu collect the dates without tending the trees.[2]

Although there are no permanent buildings in the Līwā (with the exception of the occasional mud-fort), the area may have been settled from an early date; for the region which an eleventh-century source tells us was called Baynūna because it 'separates' Oman from 'Baḥrayn', and which then formed part of the tribal area of the Bani Saʿd (ʿAwtabi Paris Ms. 69r: cf. also Yāqūt art. Baynūna), designates, the writer believes, this whole region of complementary economies in the western part of what is now Abu Dhabi, and not just the limited coastal area to which the name is now said to apply.[3]

FRESH-WATER LENSES NEAR THE COAST

The hydrological properties of sand also permit some settlement in the otherwise waterless coast of Trucial Oman. Because rain water has a lower specific gravity than sea water, fresh-water lenses (Ghyben-Herzberg principle, cf. Fig. 10B and in Fig. 11) may form in the calcareous sands of the littoral dunes that in places develop parallel to the shore under the influence of alternating sea- and land-breezes. But since the lenses are small, are recharged by sporadic rainfall which leaches the surface accumulation of windblown salts, and are subject to mechanical disturbances caused by tidal action, the fresh-water content is at best limited and rapidly becomes brackish.

Virtually all the settlements on the Trucial Coast west of Ras al-Khaima originally owe their existence to such occurrences of just potable water. But it was not until the 1760s that the local tribesmen discovered the most westerly of these sources of water at Abu Dhabi. Before then the Bani Yās and Manāṣir of western Trucial Oman had used Dubai as their main pearling, fishing, and trading port, but with the founding of a new coastal centre their shaikhly family (the Āl Bu Falāḥ) was able to develop an independent capital, and the break with Dubai widened (Wilkinson 1971). On such a chance discovery of a little brackish water in the coastal sands of a remote island were the fortunes of the now-famous oil state laid.

Palms can root themselves in these water lenses, but except in al-Jumayra (near Dubai)[4], where they are properly cultivated in fenced plots (*zarība* pl. *zarāyib*), they have no agricultural value and simply form an ornamental fringe to the coastal fishing and trading settlements. It is, incidentally, because of the mirage effect that a characteristic sight on approaching these coastal settlements by land is the appearance of a line of palms that seems to float on the sea.

OTHER OCCURENCES OF WATER IN THE DESERT

Apart from such special conditions of water accumulation in sand, the occurrence of fresh water in the desert foreland of Oman is extremely limited. The Eocene limestone surface that gives rise to the kind of small depressions in which fresh water accumulates (generically dayas, locally *rōḍa* pl. *riyāḍ*), characteristic of much of the neighbouring Qaṭar Peninsula and Ḥasā province of Saudi Arabia (Johnstone and Wilkinson 1960), is absent from the Oman desert, as also are the confined aquifers which underlie 'Baḥrayn' (Naʿimi 1965; Bechtel 1966; Wright 1967): the occurrence of undersea fresh-water springs (*kawkab*) in western Abu Dhabi may, however, indicate that these water-bearing formations just extend into the extreme west of our region. Another occurrence of a deep aquifer, which has, so far, only been exploited by oil-drilling operations in south-west Oman, lies in the Umm al-Radhuma (a Tertiary formation). This sizeable aquifer appears to be recharged from the Dhofar mountains, and so the water is only just potable by the time it reaches the outer fringes of our area: further into the area it becomes highly sulphurous and quite unusable (information from Petroleum Development (Oman) Ltd.).

Such concentrations of rain water as do occur from rare showers are highly localized, and for the most part are quickly contaminated by contact with the ground water whose salinity rapidly increases away from the mountains. (In northern Oman there is a regional increase of salinity from an electroconductivity of 2,000 to 6,000 μmhos within the first ten to twenty kilometres from the edge of the outwash fans: cf. Halcrow 1969, map 13.)

WATER QUALITY

While fresh water accumulations are unusual in the desert, there is rarely any shortage of salty water. The ability to use low-quality water must therefore play as great a role in the adaptation of life to the desert environment as the ability to economize in the quantities of water consumed. The bedu are fully aware of this, and consequently there is always a large range of terms in their dialects to describe water quality: words like *ghazīr* (the quality of rain water), *khōr* (brackish), *murr* (bitter), *kharīj* (contaminated, no good), and *māliḥ* (salty) frequently occur in some form or other in the place-names of the Trucial Coast and, along with a similar use of plant-names, may prove useful indications of the water- and grazing-resources of a locality.

While differences in water quality may arise from local variations in the concentrations of particular minerals, regionally it is the over-all content of dissolved salts that may be considered to determine the quality. A useful measure for studying spatial variations in desert land-use is therefore provided by the T.D.S. in ppm of a water sample (total dissolved solids by weight of dissolved matter per million parts by weight of solvent). Since the T.D.S. of desert waters can range from 300 ppm to a thousand times that figure in some connate waters, a figure of 35,000 ppm (75 per cent of which is $Na^+ Cl^-$) for average sea-water may be found a useful point of reference.[5]

Another parameter commonly used, because it is easier to measure in the field than T.D.S., is the elctroconductivity (E.C.) of the solution (here given in micromhos (μmhos) at 25°C.). A rough equivalent for the ranges of salinity which affect the economically utilizable parts of the desert may be obtained by multiplying μmhos by a factor of 0·7 to obtain T.D.S. in ppm (e.g. an E.C. of 1,000 μmhos is roughly the equivalent of 700 ppm T.D.S.).

LIMITING FACTORS IN DESERT LAND-USE

The limiting factor in where and how man can live in the desert is man himself, for basically he remains physically unadapted to the environment.

The maximum salinity he can tolerate for any length of time is only in the order of 3,000 ppm T.D.S., but this figure should be compared with the 500 to 750 ppm recommended by the World Health Organization and the United States Public Service. Medical opinion in the Gulf, however, is that no permanent ill-effects amongst the local inhabitants are attributable to drinking the more brackish water, and even Europeans appear to have no difficulty in adjusting to 2,000 ppm (Bechtel 1966).

Man needs to drink frequently, and his total consumption in a year is some 50 per cent more than that of a camel (Evenari, Shanan, and Tadmor 1971[6]). He is also extremely wasteful of water, and the more he is given the more he uses. For example, while under the environmental constraints of an oasis settlement he will tend to use between 2,000 and 3,500 m^3 per head per year for his domestic purposes, he will happily dispose of ten times this much in an oil-boom town where expense is no object. Yet his survival level is just 1·5 m^3. So wherever regular supplies of water of the quantity and quality sufficient to cover the most basic needs are available, some form of human settlement will normally be found in Oman, provided, of course, that there is some economic resource to be exploited. Communities will drink the vile water on the desert coasts because there they can fish and pearl, while others survive on the brackish wells inland because there they can graze livestock: perhaps the most extreme example of the use of water is provided by some of the Ḥarāsīs tribe, who reputedly survive in parts of the southern coast (seasonally affected by the monsoonal air mass described in Chap. II) by means of hanging out blankets to collect dew.

Obviously the possibilities for an agricultural economy in the desert are very limited. Whereas natural vegetation makes extraordinary use of soil moisture and can adapt to drought (xerophytes) and high salinities (halophytes) all cultivated plants that grow in the type of environment with which we are concerned require large quantities of relatively high-quality water.

The extreme limits for agricultural settlement are more-or-less determined by the requirements of the date-palm, a remarkable tree which might be regarded as the agricultural equivalent of the camel in the desert regions of the Old World. It thrives in dry heat and is highly salt tolerant. Experiments (reported in Furr, Ream, and Ballard 1966) in irrigating date-palms over a period of 380 days with concentrations of 6, 12, 18, and 24 thousand ppm of chloride salts (giving osmotic pressures of about 4·3, 8·0, 12·5, and 16·4 atmospheres respectively) showed no permanent ill-effects, and the authors' conclusions were that 'the date-palms were resistant to injury from high concentrations of chlorides for relatively long periods, but did not grow well at concentrations above 6,000 ppm.' The extreme limit of economic viability would appear to be in the order of 8,000 ppm T.D.S., for this is the maximum salinity of a regular irrigation supply the writer has been able to trace anywhere in Oman.

But while the date-palm, compared with other crops, is highly tolerant in respect of water quality, it is very demanding in the quantities of water it needs, and this really is its limiting feature for use in the desert environment. Just how limiting may be appreciated if the water consumption of a bedu group living at subsistence level by livestock-herding (as given in footnote 6) is compared with that of a similar group living at the same level cultivating the palm: the latter will consume getting on for a thousand times more water than the former, and what is more the salt content will have to be some 50 per cent lower!

LIVESTOCK-HERDING

By far and away the most profitable use man can make of desert land-resources is to herd livestock. The factors which limit the possibilities for such an economy cannot be determined simply in terms of quantity and quality of water alone, because the nature of the grazing is equally important, and this in turn can affect the water requirements of each breed of animal.

Even harder to define are parameters for assessing the economic value of desert land, for while the domesticated animals of the hot deserts are capable of surviving in extremely hostile conditions, their economic yield is best when grazing and fresh water are plentiful, and rapidly declines once certain physiological thresholds peculiar to each breed are exceeded. All animals compete for optimum conditions, but the fact that there is a difference in the 'fall-off' point between the different species allows some to live in areas where there is less competition for resources and enables others to survive under even more rigorous conditions.

Perhaps the best indication of when this fall-off point occurs is provided by the body-temperature curve, because in large ruminants adapted to a desert environment this can rise above the normal so as to reduce the need for evaporating body water in order to maintain the core at a constant 37°C. (The stored heat is dissipated when the ambient temperature drops at night).

Observations on animals like the oryx and gazelle, which are found living in the most extreme desert conditions in Oman, show that their body temperatures automatically rise 6–8°C. when the ambient temperature is kept at 40°C. for twelve hours, regardless of the watering conditions; this is a major factor which accounts for their ability to exist permanently in their habitat without free drinking water (Taylor 1969). On the other hand, similar experiments with the camel (Schmidt-Nielsen 1964, chap. 3) showed that whereas its body temperature ranged 6.2°C. in eleven hours when deprived of water, it only varied 2°C. when allowed to drink freely; this indicates that it is essentially less suited to extreme aridity than are the wild animals of the desert. This is not to deny the camel's remarkable adaptations to its environment which also include tolerating a water loss exceeding 25 per cent of the body-weight without explosive heat-rise (cf. man, who cannot take care of himself at 10 per cent and is unable to reçover from 12 per cent dehydration without assistance (Schmidt-Nielsen 1964, p. 15)); being able to lose up to 20 per cent of its body-weight without a notable diminution in feeding (controlled experiment was with a dry feed of dates and hay); and being able to ingest water at a single session equal to 30 per cent of its body-weight. These abilities show why the camel is the domestic animal of the desert *par excellence*: nevertheless, the beast does not thrive when put to such stresses, and this is indicated by a rise above the normal temperature pattern. However, measuring the rectal temperature of camels presents problems, so until some enthusiastic researcher is prepared to obtain the necessary observations in different natural environments, rather less exact measures of changes affecting the economic value of the beast will have to suffice.

All the domesticated animals of the desert have high salinity tolerations. It has been observed of sheep in the Australian desert, for example, that they can tolerate up to 25,000 ppm NaCl and that some actually appear to thrive on salinities of 19,000 ppm. But at the same time the experiments also showed that, while there was a degree of adaptation to inreasing salinity and 10,000 ppm had no long-term ill-effects on any of the herds studied, 15,000 ppm was detrimental to some, and all suffered at 20,000 ppm. Furthermore those sheep which appeared to thrive at 19,000 ppm were on green feed, but when they were placed on dry feed their salt toleration fell to some 10–12,000 ppm (Denton, Goding, McDonald, Sabin, and Wright 1961; Schmidt-Nielsen 1964, chap. 6). Once again it is the camel which proves to be the domesticated animal most adapted to the hydrological resources of the desert, for just as it is capable of going without water for long periods without its feeding habits being affected, so it is capable of tolerating far higher salinity concentrations than the smaller domestic animals (MacFarlane 1971). Nevertheless, variations in the mineral content of both free water and grazing is reflected in the quality of its milk yield, as the following comments by bedu illustrate; these remarks also emphasize the point already made that there is an extremely close relationship between the effects of water, grazing, and salinity on the performances of domestic animals in the desert.

Gurmīyāt, that is camels fed on *gurm*, the local name in Abu Dhabi for the relict communities of *Avicennia marina* (mangrove) which grow on the mud-flats of tidal lagoons of the Gulf (Djezirei 1961; Firmin 1965),[7] produce a milk which is noticeably salty, and they have to be watered daily. Similarly *hawārim*, camels that feed on the halophyte *harm* (*Zygophylaceae sp.*), the main grazing south of the Līwā, yield a milk which tastes salty; they too have to be watered daily, and in addition suffer from an almost permanent diarrhoea. In the case of *awāḍi*, camels feeding on *rimth* (*Haloxylon sali-cornicum*), the milk is characterized by a markedly bitter taste; this is probably due to concentrations of SO_4.

Since the factors involved in assessing the economic potential of the desert foreland of Oman for grazing animals cannot easily be measured, perhaps the simplest way of assessing this potential is to examine the actual practice of the inhabitants. The following observations of bedu grazing-practices in Oman tend to confirm reports from other similar environments (e.g. Asad 1964 for the Kabābīsh; Musil 1928, p. 338, for the Rwala; Gauthier-Pilters in Schmidt-Nielsen 1964, p. 68, for the Chaamba; Evenari *et al.* 1971 for the Negev).

In summer, those camels which graze in the bajada zone, even though they may be capable of going without drinking water for a week when feeding on the very good vegetation that occurs in some wadi beds, are nevertheless normally watered every two days (there is a special verb, *ghabb*, which applies to a camel going without water for two days); in full desert conditions, where halophytes predominate, they are watered daily. On the other hand, in winter a camel can go without any free drinking water at all if the rains produce good fresh grazing (water content 70-80 per cent), and under these conditions it may range as much as 25 km a day as it browses. Since the animal is then no longer tied to its water supply and appears to have no territorial instincts, this presents problems of herding: as a result *ṭawāzi* (camels in a state of water in-dependence) have to be hobbled, either by tying their legs together (*mugayyad*) or by tying one leg up against the body (*maʿgūl*) in order to prevent their wandering too far. Camels are never penned.

It can be seen that it is human adaptation to the environment, rather than that of the camel, which limits use of the winter grazing resources of the desert, and so the terrain is not fully exploited in this season. In summer, on the other hand, the picture is quite different. Camels then automatically return to water and thus spare the bedu the hardships of herding at the time when physical conditions are at their most trying. In this season too the grazing potential of true desert is extremely limited: this is not just because there is a paucity of vegetation and water, but also because the area over which the camel, when watered every day, can range, is only a quarter of that which it covers when the grazing permits watering every other day. Areas like the barren Miocene plain of central and southern Oman are therefore completely deserted in summer, and the camel-herding nomads withdraw either into the favoured areas near the mountains or into the sand desert.

The herding of sheep and goats gives rise to a very different pattern of land-use from that of the camel. In the case of sheep, suitable pasture simply does not exist in summer in full desert conditions, because the animal is essentially a grazer and not a browser; moreover, sheep need watering daily and their range of movement is more limited than that of the camel (15-20 km according to Evenari *et al.* 1971, p. 307). To some extent these limitations apply also to the goat, but because goats are browsers as well as grazers, are more tolerant of water deprivation, and are generally hardier and more intelligent than sheep, they are better-adapted to living in the desert borderlands of Oman and are ideally suited to the mountain pasture. One thing both sheep and goats do have in common however, is that they only lactate when there is ample fresh grazing, whereas the camel lactates during eleven months of the year (Sweet 1970, p. 273).[8]

LAND-USE PATTERNS AND SOCIO-ECONOMIC GROUPINGS

Two important conclusions have emerged concerning land utilization and socio-economic organization in Oman. The first is that sheep- and goat-herding is virtually confined to the borderlands of the desert, that is to the vicinity of the settled areas. Since sheep and goats,[9] when grazing on natural vegetation alone, cannot provide a basic foodstuff by which man can live throughout the year, they are therefore kept either by groups attached to the villages, or by pastoralists who also graze camels.

In the bajada zone it is mainly the bedu groups who herd sheep and goats; coupled to keeping camels this gives them a viable livelihood. There the smaller animals exploit the finer grazing, while the camels feed, for the most part, either on *ghāf* (*Prosopis sp.*), which is the most important permanent grazing in the sandy terrain, or on *samra* (*Acacia sp.*), which predominates in the *sayḥ* (gravels): since this permanent grazing has a high moisture content (acacia up to 58 per cent moisture in severe drought; Taylor 1969) the camels need only be watered every two or three days in summer. So we can see that, in the case of a mixed pastoral economy, it is the pattern of sheep- and goat-grazing that limits the range of land used, and the potential of the camel is not fully exploited. This is why the majority of the bedu groups based on the bajada zone normally have a fairly small range of seasonal movement. While they may move some way out into the outer bajada zone in winter, most of them keep fairly close to the relatively rich savanna country near the mountains, and it is only a few groups that will take camels to the outer part of the *dār* in search of the grazing which sheep and goats cannot use (thus, incidentally, introducing an element of differentiation into a tribe's social organization).

Within the mountain zone the herding of *petit bétail* is in the hands either of the villagers, who supplement the natural grazing with crops (alfalfa and the lowest quality dates), or of the *shawāwi*, who also breed camels and large numbers of donkeys, an animal in many ways more adapted to this particular environment. Although they are not hadhar, these *ṣhawāwi* groups have a number of characteristics that distinguish them from the bedu of the desert fringe: first, they are more or less incorporated into the tribal structures of the settled people, second, they have peculiar rights in the village with which they associate, and third, they act as the main long-distance transporters of goods between the settled communities.

The second conclusion is really the converse of the first; that camel-herding by itself can just provide a viable living, but if the animal's adaptation to the desert environment is to be exploited fully, then it is not possible to keep sheep and goats as well. So it is that the pure camel-herders tend to occupy the outer desert, notably the sandy regions where grazing and water are available in summer; but because resources are scarce and widely dispersed there, so too is the settlement pattern and tribal *dārs* are correspondingly extensive. Such differences in land-use organization also help explain why the bedu of the outer desert and the pastoralists of the bajada zone and mountain have different social attitudes towards each other; but these, it should be noted, are nothing like as marked as those between the true bedu and the sheep-herders (the equivalent of the mountain *shawāwi* of Oman) in the Syrian desert. Nor should such differences be equated with the distinction that is sometimes drawn between nomadic and semi-nomadic groups. Indeed, once something of the structure of the tribal groups of Oman and of the processes of sedentarization is understood (see Chapters VIII and IX), it will be realized that it can be positively misleading to label the inhabitants of the desert foreland in such a way. A rather more useful classification would be to distinguish between camel-herding groups, who tend to live in the sand desert, and mixed-herding groups, who tend to concentrate along the fringes of the settled zones. And it is because the associations of the mixed-herders with the settled core of Oman are much stronger than those of the true camel-herders, that the edge of the sand desert has more or less, become the political boundary of our region. But the fact that this line has been drawn for modern political convenience should not obscure the fact that there is a continuity in land-use which extends from the settled zone towards the core of the desert, and that the inhabitants of the outer frontier are also to some extent involved with Oman in its centralizing regional organization.

ZONAL ORGANIZATION AND DEMOGRAPHIC EQUILIBRIUM

The fact that the desert foreland can be divided into zones of different potential land-use does not necessarily mean that its inhabitants are content to organize themselves according to such a simple economic order. Because all forms of life in the desert biome seek optimum and not marginal conditions there is, on the contrary, competition for the best resources. This at its crudest may be viewed as the conflict between the desert and the sown, between the bedu and hadhạr: indeed, Ibn Khaldūn, in his famous *Prologomena* (*Muqaddima*) to world history, saw the difference in wealth between the hardy inhabitants of marginal land and the city-dwellers drawing off the wealth from the rich agricultural regions as a permanent incitement for a new bedu dynasty to take control of the settled lands as soon as the previous one had become softened and corrupted by the luxuries of high-living.

In the Oman region, this potential for conflict between the 'desert' and the 'sown' is more limited than the Ibn Khaldūn model might lead one to suppose. There are three main reasons for this: first, differences in the economic resources of the various zones of land-use tend to produce demographic equilibrium between the socio-economic groups which occupy them; second, there is no real urban society in interior Oman to accumulate the surpluses of production; third, all the inhabitants are incorporated into a 'tribal' society. These last two reasons will be discussed later; only the first will be elaborated here.

We have seen that three general zones of land-use may be distinguished on the desert fringe; an outer camel-herding zone, which passes into one of mixed-herding, which in turn merges into a zone of predominantly agricultural organization. These roughly correspond with the three broad physiographic regions of interior Oman, the desert foreland, the bajada zone, and the mountains; the fact that the sea is a clearly defined physical feature which cuts across all three adds a further dimension to this picture, permitting those inhabitants living near the coast to combine their basic economic occupations with maritime activities.

The drive to move from the 'desert' towards the 'sown' is manifested in a tendency for the inhabitants of zones of lower economic potential to try and establish territorial rights in the nearest neighbouring area of greater land potential (as will be discussed further in Chapter IX, the process of sedentarization is initiated by this interzonal movement); thus the camel-herder seeks to obtain a foothold in the better pastures of the bajada zone or to improve his lot by fishing and pearling, while the mixed-herding bedu of the bajada zone similarly seek to obtain rights in the villages of the settled zone. Yet the possibilities for their doing so are limited for two demographic reasons.

The first is that (assuming that we are not dealing with an 'invasion' from outside) conquest is virtually impossible. While it is true that the bedu tend to increase their holdings in the settled lands in times of political unrest in Oman (cf. Chapter IX), the fact that the settled population outnumbers the nomads by something like 20 to 1 means that any serious incursion can easily be resisted. The second is that each zone of land-use can only support a population of a certain size. Since none of the three socio-economic groups of Oman in reality lives much above subsistence level (whatever the bedu may think), this population cannot be increased without a corresponding increase in the yield of the land. Now it is a basic premise of this study (cf. in particular Chapters VI and VII) that there have been no such increases since the seventh century (on the contrary there has been a long-term, if intermittent, decrease in the cultivated areas, and a decline in the standards of water- and land-management), and so it follows that no zone can accept newcomers unless there is a corresponding decline in the numbers of the existing population.

Such a decline might occur as the result of various 'Malthusian checks', and *a priori* it might be reasonable to expect that levels of population did, in fact, fluctuate considerably in the pre-modern era. Yet the interior of Oman was probably less subject to the outbreaks of plague and other epidemics from which the inhabitants of a port like Muscat suffered, and such disasters as are reported in the local sources are usually concerned not with disease, as in other Gulf chronicles, but with natural catastrophies affecting the yield of the land (e.g. flood and drought). Furthermore, there is no reason to suppose that there was any regular difference in death-rates between the three economic zones of interior Oman. Should, however, the inhabitants of a particular zone happen to escape a demographic catastrophe which struck the others, then a situation could arise in which interzonal migration might occur.

A second possibility arises from outward migration. The evidence on this particular subject, as indeed on all this demographic discussion, is exceedingly scanty. Certainly Omanis are found living overseas, and we do read, particularly in the earliest period of the country's written history, of sizeable tribal movements both into and out of the region (the major period of Arab migration into Oman, however, took place in the period of Persian occupation, when the land-organization was quite different: cf. Chapter VI). Fortunately there are just enough hints in the available material to permit us to discount certain possibilities and look to others for explanation of such movements in Islamic times.

The first conclusion is that population pressures, initially at any rate, seem to be relieved by movement to another area of similar economic environment and not by interzonal movement. If, therefore, some of the socio-economic groups with which we are dealing do in fact produce the kind of natural growth that some authors have argued (cf. Barth 1961, Ch. 9; de Planhol 1968), then any increase of population above the number that the zone can support at subsistence level must lead to outward migration. In other words, a growing bedu group would tend to throw off a section which would move away to find new pastures elsewhere, rather than the group as a whole trying to force itself into the neighbouring settled area (*a fortiori* if the growth is in animal rather than human population).

The second conclusion is that overseas migration appears to originate from the inhabitants of the settled zone. The fact that a high percentage of Omanis who have gone to live in East Africa seem to come from the Sharqīya (cf. Nicholls 1971), environmentally the most precarious settled region, is perhaps evidence that it is failure of the land-resources, in other words a 'push' factor, which leads to such overseas migration. The only occasion that 'pull' factors might operate is when overseas trade is prosperous. Under those circumstances there might be some movement into the developing commercial centres, both at home and abroad, and should this happen a demographic vacuum might develop in the interior, which could result in inward migration from the desert (in so far as it was not filled by the natural growth associated with the increased prosperity). Also, in such periods of maritime activity there is some tendency to invest in the land, and this in turn would expand the demand for new population. Unfortunately, the occasions on which these circumstances have been fulfilled in Omani history are all too rare, and in the last thousand years the only period in which we may assume that the country's population increased noticeably is in the latter part of the Yaʿāriba period (late seventeenth, early eighteenth centuries).

Clearly, the opportunity for interzonal movement in Oman is very limited. While theoretically demographic disaster can occur in one zone and not in another, the probabilities are that in reality all will be affected simultaneously, and that the worst-hit areas will be those of most marginal land use, in both the desert and the settled regions — in other words, the sand desert and the outlying *qanāt* settlements in the bajada zone. Since the numbers of people living in these places are relatively small, the population forced to move may be absorbed without too much dislocation in the more prosperous part of the country. But if it is a prolonged drought which is leading to the collapse of marginal settlement, then the effects will almost certainly be felt throughout the country as a whole. In such circumstances the settled peoples will also be forced to move, and those that do not migrate overseas will swell the already hard-pressed bands of nomads. In the view of the writer it is this kind of mechanism which sets off the type of major migrations that seem to have characterized certain periods in the history of the Arabian Peninsula, and which on a smaller scale have drained off from Oman any major increase in population relative to the economic resources of the land.

Under normal circumstances, however, we may assume that the demographic pressures exerted by the inhabitants of the various economic zones in Oman are self-balancing. While there are mechanisms which allow the inhabitants of the desert to filter into the settled lands, the process is slow and conflict is limited. It is, therefore, more profitable to view the occupants of the different natural regions of Oman as forming complementary groups specializing in the country's different land-resources, rather than to consider them as comprising a series of competing socio-economic units. Such specialization leads to exchange, economic interdependence, and so to a measure of political integration: Table 7 presents a very broad indication of what goods and services are exchanged between the various regions of Oman.

THE DESERT FRONTIER

The fact remains that the western bajada zone of Oman does represent a zone where some conflict between the desert and the sown may develop, because it is here that the bedu groups compete most strongly among themselves for territorial rights, and it is here the drive from the desert builds up against the outer settlements of the hadhar. Up to now this economic drive has been

Table 7 *Economic Specialization and Potential Exchanges in Different Land Use Zones of Oman*

		Primary	*Manufactured*	*Services*
I	The Desert (Bedu and Shawāwi groups).	Meat, fats, salt, wool, firewood, dyes.	Charcoal, woven goods (mainly carpets and bags).	Long distance transport, military, labour (harvest-time, and maritime activities).
II	Villages of the Interior.	Dates (carbohydrates), fruit (fresh and dried), fodder (alfalfa and low-quality dates).	Textiles, *Sūq* crafts.	Local exchange and administrative centres.
III	Coastal Villages (a) Agricultural and fishing (Batina).	As II above, plus dried fish (food, fodder, and manure).	As II above	Local exchange by land and sea.
	(b) Non-agricultural (Trucial Coast).	Fish products (as in (a) above), pearls.	As II above, plus construction of small ships.	Local exchange by land and sea, and administrative centres. Summer labour surplus.
IV	Major Ports.	—	As III (b).	Major coastal administrative centre; major exchange centre for international trade; government, military, and naval centre.

examined from the point of view of the bedu. The situation must also be viewed through the eyes of the settled villagers if the relationships of the two is to be seen in perspective.

In contrast to the bedu, who see the grass ever greener in their neighbours' land, the hadhar might well view the whole of Oman as a desert in which settled man struggles in isolated communities to maintain a precarious foothold. For the villagers the land might be portrayed as forming a series of rings of ever-less-productive land (cf. Fig. 12). In the centre are the permanently irrigated gardens; then comes an area of seasonal agricultural occupation; then a ring of commonly-held non-agricultural land in which small livestock are grazed; and beyond this lies the desert, in which settled man has no place. It is this point of view which is enshrined in the *sharīʿa*-(Islamic law) which regulates the rights of land-ownership and establishes the territorial relationships of the nomads and the villagers, as may be seen from the following summary.

RIGHTS OF OWNERSHIP (*MULK*)[10]

Property that can be bought and sold in full right of personal ownership (*mulk*) may be divided into *amlāk* (possessions, mobile property) and *arāḍi* (land, fixed property). For the latter a document (*ṣakk*) should be held. Land which can be held in *mulk* is confined to the following six main classifications in the village: *arāḍi, atlāl, ashjār, miyāh, aflāj*, and *sawāqi*.

The first two classes refer to the land itself, and in such a context *arāḍi* basically means the economically valuable parts and *atlāl* (literally hills) the barren parts. The former subdivides into occupied land which is not cultivated (buildings, tracks, bridges, and so on), and agricultural land, permanently cultivated gardens (*mazraʿ pl. mazāriʿ*), and seasonally cultivated land (*ʿābi* pl. *ʿawābi*). In addition there is a further sub-classification, *ramm* (pl. *rumūm*), about whose exact meaning there is a degree of confusion but which, in fact, simply designates deserted property (water channels, fields, gardens, buildings, etc.). While vestigial *mulk* rights may be invested in such land it is basically treated as *mawāt*, dead land, and so possession can pass to someone who re-develops it. Outside these types of property which may be held in full personal ownership is the *ḥaram* of the village, sometimes referred to as *ḥudūd* or *ṣawādir al-bilād*, in which the village community as a whole holds the grazing rights; beyond this lies the general grazing area (*marʿa* pl. *marāʿi*) in which anyone may establish preferential rights through customary usage, but which cannot be held in *mulk* ownership. This is the land occupied by the bedu and *shawāwi* groups.

Ashjār, which means large plants and trees, represents the second element in land production that can be bought and sold. Here it is only cultivated fruit trees that may be owned in *mulk*, and this specifically excludes large non-cultivated trees with some sort of economic value (e.g. *sidr* (*Zizyphus spina-christi*)): these belong to the *Bayt al-Māl* (the property of the Muslim State

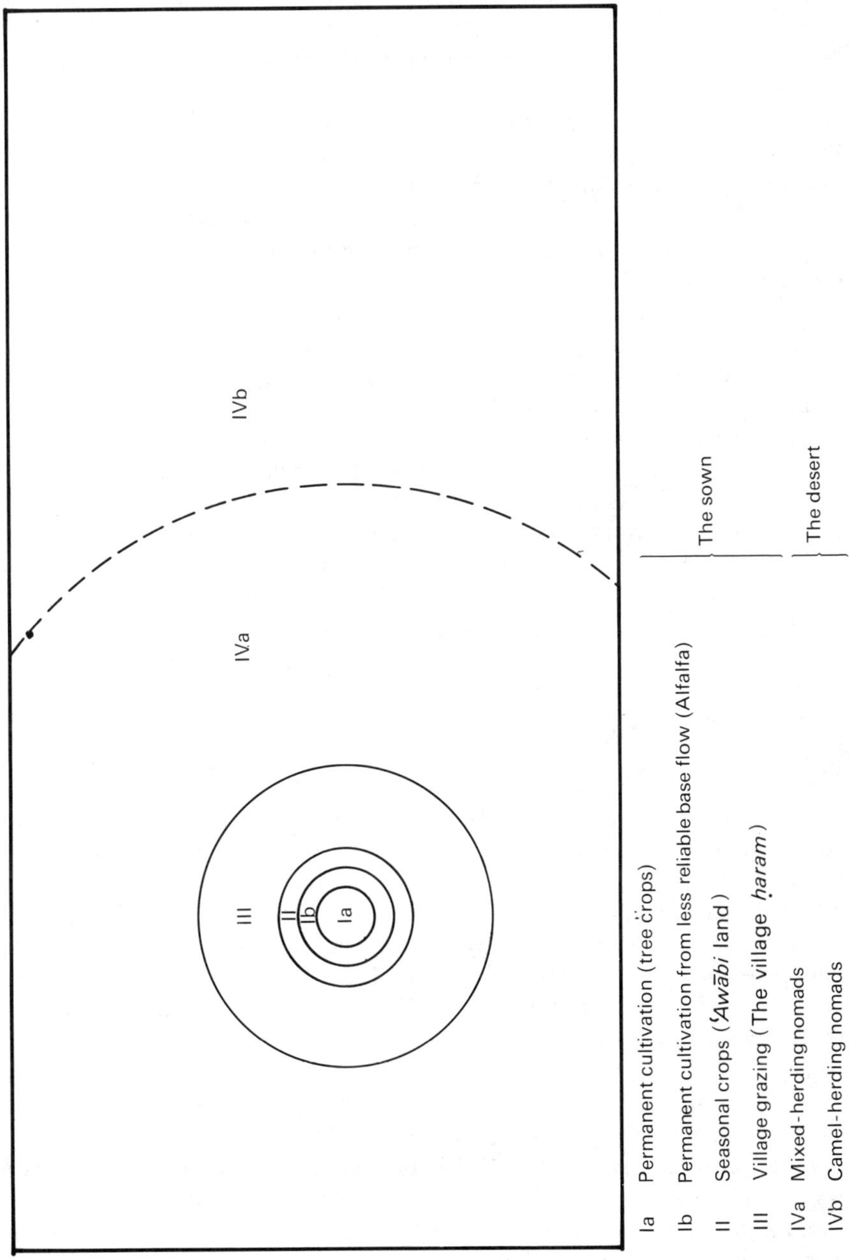

Fig. 12 The villagers' view of the land.

administered by the Imam: cf. Chapter VII), and should they fall down, the wood is sold by auction (*munādā*) and the revenue devoted to the local poor.[11] Normally the government (whether that of Imam or Sultan) is very strict about cutting down trees and only certain types of bush may be cut for firewood. At the time when the writer was living in Oman (1965), for example, the Sultan would only allow *samra* (*Acacia sp.*) to be cut for specific local needs in designated spots like the Sayḥ Ḥattāt (where it was the main source of fuel for Muscat), but in the bedu territory customary rights were recognized, and tribes like the Āl Bu Shāmis were allowed to cut the trees in order to make the charcoal that they sold in the villages.

Miyāh (wells of all types), *aflāj* (irrigation systems) and *sawāqi* (distributory irrigation channels) make up the three subdivisions of water, the third element in agricultural production that may be bought and sold in *mulk*. Details of ownership are discussed in the next two chapters.

This classification of property that may be owned in *mulk* regulates not only what land may and may not be owned by individuals, but also clearly defines the territorial rights of the villagers and thereby reduces the potential for conflict with the nomads. But while Islamic law provides a general safeguard which protects the hadhar struggling against the incursion of the desert and the bedu, it should be realized that in fact the *sharīʿa* is only really reinforcing what is already a naturally established order, for it is a fundamental error to believe that the bedu deliberately seek to destroy the settled land in order to turn it into grazing land. On the contrary, they will help to preserve it, provided, of course, that they can obtain rights in it for themselves.

THE FRONTIER OF SETTLEMENT

It would appear that within the context of the Omani region it is the bajada zone which really represents the frontier between the desert and the sown. On the one side of this physical feature lies a vast area inhabited only by a few nomads, on the other are concentrated the settled peoples of Oman. It is not however, a clear-cut boundary, but rather a zone of transition where the people who live a nomadic existence based on livestock-herding come into contact with the inhabitants of an area where man has succeeded in establishing a little cultivation in a few discontinuous settlements.

Yet this picture of a frontier of settlement really portrays what Oman as a whole is about. In this essentially arid land, man, at great cost, has established the few enclaves of settlement around which he has built up a particular form of community organization. While the rest of this book will concentrate on the way he has achieved this, it must always be borne in mind that, whether in the mountains or on the plains, the desert is always with him. His existence is essentially precarious, and his survival depends on achieving a balance not only with his physical environment, but also with the interests of the nomadic groups. While there is a distinction to be drawn between the social organization of the nomads and that of the settled peoples, both are drawn into a single unit of regional organization by their complementary interests in the land which they share.

NOTES TO CHAPTER III

1 When the Omani bedu speak of the western tribes they mean the tribes which are orientated towards the region which the old Arab geographers termed 'Baḥrayn' (that is the area of Eastern Arabia focusing on the oases of al-Ḥasā and underlain by the confined aquifers which form the second 'water' from which the region's name arises; cf. Bibby 1970; Goudie and Wilkinson, in press).

2 These trees are quite different from self-seeded palms, known as *khīs*, which grow from the stone (*ṭaʿam*) of the fruit.

3 Great care must be taken to check regional names with several sources, and to beware the possibility that modern local usage has been affected by Europeans, who sometimes apply place-names to something rather different from the feature originally designated. Such changes may arise from misunderstanding, but more often they are caused by a different perception of the terrain. For example, European map-makers like to give a single name to the whole course of a wadi because they are brought up to view a river basin as an integrated unit of drainage; so on maps of Oman the name for one part of a wadi is frequently transferred to the whole. This is doubly misleading when the proper name is a tribal one, for it distorts the social as well as the geographical picture of the area.

In the particular case of the region with which we are dealing the origins of the names are basically topographical (cf. Fig. 11). Līwā is probably a contraction of al-Jiwāʾ, and derives from the hollows (sing. *jaww*) which form it. Sārūq is so-called because it is an area of *sārūq* (pl. *sawārīq*), the corridors of hard sand between dune ridges (the 'going' of a route is often classified as *sārūq*, *sabkha*, or *sēḥ*). Its areal application therefore specifically refers to the strip of land where the Ṭaff, 'the coastal region' (here characterized by its white calcareous sand), gives way to *sārūq*, which in turn passes into the waterless, rolling redsand-dune country of al-Qufā, sometimes called al-Ẓahāra 'the outer side' because it contrasts with al-Baṭāna or al-Baṭīn the 'inner' side of the Līwā. (Cf. (1) the local nickname of Abu Dhabi, al-Ẓahāra, which is on the 'outside' of the island facing the sea, and al-Baṭīn, the settlement on the 'inner' western creek; (2) al-Ẓāhira (Dhahira) and al-Bāṭina (Batina), the trans- and cis-montane regions in northern Oman; (3) al-Jawf and al-Ghadaf the 'inside' and 'back' of the Jabal Akhdhar.)

It can be seen that the origin of these local names is quite distinct from that implicit in Baynūna, the use of which pre-dates by centuries the tribal groups who now divide the area by topographical nomenclature. Furthermore these groups have also introduced a new regional name, al-Zafra (first featuring in the seventeenth or eighteenth centuries: cf. *Kashf* tr. Ross, p. 182), to designate 'the whole area between the Sabkhat Matti and Khatam and from the sea to the Rub' al-Khāli' (*British Memorial* i. 17), and that is why Baynūna now only survives in a vestigial form as the name for one part of the coastal strip.

4 This is the area of the caravanserai which the early Arab geographers refer to as 'al-Sabkha' in their route descriptions and which is discussed in Wilkinson 1964. A recent archaeological expedition from the American University of Beirut has uncovered the actual site and confirms that it appears to have been abandoned about the end of Umayyad times.

5 A general classification of water that is sometimes used is 0-1,000 ppm fresh, 1,000-10,000 brackish, 10,000-100,000 saline, over 100,000 ppm brine.

6 They give the water requirement of a typical bedu family-group made up of 6 persons, 2 camels, 10 sheep/goats, 1 donkey, and 2 dogs as about 18 20 m^3 per year. This is made up as follows:

	Daily consumption per head	*Approx. annual total*
man	2 l winter, 7 l summer	$1\cdot5m^3$ x 6 = $9m^3$
camel	1-2 l ,, 4-5 l ,,	$1\cdot0m^3$ x 2 = $2m^3$
donkey	about the same	$1\cdot0m^3$ x 1 = $1m^3$
sheep/goat	1-1½ l winter, 2-3½ l summer	0·5 x 10 = $5m^3$
dog	about the same	0·5 x 2 = $1m^3$
	Total	$18m^3$

[7] The main community grows at Khawr al-Ghanādha near the Dubai frontier, but small clumps are also found on some of the islands in the tidal creeks. A common sight at Abu Dhabi town, before the oil era changed the traditional pattern, was the *gaṣīl* (a man who collected *gurm*) arriving in his little boat laden with branches of mangroves cut from further east along the coast.

[8] According to Evenari (*et al.* 1971, p. 307) sheep grazed in typical bedu conditions yield about 100 l of milk a year: this may be raised to between 800 and 1,000 l with modern husbandry. The camel yields between 4 and 10 l per day (Stein, L. 1967).

[9] Collectively referred to as *ghanam* amongst the hadhar and *dhōḍ* amongst the bedu.

[10] This account is based on the following two main sources. First, discussions with one of the leading Qāḍis in Muscat, who based his own knowledge mainly on a work called *Uṣūl al-Amlāk wa 'l-Arāḍi* (The Principles of Possessions and Lands) by Saʿīd b. Ḥamad al-Aghbari/Laghbari, an important *ʿālim* who lived sometime in the last century: the Qāḍi had not seen the work for some years, but believed a manuscript still existed in Nizwā. The second is al-Sālimi's *bāb al-mawāt waʾl-awdīya* (chapter on *mawāt* (dead) land and *wādis*) in his *Jawhar al-niẓām* (pp. 428-31): this is written in *urjūza* verse and is extremely difficult to understand, even for the *'ulamā'* of Oman. It was probably designed as an *aide-mémoire* for those who had already studied the subjects covered, but when its meaning can be unravelled with the aid of other *fiqh* works (cf. Muḥammad b. ʿAbdullāh al-Khalīli *al-Fatḥ al-jalīl*, Ṣāʾighi *Kanz al-adīb*, and Ḥārithi *Khulāṣa*) it proves a valuable source of information.

[11] The same applies to palms that have established themselves in a seepage along an irrigation channel or in a wadi.

CHAPTER IV

The Traditional Techniques of Water-Exploitation

The water resources of Oman are traditionally exploited by three techniques: wells, *ghayl aflāj*, and *qanāt aflāj*.

WELLS

Although wells are used throughout the whole country for domestic, pastoral, and irrigation purposes it is only near the coast that they form the sole means by which land is extensively cultivated. On the Batina littoral strip, as well as in most of the villages of the interior, the majority of these wells are of the type called *jāzira* (northern dialect), *manjūr* or *zigra* (central Oman).[1] In this system a pair of yoked (yoke = *wayl*) bullocks or donkeys draw to the surface, by means of a rope (*ʿidda*) which runs over a creaky wooden cog (*manjūr*) fixed vertically on a tripod or similar superstructure above the shaft, a skin bucket (*dalw*) which collapses when it enters the water; as the animals descend an excavated ramp (upper point *marjal*, lower *khubb*) the skin tightens and the filled bucket is raised and tilted into a basin (*ghamīla*) from where a channel (*falaj*) carries the water to the garden. The whole well unit and its cultivated area is referred to as a *ṭawi* or *ḍāḥīya*. Dowson (1927) estimated that the average single-hoist well in al-Sīb irrigates a couple of acres of permanent crops (date-palms and fruit trees), and the double hoist perhaps half as much again.[2]

Elsewhere on the coast water is generally drawn by hand and in al-Ṣīr, where there is an extensive area of palm cultivation, such wells may go as deep as 45 m.

In the interior wells are of much more limited importance, and in parts of central Oman they are hardly used for cultivation at all. In the Sirr and northern Jawf, however, they do form an important supplementary supply of irrigation water, and are extensively used for growing seasonal crops in *ʿawābi* land.

Today pumped wells are of rapidly increasing importance. Throughout the Trucial States mechanical power has entirely replaced the traditional means of raising water,[3] and extensive new areas of cultivation are being opened up by such means. Now that there has been a change of government in the Sultanate similar conversions are rapidly taking place there: this is fortunate, for the crucial factor in the agricultural economy of the region is shortage of labour. Nevertheless, the pumped well is not entirely an unmitigated blessing, for not only is over-enthusiastic and unplanned use of the new technique threatening the water supply of the *aflāj*, but it is also introducing an element of individual land-holding which is tending to break down the sense of village community which arises from operating a shared irrigation system. These changes, however, form part of the revolution in agricultural techniques and organization that stems from the discovery of oil, and are therefore not relevant to this study. Nor will the systems of well irrigation on the coast be described in any more detail, for it is with the traditional irrigation organization in the mountain and bajada zone that we are primarily concerned. This is the region of *aflāj* irrigation.

AFLĀJ

As used in Oman, the word *falaj* pl. *aflāj* is a generic term for a complete irrigation system. The word derives from an ancient Semitic root (*plg*) which means to divide: in Genesis (x. 25), for example, we read, 'And unto Eber were born two sons; the name of one was Peleg; for in his days was the earth divided; . . .'. In classical Arabic the cognate form *flj* means to divide property into shares, and, as in the other Semitic languages, may be applied to a system for dividing water amongst shareholders.[4]

This, in Oman, is basically what a *falaj* is — an organization for distributing water amongst those who have rights to it. Since the word in itself tells nothing about the form of water supply, the writer has introduced the terms *ghayl falaj* and *qanāt* to distinguish between two quite different types of *aflāj* that exist in Oman. The fact that the local terminology itself makes no such distinction is indicative of local attitudes towards the land, a theme which will be elaborated later.

Unlike *qanāt*, the word *ghayl* is in local use, and means the perennial flow in the surface gravels of a wadi (cf. Chapter II). In a *ghayl falaj* this flow is diverted (verb *radd*) into a channel either by a low bund (*sibya*; *maᶜqad*), or through a short collector gallery; the amount of water that can be diverted in this way is limited by Islamic law, and it is an offence completely to dam the flow of a stream. Sometimes *ghayl aflāj* (cf. Fig. 13) are no more than simple diversion channels that bring the water direct from the wadi to the nearby gardens, but because in many areas the wadi beds are incised and land suitable for cultivation may be located well downstream from the point of surface flow, a special channel often has to be built or cut into the rock for considerable distances along the side of a wadi; it is for the same reason that the above ground and 'cut and cover' sections of a *qanāt falaj* may also be far longer than the underground section in the mountain zone. Indeed, the problem of finding a suitable site for cultivation is sometimes more difficult to resolve than that of finding water: the great piles of stones and silt (*kabs*) which surround the gardens of so many villages in Oman bear witness to the work required to create gardens in outwash fans, while the systems of terracing which have been developed along the wadi banks in places like Maqūnīyāt,[5] or in the settlements on the edge of the Jabal Akhdhar plateau show what may have to be done if precious *ghayl* and spring flows are not to be wasted.

Although *ghayl aflāj* sometimes supply considerable quantities of irrigation

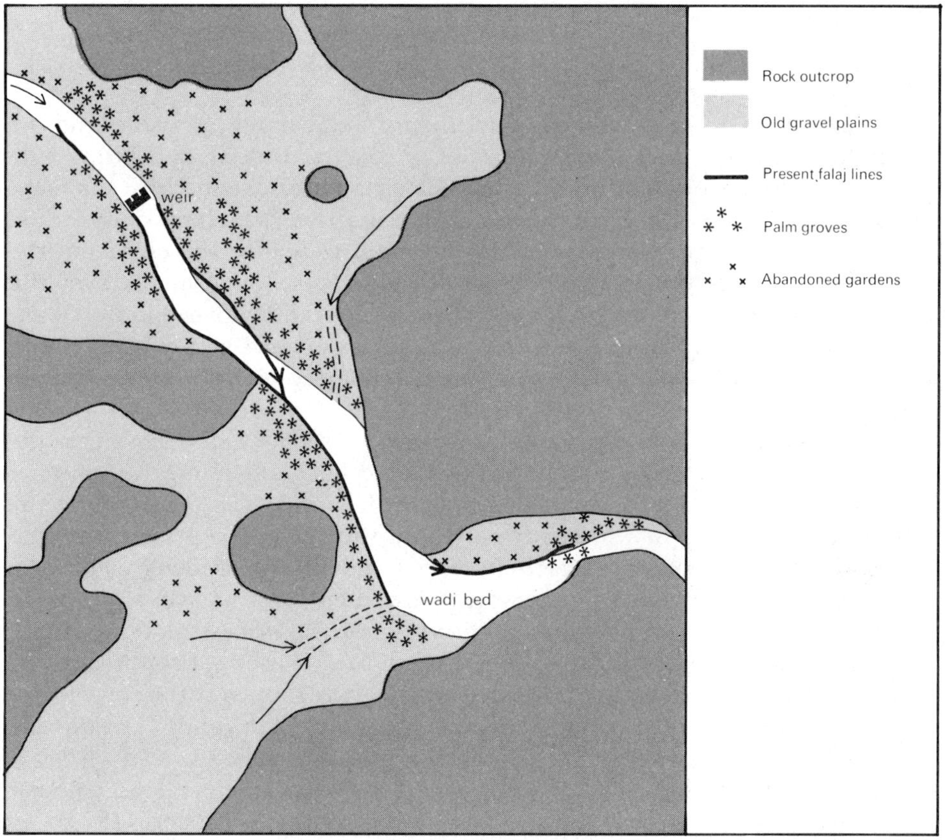

Fig. 13. The *ghayl aflāj* in the Bithnā area (northern Oman).

water, as in the case of the villages in the Wadi Sumāyil, and may be the sole source of water for some of the small villages located in the upper reaches of a wadi basin, virtually all sizeable settlements have their *qanāt* as well. Indeed, the writer knows of no major village in the mountain zone of central Oman that does not have a *qanāt*; and while there are some settlements in northern Oman which today rely entirely on *ghayl* or wells for their water supply, closer examination of their sites nearly always reveals the line of an abandoned *qanāt*.[6] A good example is provided by the very ancient port of Dibā, one of the most important places of pre-Islamic Oman; now it draws its water entirely from wells, but the line of the abandoned *qanāt* system which once supplied it may still be traced in the plain behind the village. As for the western bajada zone, virtually all the villages rely on *qanāt* alone for their water supply.

Since it is this form of *falaj* which serves as the basis for so much settlement in interior Oman, the rest of this chapter will be more-or-less confined to a discussion of the physical characteristics of *qanāt*.

QANĀT

Qanāt are really galleries which tap an underground supply of water, and the techniques used to build them are those of miners. Indeed, the rather surprising occurrence of *qanāt* in areas like Bavaria and Bohemia is probably to be explained by the history of medieval mining there (Klaubert 1967), while the *'areines'* of Liège, which supplied the main water for the city from the eleventh to the nineteenth centuries, were originally built in order to drain the nearby coalmines (Goblot 1968): the *'soughs'* that were developed in the seventeenth century to evacuate water from the lead mines of Derbyshire (Nixon 1969) may be considered as an example of an adaptation of this technique in England.

Goblot (1963, 1965, and personal discussion) is inclined to believe that the origins of *qanāt* are to be sought in the late-second-millennium B.C. mining areas of the northern Elburz and Armenia, and thinks the towns along the southern edge of the mountains from Ṭehran to Qazwīn represent the first major settlements to use this technique as a means of supplying water. An early diffusion from this centre may have resulted from Sargon's campaign against Urarṭu in the early eighth century B.C.,[7] for his successor Sennacherib certainly appears to have planned to use *qanāt* for furnishing Erbil with water (Laessøe 1951): the Etruscan drainage *caniculi* may represent the early introduction of the basic techniques into the Mediterranean lands (Judson and Kahane 1963). However, it is probable that the first major spread of *qanāt* was associated with the Achaemanids, who used them extensively to colonize new land throughout their empire (Goblot opp. citt.): Mazaheri (1973), on the other hand, maintains that this did not happen until Parthian times. (Further stages in the general spread of *qanāt* have been described in Cressey 1958; Goblot 1963; Troll 1963; and English 1968, *inter alia*.)

THE MOTHER WELLS

The first requisite for building a *qanāt* is to locate a suitable aquifer and sink a mother well (Omani *umm* pl. *umahāt* cf. Persian *mādar chāh*) to it, as may be seen from Figs. 14 and 15. On the choice of this site depends the success or failure of the water supply. The exact location is a compromise between a number of factors (cf. Fig. 16). To minimize the costs of excavating the shafts for the tunnel section it is obviously desirable to exploit the water high up the drainage basin. But the advantages of doing this are offset by the fact that the volume of water held in storage at the head of a fan is less than it is further downstream; the flow of *qanāt* supplied from such locations is therefore variable, and liable to cease altogether in times of drought (*ayyām al-maḥal*). Just as water can be found at no great depth at the upper end of the drainage basin, so it is also easily accessible at the downstream end; here however, the disadvantages of a fluctuating water-table are added to by the drop in hydrostatic pressure and the fall in the quality of water obtained.

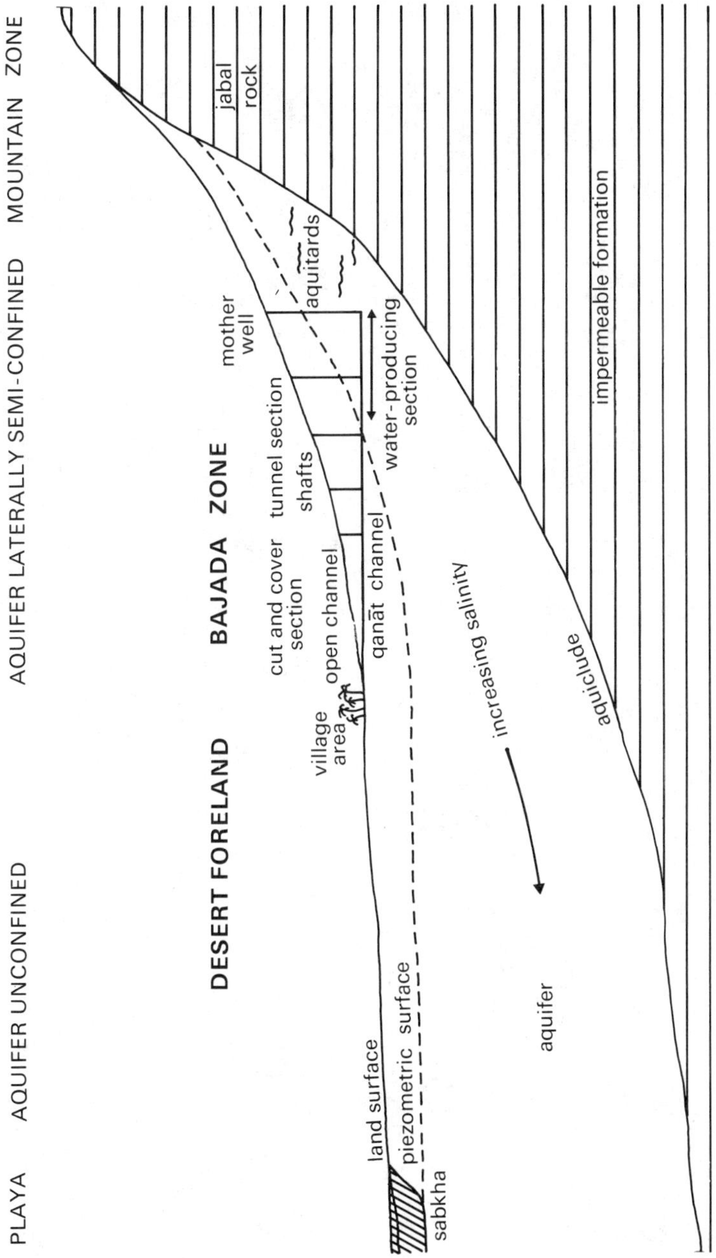

Fig. 14. Qanāt: in cross section.

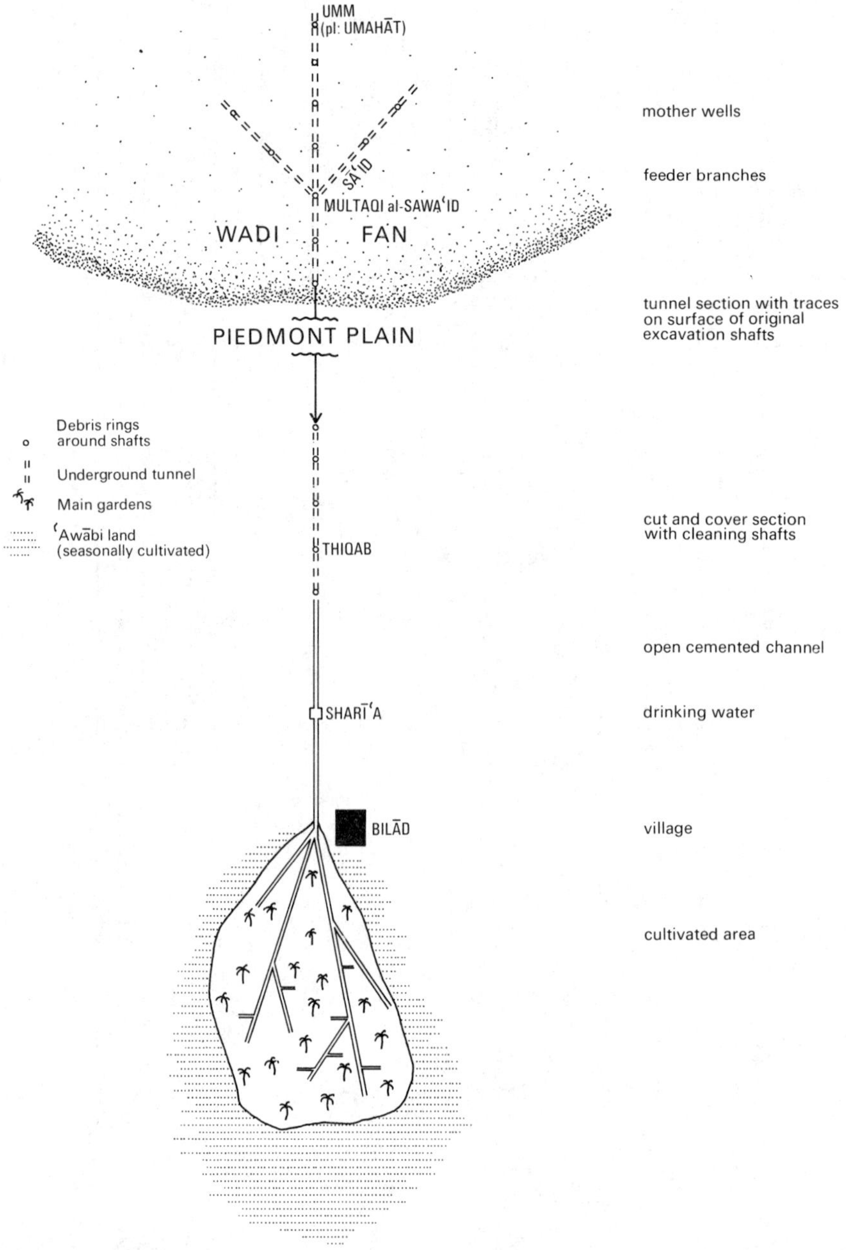

Fig. 15. Qanāt: in plan.

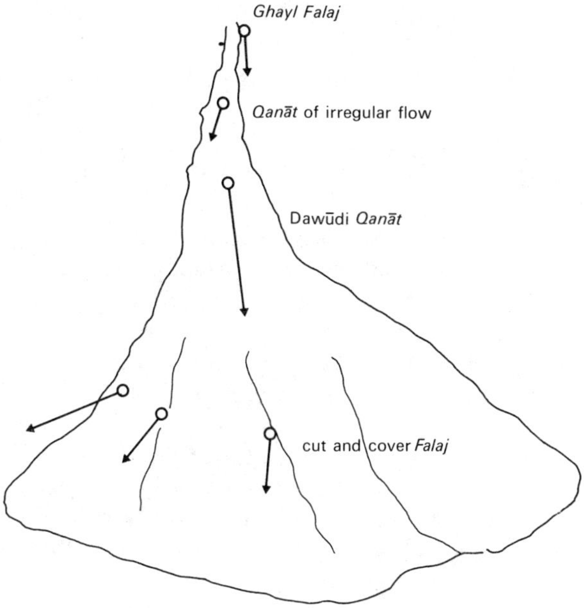

Fig. 16. Exploitation of water resources in a fan by *aflāj*.

Obviously, therefore, the best area to locate the mother well is a little distance downstream from the head of the fan. Here the volume of water in storage is considerable but does not lie too deep, the quality is good, and the hydrostatic pressure is still reasonably high. *Qanāt* supplied from such a site will thus have a dependable base flow, while seasonal variations will tend to be evened out by transmission delays so that the minimal discharge will occur in early winter, when demand is least, and the maximum in early summer, the critical period for the development of fruit on the date-palm.

Furthermore, since in this zone of offtake the slope is usually in the order of 6–7 degrees but rapidly flattens out to about 2 degrees (which is the regional gradient of the water-table in the outer bajada zone), the water is brought to the surface within a reasonable distance and the total length of the *qanāt* is not excessive. This is not only an advantage from the point of view of the cost of building the system, but also because it means that transmission losses in the underground section and evaporation losses in the open channel are minimized. Another advantage is that in the area to be cultivated, the land is well drained, and this, when combined with the high quality of the water (good *aflāj* contains only a few hundred parts per million of dissolved solids), means that there is very little risk of salt accumulation. The corresponding disadvantages are that the soil tends to be thin and stony in the area of cultivation, while the upstream gardens may have to be excavated to a considerable depth.

Because of the possible variations in locating mother wells it can be seen that no hard and fast statements can be made about their depth: 20 metres, however, does seem to be a fairly typical figure for many of the high-quality Dawūdi *qanāt* (for the origin of this name see Chapter VI). The deepest, according to local reports, is one of the Rustāq *qanāt* which goes down to 60 metres; at Nizwā the deepest is said to be at 40 metres, but the most prolific at only half this depth.

Many *qanāt* have more than one *umm*, and sometimes these may have been added since the original construction. On occasion there are two distinct areas of water offtake, one in which the mother well (or wells) taps a dependable supply of water and provides dependable base flow, the other, tapping shallow water higher up the wadi, provides supplementary flow in times of good rainfall (*ayyām al-khaṣab*). Such an arrangement has the advantage of combining some of the different water resources of a wadi basin in the same irrigation system. Another way the different resources of a drainage basin may be exploited without the disadvantage of having a series of scattered settlements each with a different flow régime (as is the case in Fig. 16) is to concentrate a number of *aflāj* at a single spot (cf. Fig. 17 of the Buraimi oasis). In cases where the drainage is confined for a considerable distance out into the piedmont zone, as in some of the westward draining valleys of central Oman, a number of such grouped settlements may be found along the same wadi.

THE TUNNEL AND MAIN CHANNEL SECTION

Having located a suitable supply of water, the line of the *qanāt* is then surveyed and a tunnel is dug back to this source at a gradient of between 1/500 to 1/2,500; this angle allows the water to flow without causing erosion of the tunnel wall or siltation.[8] Where necessary the channel is cemented. As the tunnel is dug shafts (*thuqba* or *thiqba* pl. *thiqāb* or *thiqab*) have to be sunk for ventilation and to allow removal of spoil (*kabs*); these may later serve as access points for repair and maintenance.[9] At the lower end of the *qanāt* tunnel, where it approaches the ground surface, or where it crosses unconsolidated ground (notably in *wādi* gravels), tunnelling techniques give way to those of 'cut and cover'; in some small *qanāt* where the water supply is at no great depth the whole underground tunnel may be constructed in this way. In these 'cut and cover' sections the invert is excavated from the surface, lined, and recovered with spoil. In Persia baked-clay hoops are often used here to prevent collapse, but the writer has found no signs of these in Oman; instead the weak sections are usually lined (*masmūm*) with stone blocks (*saqf* pl. *suqūf*), and the inspection shafts (*furḍa* pl. *furaḍ*) strengthened with cemented stone or masonry. The final section of the *qanāt* which leads to the village is, of course, above ground, but sometimes parts of this section may be covered over to prevent pollution and decrease evaporation, and normally this part of the channel is also cemented (*tasrīj*, noun *sahrūj*).

The relative lengths of the tunnel, cut and cover, and open channel sections

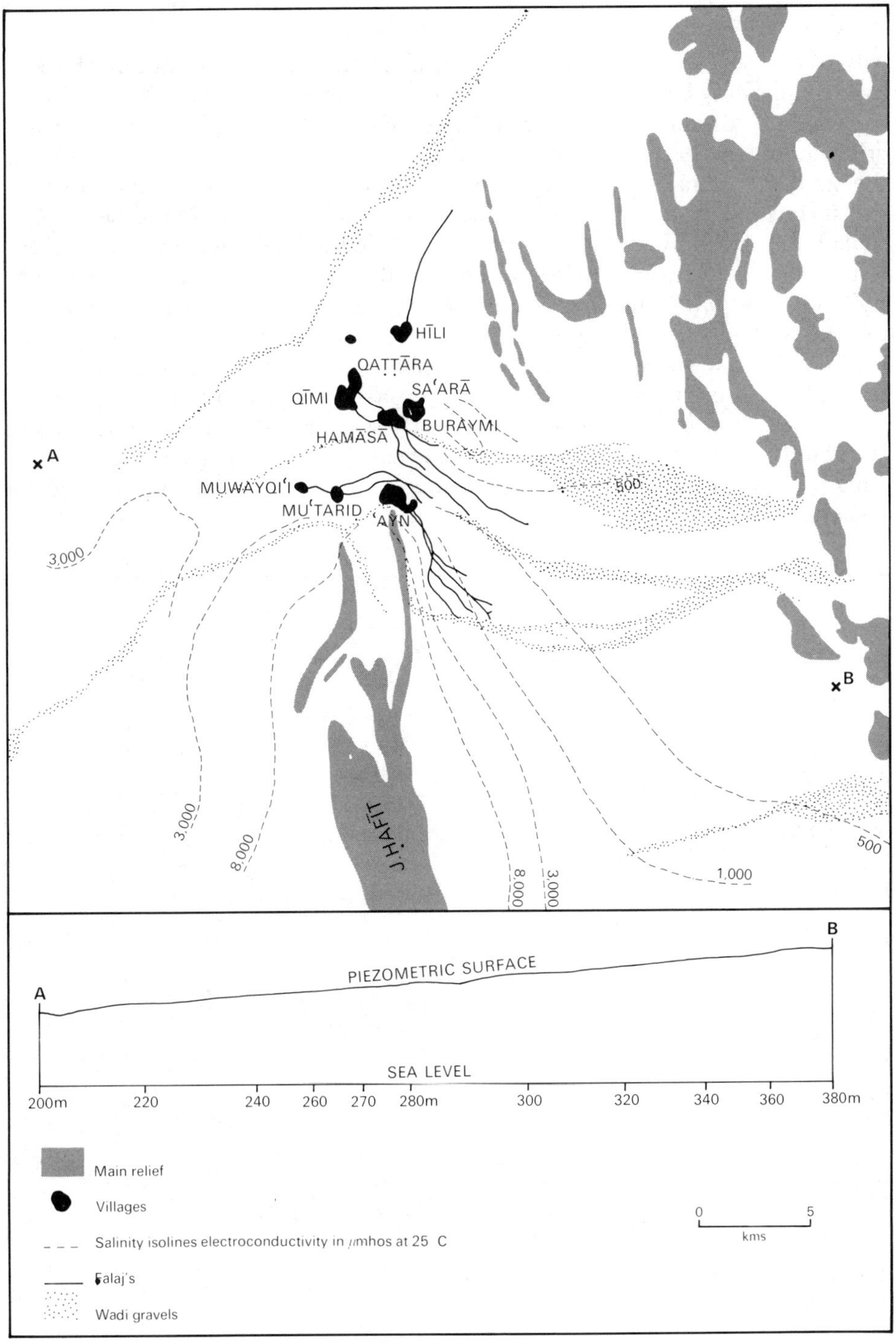

Fig. 17. The Buraimi oasis: water supply.

will, of course, depend on the nature of the terrain. In the mountains the first two sections may be so short and the third so long that it is sometimes difficult to make a distinction between *qanāt* and *ghayl aflāj*, except on the arbitrary criterion of whether the aquifer has had to be tunnelled or not; in both cases the open section may go underground from time-to-time and wind around on the surface (such a *falaj* is sometimes called *ummat ṣulayl*, mother of the snake) in order to make the best use of the lie of the land. In such terrain there is a strong risk of flood damage, and so overflow points (*miflāḥ*) are sometimes built into the *falaj* and low bunds constructed to divert the flood spate. A technique used for crossing wadi beds is the inverted siphon (*gharrāq fallaḥ*; cf. Fig. 18) but there is evidence (cf. Chapter VI) that this technique was introduced into Oman with a particular phase of *falaj* construction, and it is to be noted that its occurrence is more-or-less confined to the eastern half of the mountain area.[10] (N.B. the curious sealed *falaj* at Ḥayl Ghāf seems to work on a proper siphon system and is unique in Oman: it may be of Yaʿāriba construction).

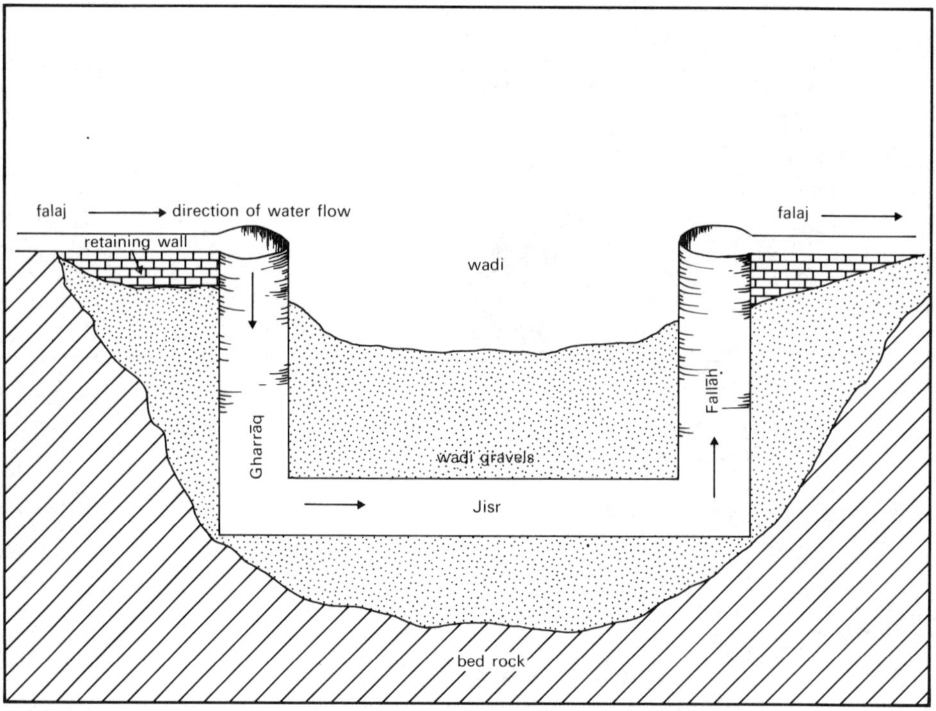

Fig. 18. Sketch of an inverted siphon (*gharrāq fallaḥ*).

In contrast to the rugged mountain zone where the underground sections of *qanāt* are often short, tunnelling techniques are put to full use in the bajada zone. Measurements of the underground sections of ten *qanāt* in the Buraimi oasis show a range from 3.1 to 9.5 kilometres, (unpublished survey of 1962), and these figures are probably fairly representative of the length of most *qanāt* in the country. They are by no means sensational when compared with figures quoted in many articles about *qanāt* in Persia, but such statistics apply to exceptional examples and are, in some cases, suspect; certainly one of the more reliable writers (Wulff 1968) gives much more credible figures, and the longest *qanāt* mentioned by him is 29 kilometres long. Without any doubt the depth and length of Omani *qanāt* are well up to Persian standards, as too are (or were once) their reliability and discharge.

AREAL DISTRIBUTIONS OF THE TECHNIQUES OF WATER EXPLOITATION

It is clear that the three main techniques by which water resources in Oman have been exploited complement rather than challenge each other. *Ghayl aflāj* make use of surface flow, while *qanāt* utilize subsurface flow and stored water. Both are therefore employed in the mountains, but in the bajada zone the *qanāt* has no rival. However, as the slope of the land flattens out all forms of irrigation by gravity flow must give way to some form of artificial lift. The fact therefore, that the Batina coast is cultivated by wells and not *aflāj* in no way implies that the people who developed the area were necessarily different from those who built the *qanāt*, any more than the fact that *ghayl* flow can be harnessed by simple diversion channels argues that the builders of such *aflāj* were ignorant of more complex techniques.

While we can argue little, therefore, about the relationship of the peoples who developed the cultivated lands of the Batina and those who developed the *aflāj* settlements in the interior on the basis of techniques alone, the fact that the coastal settlements were also once supplied by large cemented channels (the ruins of which can still be traced running from the mountains all the way across the plain in both the Batina and the Ṣīr) does surely indicate that the people who lived there had something of the same sort of 'belt and braces' approach to the security of water supply that was encountered in the mountain zone where villages with a liberal supply of *ghayl* water were also provided with *qanāt*. Again, while it is true that the systems of irrigation used in the settlements on the edge of the plateau of the Jabal Akhdhar (al-Sayq and al-ʿAyn) are somewhat different from those used in the valleys and plain, this can be explained by the fact that the problems of exploiting the springs which issue from the limestone into steep ravines are almost unique to this area. Yet a glance at the work that has been invested in the network of channels, tanks, and terraces of this particular irrigation system convinces one that whoever developed the water resources for these highland settlements displayed the same kind of approach to land management that is found in the lowland.

Indeed, whatever area of settled Oman is examined, one is liable to conclude that the main exploitation of the land is (or was once) based on a very high level of skill in water management, and the investment of effort has been remarkable; at the same time a rider would be added, that it is improbable that this work could have been carried out by the people who now use these irrigation systems, at least not with the levels of skill, knowledge, attitudes, and methods of land organization they currently display.

Areal anomalies in the distribution of irrigation techniques similarly call for explanation. For example, if we examine the map of Oman and wonder why there is no equivalent on the other side of the mountains of the strip of well irrigation that occurs in the outer part of the eastern bajada zone, the answer will be found in the hydrological differences between the two areas (cf. Chapter II); but if we also happen to notice that the line of piedmont *qanāt* settlements which characterizes the inner side of the mountains is almost entirely missing on the coastal side, then the explanation is less obvious. At first sight it might be postulated that the ease of exploitation of the Batina littoral zone has removed the stimulus for the laborious work of *qanāt*-building further inland: but this explanation will only partly satisfy, because, if this were so, why is it that there are considerable areas of *qanāt* development further up the valleys? Why too are these developed with the use of the inverted siphon, a technique which is almost completely absent on the western side of the watershed? Obviously capital and labour costs were not the limiting factor in a society that was prepared to build the great cemented channels that once crossed the Batina plain to supply the coastal settlement with what was probably little more than a supplementary source of water drawn from a different hydrological environment. The areal variations in the siting and techniques of the irrigation systems of Oman are not entirely to be explained on physical grounds alone, and some explanation must also be sought in the history of the colonization of the region.

Areal variations on the larger scale may also provide clues about where to look for the origin of this land-development. Clearly not to the western side of the Peninsula, where the ancient techniques of terracing, water-storage, run-off farming, and *sayl* (flood and silt) control predominated, because these could equally well have been used in Oman, just as the Omani systems of exploiting ground-water could profitably have been used by the Old South Arabian and Nabatean civilizations which specialized in surface-water techniques, as is proved by subsequent introductions into their settlement area. To the east on the other hand lies Persia, generally acknowledge as the home of *qanāt*, and so it is in this direction that we would tend to look for explanation of the basic land-development of Oman.

RELIABILITY OF *QANĀT*

The quality of a *qanāt* is not measured in terms of its length and depth but of its reliability. While all *qanāt* are affected by long periods of drought and some show marked seasonal variation in their discharge, the criterion by which good *qanāt* are judged by the people themselves is continuity of base flow in times of general water scarcity (*maḥal*). Unfortunately specific data do not exist for developing this point statistically: some measurements of flow rates taken sporadically over the last decade for the nine working *qanāt* which supply the Buraimi oasis do exist, but these are of little value because during that period a number of improvements have been carried out on the *falaj* system and it is impossible to elucidate what part these and other developments affecting the hydrology of the area have played in accounting for the variations in the flow.

Associated with this characteristic of reliable flow in a well-constructed *qanāt* is its extraordinarily long life. This is attested everywhere, and no more so than by the *qanāt* system of the Kharga oasis, which appears to date back to the early Achaemanid period and is still in working order (Beadnell 1909; Caton-Thompson 1931; Caton-Thompson and Gardner 1932). The reason for this longevity lies in the simple fact that the upper part of a *qanāt* is virtually immune to the vicissitudes that affects its lower 'cut and cover' section. Once a *qanāt* has been completed and any necessary adjustments made as the cone of depression stabilizes, no further work is required, and so the excavation shafts are sealed. In Oman the upper sections of many *qanāt* have been completely ignored for centuries; indeed, the location of the mother wells is sometimes unknown. One is reminded of Polybius' description (X. 28) written over 2,000 years ago of the *qanāt* which amazed the army of Antiochus the Great during their campaign (212–205 B.C.) against the Parthian king, Arsaces III: 'These people at infinite toil and expense constructed these underground channels through a long tract of country, in such a way, that the very people who now use the water are ignorant of the sources from which the channels are originally supplied.' Who 'these people' were in the case of Oman will be discussed in Chapter VI, but since the writer will claim that there some of the *qanāt* are as old as those of al-Kharga, that the whole system was completed in pre-Islamic times, and that for the last 1,200 years it has been woefully neglected, it is important to try and evaluate any physical factors that might have affected their water supply over such a long period.

LONG-TERM PHYSICAL CHANGES THAT MAY HAVE AFFECTED QANĀT FLOW

Among the natural causes which might be put forward for explaining why it is that so much land irrigated by *qanāt* has been abandoned in Oman are changes in the hydrology of the region. At first sight it might appear impossible to assess this factor, for the kind of information needed has simply not been collected. However, because the *qanāt* of Oman take their rise in the upper sections of wadis and do not tap 'fossil' water sources, the ecology of the water supply need not be considered for anything like the kind of time-scale that would be necessary for a study of physical changes that might have affected the irrigation systems of, say, the Kharga or Ḥasā oases. If enough evidence to cover the last three millenia can be pieced together this is more than adequate for our purposes.

Climatic Change

The subject of climatic change will be considered first. Here there is as yet very little direct evidence concerning Oman, but the general scheme of climatic variations for the Near East in the Holocene proposed by Butzer (1957), which is still held to be generally valid, does have a certain broad relevance to the region. The over-all picture Butzer paints is one of arid conditions, sometimes more arid than those of the present day, going back well beyond the first settlement of man in village communities. From 6500 to perhaps 5000 B.C. there was a minor improvement in precipitation, and from 5000 to 2400 B.C. the Near East generally enjoyed a rainfall somewhat greater than that of the present, albeit possibly with higher temperatures. In the Sahara Butzer (1961) sees the effect of this moister period as a shift of the margins of vegetation belts 100–250 kilometres towards the core of the desert, with the highlands featuring as rather more favourable reservoirs of life and water than at present. This was the period of the Neolithic cultures which were also of considerable importance in Eastern Arabia. No fewer than 200 settlement sites have been found in Qaṭar alone (Kapel 1967) and smaller finds have been discovered well into the Empty Quarter (cf. notes in *Man* 1954, 1958, 1960–3): present investigations are revealing more and more such sites in Oman.

Butzer's post-pluvial III, from 2400 to 850 B.C., was arid, with rainfall less than the present, but it was interrupted by at least one moister interval (in the twelfth century B.C.). In Oman this period covers the time of the main pre-*qanāt* civilizations, the earliest of which appears to be the Umm al-Nār culture (Frifelt 1970) which begins to feature in northern Oman sometime between the middle and the end of the third millenium (for dating see Bibby 1970 and comments by Tosi 1971). Here however, archaeology may have some interesting surprises, for a little further up the Gulf, settlements of the much earlier Obaid cultures have been discovered (Bibby 1973).

850 B.C.–A.D. 700 represents Butzer's post-pluvial IVa, and covers the period of *qanāt* building in Ōman (cf. Chapter VI). Ushered in by somewhat moister conditions (the time of the proto-*qanāt* builders?), rainfall for the rest of this period was about the same or a little less than in the present day, except for a period of very severe drought from roughly A.D. 590 to 645. The only features of note in post-pluvial IVb (A.D. 700 to the present) were slightly moister conditions in the early part of the period, and a recent deterioration of climate destructive to organic life in marginal areas, which dates up to the beginning of the present century.

These variations in climate must be seen in perspective. Climate is not static, and the variations outlined by Butzer are small in comparison with the changes that took place during the Pleistocene. But such fluctuations might be significant in areas of marginal settlement. A northward shift in the monsoon belt, such as probably occurred in the post-glacial 'climatic optimum' of the Neolithic (Lamb 1968; Glennie 1970), could be highly significant in Oman, because it would affect the period, frequency, and intensity of rainfall in a way that would not necessarily be shown up in gross statistics or in broad considerations of climatic change in the Near East. Changes in drought cycles would certainly affect the small *qanāt* on the fringes of the settled area, for these are the first to suffer from fluctuations in the water-table: but even the bigger *qanāt* would eventually succumb if drought was prolonged (cf. Fig. 19).

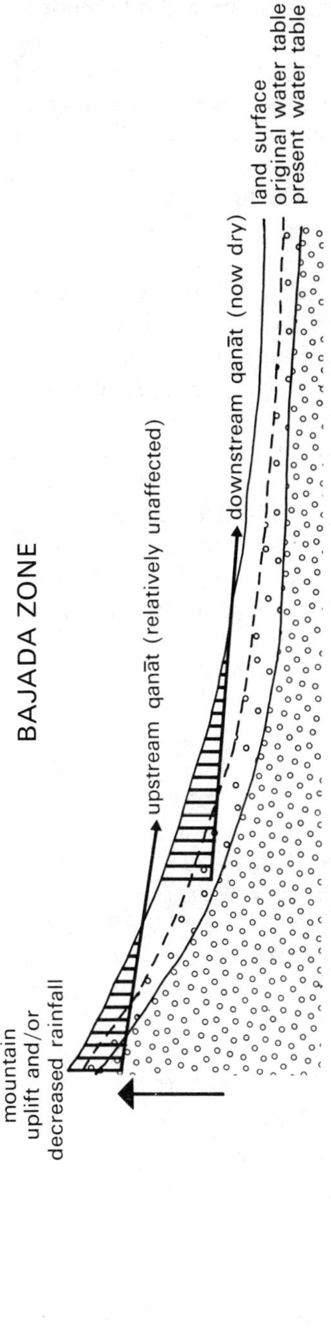

Fig. 19. Effect on *qanāt* of a falling water table.

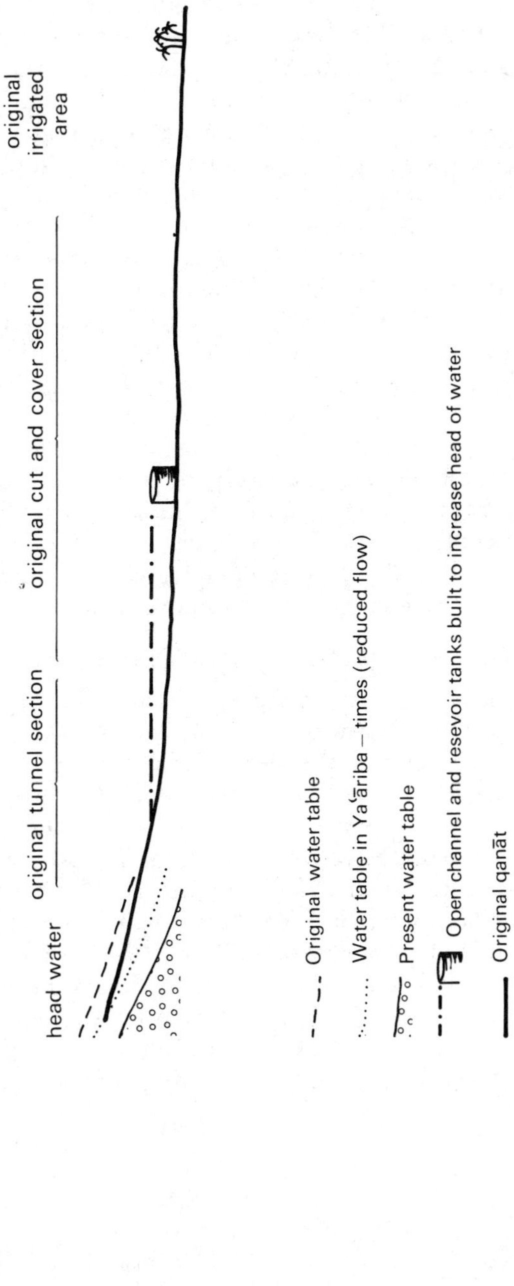

Fig. 20. Possible explanation of the Siḥāma *falaj* on the Najd al-Maghbarīya.

The impact of drought cycles may certainly be observed in south-east Oman, the region most susceptible to shifts in the inter-tropical convergence zone. In the Sharqīya, which may be considered as the main area of marginal *qanāt* settlement in Oman, villages are always being abandoned and reopened up by new groups; the author of the *Nahḍa* (p. 71), for example, attributes the rise of the fortunes of the shaikhly family of the Ḥārith (who dominated so much of Omani politics in the nineteenth and twentieth centuries) to the fact that sometime in the first half of the eighteenth century one of their forebears was able to break away from the clans of Lower Ibrā to found an independent 'capital' at al-Qābil when the *qanāt* there started to flow again after being abandoned for many years. It is also worth noting that the unreliability of water supply in the Sharqīya has caused many of its inhabitants to migrate to East Africa, and this in turn has led to absentee landlordism and other forms of economic and political structures in the area that are not typical of the rest of central Oman. There is however, no evidence from the histories that the unstable climatic conditions which typify the Sharqīya have ever affected settlement further north.

Yet while extended periods of drought may have caused fluctuations in the water-table, leading to the abandonment of some of the *qanāt* settlement on the outer fringes of the bajada zone, and while shifts in the inter-tropical convergence zone could, perhaps, have contributed to a partial collapse of settlement in the south-eastern part of the country, the writer is certain that the majority of *qanāt* settlements have not been seriously affected by climatic change, and does not believe that such change should be invoked as an important cause for the decline in the cultivated areas of interior Oman. That is to say, not as a direct cause: indirectly, it might be argued that minor climatic fluctuations may have been one of the factors that triggered off Arab migration from areas of marginal settlement into the region and so led to profound change in the human organization of its settled lands.

Changes in the Base Levels of Drainage Basins

Possible changes in the hydrology of the region through variation in the base levels of drainage may be dealt with more briefly. Eustatic sea-level fluctuations in the period with which we are concerned may be ignored. Certainly in the late Pleistocene and early Holocene there was a dramatic rise in sea-levels; indeed, at the maximum of the last glaciation some 20,000 years ago, virtually the whole Gulf was dry land, and the Shaṭṭ al-ʿArab extended to reach the shelf margin in the Gulf of Oman, that is some 800 kilometres further to the south-east (Sarnthein 1972). The present sea-level, however, was attained between 3400-3700 B.C. (Mörner 1971), and subsequent changes have at most been of the order of the one metre above present sea-levels which Evans *et al.* (1969) detected in an apparent temporary high, dating back to some 4,000 years ago at Abu Dhabi. Such minor eustatic changes might have a marked affect on a low-lying *sabkha* coast-line (and could be important when looking for the site of an old port like Gerrha: cf. Bibby 1970, chap. XV), but the impact on the hydrology of a region with aretic drainage would be neligible: only at the fresh-water/sea-water interface would the effect be detectable, and that would only affect the seaward edge of coastal settlements.

Diastrophic Change

Of greater importance, but rather more difficult to evaluate, are the effects of diastrophic change, that is, of movements of the land itself. Oman is not in a zone of recent seismic activity; the only references to earth-movements in the histories is one to a severe earthquake at Ṣuḥār in Jum. II 265/Jan. 879 (*Tuḥfa* i. 166) and a dubious statement that the main decline of the port of Qalhāt in south-east Oman was due to an earthquake (Wilkinson El_2, art. Ḳalhāt). But the orogenic zone of Oman is certainly still active in places, notably north of the Ras al-Khaima-Dibā line where subsidence of 60 m in 10,000 years has been postulated (Vita-Finzi in Cornelius *et al.* 1973). In contrast, the evidence of the wadi beds (which show downcutting since the last major pluvial, despite a decreased rainfall and a rising sea level) argues continued uplift in the last 15,000 or so years in much of the main part of the range. The important question is just how much of this has occurred in the last three thousand years.

At first sight the answer is not much, because both the *qanāt* settlement and the earlier third-millennium sites appear to be more or less related to the present drainage profiles. However, on the plateau of the Jabal Akhdhar the writer found evidence that both the open channels which once watered a small area of settlement on the plateau itself, and the channels irrigating the main villages below the lip of the promontory are now misaligned with the point of offtake in the Wadi bed. It may be for this reason that tanks (*legil < al-ijl*) have had to be constructed (added by the Yaʿāriba?) at the entrance to each of the main cultivated areas in order to build up the head of water to irrigate the dowstream gardens. On the other hand, the reason for these tanks may be the variable seasonal discharge of the spring which feeds them.

Another interesting example of what may also be an adaptation to a falling water-table is to be found at a place called al-Siḥāma on the Najd al-Maghbarīya, the water divide between the Wadis al-Ḥalfayn and al-Sumāyil (cf. Fig. 20). Here the main feature is a very large tank half-way along the *qanāt*, which (as the writer reconstructs the evidence) seems to have been built (again by the Yaʿāriba?) in order to build up the head of water sufficiently to carry the reduced flow in the underground gallery to the original settlement: the fact that the water-table has continued to fall may account for the fact that the whole system is now completely abandoned.

It is relevant to note, however, that in both these cases the water-supply came from the limestone/dolomite bloc of the Jabal Akhdhar proper so that the change could result from the peculiarities of limestone hydrology rather than from uplift.

Uplift in the mountain zone would, of course, produce a change all along the profile of the water-table, and this could affect downdownstream *qanāt* (even if the results were less noticeable further up the gradient), particularly if the original galleries did not extend far into the zone of saturation (cf. Fig. 19). However, before we accept such an explanation of why some of the *qanāt* in Oman may have been abandoned or have reduced flow, it should be remembered that, on the scale of change suggested, the cost of the modifications necessary to restore flow by tunnelling further back into the aquifer are very small in comparison with the initial costs of building the *falaj*. It seems hard to believe therefore, that the people who originally developed the land of Oman would have abandoned the fruits of their labour for want of a little special maintenance from time to time. Again, when we look at the settlement on and around the Jabal Akhdhar, it will be found that there any decrease in yield due to physical changes is as nothing compared with the effects of British bombing and of the Sultan's punitive razing of Nabāhina settlements in the so-called 'Jabal war' at the end of the 1950s. The last twelve hundred years of Omani history is by no means short of other examples of such wanton destructiveness by Omanis and foreigners alike.

Even if the possibility that some outlying *qanāt* may have been abandoned due to changes in the physical environment is accepted, this amounts to little more than saying that a man dies because his heart stops beating: such explanations are superficial, and like the statement that the granaries of North Africa were turned into desert wastelands because of the goat, they raise more questions than they answer. To understand the real reason why the goat was allowed to invade the settled lands, or why so much land has been abandoned in Oman, it is necessary to investigate the changes in human organization that have allowed physical factors once again to take control of areas where settlement had only been wrested from the wilderness by the investment of 'infinite toil and expense'.

Other Physical Factors Affecting the Flow of Qanāt

There are a number of reasons why *qanāt* may fail locally: a fall in the level of the water-table due to over-exploitation (since for nearly a millennium and a half there was no major new exploitation of the land until the advent of the mechanical pump, this is a factor that can be ignored in Oman), or the downcutting of a wadi,[11] or even of the *qanāt* itself.[12] The water-supply may also be affected by land alluviation or by highland gullying as a result of over-grazing (cf. Vita-Finzi 1969), but it should be noted that anything that increases runoff in the mountain is liable to be beneficial to the underground water storage tapped by *qanāt*. A more insidious cause of decreased flow could be scaling and deposition in areas of carbonate rocks. Records show that probably the most frequent maintenance required for ancient Rome's water supply was the cleaning of encrusted channels, and investigations of Roman irrigation channels in Jordan show just how rapidly extensive scaling can take place (Underhill 1969). But the places where this could occur in a *qanāt* are limited, and are more or less confined to points of rapid aeration such as an inverted siphon. There is also a possibility that the 'pores' in the aquifer at the point of off-take may become 'clogged'; if this has, in fact, happened then there is an interesting possibility of increasing yields by acidizing or fracturing the water-bearing formation.

In certain places shifting sand has engulfed *qanāt* settlement. Bagnold (1941) has shown that the sand-moving power of a wind increases by the cube of the velocity once the threshold of approximately 20 km/hr has been exceeded, and figures for the year 1966 show that at Sharja winds greater than this speed blew for 1,975 hours, 70 per cent of the time from the north-west quadrant. In other words, for almost a quarter of the year there was some sand movement, and most of the time it would be moving toward the mountain zone. This gives some idea of the order of the sand threat in parts of northern Oman and perhaps also the Badīya. The problem of combating sand is enormous, for it is not just the thin line of the *falaj* which is at risk but the entire settlement. Windbreaks of palm fronds and mud walls have constantly to be rebuilt, and since the gardens have often been sunk into the gravels of the outwash fans the risk of their being overrun increases as the tide of sand continues to pile up against the frail barricades which protect each hollow.[13]

With the exception of this sand threat, all these factors which could have affected *qanāt* flow in Oman are of fairly minor importance, and are at most of very localized concern. In no way do they compare with the damage that can occur to the one really weak point which affects virtually all *qanāt*, the lower tunnel.

DAMAGE TO THE LOWER SECTION OF A QANĀT

While the upper section of a *qanāt*, excavated out of rock or cemented coglomerates, may continue to operate satisfactorily, once it has been sealed, even after a couple of thousand years' neglect, the lower part, and in particular the cut and cover section, is the Achilles heel of the whole system. It is highly susceptible to damage by both man and nature and it needs constant maintenance. The main threat is a major flood, but even the normal increase in flow following rain may bring down sand and silt that will rapidly clog the channel course if it is not cleaned out regularly. Although the frequency of flooding is greatest in the mountains, the fact that *qanāt* follow natural drainage courses for much of their length means that they are not immune to dangers of collapse and siltation in the bajada zone.

The damage caused by flooding in their lower sections therefore accounts for the abandonment of most of the *qanāt* of Oman. But once again, while the immediate cause is physical, the reason behind it is the failure of the traditional *falaj* maintenance system: so it is not changes in the physical environment but rather in the human organization that have caused disaster.

THE SIZE OF QANĀT SETTLEMENT AND WATER USE IN THEM

Before moving on to this question of human organization, it will be profitable to consider the size of *qanāt* settlement and the uses to which the water in them is put.

In the absence of proper surveys the writer has found that the following figures give a reasonable basis for estimating the size of *qanāt* settlement in Oman:

(a) water duty in permanently cultivated land is between 3 and 4 m p.a.

(b) virtually all the most reliable base flow is used for date-palm cultivation, and the average density of these is 200 to the hectare.

(c) One litre a second (ls^{-1}) of base flow discharge irrigates roughly one hectare or 200 palms.

(d) 40 to 50 palms support a family-group of five persons.

There are, of course, enormous differences in the minimal base flow discharge of a *qanāt*, but few would seem to produce more than 120 ls^{-1}.[14] In central Oman the regular discharge of quite a number of the better *qanāt* in their present state of repair is probably in the order of 60 to 80 ls^{-1}, but in general it would be unwise to place the average figure of the better *qanāt* in the bajada zone at much more than 40 ls^{-1}, while the average for all working *qanāt* in the area might be about 15 to 20 ls^{-1}: these figures it should be remembered are for regularly sustained base flow; they can possibly be doubled if there has been a series of good rainfall years.

This means that a reasonably sized *qanāt* settlement in the bajada zone covers some 40 ha of permanently cultivated land and has a population of about 1,000 souls (that is before the relatively recent rural depopulation), while the larger settlements may typically be considered to support about 2,500 inhabitants. In multiple settlements where there are a number of *aflāj* concentrated in one place, the population may reach 8,000 people. It is worth emphasizing here once again that *qanāt* produce nucleated settlements well separated from each other, and that even where they are clustered each irrigation system still tends to produce its own self-contained community. The population of interior Oman is therefore condensed into isolated settlements of small size, and few of the villages, for reasons which will be discussed in Chapter VII, have developed into anything more than a local market centre.

The traditional use of agricultural land in *qanāt* settlements varies little from place to place. In the Sirr and Upper Jawf, where the flow of *qanāt* tends to be rather more variable than in central Oman, there are considerable areas of *ʿawābi* land in which wheat and barley are cultivated, but much of this seasonal flow is at present wasted in central Oman. In some measure this may be because the more ample base flow provides an adequate living for the inhabitants, but it is probably chiefly due to the effects of population change, for certainly there are signs that even this area had a great deal of seasonal cultivation at some time in the not-too-distant past.

Virtually all the most regular base flow (that is, with a reliability of perhaps 95 per cent) is used for cultivating dates. Where water is plentiful and the emphasis is on producing high-quality dates, the palms are well spaced and the ideal of 10 metres between trees (100 per ha) is approached. The Omanis are well aware of the importance of not overcrowding, and consider 17-20 *dhraʿ* (9 to 10 m) to be good (this is the spacing used in the United States), and 15 to 17 *dhraʿ* to be reasonable: the better figures are reputedly achieved in some of the gardens in Nizwā and in the Badīya. In most cases the ideal has to be tempered and the average is about 6 to 7 metres apart (200 per ha): this figure is still considerably better than the figure of nearly 450 to the hectare which characterizes the traditional gardens in the world-famous date groves of the Basra area (Dowson FAO 1965).

The basic reason why palms are packed more densely than the ideal is scarcity of water. Whilst it is true that the average yield per palm may fall below its best in the more closely planted groves, it should be remembered that the land and water needed for the ideal spacing is virtually twice that required for the normal spacing, and so the yield per unit of irrigated area is less than with the closer spacing. There will however be a marked decline in quality, even if not necessarily in total quantity, in an overcrowded grove.

Palms are also closely packed in places where the base flow is variable, because under these circumstances the tree itself is at risk. Newly planted off-shoots (*ṣarm*) do not start yielding for two or three years, and only reach full yield after five years (some varieties take eight or ten years before they even start to bear fruit); thereafter the crop will be good for a further thirty or forty years, and may not finally cease until the tree is a hundred years old (Popenoe 1913). Since, therefore, no landowner can afford to risk losing his trees due to water failure, the tendency is to pack the palms tightly to minimize transmission and evaporation losses wherever there is the slightest chance of this happening. This crowding can reach ludicrous proportions in some bedu settlements in northern Oman, where the effects of water shortage and unreliable base flow are exacerbated by the desire for the short-term profits which can be made from placing quantity before quality.

Close packing also saves labour, for if a plot (*jilba*) contains eight or nine palms it can be irrigated as a single unit, and the amount of manure (*samad*) that has to be ploughed in (rad. *hys*) each year in order to maintain the fertility of the soil is reduced: this is an important factor in an area where manure is expensive and often has to be transported considerable distances. It also saves valuable land, for in Oman no crops are grown under the palms except occasionally a little self-sown *bersīm* (*Trifolium spp.*).

The result of this land-usage is that in times of plenty, water is simply poured on to the land and the application can even exceed 4 m p.a. Such an excessive application may pose a salination risk. In most places this is not great because the water is sweet and the soil well drained, but near the coast there are noticeable signs of salt incrusting due to excessive irrigation, while in the interior settlements of the Trucial States, where there has been a recent rapid increase in water exploitation, there are signs both of increasing soil salinity and of sweet wells becoming brackish. To some extent this does not matter because palms are salt tolerant, but where salt-sensitive crops like citrus fruits are grown in close proximity to the palms then these may well be put at risk.

Unfortunately it is not possible to say what the correct watering of palms should be. United States irrigation manuals give certain recommendations but, although couched in impressive terms of suctions at different root depths, in reality they tell us little that is of general application. A FAO report for Saudi Arabia (1952) recommends irrigating palms growing on light soils every 6-8 days in summer and 15-20 days in winter (slightly less frequently on heavier soils); it also speaks in terms of a total annual water duty of 9-12 feet (3-4 m), but these figures are, in fact, no more than a reiteration of the actual practices observed in the better gardens of the Ḥasā province. Furthermore it should be remembered that it is almost impossible to over-water a palm: this is illustrated by the much-quoted saying about the palm (reputedly Arabic in origin) 'feet in heaven [water], head in hell [heat]'. So while the date-palm can survive (without fruiting) fairly bad drought conditions, there is virtually no limit to the amount of water it can take. Experiments on excessive irrigation show little difference to growth and yield, although there are some signs of vegetative growth at the expense of fruiting if water is applied continuously (Gibb 1969).

For all these reasons there is a wide variation in the practices of irrigating palms in Oman, both with respect to frequencies and volume of water application. Thus in northern Oman the *dawrān* (cycle of distribution of water amongst shareholders: see Chapter V) changes so that the palms receive a longer but less frequent soaking in summer than in winter, but it is normally fixed throughout the year further south. At Buraimi, one of the ʿ*arīfs* (the man in charge of water distribution) maintained that the correct watering for a large palm was three hours every twenty days in summer, but this figure is certainly exceeded in many places. For example, in the Badīya palms are watered every three days 'because water is now plentiful', and on the Batina the general practice appears to be to water every four or five days throughout the year. When water is scarce, on the other hand, all the palms tend to suffer because of the system by which water is shared on a *falaj* (cf. Chapter V). Instead of some being saved and the rest abandoned, the normal practice is to extend the *dawrān* in order to distribute the diminished flow equitably among all shareholders. For example, not long ago when some of the Buraimi *qanāt* had been allowed to fall into a bad state of repair, the *dawrān* of the Falaj Dawūdi, which is now fifteen days, fell to thirty-five days, while that of al-ʿAyn, presently twenty days, was cut back to seventy days! With so little water both settlements were at the limit of survival. The only general rule that would seem to apply to irrigating date-palms in Oman is 'give them all you have got'.

Apart from the palm and other less-important tree crops, the only perennial crop of any importance grown in Oman is alfalfa (*jatt*).[15] Since this needs plenty of sunshine, and thus cannot be grown under trees, it is normally cultivated in basins beyond the palm groves, and so (along with vegetables) tends to occupy the outer zone of a village's permanently irrigated land. Yet while alfalfa serves as a 'mopper up' of the less reliable base flow, it is even more demanding of water than the palm, and frequently it receives waterings of 10 cm every three or four days (that is, a water duty of some 9 or 10 m p.a.), which is almost 50 per cent more than it requires for optimal production (Gibb 1969, p. 57). Part of the reason for this excessive application is that alfalfa too represents something of a capital investment and is not readily abandoned.

It can be seen that the general practice in Oman is to over- rather than under-water crops. While the date-palm has a very high yield in terms of calories its virtual monopoly of the base flow introduces an inflexibility to agriculture that is wasteful of hard-won land-resources. More annual crops are needed if the water use in *qanāt* oases is to be optimized. To introduce them, however, involves a whole range of organizational changes, and the effects on the social structure of the village is something that planners will have seriously to take into consideration when considering the future course agricultural development is to take in Oman.

Notes to Chapter IV

[1] This is typologically identical with the Mesopotamian *čerd* or *bakra* described with photographs by Dowson (1921), and with the Persian *gāv-čah* (and variants of the name) described with a photograph by Wulff (1966). There is also a good photograph reproduced in Cressey (1960, p. 161) of such a well in Kharj, Saudi Arabia. It is worth noting that the origins of this kind of well system (like *qanāt*) appear to be associated with the land of the pre-Islamic Persian Empires. The Omani name *manjūr* strictly refers to the cog itself, and its substitution for *jāzira* by synecdoche is similar to the way *bakra* sometimes replaces *čerd* in parts of Iraq (Laessøe 1953).

[2] Wulff (1966, pp. 256 7) estimates that a good working day of 250 runs will produce 7500 gallons from such a well. Assuming a water duty of 4 m p.a., this would be adequate for irrigating about an acre.

[3] During a visit in 1970 to the Trucial States the writer was unable to find a single working *jāzira*.

[4] The cognates of *palgu* (and variants) in ancient Semitic languages, although often translated simply as 'water courses' or 'rivers of water' in the Bible (e.g. Psalms i: 3), appear rather more exactly to mean distributory water channels. Laessøe (1951) reads *palgu* in line 203 of Sargon's campaign (in 714 B.C. in the Lake Urmīya region) as meaning the open ditch which collects the output of the *qanāt*.

[5] Despite these examples, the techniques of terracing have not been extensively applied in Oman. In the gardens, however, plots (*dakk* pl. *dukūk*) may sometimes be built up by means of small retaining-walls (*ḍifr*): where this results in a plot receiving its water from a higher one it is then termed *salīl* in central Oman and *ʿaqad* or *badʿa* further north.

[6] The writer has been unable to examine the sites of villages in south-eastern Oman, where, for reasons that will be discussed in Chapter VI, *qanāt* were probably less developed than in the

central and northern parts of the country.

7 The account of this campaign in 714 B.C. (text in Thureau-Dangin 1912, $202 et seq.) provides the earliest fairly definite piece of evidence for dating the origins of *qanāt*.

8 The techniques of *qanāt* construction are not discussed in detail here because they have long since been forgotten in Oman. For those interested, attention is drawn to a fascinating work called *Anbāṭ al-miyā' al-khafiya* (translated into Persian, 1966 as *Istikhrāj-i Ābhā-yi Panhānī*) written in A.D. 1017 by Abu Bakr Muḥammad b. al-Ḥasan (al-Ḥāsib) al-Karaji which analyses ground-water occurrences and the engineering and surveying techniques involved in exploiting them. This has now been translated into French, accompanied by a detailed commentary, by Mazaheri (1973).

9 It is the mounds around the entrance to these shafts that characterize the *qanāt* landscape and have led some authors to describe *qanāt* by the misleading term of chain-wells (e.g. in Cyprus).

10 It is unfortunate that on the main road through the Sumāyil Gap there is an inverted siphon at Izki which every visitor to Oman sees. This in fact is on the Qasawāt *falaj* which is of eighteenth-century construction (cf. Chapter X); it is not typical of the *qanāt* on the western side of the mountains.

11 Stein (1937, p. 126) has noted this as a probable cause for the drying up of *qanāt* at one place on the Makrān coast.

12 Tresse (1929) saw this as a cause of abandoned *qanāt* in an area of soft, chalky rock he studied in Syria: normally the slope of approximately 1:1,000 which characterizes the invert of most *qanāt* ensures flow without erosion (Goblot 1963).

13 The threat of sand encroachment is dramatically treated in Hammond Innes's novel *The Doomed Oasis.*

14 Wulff (1966) gives the discharge of the average *qanāt* in Persia as 40 80 $1s^{-1}$, of a good *qanāt* as 200 $1s^{-1}$, and of an exceptional one as 400 $1s^{-1}$.

15 After the first two cuttings, respectively known as *al-dhikr* and *al-jizz al-thāniwi*, the *jatt* stem becomes fully developed and woody (hence the third cutting is called *al-ʿirq*). The foliage may then be cut every month. Stevens (1970) states that under the present improved practice in the Buraimi oasis up to 14 cuttings per year may be made, yielding up to 145 metric tons per ha (fresh weight: cf. 3 tons dry per acre for the Qaṭīf oasis, quoted in Ebert 1965).

CHAPTER V

Falaj Organization[1]

It is obvious that a system of irrigation as remarkable as *qanāt* must impose certain characteristics on its dependent communities. The interests of the inhabitants of an isolated village who survive in the desert by a thin life-line of underground water are evidently going to produce a quite different social organization from that, say, of the one-well, one-garden land-owning system characteristic of the Batina coast. The arrangements in these two types of Omani settlement will, in turn, be somewhat different from those in other areas of the Middle East where the society is organized to exploit the water resources of a river or of ephemeral *sayl* floods. Yet even though the physical requirements of *qanāt* do account for many important aspects of the economic, social, and political organizations in Oman, the fact remains that these have few features in common with the organizations in other similar areas of settlement; and in particular is this true of neighbouring Persia, the real homeland of *qanāt*. To understand why such differences should exist it is necessary first to study in some detail how *aflāj* are organized in Oman.

We will examine first the layout of a *falaj* settlement, then the principles of water shareholding and the way in which the finance and maintenance of the *falaj* are arranged, and finally the division of labour and responsibilities in the irrigation system. The emphasis will tend to be on the methods of organization in central Oman, where the influences that will be discussed in Chapter VII have led to much more carefully regulated systems than is the case further north.

I THE *FALAJ* LAYOUT

THE *FALAJ* AND THE *BILĀD*

The layout of a *qanāt* village varies considerably from place to place in Oman, but the following scheme has a certain general validity (cf. Fig. 15).

At the very top of the *falaj*, where it first comes to the surface, is an opening from which drinking water may be drawn, the *sharīʿa*. This is the first permitted use of water, and access is free to all. From here the water runs in a well-constructed channel towards the village, and quite often this section is partially covered. On a large *falaj* the first split may occur high up this main stream (*qāʿid, ʿāmid*), but in smaller ones division does not take place until the *falaj* reaches the cultivated area. The location of the residential area (*bilād*) itself varies, but it is quite often close to the upstream end of the gardens: in those cases where the *falaj* actually flows through the built-up area the channel is normally covered and special access points to the water constructed. The order of domestic usage for which communal facilities on the main stream may be provided is first drinking water, then bathing facilities (with the women's sections clearly separated downstream from those of the men), and finally the *mughsila* for washing the dead. In the residential area no diversion of the *falaj* for private or public purposes is permitted, nor does the *falaj* normally pass under buildings. An exception sometimes occurs in the case of a major fort; mosques too may have direct access to the *falaj* water supply for the purpose of ritual ablutions.

From this brief description it is clear that the *falaj* water in the *bilād* is very much regarded as communal property. No individual has particular rights in it, and the drawing of water for domestic purposes and the watering of animals is free to all. Because no diversions of the *falaj* are permitted, wells are often dug to provide more accessible sources for domestic water, and mosques, too, often have their own well.

These wells, however, also serve another purpose, that of providing an alternative *in situ* supply of water for defensive purposes. However well fortified a village might be, it is obvious that the *falaj* is going to be a highly vulnerable point in its defences; even the great forts, despite alternative water supplies, may eventually be reduced by cutting the main *falaj* supply, as a study of the history of the fortress of al-Ḥazm (constructed by the Yaʿāriba to control access to the Ghadaf from the Batina) all too clearly shows (cf. in particular *Kashf* tr. Ross, p. 170; *Nahḍa*, p. 256). Indeed, mastery of the upper reaches of a *falaj* is often the key to controlling the turbulent inhabitants of the settlements they supply. This was why, for example, Sālim b. Suwaylim, the powerful and unpopular *mawlā* of the Sultan Fayṣal b. Turki (ruled 1888 1913), built a fort in Lower Qārūt, because from there he was able to command one of the feeders of the Izki *qanāt* and so bring the Bani Riyām living in this strongly defended settlement under governmental control. Since the fort subsequently passed into the hands of the Riyām's tribal enemies, the Bani Ruwāḥa, fighting for possession of it became endemic, and it was not until the Imamate was restored in 1913 that the fort was razed on the orders of ʿAbdullāh b. Ḥummayid al-Sālimi, 'because it represented a permanent threat to the peace of the Muslims' (*Nahḍa*, p. 184 et seq.).

Precisely because a *qanāt* does represent the life-blood of a community, certain conventions tend to be adhered to in local warfare. Cutting a *falaj* is acceptable and standard practice, while government retribution may go as far as the cutting down of palm trees — for did not the Prophet so act against the Bani Naḍīr? (Cf. debate in *Tuḥfa* i. 112-13) — but the full-scale destruction of a *qanāt* is an extreme action. Reports of such acts in the histories are clear indications that the political situation had got seriously out of hand, while the worst excesses often prove to be the work of foreigners.

Normally, tribal fighting, although chronic, is not sustained, so the tactics of reducing one's enemies by a prolonged siege and cutting the water supply until the palms die is not characteristic. However, in a short attack the importance of an alternative source of water supply is obvious; it is then that wells may prove essential for the survival of the inhabitants of a *falaj* community.

THE *FALAJ* AND THE GARDENS

The number of divisions of the primary water channel for irrigation purposes obviously depends on the volume of flow in the *falaj*. Where there is considerable variation in base flow some of the channels of this primary network are opened only when water is plentiful (*ayyām al-khaṣab*): obviously on the land watered by such channels it will be alfalfa or vegetables rather than tree crops that will be grown. Division takes place at certain fixed points, and the resulting network of channels (*ghayz*, pl. *ghuyūz*; *sāqīya*, pl. *sawāqī*) takes one of two patterns. By far and away the more common of these is the bifurcation pattern shown in Fig. 21A. The other is the rectilinear pattern shown in Fig. 21B, which is an example taken from the description given to the writer by an inhabitant of Mintirib who stated that it was fairly common throughout the Badīya (not visited by the writer). In the bifurcation pattern the points of primary division are called *ṣiwarayn*, in the rectilinear pattern, *farāsha*.

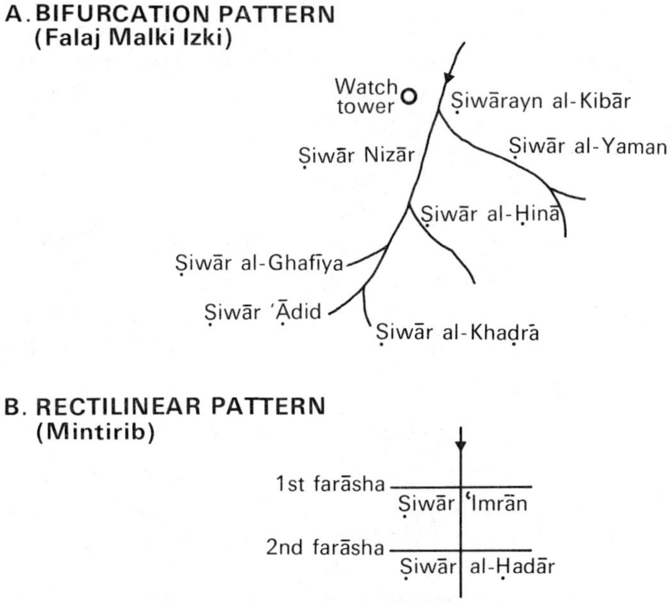

Fig. 21. The two basic patterns of a *falaj's* primary distributory channels.

Branching out from the primary channels of the main irrigation network are the laterals which feed the gardens (*māl, ḍāḥīya, maqṣūra*), and these in turn split into yet smaller channels which water the individual plots (*jilab*).

Upkeep of the main network of primary channels is the responsibility of the *falaj* organization, while individual owners are responsible for the garden channels. Just as the underground section of the *qanāt* must be cleaned (*shiḥāba*), so the open channels have to be kept in a good state of repair, for loss of water through percolation and evaporation in a badly aligned and clogged *falaj* can amount to double that in a properly engineered system; this means not only a decrease in the volume of water supplied to the downstream gardens, but also an increase in its salinity.

The Omanis are fully aware of this need to maintain the channels in a good state of repair, as the following little story from the time of the First Imamate shows (*Tuḥfa* i. 125-8). One day, while the Imam Ghassān b. ʿAbdullāh al-Yaḥmadi (192/808-207/823) was walking in Nizwā, he noticed that water-moss (*ṭuḥlub*) was beginning to grow in one of the main irrigation channels. Realizing that this was indicative of detrimental changes, he determined on discovering why. By pretending that he wished to raise a loan for a war against 'Hind', the Imam was able to sound out various groups who might have been responsible. Eventually he discovered that it was neither the merchants nor the land-owners (who, it is of interest to note, are described by the merchants as being mostly small farmers) that were to blame for this deplorable state of affairs, but his own officials. These he therefore changed, and thereafter it was to be seen that the water flow of the channel increased.

The importance of cementing (*tasrīj*: noun *sahrūj* or *sārūj*) channels is also appreciated. So we find that among the important works carried out by Abu Zayd ʿAbdullāh b. Muḥammed al-Riyāmi at Bahlā, where for thirty years he was *Wāli* (governor) on behalf of both of the twentieth-century Imams, were a number of major improvements to three of its five *qanāt*, and these included cementing all the branches of the Falaj al-Maytā (Maythi) from the 'Khaḍr quarter to the walls of Lower Bahlā' (cf. further Chapter VII). We should note, however, that the *falaj* organization may not use its money to cement the lateral channels within the gardens unless the shareholders agree to such work, in which case all, and not just some, of the channels must be done (cf. Khalīli *al-Fatḥ al-Jalīl*, pp. 556-7).

II. THE PRINCIPLES OF WATER SHAREHOLDING

The systems of shareholding and the ways in which *falaj* water is distributed are complex. Faced with the combinations and variations of methods used in each village and with a horrifyingly confused terminology, the field-worker may well despair of ever understanding how the system or systems work. The following account of the organization of water rights in Oman is no more than an attempt at examining the basic principles upon which each village develops its individual system of water organization.

The attempt is worth making in some detail because it is only in so far as we understand the nature of the compromises involved when a *falaj* community produces its own particular solution to the problem of how to divide an irrigation supply fairly amongst a large number of shareholders, while at the same time trying to make efficient use of the water and ensuring that the irrigation system is properly maintained, that we will be able to comprehend some of the fundamental aspects of social organization in an Omani village.

Only from a detailed study can the real differences between social organizations of oases settlement be appreciated. When, for instance, the writer first glanced at Dr Lars Eldblom's magnificent study on Ghadamès, it immediately struck him, just from reading Eldblom's account of how water rights are organized (Eldblom 1968, pp. 130-43), that the social structure in that area must be basically different from that in Oman. A superficial account, on the other hand, would only have brought out the similarities. So, for instance, while the *zjedd* in Ghadamès appears at first sight to represent the same principle of shareholding as that of the Omani *khabūra* (see below), the fact that in Ghadamès the water is now distributed amongst the usufructs at an annual *zjoumla* indicates a quite different evolution of the tenure system (albeit with some interesting parallels to the Omani system of auctioning the share of water belonging to the *falaj* administration each year). A superficial description of the duties of the *amin-n eddafter*, the *ennāyib n-āman*, and the *moujarri* of the Ghadamès organization might again lead one to suppose that they were respectively the same as the *wakīl*, *ᶜarīf*, and *bīdār* in Oman: yet this would be misleading, for in the details of their duties the subtle variations show up and reveal that the two areas have fundamentally different attitudes to the basic principles of land organization.

The Standard Dawrān and its Shares

Basic to all Omani systems of water shareholding is the *dawrān*, that is, the cycle by which the *falaj* water is distributed around the irrigated land. A *falaj* is said to 'rotate on such and such a period'. If, for example, it is said of a *falaj*, *yadūr ᶜala tisᶜa* or *dawrān al-māy ᶜala kull tisᶜa*, it means that the cycle takes nine periods (usually days) to complete. In most systems this water is distributed to the gardens in a set order, and each plot of land has a set period of time allocated to it.

The basic organization of the *dawrān* is rooted in the original shareholding of the *falaj*. This may be illustrated by taking the following simple example. Suppose eight shareholders build a *falaj* and share the land and water among themselves dividing the land on either side of the channel into eight plots and allocating the whole discharge for a complete day to each in turn; then it will be seen that the *dawrān* will be eight days and each day will constitute a share of the *falaj* water. Each of these days may well be identified by the name of the shareholder, and these are likely to be on the pattern of one or more of the following names: *raddat fulān* (A's turn), *bādat fulān* (A's day: cf. meaning of *bāda* below), *qiṭᶜat fulān* (A's portion), *mā fulān (A's* water), *khabūrat fulān* (A's share), and so on. Sometimes the name of the share is associated with an area of land or of some characteristic of the garden. So, for example, at al-Rassa in the Wadi Bani Ruwāḥa some of the various days of the *falaj*'s *dawrān* (nine and a half days) have names like *raddat Ṣāliḥ* (Shaikh Ṣāliḥ's turn), while others are called by the name of the land, e.g. *jīl farūḍ*, the plot with the *fard* date-palms. In some places these names may be picturesque, as for instance *māl al-afārīt*, the field of the *afārīt* (small devils) on the *dawrān* of the Falaj Dawūdi at Buraimi. For convenience these basic shares of the *dawrān* will be referred to as *khabūras*,[2] the form most commonly used in legal texts: in local parlance such a share may be called *radda* or *rabīᶜ*, while in central Oman a Persian survival word, *ād*, is often used.

It can be seen that in this organization of the standard *dawrān*, the basic principle is that the individual shareholder's water is delivered to him at an appointed place and at an appointed time by means of the network of distributory channels that belongs to the *falaj* itself. What happens to the water inside the plot of land is not the affair of the *falaj* administration, nor is it affected by the fact that gardens may become subdivided as shareholding changes. As far as the community organization is concerned this is an individual arrangement, and, unless all the shareholders agree on a complete reorganization, the *falaj* will continue to deliver water in the way originally laid down. It is for this reason that the names of the *khabūras* tend to perpetuate earlier landholdings and thus provide valuable clues to the history of settlement (cf. for example Table 10).[3]

LAND AND WATER

It is apparent from the basic prinicples of how the *dawrān* works that water and land are intimately linked. While the three elements involved in *mulk* ownership of land (the ground, the crop, and water) may be held quite separately, a garden is usually owned with water rights (*shārib*, literally 'drinking'), and rarely changes hands *yābis* (dry) unless it is irrigated on the Izki system (see below). For example, documents of land sales from Buraimi quoted in the *British Memorial* (Annexe F, pp. 256-7) are all of the pattern 'I, A, have sold a garden, plot etc. called B for so much: it is watered by X time units of Y *falaj*, and is also includes rights-of-way, hills [i.e. uncultivated land], and irrigation channels.'

The *falaj* certificate held by a shareholder, on the other hand, will only show his water rights and will probably be based on the following pattern (example from ᶜIbri): *li fulān b. fulān al-fulāni rubaᶜ athar min rabīᶜ nisf al-nahār al-manthūra*, which means 'A has a quarter *athar* (time unit: see below) from the half-day share (*rabīᶜ*, the local equivalent of *khabūra*) called Manthura. In other words this man receives an allocation worth about seven and a half minutes on the Manthūra *khabūra*, which is the one that supplies water to his area of the irrigated lands on a specified day of the *dawrān*. The value of this quarter *athar* share relative to others will, of course, depend on the place where this water is received. This in turn depends on the layout of the network of the *falaj*'s primary distributory channels.

THE PROBLEM OF EQUAL SHAREHOLDING IN LAND AND WATER

The natural layout of cultivated land around a source of static water like a well is a circle, and the most convenient way of subdividing it amongst shareholders is to split it into segments each irrigated by a radial channel (cf. Fig. 22, pattern A). Such an organization provides a simple and equitable division of both land and water, and at the same time minimizes water losses through transmission. However, in a *falaj*, where water is flowing by gravity, the natural system for irrigating the land is to divert the stream successively to the shareholders' gardens on either side of the channel. The resulting shape of the cultivated land tends therefore to be rectangular, as in Fig. 22, pattern B, rather than circular, as in the fixed-point distribution of pattern A.

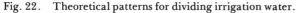

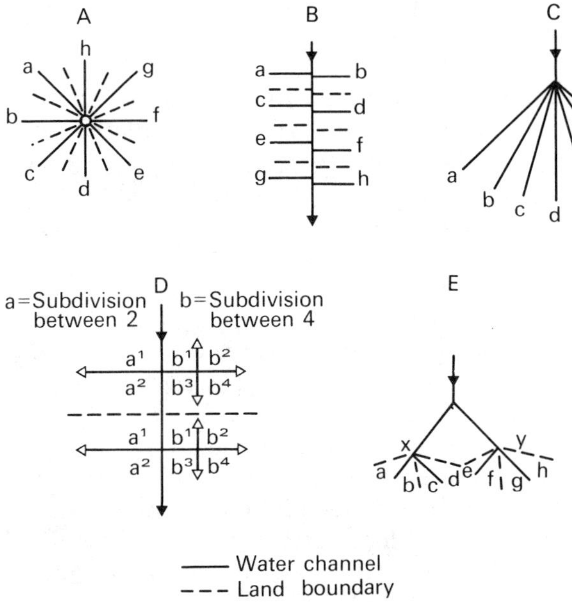

Fig. 22. Theoretical patterns for dividing irrigation water.

The obvious disadvantage of pattern B is that while the area of the plots can be made equal, the volume of water per unit of time received at the point of use decreases downstream owing to losses in transmission and evaporation: these, as already shown, can be considerable, even on a well-kept *falaj*.

Now this basic problem of achieving parity in both land area and water available at the point of use is, in fact, raised in Islamic law, where it is stated in a generally accepted *ḥadīth* (reputed saying of the Prophet) that each plot of land should be watered in sequence downstream to the depth of a man's ankle (two ankles in Khalīli *al-Fatḥ al-Jalīl*, p. 553). Unfortunately this ruling often clashes with established practice, and this is why a somewhat ambivalent answer is usually given by the jurists as to whether the Prophet's ruling or customary law prevails (cf. Maktari 1971, p. 34 in connection with *sayl* flood irrigation in South Arabia). In Omani legal works, on the other hand, the writer has never seen this ruling discussed, except in the case of *sharāja* (that is, ephemeral flow in a wadi), for there it seems generally to be accepted that customary law applies, and the attitude of the religious authorities (*ʿulamāʾ*) is that any arrangement is valid, provided the agreement satisfies all parties (cf. Sālimi *Jawhar, bāb al-sawāqi*).

Even so the local solutions do tend to fulfil the spirit, if not the letter, of the Prophet's ruling, for *khabūras* have normally been designed to obtain a reasonable degree of parity in both the land and water apportionments. This is achieved by the simple process of channel-splitting without recourse to such complex solutions as a variable time-schedule, or mechanical devices for measuring the volume of flow, or a pattern of divided holdings (cf. Fig. 22, pattern D, which is obviously wasteful of both land and water).

However, the number of equal shares that can be accommodated in this way is limited, for two reasons. First, the greater the number of divisions, the greater the ratio of channel to cultivated area, and so the less the effective use of water. Second, the number of splits that can occur at any one point is limited because the wider the arc of distribution (see Fig. 22, pattern C), the less the natural gradient of the land can be effectively used, and the more sluggish the water movement in the outer channels.

Splitting can be carried out either by means of sluices, in which case the total flow is directed down each channel in turn, or by means of a weir which divides the flow itself. The latter solution, although occasionally used on *qanāt* in Persia (cf. Wulff 1966), is, nevertheless, unsuited to their relatively small discharges for the obvious reason that spreading the water reduces its velocity and so increases losses in transmission. Temporarily, however, a channel may be split and the flow divided into proportions of a third or a half by inserting a specially designed block at the point of primary division.

So the normal pattern for distributing water tends to be a modified form of pattern E in Fig. 22 (cf. also Fig. 21A). The main bifurcation takes place upstream of the gardens, and in this way divides them into two distinct parts (equal or unequal acording to the proportion of the time-schedules allocated to each channel); this split also tends to be reflected in the social organization of the settlement (further discussed in Chapter X). If the volume of flow allows, the channels may be bifurcated again, in which case the number of equal *khabūras* may be raised from four to eight (two on either side of each channel).

It will be noticed that if the principle of equal land and water at point of use is to be maintained, then no irrigation can be permitted upstream of the point where the subdivisions of the *falaj* network are completed (i.e. above points x and y in Fig. 22, pattern E). This, however, poses a problem, for not to cultivate here is wasteful of both land and water. In general, therefore, some sort of compromise solution is achieved and an upstream share or shares is created with a somewhat shorter time allocation to compensate for the additional volume received: similar juggling with the time shares (see below) also allows the type of rectilinear network shown in Fig. 21B to be operated without too much difficulty. These adjustments only remain simple, however, so long as channel-splitting does not occur more than twice; it is for this reason that the number of distributory channels carrying base flow in a *falaj* network is rarely more than four (or six in the rectilinear pattern). Indeed, there are special legal terms used to distinguish between *aflāj* which divide into four or less channels and those that have more. A distributory channel in the former is called *jāʾiz* (pl. *jawāʾiz*) and has a different *ḥaram* (that is the land belonging to the *falaj* which separates the channel from the individual gardens) from the latter, which is termed *ḥamlān* (cf. Sālimi *Jawhar, bāb al-sawāqi* and Khalīli *Fatḥ al-jalīl,* p. 550).

Thus, on the Omani system of laying out a *falaj* network the maximum number of *khabūras* into which the ordinary-sized *qanāt* settlement can be divided (always according to the principle of equal sharing in land and water at point of use) is really limited to some eight or ten. The smaller the number of shares, the greater is the mathematical accuracy with which division can be measured and the more efficient the use of both land and water (for rational use ideally there would only be one owner). The higher figures, however, may be achieved without greatly affecting the basic principles of shareholding, by ensuring that the cultivated area is kept well within the capacity of the *falaj* base flow so that everyone receives plenty of water; this, on the other hand, tends to result in inefficient use of water through over-irrigation (as described at the end of Chapter IV).

If the number of shareholders is to exceed eight or so, then the principle of equal water rights at the point of cultivation will be lost. This is why within the *khabūras* themselves (whose fragmentation is largely due to the changes in the land-tenure system brought about in Islamic times) there is considerable variation in the values of holdings. Here too, water and land rights are liable to become separated, because holders of the land on the outside edge of the *khabūra* plots may have to acquire extra water either by renting (rad. *rhn*) from their neighbours or by purchasing temporary shares in the annual or weekly sale of the water that belongs to the *falaj* organization (see below). These outside gardens are also the first to suffer when there is a decrease in base flow.

One other solution to the problem of providing parity in land area and volume of water at the point of use is found in Oman. This is the special case where tanks have been installed in order to build up the head of water to a set of gardens (see Chapter IV); under these circumstances it is possible to control the delivery to each dependent set of gardens by direct volumetric measurement (cf. Rossi 1953 for detailed description of this use of the *mājil* at Ṣanʿāʾ). It must, however, be emphasized that this system has not been designed for shareholding purposes: it is merely an adaptation of a costly device that has had to be introduced to deal with the problem of variable or diminished *falaj* flow. No other devices for measuring water flow volumetrically exist in Oman so far as the writer knows, and even the tank system occurs only in a very few places.

To sum up the main points discussed so far:

1. A *falaj* is a network of canals designed to deliver water at certain places on a fixed time-schedule (the *dawrān*). While the organizers of the *falaj* are responsible for ensuring that the delivery system works efficiently, they are not concerned with what happens to the water within the gardens. The primary network of *falaj* channels is therefore fixed, and is quite separate from the distributory network whose layout can be altered as the various landowners wish.

2. The simplest way of dividing the *falaj* flow into shares of equal water volume at the point of use is by a series of bifurcations of the main channel, with no irrigation allowed upstream of the final point of division. The flow is then directed down each channel in turn by opening and shutting sluices: permanently splitting the flow itself is rarely practicable because the discharge of *qanāt* is inadequate. But because there is limit to the number of times the channel can be divided if serious inefficiencies in land and water-use are to be avoided, the primary channel of a *falaj* does not normally split at more than two levels to give four primary subdivisions; a special legal term has been introduced to distinguish those that have more.

3. The maximum number of primary shares (*khabūras*) into which land irrigated by a *qanāt* can practicably be divided, according to the principle of equal shares in land and water, is therefore eight (two each side of the four channel divisions). Less than this number of divisions provides a more rational use of the land and water. If more than this number of divisions is required, then the basic principle of shareholding will be lost. The greater the number of subdivisions of the *khabūras*, the greater the inequalities in the shares become.

4. One or two extra *khabūras* upstream of the final set of bifurcations can, nevertheless, be achieved by making minor adjustments to the amount of water allocated to this more favoured land. Risk of inequalities may be further minimized by ensuring that the area of land divided into *khabūras* is kept well within the capacity of the *falaj*. This can lead to overcrowding of date-palms and over-watering when the flow is abundant.

5. Devices for measuring the volume of water allocated to shareholders are not used in Oman, except in the special case of tanks constructed to build up the head of water in the *falaj*.

Subdivision of the Khabūras into Time Shares

Basically, there are two methods that can be used for measuring time. One is by the movement of the celestial bodies, the other is by a mechanical device which measures an arbitrary unit of time (which may or may not be related in its original design to sidereal time).

In traditional irrigation practices in the arid lands of the Old World both methods are used, sometimes together (by day the movement of the sun is measured, while at night a mechanical device is in use: Caponera 1954); in Oman, however, the usual mechanical devices of water- and sand-clocks (*gadous, mechkouda, ṭāṣa*, etc.) are traditionally unknown. Indeed, it is said that when one of the Āl Bū Saʿīd Sultans tried to introduce the *ṭāṣa* it was strenuously resisted as an innovation (*bidaʿ*). Nevertheless, the writer has heard reports that in one or two places (notably Firq) a form of *ṭāṣa* is now in use (the device is a container pierced with small holes which fills when placed in water), and certainly today more and more *aflāj* are operating on watches. These exceptions apart, time is always measured by direct observation of celestial bodies.

The reason for this can only be a matter for speculation. The writer suspects that while there was a rapid spread of techniques and scientific ideas between the Mediterranean, Arab, and Persian worlds in medieval Islamic times, the basic laws concerning *qanāt* in Oman, albeit modified and brought within an Islamic framework by Ibāḍi government, were probably never radically altered, and new methods were resisted in this land which was already developing in isolation by the middle of the eighth century A.D. Certainly in other areas the changes in the organization of land and water brought about by the overthrow of the pre-Islamic order caused chaos. In Persia, disputes on *qanāt* became so frequent, and the rules so complex and inconsistent, that ʿAbdullāh b. Ṭāhir (governor of Khurāsān 213/828–230/844) found it necessary to assemble the jurists of Iraq and Khurāsān so as to clarify the laws in the *Kitābi Qanī*, the *Book of Qanāt* (Lambton 1953, p. 217). Perhaps therefore the Omanis learnt their lesson from other areas and chose to preserve, rather than to change. (If so, the Omani system of *falaj* organization may retain elements of the original Persian system and indicate how water was administered in the homeland of *qanāt* in pre-Islamic times.)

It is necessary at this point to outline the principles and associated terminology of the units of time used for creating secondary water shares in Oman. At first sight the use of these terms is highly confusing. For example, the writer has found that while it is usual to divide the 24-hour day (*yawm*) into two *bādas*, in one place the *bāda* represented the complete day, and in another a third of a day.[4] The reason why so basic a unit of shareholding should vary in such a way lies in the fact that the time units are really subdivisions of the primary *khabūra* shares, and these, in theory, have no universally fixed period of duration: in practice, however, they are related to some readily observable phenomenon of the passage of time. The 24-hour day is one such unit of time, and many *falaj dawrāns* are accordingly divided into *khabūras* of this length. And so where this is the practice it is possible that the word *khabūra* might itself come to signify a period of 24 hours: but this is a case of transferred meaning, and the word essentially means a share and not a division of time (in fact the writer has only once come across *khabūra* used as a unit of time). Conversely, because the 24-hour day divides into two parts, each of which has a different system for measuring time (sun and stars), the largest time unit used for subdividing a *khabūra*, and one that is in almost universal use, is the *bāda*, the day- or night-half of the 24-hour day.[5] Thus in some places the basic *khabūra* units may have been designed with a half-day duration and in such places the word *bāda* may have become synonymous with *khabūra* and so subsequently have assumed a different time-value as the shareholding system changed. Here, however, the terms *khabūra* and *bāda* will be used in their normal and etymologically correct way to indicate respectively a share and a half-24-hour-day time unit (over the year, of course, it averages out at 12 hours).

The terminology for the time units which subdivide the *bāda* falls into two sets. One, in use chiefly in northern Oman, clearly indicates that its origin lies in simple mathematical fractions. So, for example, at Buraimi the *bāda* divides into four *rabīʿ* (pl. *arbūʿ*), each of which in turn splits into six *suds* (pl. *asdās*), the words literally meaning 'quarter' and 'sixth' respectively. There are therefore twenty-four *suds* in a *bāda*, and a *suds* is effectively a period of half an hour. This is the most useful unit of time for allocating water, and as a result time shares are frequently expressed in terms of it alone. Its equivalent from the other set of terms is the *athar* and this is in general use throughout central Oman; for the same reason many *aflāj* there are described as *maqsūm athāri*, that is divided into *athar* shares. Everywhere in Oman the *athar* is invariably used purely as a time unit, the forty-eighth part of a 24-hour day: thus at al-Rassa, where there are three *bāda*s per 24-hour day, each divides into sixteen *athar* instead of the normal twenty-four.

Although the *athar* or the *suds* is the most practical unit of time for sharing water it is sometimes broken down into smaller units. Before the twentieth-century reform of the water-holding system at Izki (see below) the *bāda* divided into the following series of units, each worth respectively one twenty-fourth part of the larger: *athar* (pl. *athār*), *qiyās* (pl. *qiyāsāt*), *daqīqa* (pl. *daqīqāt* or *daqāyiq*), and *shaʿīra* (pl. *shaʿīrāt* or *shaʿāyir*; there were even vestiges of a still smaller subdivision, the *iṣbaʿ shaʿīra* or *jalīla*). Just how small these subdivisions were, may be appreciated by the fact that the smallest share recorded in the Izki *falaj* book in 1825 was half a *shaʿīra* (i.e. about $\frac{1}{16}$ of a second), and even that was shared by three relatives! Sometimes the names used for these small subdivisions are simply the fractions of the *athar* or *suds*; such are the *sādisa* and *thāmina* (a sixth and eighth of an *athar*) in the Badīya, or the *nuṣṣ suds* (half *suds*) in Buraimi. Normally the need for such small time units arises from the complex Islāmic inheritance laws, and they are only employed to keep the mathematics of the *falaj* shareholding straight; but on some of the larger *aflāj*, a smaller unit than the *athar* is required for practical reasons, and at Rustāq, for example, the *qiyās* is a meaningful unit of shareholding.

The names associated with the two sets of time units are sometimes joined in the same system. At ʿIbri, for example, the basic unit of shareholding is the *athar* (which subdivides into four *qāma*), but, borrowing from the northern

Oman system, six *athars* make up a *rabīʿ*: *suds* does not appear to be used much further south than Buraimi, while the *athar* is still in use at least as far north as al-Sunayna in the Dhahira. In the Badīya some other terms are used: for example at Mintirib six *athars* equal a *rabʿ* (pl. *arbūʿ*), twelve *athars* make up a *bāḥa*, and twenty-four *athars* a *waḍḥ* (the equivalent of the *bāda*). Doubtless there are other names employed elsewhere in Oman, and this list is not meant to be exhaustive. The most important time units for practical consideration are the *bāda* and its half-hour division the *athar* or *suds*.

MEASURING TIME (*MAḤĀẒARA*)

The length of the two *bādas* of the 24-hour day is obviously governed by the rising and setting of the sun. Subdivisions of the day *bāda* are therefore assessed by observing the sun's shadow, while those of the night are measured by the movement of the stars. These observations are by no means in continuous use: the need for accurate observation only really arises in times of water shortage, while in periods of cloudy weather (*ghaym*) such measurement is, in any case, impossible and experienced judgement has to be relied on. While the techniques of measurement are based on sound astronomical principles, the *ʿarīfs* and *bayādīr* who operate the system (see below) are not normally acquainted with the mathematics involved. The writer was never once shown an astronomical work, nor did he meet a *falakī* (astronomer), and it is quite clear that lore is simply passed on from generation to generation and that the measurements for sundials are similarly copied from place to place.

There are two methods in use for measuring the units of time during the day. While both are based on the same principles, the geographical distribution of the two practices illustrates once again a difference between northern and central Oman. In the north the system, as described by one of the *ʿarīfs* from the Buraimi oasis, is that the units of time are measured by observing changes in the length of a man's shadow. This is said to shorten forty *qadam* during the first *suds* (that is, after the sun is sufficiently high for a man to cast a clear shadow), twenty in the second, five in the third, three in each of the fourth and fifth, two in the sixth and seventh, and one in each of the remaining *asdās* leading to the middle of the day (*wuqūf al-shams*: the standstill of the sun). The order is reversed in the afternoon. The word *qadam* means literally a foot, and the name *athar* arises, according to the *ʿarīf*, because it is the 'trace' or 'print' of the foot (*qadam*) measuring out the *suds*.

The second system, in use in most of central Oman, is a form of sundial (*ʿalam*) in which a stick of a standard length is placed in a convenient spot and the *athar* divisions scratched out on the ground: the day *bāda* starts when the sun is sufficiently high for its shadow to reach a landmark fixed in each village. In both systems seasonal adjustments are made, and while the measures are somewhat rough and ready, they do provide a reasonably accurate system for work in the field.

The systems used for measuring times at night are again based on sound astronomical principles, and require from the operators a considerable practical knowledge of the stars. The stars used in northern Oman appear to vary from those used in central Oman, but this may be partly due to differences in nomenclature, a matter which is made even more complex by the fact that, in northern Oman at least, the same star sometimes has a different name according to whether it is increasing or diminishing (al-Nisr is so called when it is in *ṭulūʿ*, but becomes al-Samak when it is in *ghurūb*, for example). In central Oman twenty-four basic stars are used, twelve in summer and twelve in winter. The stars used and the time-values associated with each are normally altered each *dawrān* (where there is no *ʿarīf*, the *bayādīr* agree on the change and announce it on the day the *qaʿāda* (see below) is distributed): in Buraimi the stars are altered according to the *darr* system (Tables 8 and 9).

Table 8 *Falaj Star Calendar from Central Oman (Qārūt)*

1. al-Shaʿara	9. Zabān	17. al-Ṣāra
2. al-Janāb	10. Ghaḍīr	18. al-Saʿd
3. al-Dhira'ayn	11. Kuwi al-awwal	19. al-Kawkabayn
4. al-Buṭayn	12. Kuwi al-thāni	20. al-Fatḥ
5. al-Waqurt	13. al-Munṣaf	21. al-Najm
6. al-Mithāb	14. al-Mūfi	22. bu Qābil
7. al-Dhakarayn	15. al-Ghurāb	23. al-Shābik
8. al-Ghufar	16. al-Ladam	24. al-Ẓalmi

Table 9 *Falaj Star Calendar from Northern Oman (Buraimi) in Thamānīn of the Darr Calendar (February)*

Order from Sunset	*Star name*	*Period of time measured*
1	al-Najamāt	2 *suds*
2	Suhayl	2 ,,
3	al-Sāta	2 ,,
4	al-Sābiʿ	2 ,,
5	al-Ḥayar	2 ,,
6	al-Dhrāʿ	2 ,,
7	al-Ḥayra	2 ,,
8	al-Thurayā	1 ,,
9	al-Tuwaybi	1 ,,
10	al-Mirzam	1 ,,
11	al-Mīzān	1 ,,
12	al-Najim	½ rabīʿ (3 suds)
13	al-Nisr	½ rabīʿ (3 suds)

THE ANNUAL CALENDAR

The *darr* systems of northern Oman are really the local equivalent of (Persian) *Rūznāmeh* calendars, and meet the need to fix seasonal activities and occurrences by reference to the solar (and not the Islamic lunar) year. However, because the ordinary Omani knows nothing of the principles on which the *Rūznāmeh* is based, each group has tended to develop a partial calendar for those parts of the year in which it is interested, and ignores the rest. So the fundamental differences between them lies in whether the hundred-day period called the *mīya* is calculated from the rise of *Suhayl* (Canopus) or from some other starting-point; in how many of the potential thirty-six *darrs* (of ten days each) are used and what is done with the five or six *masārīj* (the intercalary days); and in the numbering order given to these periods. Thus the Bani Kilbān use two *mīyas*, that of winter (the *dirrat al-shitā*) and that of summer (the *dirrat al-qayẓ*), while the people of Buraimi have only one, which, because it starts with the rise of Canopus, is adequate for covering the critical period of agricultural activity.

An interesting point about the *darr* calendars is that they are entirely confined to northern Oman. A man from central Oman, who was present when the writer was questioning a group of the Kilbān, was highly intrigued by the idea, and was just as confused as the writer by the explanations offered. In central Oman the calendar follows more orthodox lines. At Izki, for example, the year is divided into four main seasons; *rubᶜ*, autumn (not spring: cf. *ṣfiri* in northern Oman and the Lower Gulf), which is the time when the annual crops are planted; then comes *shitā*, in which *ṣardat al-arḍ*, the time of cold winds, passes into *ṣardat al-hawā* (cf. Reinhardt 1894, §405), when the new buds start appearing on the trees. This is followed by *ṣayf* when the annual *ṣayf* crops ripen and are harvested, and *ṣayf* gives way to the real heat of summer, the *qayẓ*: first *al-tibishshira*,[6] when the first *ruṭab* dates ripen, and then the hottest months, *al-qayẓ al-mutawassiṭ*.

ALTERATIONS TO THE *DAWRĀN*

Alterations to the *dawrān* may be necessary for a number of reasons. Amongst these is the fact that the length of day- and night-*bādas* changes during the course of the year. Thus, while the value of an *athar* share held in a particular *bāda* averages out at half an hour, its length will vary around the mean by up to some nine or ten minutes during the course of the year (in the latitudes of Oman). This is enough to be significant, because differences in day and night evaporation-rates do not compensate for drawing a short *athar* at night in summer, nor does the long *athar* received in winter, for then the need for water is reduced: furthermore, social disadvantages may result from being permanently allocated a water share at an inconvenient time.

The simplest way of avoiding these difficulties is to design the *dawrān* with an odd number of *bādas*, so that a shareholder will automatically receive his water alternately night and day on each successive *dawrān* (e.g. a *dawrān* of nine-and-a-half days, rather than nine). This is the solution most commonly adopted in central Oman. Other systems require juggling with the order of the *khabūras* within the *dawrān*, and on some *aflāj* there are quite complex methods of slipping *khabūras* during the course of successive *dawrāns* with the object of gradually changing the period when the individual receives his share of water.

Nor is the length of the *dawrān* itself necessarily rigid. It is altered annually in northern Oman to meet the changing requirements of summer and winter irrigation (cf. Chapter IV): for example, in Darīz (Sirr district) the *dawrān* is changed from ten to twelve days; on one of the ʿIbri *qanāt* from four to five days, and on one of the Buraimi *qanāt* from ten to fourteen days. And it may also be altered to adapt to variations in base flow. Changes can also be made with the purpose of altering the shareholding: as we shall see, this is a device that is commonly used for increasing the allocation of funds for maintaining a *falaj*.

THE *FALAJ* SHARE (*QAʿĀDA* AND *ZĀYIDA*)

All *aflāj* must have some organization for ensuring that the irrigation system is properly maintained. On small *aflāj*, where there are only a few owners, this can be arranged on an *ad hoc* basis, while in areas with capitalist land tenure the landlord will carry out the necessary maintenance and repairs.

On the big *aflāj* with a large number of shareholders, however, some form of system has to be set up to ensure that this work is carried out automatically, without recourse to the owners each time money has to be spent: on the effectiveness of this organization depends the continued survival of the whole *falaj* community.

The following account is of the basic system that applies throughout much of central Oman, where the organization of the *qaʿāda* has been more-or-less-formalized by the rulings of the *ʿulamāʾ*. It is based partly on notes collected in the field, and partly on the rulings given in the chapter entitled *qaʿādat al-falaj* of al-Ṣāʾighi's *Kanz al-Adīb* and the section on *anhār* (etc.) of al-Khalīli's *al-Fatḥ al-jalīl* (pp. 539–70).

The *qaʿāda* is a share of the *dawrān* which is allocated to the *falaj* organization and is administered by the *wakīl* (see below). On some *aflāj* where water is plentiful (e.g. Sumāyil), this will be allocated with land so that a regular income may be had from the sale of the produce. In most cases, however, the *falaj* share is in water only and is auctioned, usually by lots of an *athar*, each year: in Mintirib for example the day (*yawm al-qaʿd*) is fixed on the second of Muḥarram (N.B. a lunar date), but in some places the sale is fixed, at the time the *wakīl* adjudges will be most profitable to his organization. Sometimes the water may be sold weekly (more exactly once per *dawrān*), while on some *aflāj* (e.g. Izki) part is sold annually and part weekly. The price of the water will depend on the state of the *falaj* flow and, in the case of weekly sales, also on the season and whether it is a day- or night-share.

Normally *qaʿāda* shares may not be re-sold.

On some *aflāj* the *wakīl* fixes the price of the *falaj* shares according to demand; at Mintirib for instance its recent value (1970) was twenty to twenty-two *qirsh* (Maria Theresa dollars) per *athar*, which contrasted with the price of a permanent share (*athar aṣli*) that tended to change hands at between 600 and 1,000 *qirsh*. At Buraimi, where the *falaj* share is called *mushāʿ*, the water used similarly to be disposed of on an annual basis, but the present ruler of Abu Dhabi reorganized the system when he was governor in the oasis, and now (1970) it is sold at a fixed price each rotation cycle (*dawr*). In many places in central Oman, however, it is sold by auction. At one such auction which the writer attended (at Izki) this worked as follows. The auctioneer (*dallāl*) sat in the middle of a ring of bidders calling the price (verb *nād*): those interested in the particular lot placed their camel-sticks so that they were touching him. As his calls increased the bidders would drop out by lifting their sticks until eventually only one remained: his name was then registered with the purchase price by the *wakīl* (agent), who also collected payment on the spot. The annual auction is, naturally, a much more serious affair, and in Izki it is interesting to note that the calls are still traditionally made in antique currency denominations (*ʿabbāsi, muḥammadi, rālīya*, and *shākha*).

The creation of a *qaʿāda* share requires the general agreement of the main *falaj* shareholders (the *jubā*). If certain groups object, the affair may be referred to the *qāḍi*, who will base his decision on what he considers to be the general interest of the *falaj* community. Once the agreement has been made and confirmed by this religious authority, the *qaʿāda* then becomes *waqf* (the Islamic equivalent of mortmain, or inalienable tenure) and so may only be used for the specific purposes for which it was created. The primary use is, of course, for the upkeep of the *falaj* (*khidmat al-falaj*), but in some villages a proportion of the water is bequested for education purposes, for providing for guests, for the poor, and the like.

The rules of *waqf* also mean that, even should the *falaj* come to own more water than the ordinary shareholders and have no need of the money for repairs, the *qaʿāda* may not be abolished or redistributed; at best the price at which its shares are sold, and which normally has to be paid in cash at the time of sale, may be registered in the *falaj* accounts as a deferred credit against the purchaser. Furthermore, should the *falaj* have to raise funds for repairs the *qaʿāda* may not be sold absolutely but only disposed of on lease (cf. in particular rulings in Khalīli *al-Fatḥ al-jalīl*, 552 and 555).

However, a *falaj* share may be created which is not treated as *waqf*, and this is usually called *al-zāyida*. In this case, should the needs for which the share has been 'added' disappear, the *zāyida* may be dropped from the *dawrān*: conversely, should further income be required, an additional share may be created and this is sometimes called *al-muzayyida*. *Zāyida* shares are therefore often found in the *falaj dawrān* both in addition to, or in place of, *qaʿāda* shares (cf. Table 11). Options on the sale of *zāyida* water may be agreed by prior arrangement amongst the shareholders so long as this is considered to be beneficial to the *falaj* community as a whole (cf. rulings of al-Sālimi in the case of the Muslimāt *falaj* quoted in Khalīli *al-Fatḥ al-jalīl*, p. 547).

The *qaʿāda* and *zāyida* shares should meet the normal requirements of *falaj* maintenance and provide some kind of reserve funds for emergencies. If, however, the *falaj* flow decreases seriously and requires expensive work to restore it, extra money will have to be raised. This may be achieved by a proportional levy (*rammīya*) on all the shareholders. If the repairs cost more than originally estimated, all who were party to the agreement must make up the difference; absent shareholders, minors, etc. are not so obliged, but if they exercise the right to be excluded then they lose their shares in the *falaj*.

THE IZKI SYSTEM

Before we can conclude this section on the principles of water shareholding we must consider what has been referred to as the Izki system. This is the method by which the Malki Falaj (cf. also Chapter X), the main *falaj* of Izki, is organized. While the system is peculiar to a few places in central Oman,[7] it is of particular interest, for it combines several of the principles of water organization already discussed into an arrangement which presents quite different features from the fixed land- and water-apportionments of the standard *dawrān*.

The writer has been able to study the system in some depth as a result of being allowed to see one of the old *falaj* books (but unfortunately not the recent ones) in which are recorded the names and holdings of the owners of the *khabūra* shares (*aṣḥāb al-uṣūl*) with the history of their holdings during some fifty or so years. This document (*nuskhat/daftar al-falaj*) is of almost unique value for studying water holdings in a village, for it is only where the organization is along these Izki lines that such a detailed record has to be kept of the water shares.

As may be seen from Table 10, the primary shareholding is divided into fifteen *khabūras* to which should be added the *falaj qaʿāda* and *zāyida* which was probably then of four *bāda* duration. Each *khabūra* makes up a section of the *falaj* book, and everyone who has a share in it (at the time this particular book was opened, *c*. 1825) has his own page (however small the share) on which is recorded changes in the holding: an example of the entries (albeit a rather exceptional case, selected for other reasons) is shown in Fig. 24. By about 1875 the holdings had become so changed and the entries so confused that a new book was opened (not seen), and this once again presumably started with clean sheets for each shareholder at that time.

To obtain the total amount of an individual's holding in the *falaj* his water rights on all the *khabūras* must be traced. So, for example, if the example of Sulaymān b. Aḥmad b. Ḥabīb Umbārūmi is taken he is found to hold water rights as follows:

1st	*Khabūra*	10 *qīyās*
2nd	,,	¼ *athar*
3rd	,,	11 *qīyās*
4th	,,	4 *athar*
6th	,,	8 *qīyās*
11th	,,	¾ *athar*
13th	,,	1 *athar,* 10 *qīyās,* 18 *daqīqa,* and 12 *shaʿīra*
14th	,,	1 *qīyās,* 5 *daqīqa,* and 12 *shaʿīra*

In sum he owned seven *athar*s and seventeen *qīyā*s (assuming no lacunae), that is getting on for four hours of water rights spread somewhat unevenly over eight days of what was probably a seventeen-day *dawrān*.

Despite the defective nature of the document a detailed insight into the social structure in Izki can be obtained by examining the family and tribal relationships of the 200 or so owners of *khabūra* shares (*aṣḥāb al-uṣūl*), the way water rights have changed hands, and the purposes for which *waqf* bequests have been given. This will be discussed in Chapter X.

Unfortunately it is not possible to be certain of all the details of the way in which the organization of the *falaj* worked at the time of the *falaj* book: this is first, because the document does not indicate the principle of shareholding, and the opening pages which may have given important details are missing or torn; second, because the system was subsequently reorganized during the life of Muḥammad b. ʿAbdullāh al-Khalīli (b. 1881-2, Imam 1920–54); and third, because detailed field work was difficult due to the political situation in the village. However, the evolution of the basic organization is clear.

Originally the Falaj Malki was divided along standard lines, with the water shares of the *dawrān* allocated to specific land. Some of the names of these early divisions are still preserved in the titles of the *khabūra*s used in the Falaj Book (cf. Table 10), and may date right back to very early Islamic times, for amongst them we find those of both Persian groups (No's 3, 9, 15 probably) and of certain early Arab settlers who were important in the time of the First Imamate (cf. Chapter VI and VII).

During the terrible civil war at the end of the ninth century, most of the Falaj Malki was destroyed and major changes in the tribal composition of the village took place. Since this must have entailed a major redistribution of the remaining water supply it is possible that it was in the relative peace of the eleventh-century Imamate that the new system of water organization was introduced; but more probably it occurred during Yaʿāriba times, for certainly the present *qaʿāda* agreement, like that in many other villages, is based on that drawn up by one of their Imams.

Under this new system, water was completely divorced from land and a shareholder was deemed to hold his share above the *Ṣīwarayn al-Kibār*, that is

Table 10 *Khabūras of Izki Falaj Book* (*c.* 1825)

Number	*Name of Khabūra (B.=Bani)*	*shilla*	*Approx. total in athars of mulk*	*waqf**	*Estimated size of Khabūra*
1	al-Awali	no	18+	?	2 *bādas*. The record is complete but badly damaged. There is a very sizeable *waqf* page, but the actual values are torn.
2	al-Ukhrā	yes	18	29	2 *bādas*
3	B. Hormuz	yes	24	7	2 *bādas*? but if so 17 *athars* are missing.
4	B. ᶜAli	yes	19	30½	2 *bādas*
5	B. Muḥammad	no	17 }		Incomplete. No. 5 is probably two *bādas* in length and No. 6 one *bāda*.
6	Ād al-Ṣaghīr	yes	22 }		
7	B. ᶜUzra (i.e. ᶜUzūr)	yes	45½	2½	2 *bādas*
8	B. Ḥusayn	no	40½	4½	2 *bādas*
9	B. ᶜAqba	yes	26	22	2 *bādas*
10	B. ᶜAbdullāh al-Ūlā	yes	40	10	2 *bādas*
11	,, ,, al-Ukhrā	yes	27½	20½	2 *bādas*
12	al-Bāda	yes	16		1 *bāda*
13	Ād al-Kabīr	yes	29	19	2 *bādas*
14	al-ᶜIyzār (i.e. ᶜUzūr)	yes	20	28	2 *bādas*
15	B. Mī	no	41	7	2 *bādas*

* included in *waqf* figures is *bayt māl* water and other institutional grants that should not strictly be classified as *waqf*.

above the point where the main channel first divides: he may therefore draw his water wherever he wants from the main network of *falaj* channels (cf. Fig. 21A).

The advantages are obvious. In the standard system a man draws his water for a fixed period on a fixed day at a fixed point, and the only changes he can make to his water supply are either to acquire some of the *falaj* shares (and even then this water may be delivered at an inconvenient time), or to make special arrangements with his neighbours. In the Izki system a man acquires a share of water on whatever day he wants for the period he wants, and can draw it at the place he wants.[8]

On the other hand there are two disadvantages in such a system: first, there can be a tremendous waste of water in the channels, because the supply is always being switched from point to point, and second, there are considerable time delays in getting the water from one place to another. This is illustrated by the example of what is called *shilla*, or *shilal*, that is, the opening of the long main channel to (al-)Yaman, which, as can be seen in Table 10, occurred on no less than eleven of the fifteen *khabūras*, even though the volume of water delivered was probably in the order of a fifth of the total.

To some extent these disadvantages were reduced under the reforms introduced in the time of Imam Muḥammad b. ʿAbdullāh al-Khalīli. Under his modifications the holdings in the old *khabūras* were reshuffled and renamed, the Yaman holding (*shilla*) was rationalized, and the *dawrān* was divided into two halves (cf. Table 11): at the same time subdivisions of the *athar* were abolished and a new *falaj* share, subsequently increased again, was added. In effect these modifications meant that a man who held land in say Nizār (Nizār and Yaman land are quite separate, it should be remembered) would now draw his water in one of the periods which the *falaj* was 'running' (*ridd al-falaj*) in the Nizār branch, and could either take all of his share on a *khabūra* once per full *dawrān* of eighteen days, or half of it every nine days. So even though the number of days in which the *falaj* was running in the Nizār or Yaman channels was reduced, a shareholder still had a wide range of *khabūras* from which to purchase a water right in order to plan his holdings to suit his land-needs, and he could still draw his water from wherever he wanted on the channel. At the same time the wastage of water was decreased and the *falaj ʿarīf* (administrator, see below) could, by careful manipulation, arrange the sequence of delivery within each *khabūra* so that gardens were watered in a logical order and thus keep the transmission losses to a reasonable level.

Even so, the *ʿarīf*'s task is made very complicated by the allocation of temporary shares of water as landowners buy or sell their water to meet variations in their needs (these requirements will be affected by changes in the size and distribution of their holdings, by the season, and by the type of crops grown). The amount of water that changes hands in this way can be considerable; at the time the writer was investigating this, he was told that although the Yaman holding of permanent shares was only 100 *athars* their allocation as the result of temporary transactions was in fact 156 *athars*. In addition to this 'floating water', if such a term may be permitted, there is also one day of the half *dawrān* in which holdings change each cycle (cf. the *qaʿāda* share on day 2/11 of the *dawrān*), and another in which it changes annually (cf. the *zāyida* share, day 9/18 of the *dawrān*).

All this organization places a heavy responsibility on the *ʿarīf* on whose efficiency depends the effective use of water. In fact the whole administration of the Falaj Malki is considerable. On this *falaj* alone there is a secretary and a guardian of the Falaj book (in which are recorded changes in the permanent water holdings only), an agent (*wakīl*), and two *ʿarīfs*, the senior in Nizār (who also has an assistant) and the other in Yaman. The number of these officials should be compared with the simple organization of the standard *dawrān*, where there is often only one employee. The roles of these officials will become clearer from the following discussion of the way work on the land is organized in Oman.

Table 11 *The Present Dawrān at Izki*

	Name	*Period*	*Comment*
1 & 10	Futūḥ al-Qaᶜāda	24 hr	On this day the *qaᶜāda* share is auctioned.
2 & 11	al-Qaᶜāda	24 hr	Distribution of the *qaᶜāda*-share.
3 & 12	Bani Ḥusayn	24 hr	cf. the name of *khabūra* no. 8 in the earlier *falaj* organization.
4 & 13	al-Khabūra	24 hr	Vestigial name from the earlier organization.
5 & 14	Badāwat or Futūḥ al-Shilal	24 hr	'Beginning' or 'opening' of *shilla*, that is the Yaman share of water.
6 & 15	Wasāṭ al-Shilal	24 hr	The middle of *shilal*
7 & 16	Bāqiyat al-Shilal	24 hr	The remainder of *shilal*.
8 & 17	al-Habṭa	24 hr	
9 & 18	a. Nuṣṣ al-Radda	Day *bāda*	Distribution of the *falaj* water which is sold annually (9a was a *Zāyida share* created by the original reform and
	b. al-Muzayyida	Night *bāda*	9b subsequently?)

III. DIVISION OF LABOUR AND RESPONSIBILITIES IN OMANI VILLAGES

Basically every village in Oman is self-supporting in its organization of agriculture and irrigation. There are two minor exceptions to this general rule. The first is that migrant labour from nomadic groups in the interior and from fishing villages near the coast may be used in some places to help out at harvest-time (such help is paid for with a share of the produce), and the second is that the village may have to make use of certain outside experts for very specialized work on the *aflāj* (see below).

The following account is a summary of the way agricultural and *falaj* work is organized in the villages of central Oman. It will, of course, be appreciated that even there this division of responsibilities varies somewhat from place to place.

CULTIVATION AND HERDING

Within the *falaj* village community most agricultural and irrigation work is in the hands of the men. Women and children are entrusted with simple tasks like cutting *jatt* (alfalfa) or looking after the flocks of sheep and goats, but the serious work of irrigating and tending the palms is a man's job!

Although the majority of land-workers in Oman are called *bayādīr* (sing. *bīdār*), the *badāra* duties are quite distinct from the other work a *bīdār* may do (the origins of this work organization go far back into antiquity and it is a partial survival of the old Persian land tenure system: cf. Chapter VI and Wilkinson 1974). True *badāra* duties are entirely confined to irrigating and tending the palms. So the *Bīdār* pollinates the female flowers (*ynabbit*), ties back the bunches as they form (*yeḥaẓẓar, yukhallij*), cuts the ripe dates (*yajidd*), and irrigates (*yasqi*) the palms: for this he receives the *bīdāra* (sometimes called *ṭalīʿa, ṭalʿān*) of one bunch (*ʿisqa*)[9] of dates per palm. Although a *bīdār* receives this payment from the individual palm-owner, he is not in fact tied to any particular landlord and may work in a number of gardens: furthermore it is the *ʿarīf* who supervises his irrigation duties. For all the other tasks, such as ploughing under the palms and looking after other crops, he receives a proportion of the produce or a cash payment. (This system is today rapidly breaking down as a result of the labour crisis in the villages).

Whilst the *bayādīr* and the property-owners between them look after the irrigation and cultivation of seasonal crops grown on *ʿawābi* land, the *dawwās* are responsible for threshing. These labourers receive as payment one-tenth of the grain (*ḥabb*), and as much of the chaff (*tibin*) and straw (*ghuffa*) as they want. Because their work is seasonal the *dawwās* are also expected, in return for this fixed payment and various gratuities given at the *ʿiyd*s (the two great public feasts at the end of the fasting month of *Ramaḍān* and of the annual *Ḥajj* pilgrimage), to act as grave-diggers for the village.

The job of grazing the village's livestock is normally entrusted to a shepherd (*rāʿi*) who receives a fixed payment per head per month, plus the usual *ʿiyd* gratuities; but in some villages each house (*bayt*) in turn takes over the responsibility of the village flock: the richer inhabitants hire labour for this duty. The flocks are sent out every morning to graze on the natural pasture of the village territory (*ḥaram*) and are brought back in the afternoon to be handed over to the individual owners, who milk them and give them supplementary feed (dates and alfalfa).

FALAJ OFFICIALS

The number of officials involved in running a *falaj* depends both on its size and on the method by which it has been organized. On small *aflāj* many of the jobs are done by the same man, but on a major system, such as the Falaj Malki at Izki, the responsibilities are divided amongst a number of officials.

At the head of the organization of a *falaj* in which such duties are divided is the *wakīl* (agent). His basic responsibilities are financial: it is he who organizes the sale of the *falaj* water (*qaʿāda* and *zāyida* shares), and it is he who arranges that the *falaj* is properly maintained (*khidmat al-falaj*). For this he receives a salary from the *falaj* income: this varies according to local arrangements, but is quite often assessed as the equivalent of one labourer's wages when he merely administers the *falaj*, and of two if he actually supervises the repairs himself.

Ordinarily he carries out his duties without consulting the shareholders (*arbāb*), but if he considers special expenditure is necessary he arranges an assembly of the leading owners (collective noun *jabha* pl. *jubā(h)*) and the matter is discussed. If there is a substantial majority in favour of the work being carried out the decision is binding on all.

Although most of the routine maintenance of the *falaj* is carried out by labourers (including many of the *bayādīr*), who receive a daily wage for their work, specialists on occasion have to be called in. One of these is the *bāṣir*, the water diviner, who advises on where water is to be found and how the *falaj* supply can be improved. He is normally paid according to results. The second group are the ʿAwāmir (cf. Chapter IX) who, along with one or two smaller groups, are considered as the greatest experts in working underground in the hard rocks and conglomerates at the head of the *falaj*: they normally work on a contract basis. In charge of the distribution of water is the ʿ*arīf*. On small *aflāj* there is no need for such an official, as the *bayādīr* can arrange the time schedules of the *dawrān* adequately amongst themselves. But on a big *falaj* the problems of organizing the adjustments to the time schedule, and of supervising the *bayādīr* in the opening and closing of the sluices according to the rights of each garden, make the ʿ*arīf* a very busy man indeed and demand a high level of expertise in the methods of measuring time. As a result the position of ʿ*arīf* has run in the same family since time immemorial in many villages, and his word is law. His pay may come, partly or wholly, either from the land-owners who share the cost in proportion to the size of their holdings, or from the *falaj* share, or from water rights allocated to him.

Other minor officials connected with the *falaj* organization that may be found in a village are the holder of the *falaj* book (*Amīn al-daftar/nuskha*) and his clerk, and the auctioneer (*dallāl*) who helps the *wakīl* in the sale of the *qaʿāda* and *zāyida* shares. We should also note that in the villages there may be other *wakīl*s responsible for other institutions (education etc.) that, partly or wholly, derive their income from the *qaʿāda* and other *waqf* shares.

JUDICIAL RULINGS

Normally the village community works in comparative harmony over the administration of the *falaj* and its lands, even though there can be considerable rivalry over other matters (cf. Chapter X). When, however, a dispute arises which cannot be settled, the affair is referred to the *qāḍi* or other government official.

The decisions reached nearly always derive from custom rather than from the fundamental rulings of Islamic law (*uṣūl al-fiqh*). In virtually all cases the judgements have been decided on two principles: first, that water is an essential need of the community and nothing must impede proper use of it (such, for example, is the first recorded ruling which forbids anyone from preventing access to *qanāt* headwaters, even though these may lie in the territory of a group other than the usufructs); second, that if the measures disputed are in the general interest of the *falaj* community then they are permitted and are binding on the dissidents. As al-Sālimi has pointed out in the *Jawhar al-niẓām*, 'co-operation is of the essence in the organization of agriculture and irrigation.'

NOTES TO CHAPTER V

1 Part of this chapter was used in *Research Papers*, No. 10 published by the School of Geography, Oxford (1974).

2 Cf. the definition (Lane): *takhabbarū khubra*, they bought a sheep or goat for different sums and slaughtered it, and divided its flesh amongst themselves, each of them receiving a share proportional to the sum he paid.

3 There is an interesting parallel here with the names of the various *zjedd* (*jadd*, the very word means forebear) at Ghadamès.

4 At ᶜIbri an informant stated that there were two *bādas* in use there, a *bāda ghāfi* (24-hour day) and a *bāda ṣāfi* (which was a half a *bāda ghāfi*). He was of the opinion that ᶜIbri was the only place to have a 24-hour *bāda*, but in fact the writer came across such a *bāda* at a place in the Wādi Sumāyil, while only a short distance away at al-Rassa there were three *bādas* to the 24-hour day.

5 Further subdivisions of the 24-hour day occur. At Izki, for example, it is divided into four parts: the first half of the night is called *khalyān* and the second simply *layl*; daylight time is similarly divided by the passage of the sun past its zenith (*qiyām*) into *rafᶜān* and *rawāḥ* (cf. bedu *rawaḥ*, to travel in the afternoon). In al-Khaṭṭ, according to some notes Professor R. B. Serjeant kindly lent me, there are eight such divisions. The names, however, only indicate the parts of the day when a water right is drawn; they are not used as subdivisions of the basic *bāda* time unit.

6 Cf. definition in *Līsān al-ᶜArab* of verb *tabassara*; for the *sīn* to *shīn* change in Omani dialects cf. Sālimi *Jawhar*, p. 435.

7 At least one of the *aflāj* in Qārūt is organized on this basis, and so, apparently, is ᶜAwābi and some of the Nizwā *aflāj*. There are probably a number of others as well.

8 Documents of sales from *aflāj* organized on the Izki system are on the following pattern:

(a) for water alone:

I so-and-so confirm that I have sold two *athars* of the undivided water (*mā ḍamm*) on Falaj al-ᶜAyn of the village of Qārūt al-Sāfil on the *radda* (i.e. *khabūra*) Mā al-Masrūr on each of its complete rotations (*ᶜala dawr ādi*) for so much, etc.

(b) with land:

I so-and-so confirm that I have sold the garden (*māl*) called so-and-so with its borders (*ḥudūd* cf. *ḥaram*), access tracks, channels, and all that is necessary according to the *sharīᶜa* with four *athars* of such-and-such a Falaj on the *raddas* so-and-so and so-and-so, etc.

9 This is frequently left hanging on the tree until the *bīdār* has completed harvesting his client's dates.

CHAPTER VI

MAZŪN

'The Kesrá [Khusraw/Chosroe] named
'Omân Mazún
And Mazún, O friend: is a goodly land,
A land abounding in fields and groves,
With pastures and unfailing springs.'

(*Kashf*, tr. Ross, p. 116)

We have already seen that there are certain inconsistencies between the use of irrigation techniques, seemingly well suited to the type of physical environment that exists in Oman, and the present administration of the land, which appears to be inadequately or even badly adapted to the needs of the *falaj* network. The chief of these anomalies are as follows.

First: with a system of irrigation that demands a very large capital investment, the present tenure system of small tribal *mulk* holders (freeholders) in central Oman is paradoxical: indeed, such a form of land-ownership represents almost the opposite extreme to the quasi-feudal or landlord peasant relationships which characterize the history of land-tenure in Persia, the home of the *qanāt*.

Second: the political administration in Oman is not suited to such an irrigation system. Polybius' description (X. 28, tr. Shuckburgh ii. 27) of the way the Persian rulers (Achaemanids?) orginally developed their territory through the use of *qanāt* illustrates the kind of conditions required for fostering the economic basis of empire: 'they granted the enjoyment of the profits of the lands to the inhabitants of some of the waterless districts for five generations on the condition of their bringing fresh water in.' Such political and economic acuity has hardly been characteristic of the last 1,200 years of Oman's history. There the traditional idea of state is little more than a religious transformation of tribal organization, and is opposed both to centralized administration and to the concentration of power in the hands of the few: since this encourages neither bureaucratic administration of the country's wealth, nor capitalist tenure, major investment in Oman's economic infrastructure can hardly be expected.

Third: the present population of Oman has no real knowledge of the techniques of *qanāt* building. The ʿAwāmir are the *falaj* experts, but the *aflāj* they have built are of simple design and they have little knowledge of the surveying methods and specialized constructional techniques possessed by the *muqannis* of Persia.

Fourth: the local population is completely ignorant of the history of *qanāt*: they are *shē mubhim*, something unknown, *ʿand Allāh*, from God. The answer to the query about who built them is *Sulaymān b. Dawūd (Daʾūd)*,

Solomon son of David. This, at first sight, is not very helpful, for in many parts of the Islamic world any great work of antiquity is attributed to the supernatural powers of this legendary King Solomon, one of the four great world rulers and a true believer, according to the Islamic traditions.

Fifth: Omanis do not even distinguish between their various types of irrigation system. For them a *qanāt*, like any source of running water, is a *falaj*, something to be shared. Preoccupied with the methods for distributing this God-given source of wealth to the community, they remain largely ignorant of its mechanics and have evolved only the elementary means of upkeep and maintenance described in the previous chapter. Similar attitudes are to be observed in the principles which control government administration of the land.

Now, to understand how such anomalies have arisen, and to appreciate why land organization in central Oman differs from that of northern Oman and contrasts so markedly with that in neighbouring Persia or Ḥaḍramawt, it is essential to delve below the observed surface order and to try and evaluate the processes which have moulded Omani society and influenced its attitudes towards the land. Such explanations will be the objective of the second half of this book. In it discussion will concentrate on three major factors which the writer believes are mainly responsible for the peculiarities of Omani land organization. These are: the original organization associated with the period of *qanāt* construction (present chapter); the influence of Ibāḍism (Chapter VII); and the system of social organization loosely labelled 'tribal' (Chapters VIII–X).

The primary object of the present chapter is to try and find out something about the origins of *qanāt* in Oman, to discover who built them, where and when, and what were the forms of land organization associated with the constructional periods.

THE ORIGINS OF THE *QANĀT* OF OMAN

Specific evidence from the *jāhili* period itself apart, there are a number of reasons why one is forced back to 'pre-Islamic' times in order to discover when the *qanāt* system of Oman was built. In the first place a study of the places mentioned in the early sources shows that the names of virtually all the main settlements (many of which are, in fact, arabizations of older names)[1] have featured by the time of the civil war at the end of the ninth century, and that many occur in connection with even earlier events. Since a large number of these places can only exist by reason of their *qanāt*, this of itself suggests that the irrigation network must have been more or less established at least by early Islamic times. Secondly, there are hints that at that time the irrigated area was far more extensive than it is now (air photographs certainly confirm that a major decrease in the area cultivated by *qanāt* irrigation has occurred at some time or other). One reads, for example, that during the Imamate of Ghassān b. ʿAbdullāh (192/808–207/823) Nizwā 'was so fertile . . . its water so plentiful that it was said the old Falaj Ḍawt extended as far as Dāris land'

(*Tuḥfa* i. 125). In contrast, history and local tradition speak of a massive destruction of settlement in central Oman during the civil war of the late ninth century, and recount that in the ensuing period most of the settlements of the Batina coast were abandoned and were only brought back into cultivation by the Yaʿāriba (*Tuḥfa* i. 165).

Then there is the fact that the historical sources provide no evidence of a major period of *qanāt* construction within Islamic times (except for the Yaʿāriba period — see below), even though they have plenty to say about the destruction of *aflāj*. This evidence should not be considered as simply negative, for a closer examination of the sources will confirm that the occasions when large-scale land developments could have occurred during the last thirteen hundred years are extremely limited, and that such investment as did in fact take place largely consisted in restoring the ravages of the past rather than in building anew.

There is a distinct pattern in the history of Oman such that the Islamic period may be divided into two major and a number of minor 'Imamate cycles' (cf. Fig. 23). Briefly this cycle works as follows (Wilkinson 1972; certain details are discussed further in Chapter VII). At the height of the cycle the people are united under a strong Imam, the Omanis profit from control of their coast, and the benefits of overseas trade feed into the country's economic system. Some of this wealth is invested in the land, but in such a way that capitalist land-tenure develops whilst simultaneously Imamate government declines into dynastic rule. So the ideological basis of the Ibāḍi Imamate weakens and competition for control of power and wealth grows: and as it does so, tribal factionalism revives (it may even lead to full-scale civil war in a major Imamate cycle), and the central authority of the Imam finally collapses to be replaced by the rule of local pseudo-Imams or *mulūk* who are incapable of holding the state together. Thus divided the Omanis lose control of their maritime trade, the economy of their villages declines, and outsiders begin to take possession of their land. Not until they have sufficiently 'quaffed the draught of terror, and suffered from the general destruction which encompasses religion, property and life' does the Ibāḍi ideology dormant in the central core of the country slowly reawaken and inspire the tribesmen once again to give their support to an Imam capable of re-establishing strong government.

Only at the height of the Imamate cycle do conditions favourable to major land development exist, while at other times destruction rather than construction tends to be the order of the day. There are therefore only two periods in Islamic history that need seriously be considered as possible epochs for really extensive *qanāt* building.

The first is the Golden Age of the First Imamate (ninth century). Here the striking feature is that although there is evidence that this was a period when the Arabs developed a major new land organization and *falaj* rulings first begin to feature in the records, there is no mention at all in the fairly detailed historical material of any *qanāt* construction. On the other hand, this does not mean that no *qanāt* building occurred, for there may well have been some *muqannis* left in Oman itself at this time, while clearly some important restoration work did take place to make good the neglect of the preceding Julandā period. But the only positive evidence concerning a major extension of the cultivated area comes from the Ṣuḥār area, a rather special case because even though this port did prosper during the First Imamate, its major development occurred during the period of foreign (largely Persianized) domination which followed the collapse of the Imamate, and it was in major decline well before Ibāḍi 'puritanical rule' (Ibn Khaldūn iv. 489-90) was re-established in the middle of the eleventh century (Wilkinson 1964; Williamson 1973b). It is unlikely therefore, that any major addition to the settlement area in interior Oman occurred during the First Imamate, even though it may have been a period of important reconstruction. Furthermore, such gains as were made were more than offset by the appalling destruction which followed the invasion of a Caliphate force in the civil war which ended the First Imamate in the last decade of the ninth century.

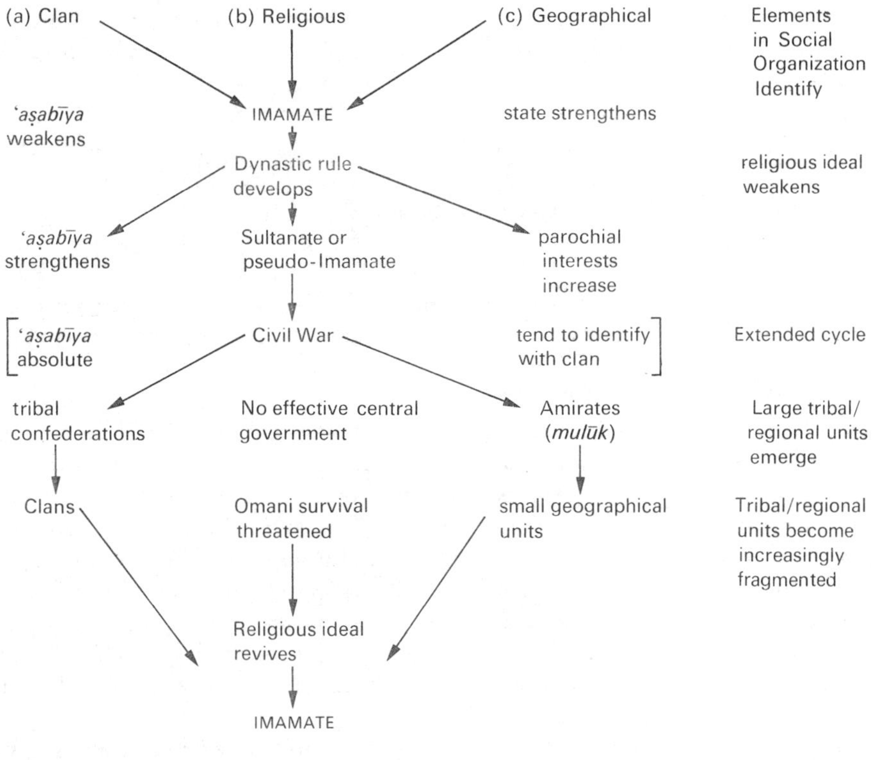

Fig. 23. The Imamate cycle.

The second potential *qanāt*-building period that must be considered is at the height of the Yaʿāriba Imamate, roughly from 1650 to 1725. Here the evidence needs examining rather more closely, for it is certain from both the written record[2] and the spoken tradition that considerable land-development did occur at this time. Amongst the works that we know were carried out was an extensive redevelopment of the Batina, the rebuilding of numerous *aflāj*, and the reconstruction of Ibrā, Birkat al-Mawz and al-Ḥamrā; we also know that new crops were introduced, that villagers were encouraged to improve their land through reorganization of the *falaj* maintenance systems, and that the merchant class, along with the Yaʿāriba family itself, invested extensively in the land: indeed, the latter became so wealthy that it is said that one of their Imams actually owned a third of the land rights of Oman (not altogether honestly acquired, to judge by the remarks in the *Nubdhat al-Maʿāwil*). But the important point is that their work was very largely confined to restoration: the Batina was re-cultivated, abandoned settlement was re-colonized, and most of the *aflāj* were reconstructed. True, such work often involved modifying the original design (the Yaʿāriba made particular use of inverted siphons, and they almost certainly employed foreign craftsmen for their irrigation works just as they did for their forts), but the development of virgin rather than abandoned land seems to have been fairly limited, and was probably more or less confined to parts of the east coast (e.g. the Ḥayl *falaj*?).

Thus, remarkable as the work of the Yaʿāriba was, it is not possible to attribute any major part of the basic settlement pattern in Oman to their efforts, but only a revitalization of the land after the all-time low into which the country's economy had sunk by the end of Nabāhina times.

So, from the evidence of the Islamic age itself, the *jāhili* period presents itself as the epoch when the main settlement pattern of Oman must have developed. Fortunately the surviving vestiges of the history of this 'age of ignorance' do provide some positive support for the thesis that the main land development of Oman was completed by the middle of the seventh century A.D.

THE ACHAEMANID AND PARTHIAN PERIODS

Omani history really begins with an account of how the first Arab tribes came to the area. It tells of the way clans of the Mālik b. Fahm Azd, accompanied by some so-called Quḍāʿa groups, left the Sarāt and the Tihāma (in South-West Arabia) and migrated along the settled fringes of Southern Arabia to arrive in Oman. This story forms a part of the legend of the Azd diaspora which began when the Sayl al-Aram, the flood which reputedly burst the Mārib dam, caused the Azd to move away by major genealogical groupings from their homeland, first into Western Arabia (from the Ḥijāz to Sarāt) and then, in the course of time, further afield into the Arabian Peninsula until they reached the fringes of the Fertile Crescent.[3]

Now the Mārib part of this story can be proved sheer nonsense (von Wissmann 1964), part of a deliberate piece of historical manipulation which seeks to identify the rulers of Old South Arabia with the 'Qaḥṭāni' tribes; nevertheless, there are some elements of fact in the legend. There does, for example, appear to have been a period of active, though intermittent, migration of Arab tribes away from South-West Arabia which started roughly at the time when the old civilizations associated with the Mārib dam were collapsing, and it lasted for several centuries. These tribes followed three main routes in their dispersal: northwards towards Shām (Greater Syria) and Iraq, eastwards through Central Arabia (Yamāma) to 'Baḥrayn' and south-eastwards along the settled fringe of southern Arabia to Oman. These major routes of migration were like three streams which, issuing from a tribal spring in the western part of the Peninsula, flowed their separate ways across the deserts of Arabia to rejoin in a whirl of complex cross-currents on the fringes of the settled areas of the Persian Gulf and the Fertile Crescent.

Thus the local story of how some of the Azdi Mālik b. Fahm clans migrated to Oman forms part of a complex history of tribal movement in which the factual elements have been expanded, compressed, personalized, transferred, and manipulated, and the whole embellished with a generous dose of legend. Nevertheless, once this story is stripped of its legendary overlay and the various strands of history unravelled, it does say something about how the first real Arab tribes came to Oman, and it does, by chance, contribute some interesting clues to the history of *qanāt* there. This basic story is as follows.

The Arab new-comers first began to make their new homeland in south-east Oman, in the Jaʿlān and on the coast around the Qalhāt area, (that is, on the outer fringes of settled Oman, away from the main maritime centres of the time, and in a region that had scarcely been settled, if at all). Soon, however, the Arabs began to penetrate into the Jawf, which led them into direct conflict with the Persians who were the 'people' of the country and who recognized 'Dārā b. Dārā b. Bahmān' as their suzerain (*Kashf* MS. 31). The Arab demands for a grant of territory with water and pasture were turned down, and the Persians joined battle with the new-comers near Salūt (in the Jawf: the account states that in this battle the Persians used elephants). The Persians were defeated and a truce was concluded, the terms of which appear to have been that the Persian forces should retire to the coastal regions and evacuate Oman within a year. The chronicles relate that in the time of grace accorded them, the Persians deliberately laid waste the land, destroying large numbers of *aflāj*, of which 'Sulaymān b. Dawūd had constructed 10,000 in Oman'. While this evacuation was in process the Persian King sent reinforcements; the Arabs, anticipating the new attack, struck first, and drove the Persians right out of their territory which the Arabs then proceeded to pillage. Following this victory, large numbers of Azd groups and other tribes started to arrive in Oman ('Awtabi Paris MS. 254^{r}-258^{v} and Johnstone MS. 187^{r}-191^{r}; Kashf MS. 34).

So runs the local story, and once again towards the end, as at the beginning, the time scale has been enormously compressed. While it is true that the first identifiably 'Arab' migrants to Oman did establish themselves in the western desert borderlands in pre-Sasānid times (possibly in the first or second century A.D.), their final success in taking control of all Mazūn (the Persian name for Oman) did not occur until the middle of the seventh century A.D., while Azd migration into the region continued at least until well into the eighth century. But having made allowances for such distortions, this story is most revealing about *qanāt*, first because it shows clearly that when the Arabs *qua* Arabs began to arrive in Oman some form of *qanāt* network already existed there,[4] and secondly because it provides two indications that this had been developed (at least in part) by the Achaemanids.

The first of these indications is contained in the statement that when Mālik b. Fahm came to Oman the land belonged to Dārā b. Dārā b. Bahmān. Now E. C. Ross, in a footnote to his partial translation of the *Kashf al-Ghumma* (p. 186), dismisses this as preposterous; but the reason he does so is that he has taken the story of Mālik b. Fahm literally. To understand who Mālik b. Fahm really was requires study of all the stories about him, and these show that he was something far more important than just the leader of the first Azd migration to Oman. Not only does he act as a key figure in Ibn al-Kalbi's legerdemain of welding the Azd and Quḍāʿa into a single genealogical group through the story of the Tanūkh migration, but he also acts as one of the links by which the Arabs, 'proto-Arabs',[5] and the peoples of the Old South Arabian civilizations are welded into a single race in Arab folklore. These Semitic races, whom the Arabs, through such genealogical manipulations, recognize as their forebears, were connected with Oman long before the first Azd arrived: this is apparent from the Arab folklore itself, from literary clues (discussed in Wilkinson 1964), and from an important new piece of archaeological evidence[6] which finally proves contact between Old South Arabia (the area of the civilization with which the Azd were associated before their diaspora) and northern Oman five or six hundred years before the particular historical migration to which Mālik b. Fahm's name has become attached. In the stories about Mālik b. Fahm, therefore, the writer believes that nearly a thousand years of history have been compressed, and in the Omani version are found elements of the history of contact between South-West Arabia and Oman which range from perhaps the fifth century B.C. down to the arrival of the second major wave of Azd migration (the Azd Shanuʾa) well on into Sasānid times. If then there was an Old South Arabian connection with so distant an area as northern Oman as far back as the middle of the first millennium B.C., it should certainly occasion no surprise to find the Achaemanids (figuratively represented by the great Dārā b. Dārā b. Bahmān) occupying this potentially fertile land, a terrain similar to their homeland of southern Persia and separated from it only by the narrow Strait of Hormuz. On the contrary, it would be curious indeed if Oman, which had already been closely linked with the peoples of the Persian mainland and involved in the trade of the Gulf from at least the third millennium, did not form part of the great Persian empire. Furthermore if the Achaemanids occupied the land, then *a priori* one would expect major development of it to have occurred, for their state was no ephemeral empire of military conquest but one that was built on the solid foundations of the land. Even the invasion of Egypt was followed up by major investment in irrigation works, while the satrapies proper were developed through the kind of encouragement for investing in *qanāt* described by Polybius (cf. p. 122, above).

The second indication that the Achaemanids had built *qanāt* in Oman lies in the statement that during the truce with Mālik b. Fahm, the Persians destroyed many of the 10,000 *aflāj* that Sulaymān b. Dawūd had constructed. ʿAwtabi (Paris MS. 260, Johnstone MS. 192ᵛ) expands this legend. The story he relates is that one day Sulaymān b. Dawūd was being carried by the winds on his daily trip from Iṣṭakhar to Bayt al-Muqaddas. On his way he was blown across to Oman where he saw a castle, seemingly only just constructed: this castle was at Salūt according to one version of the story. Sulaymān ordered the spirits to investigate. They reported that its sole occupant was an eagle who said that he and his forebears had been living there for generations (800 years in one variant of the story), and all that time the castle had been thus uninhabited. Then Sulaymān entered Oman, 'and at that time there were only nomads (*bādīya*) living there'. He stayed ten days, on each of which he ordered his spirits (*shayāṭīn*) to dig a thousand *nahr* (*qanāt*): hence the ten thousand *aflāj* of Oman.

This apparent nonsense deserves a little more attention that it might seem to merit at first sight. It is, after all, a story concerned with a very remote past, and events are almost certain to have acquired a mythical embellishment in their transmission.

Sulaymān is the hypostasis of King Solomon whose connection with the Queen of the 'Sabaean' kingdom is celebrated. Less well known, perhaps, is the fact that in Persia he tends to be partially identified with the even more legendary Jamshīd; thus in folklore it was this Jamshīd-cum-Sulaymān, and not the Achaemanids, who built Persepolis (cf. Takht-i-Sulaymān, Takht-i-Jamshīd). This is significant in the Oman context because when Sulaymān visited Oman and ordered the *qanāt* to be built, he was on his daily journey from Iṣṭakhar, that is the Achaemanid capital of Persepolis, to Bayt al-Muqaddas, or Jerusalem, the city of the real King Solomon. The place where Sulaymān stayed was Salūt, that is, the same place that the first Arab migrants and the Persians were later to do battle.

When the writer was last in Oman (February 1973) he visited Salūt, an abandoned settlement near Bisyā, to see if he could find any archaeological evidence which might throw light on this story. There he was taken by the local Shaikh to a site which turned out to be a very sizeable ruined fort (now numbered BB/15). Preliminary investigation of this discovery by a visiting archaeological team from Harvard University showed that most of the sherds were of a Persian first-millennium type, but that there were also some pieces which might have been of much earlier date. The large number of what the local Shaikh called 'Mālik b. Fahm graves' on the surrounding hills were clearly third-millennium mounds of the Umm al-Nār cultural type.

It is, of course, far too early to draw any firm conclusions, but it does seem that Salūt was once an important centre with levels of occupation probably going back to the period of the earliest civilization in Oman, and that a major fort was built there by people from Persia in the first millennium, and was abandoned towards the end of this era.

Coupling this evidence to the published archaeological data and some minor local traditions (notably that which claims that the oldest village in Oman is Izki, followed by Nizwā; cf. *Nahḍa*, p. 181, and certain stories about northern Oman recorded by Thomas, 1929), the writer tentatively proposes the following reconstruction of early *qanāt* building in Oman.

The initial network was developed along the western bajada zone during Achaemanid times, probably in roughly the same area as had been occupied by the third-millennium civilization(s) (the settlement of this early civilization was probably based on well irrigation and, perhaps, some exploitation of seasonal *sayl* and perennial *ghayl* flow). There may have been some construction of *qanāt* somewhat earlier in the Dhahira but extension into central Oman began during the Achaemanid period proper from a fortified colony-centre at Salūt, itself dependent on Julfār, then the main port of Mazūn. This work was continued during the Parthian period when a full feudal organization seems to have been introduced: this brought the indigenous population into a serf status in order to provide forced labour (*bēghār*: cf. Mazaheri 1973) for the enormous task of constructing the major *qanāt* on which the main settlements in the bajada zone are founded. It was over part of this irrigation system that the early Arab migrants were eventually to obtain a degree of control towards the end of Parthian times.

Whether or not the writer is stretching the slim evidence too far in this reconstruction, he is sure that some of the *qanāt* of Oman are themselves a living testimony to the one-time presence of early Persian civilizations there. The story of how Sulaymān b. Dawūd built the 10,000 *aflāj* symbolizes the way the newly created Persian state revitalized Oman, by creating 'unfailing springs' in a land that had been occupied only by the bedu since the ancient cultures of Magan (represented by the abandoned fort at Salūt seen by Sulaymān) had passed away, at some time during the course of the second millennium. And the name the Omanis give to a good *qanāt*, 'Dawūdi' (from Sulaymān b. Dawūd), is the Arabs' tribute to the peoples who, through 'infinite toil and expense' really began the permanent development of the resources of this country, some 2,500 years ago.

THE SASĀNID PERIOD

When we move into the Sasānid period (mid-third to mid-seventh century A.D.) the evidence about the work of the Persians becomes much less tentative.

Since the writer has already published a specialized article on this period (Wilkinson 1973; cf. also 1974 and in *J. Omani Studies*, in press), it will suffice here to summarize the relevant conclusions.

Although Persian control over Oman was clearly re-established early in the Sasānid period, inward Arab migration continued, to reach a climax during the weak and unsettled government of Kawādh (A.D. 488-531), at which time a new wave of Arab settlers (the Shanuʾa Azd: cf. Chapter IX) succeeded in carving out tribal territories for themselves in the mountain heartland of Mazūn. Subsequently Khusraw Anūshiravān once again brought the region firmly back into Persian hands, but in doing so he came to a formal understanding with the Arabs that seems to have endured right up to the coming of Islam. Under the terms of this agreement the country was divided into two parts, one of which was deemed to be full Persian territory. The main commercial and military centre here was probably in or near Ṣuḥār (possibly called Omana > Oman?), an important trading-port in the territory of the Persian maritime empire (*Arḍ al-Hind*), but a major subsidiary centre was also developed inland at Rustāq. And it was from the great fort there (the Qalʿat al-Kisra) that the Persian governor controlled rural Mazūn through a modified form of the old Parthian(?) feudal system of frontier lords (*marāziba*), a military aristocracy to whom fiefs had been allocated (*asāwira*), and the main land-colonizing class (*hanāqira*). Near Rustāq too lived the Shanuʾa Azd shaikh whom the Persians appointed as Julandā[7] over all the Arab tribes of Oman (it was probably in order to keep control over his direct tribal followers living in the Ghadaf that Rustāq was selected as the site for the main fortified centre in the interior).

Within this fully Persianized territory the Arabs, who for the most part lived as herdsmen outside the villages, were theoretically administered through their own tribal system (at the head of which was the Julandā), but in reality they were probably more or less directly controlled by the local Persian officials. Those that had settled in the villages were treated like the rest of the subject peasantry (*bayādīr, ahl al-bilād*), while those who worked in the Persian marine or earned their living in the towns were simply considered to be part of the common people (the *ʿulūj*), and they paid their taxes and dues directly to the Persians. Throughout this region the Arabs were regarded as second-class citizens, and such of them as had begun to settle were considered detribalized and incorporated into the 'subject' classes.

Rather different was the situation in that part of Oman which lay outside direct Persian rule. Here the Arabs enjoyed a degree of autonomy, with Persian control exercised indirectly through the Julandā. This Arab territory consisted of the western desert borderlands along with the two areas of the mountain region that lay at the end of their main migration routes into Oman. Of the south-eastern Arab settlement area we know little; it may have had its own Julandā (from the Bani Salīma who occupied the mountains behind Qalhāt, the Jabal Minqāl, and also lived on the Persian coast at the entrance to the Gulf), and his area of control possibly included the whole of the Jaʿlān, the lower Wadi Ṭayyin, and the outer confines of the Sharqīya. The northern area was very much more important and stretched from the borders of the Sirr as far as Julfār. The main centre here was at Tuʾām (Buraimi), but the Arabs were also allowed control of their own port at Dibā; this, along with Ṣuḥār and Damā (respectively at the northern and southern ends of the Batina coast), also formed part of the network of periodic trade fairs which covered the Arabian Peninsula (*Sūq al-ʿArab*), but at Dibā the Julandā had the right to the tithe, whereas in the other two ports it was the Persians who collected it.

Now one of the things that is clear about this second major period of Persian rule in Oman is that there has been a distinct shift eastwards in the principal area of economic activity. Whereas the main Achaemanid and Parthian land colonization appears to have developed along the inner side of the mountain chain from a bridging-point at the Strait of Hormuz, and their main ports were probably located in and around the Musandam Peninsula, the Sasānid interest focused on the development of a maritime empire based on a full exploitation of the monsoon trading pattern, and so tended to make much greater use of the eastern coast of Oman (as also Dhofar). And it was in association with this maritime interest that the major colonization of the Batina littoral strip and of its mountainous hinterland came about.

Unlike their predecessors, who developed the water resources in the bajada zone by means of classical piedmont *qanāt*, the Sasānids had mastered some of the Roman methods of water management, and put their cementing techniques to use for constructing the long channels which brought water from the mountains to supplement that provided by well-irrigation on the coast, and also for building the inverted siphons[8] which made possible the exploitation of the prolific water supplies within the valleys of the Ghadaf: this in turn partly accounts for the differences in the settlement pattern on either side of the range (cf. also the explanations given in Chapter IV).[9] On the other hand, their work was not solely confined to colonizing new land in the east, for whilst they had abandoned the Dhahira to the Arabs, their area of direct rule also included much of the rest of the most fertile parts in Oman. So the writer believes this period also saw an intensification of the old-established *qanāt* network, notably within the mountain area, a possible extension of it south-eastwards to the outer limit of reliable water supply in the Sharqīya, and a development of the water resources on the plateau of the Jabal Akhdhar. Only in the territory which had passed permanently into Arab hands were there no major new developments: on the contrary, decline may already have started there.

Thus the *mise en valeur* of the land of Oman was completed in Sasānid times, and the *qanāt* settlement pattern finally established. And up to the coming of Islam the Arabs were still largely foreigners in the villages, where they represented the threat of the desert to the sown. At best they had a worm's eye view of the organization of the land as they scratched a living as herdsmen, transporters, fishermen, sailors, and weavers. Those that had become cultivators paid heavy taxes to the Persians (cf. Chapter VII) and formed part of the lowest orders in the semi-bureaucratic semi-feudal structure which emerged in Oman after Anūshiravān's reform. Yet their very lowliness may have given them some appreciation of the problems and hardships of peasant life. The writer firmly believes that there was a genuine *rapport* between the ordinary Arab tribesmen and certain of the lower elements of society in the Sasānid lands, the *ᶜulūj*, the *ahl al-bilād*, etc., and this in turn was later to find expression both in the composition of Khawārij bands and in their attitudes towards selecting their leaders. Certain of these egalitarian ideas were thus, right from the start, built into the theory of the Ibāḍi movement, and were to play an important role in integrating the villagers and tribesmen into a single society as well as in breaking down traditional Arab attitudes towards working the soil, once the Imamate was established in Oman. But of the requirements and problems or organizing and administering an agricultural society, the tribesmen can have understood little. True, there were major *qanāt* in the Arab territory (notably in Tuʾām), but the tribesmen's role in these settlements was probably similar to that of the semi-bedu groups who own villages on the desert fringes of Oman today (cf. Chapter IX). While they took the *hanqari*'s share, it was the old subject peasantry (*bayādīr*) who cultivated and operated the irrigation system according to the establihed principles of *qanāt* shareholding. The Arabs did not have to build the *qanāt*, for these were already in existence, while the general security of the land was provided by the Persians and the Julandā. Maintaining their tribal organizations and 'bedu' attitudes, there is no reason to suppose that the Arabs did anything to expand the prosperity of the land or create new settlements in *jāhili* times, any more than they were to do so in the Islamic period.

THE COMING OF ISLAM

Overnight these people found themselves masters of the land. For the Arabs the call to Islam was the call to drive out the Persians. It was not, however, the poorer subject-classes whom they expelled, but the upper echelons of the Persian ruling organization, the governor, along with his *marāziba, asāwira*, and most of the *hanāqira*. At first all went well, for Oman was ruled by governors appointed from Madīna assisted by the Julandā (the title now became a proper name used by members of the ruling clan) who saw to it that justice prevailed and that both the Muslim and non-Muslim taxes were properly collected and correctly used (Ibn Saᶜd I. ii. 18; Ṭabari i, 1686): there was, therefore, no extensive pillaging or excessive exploitation of the property the Arabs acquired through their conquest, and the transfer of power in the villages was probably quite peaceful. Within a few years, however, this relative tranquillity declined. As the tide of Muslim conquest moved into the heart of the Sasānid lands, many Omanis moved to the new *miṣr* of Basra, where they became deeply embroiled in the politics of Iraq and the eastern territories conquered by their armies. Oman itself now lay outside the main centres of political activity and so, as central Islamic government collapsed in ᶜAli's Caliphate, the country's administration foundered in a morass of tribal politics. The Julandā tried to maintain some sort of over-all political control, but such information as we have about conditions in the country indicates that it was torn by political and ideological struggles emanating from tensions within the ruling family, the tribal system, the Khawārij movement, refugee groups from Iraq, and the rival governors nominated from time to time by the Muhallabites and the Caliphate authorities. Finally came the wars associated with the early attempts to establish Ibāḍi government.

Under such conditions the organization of society collapsed, the land was ruthlessly exploited, and centuries of investment became imperilled.

NOTES TO CHAPTER VI

1 The fact that the names of many Omani settlements have an *alif mamdūda* ending and lack the definite article indicates that they may be non-Arab in origin: furthermore we know definitely that two of the most important settlements (Izki and Sumāyil) are pre-Islamic because they changed their name with the change of religion (cf. Chapter X, n. 3).

2 Notably *Tuḥfa* i. 164-5, ii. 45-100; Maᶜwali, pp. 371, 379 80; *Nubdhat al-Maᶜāwil*, p. 432; *Nahḍa*, pp. 60, 97-9. It should be noted that the seventeen *falaj*s (variously listed by the different authors) were restored by Sayf b. Sulṭān (known as Qayd al-Arḍ) and not built by him (Maᶜwāli uses the correct verb *aḥdath*); confirming evidence also arises from the fact that some of them, are specifically mentioned in earlier history, e.g. al-Ṣāyighi (which was the *qanāt* supplying the fort complex built around the prow-shaped Sasānid Qalᶜat al-Kisra at Rustāq and al-Bizayli in the Dhahira.

3 The whole question of the Azd migrations (which is touched on again in Chapter IX) is extremely complex, and the writer hopes in due course to publish a paper devoted to sorting out some of its problems. The Omani story is ignored in the main classical sources, largely, the writer believes, because it does not fit in with Ibn al-Kalbi's manipulations of the Tanūkh migration (notably in Tabari i. 767 et seq., ii. 821 et seq.; Yāqūt art. *al-Ḥīra*) or with the 'Qaḥṭāni' myth (cf. the *Qaṣīda al-Ḥimyarīya*; cf. also Caskel and Strenziock in the introduction to the *Jamharat al-Nasab*, pp. 31-5). Ibn al-Kalbi certainly knew this story, because he is quoted extensively by ᶜAwtabi (probably from his lost work *Kitāb Tafrīq al-Azd*). Traces of the Omani story can however, be found in Ibn Durayd's compromise treatment of the Quḍāᶜa genealogy (*Ishtiqāq*, pp. 542-3: N.B. Ibn Durayd was himself an Omani by origin) and also in some of what Yaᶜqūbi (i. 232-4) says. It should be noted that for studying Arab migration to Oman ᶜAwtabi is absolutely essential: the material in the standard *sīras* (e.g. *Kashf al-Ghumma*) has been lifted from him and makes sheer nonsense out of context (notably the list of tribes that came to Oman after the Mālik b. Fahm migration: Ross's translation only adds to the confusion). One can only tentatively date this migration. The initial stages may have been connected with the turbulent conditions that prevailed in

Southern Arabia from the end of the first century A.D. onwards (cf. von Wissmann 1964, p. 452, and ibid. in EI_2 art Badw), and there is some reason to suppose that the arrival of the tribes on the outskirts of Oman coincides with the collapse of Persian rule in Eastern Arabia at the turn of the second and third centuries.

4 That *qanāt* building was still being carried on when the Arabs arrived is indicated by the fact that Mālik b. Fahm had a *qanāt* built for him at Manḥ during the period of the truce with the Persians.

5 The so-called Ṭasm, Jadīs, and ʿAmālīq who inhabited the desert fringes of settled Arabia were found in and around Oman (Ṭabari i. 213). Furthermore, the very name Oman is reputed to arise from early 'Arab' forebears, ʿUmān b. Qaḥṭān or ʿUmān b. Sinān b. Ibrāhīm who settled in the region. Other authors, predictably enough, try to find the origin of the name in the meaning of the root-letters of the name (e.g. Ibn Durayd *Jamhara* iii. 142), but local sources say the Arabs called Mazūn Oman after the name of a wadi in their original homeland at Mārib! In fact Oman is almost certainly an arabization of an old regional name (Wilkinson 1973).

6 On a visit to the Trucial States in 1970 the writer was shown pieces of pottery and an inscribed block from a major unexcavated archaeological site at Ṭawi Milayḥa (in Sharja territory). Professor A. F. L. Beeston comments on the transcription the writer made of the latter as follows:

The Sharja inscription is interesting. There is a small collection of somewhat similar texts in al-Ḥasā which are in South Arabian script though I have always had my doubts about them being properly speaking 'South Arabian' in language. The Sharja text however is undoubtedly South Arabian in every sense (except that of actual geographic *Fundort*!) and is, so far as I know, the first authentic proof of South Arabian penetration to the east coast. Palaeographically it seems to be approximately of the fifth century B.C. or perhaps a little later, but not much. It is quite clear and reads 'gravestone and grave of Dhariyyat servant of the kings' (*nafs wa-qabr dhariyyat fatā l-mulūk*).

The writer's own investigations into the pottery types confirm a dating which goes back at least to the third century B.C., if not earlier. (Cf. American University of Beirut Museum No. 1423.) The Ṭawi Milayḥa site therefore provides important evidence of an early link between the Old South Arabian civilizations (N.B. The Mārib dam was the original home of the Azd in their legends) and northern Oman.

7 Originally Julandā (variant Julundā) was a title but in Islamic times it became a proper name. The authority of this family of Maʿwali origin (cf. Chapter VIII) continued to be recognized until the Imamate was fully established; the first Omani Imam of the short-lived Imamate in the middle of the eighth century was from the family, but thereafter the Julandā family strenuously opposed the Ibaḍīs so that when their state was established the Imams were nearly all chosen from their 'cousins' the Yaḥmad (Wilkinson in *J. Omani Studies* in press). Another Julandā family, the Julandā b. Karkar of the Bani Salīma, appears to have held control of the entrance to the Gulf until Būyid times: even after this they remained influential there until at least the early thirteenth century. Their power probably finally collapsed with the establishment of Qays as a maritime power (Tiesenhausen 1875; Bergman 1876, Zambaur 1906, pp. 126-7, Iṣṭakhri 140; ʿAwtabi Paris MS. 270v; Yāqūt arts *Huzū* and *al-Dīkdān*).

8 Both Professor R. McC. Adams and Monsieur H. Goblot (personal communications) subscribe to the view that this method of bridging obstacles in *qanāt*, (which demands the same sort of knowledge of cementing techniques as do the open channels of the Batina coast) resulted from the fusion of Persian and Roman knowledge of water management which occurred when the Persians enslaved the Emperor Valerian's army and put it to work to develop the resources of Khūzistān (cf. also Adams 1962).

9 Two other minor pieces of evidence may also be relevant. First, the ancient burial mounds from the 'time of ignorance' which are so characteristic a feature on the hills surrounding the

settlement in the western bajada zone seem to be more or less absent on the eastern side. Second, as far as the writer gathers, the *qanāt* on the western side of the mountains are lined by uncemented dressed stone, a characteristic of pre-Sasānid Persian construction (Māzaheri 1973, p. 23 fn.).

CHAPTER VII

The Impact of Imamate Government on the Social and Economic Organization of the Settled Lands in Oman

'So every group benefited from the Right until God's ordinance was fulfilled; plundering of their wealth was not permitted nor the enslavement of their families' (*Tuḥfa* i. 89). These few words written about the reign of the Imam al-Wārith b. al-Kaʿb al-Kharūṣi (*c.* 179/96-192/808) sum up the social revolution brought about by the establishment of a new order in Oman, that of the Ibāḍi Imamate. For the first time since the period of the so-called Patriarchal Caliphs (*Khulafāʾ al-Rāshidūn*) law and order has been brought to Oman. The exploitation of the peasant classes, the inter-tribal raiding and plundering of the villages which characterized a century and a half of Julandā rule were at last checked, and no longer were the excesses of primitive pastoralists permitted in the settled lands to which the Arabs had fallen heir. The non-Muslim *dhimmis* were organized and protected as *raʿīya* by the Ibāḍi *shurāt*,[1] and only legal taxes were collected. The *shurāt* themselves were organized into groups of two, three, or four hundred under a commander, and over every ten such groups was placed one of the *ʿulamāʾ* trained by the Ibāḍi teachers in Basra. Each *shāri* received a stipend of seven *dirhams* a month from the state property and many used to return the money not spent. Abstinence was encouraged amongst these warriors; a commander who coveted women was instantly dismissed, and marriage was only permitted with the express approval of the Iraqi-trained leaders. In order to protect the poor the dowry was fixed at ten *dirhams*, and no man was permitted to marry a non-Muslim. Such was the reputed spirit of the early Ibāḍis who brought the new order to all parts of Oman.[2]

Although such proselytizing zeal has been somewhat idealized in the local literature and was, in any case, destined to be of short duration, some of the changes brought about by the establishment of Imamate rule were to persist. In this chapter the main objective will be to try and elucidate how far 'God's Ordinances' have played a role in influencing settlement organization in Oman, and to what extent they help to explain the attitudes of the inhabitants towards the land in which they live.

In a study of the history of land-use under the Imamate it would be necessary to examine critically the extent to which such principles have in reality been applied at different periods. But here, where the concern is with attempting to isolate the permanent influences of Ibāḍism, such an approach would be out of place. Thus, for example, interest in the First Imamate will concentrate less on the actual conduct of government than on the semi-idealized image of a golden age as presented by the *ʿulamāʾ* in Omani writings, because it is this image that has inspired Oman's inherently fissiparous tribal society to unite from time to time into some sort of political community, and it is the theoretical abstraction from it of political conduct that has provided the yardstick with which to measure the performance of all subsequent government.

That a structure of socio-political organization more or less established in the ninth century should have persisted until the twentieth century may be difficult for those conditioned to view social institutions as transforming through time to accept, but even a cursory study of Omani written records will convince the sceptic of the extraordinary atemporal quality of local history in the interior of the country. True, the presentation of this history has been formalized, but even so it is quite clear that the fundamental problems which faced Muḥammad b. ʿAbdullāh al-Khalīli in the twentieth century really had changed little from those which faced his forebears over a thousand years before; that is, how to keep the tribes in hand, how to keep the *jabābira* (tyrants, i.e. non-Ibāḍi rulers) at bay, and how to 'realize' the 'true' form of government which God ordained through his Prophet Muḥammad (the *imāma* or Imamate).

THE IBĀḌI CONCEPT OF COMMUNITY ORGANIZATION[3]

The Ibāḍi *madhhab* looks for its origin in the so-called Khawārij schism, officially the first major secessionist movement in Islam. Whatever the historical reality of the interests of the diverse groups who were so labelled after Ṣiffīn (A.H. 38), the fact remains that they did represent a movement of opposition to established government, and they did subscribe to a basic political theory which rationalized that opposition in Islamic constitutional terms. So even though the Ibāḍis themselves perhaps represent the most moderate of the Khawārij groups, and the last to become politically active (beginning of the second century of Islam: specifically A.D. 720 onwards[4]), their basic philosophy still stemmed from the original reactionary doctrine that sought to adapt the nascent principles of Islam to the concepts of a tribal society which found itself increasingly threatened by the new forms of state organization evolving in the wake of the Muslims conquests.

Thus Ibāḍi doctrine must be analysed at two levels. First; that which regulates the Islamic community at the level of the individual: here their *madhhab* shows no more variation from that of the Sunnis than the four legal schools show between each other; indeed, the Ibāḍis themselves simply consider their codification of the *sharīʿa* as the earliest, and therefore the purest, of the Sunni schools (Sālimi *Lumʿa*, and in his introduction to volume III of the *Saḥīḥ* of Rabīʿ b. Ḥabīb; cf. also Rubinacci 1957, p. 37). The second concerns the application of basic Islamic principles (*uṣūl al-fiqh*) to political organization at the level of the state: it is here that the difference between the Sunnis and the Ibāḍis is fundamental, even though there is important common ground between them. Thus the Ibāḍis reject all pre-emptive claims by a particular group to rule the state, and instead subscribe to the view that the Muslim community (*imāma*) selects the man its members deem most worthy to serve as their leader (*Imām*) and that his powers are entirely prescribed by the laws of the Islamic constitution (the *sharīʿa*). So long as the Imam rules according to these laws he has authority (*wilāya*) and his followers are divinely contracted (hence the term *ʿaqd*, which is frequently translated as election) to obey him and may impose no other terms (*shurūṭ*) on him. Constitutionally he becomes 'custodian of the Muslim community and their commonwealth' (*bayt māl al-muṣlimīn wa dawlathum*), and 'no army is assembled, no legal judgement is valid nor punishment imposed except through him'. 'Revolt against the true Imam is the worst of crimes and obedience to him is compulsory.' But if the Imam transgresses God's laws and refuses to make a formal repentance (*tawba*), then it is the duty of the community to dissociate (*barāʾa*) from him and he has lost *wilāya*.

These theoretical aspects of the Imamate, and the formalized adaptations made in Oman, are a subject which largely lies outside the scope of this work but there are certain consequences generally relevant to the theme of settlement organization which arise from them. The first is that the Ibāḍi Imamate is a hopelessly idealistic constitution to provide a permanent basis of government. The identity of the leading Muslims who are to make the election is not clearly defined, while the form of the election is largely interpretative; worthiness to be Imam is obviously debatable ground, as too are the pretexts (*ʿudhr*) for his deposing. Clearly the system contains so many loopholes that it can, and does, rapidly degenerate into secular rule once regligious fervour is undermined by the material benefits which derive from temporal power.

On the other hand, the ideology has enormous appeal. The only criterion which determines status is religious worthiness, and all can aspire to this because *ʿilm* (cf. *ʿulamāʾ*) is a personal acquisition and not transmitted by birth.[5] In theory, therefore, the system is highly democratic, and it serves as a wonderful vehicle for rallying opposition to the rule of 'tyrants' (*jabābira*). This is one of the reasons why Ibāḍi ideology persists even when the Imamate itself is in abeyance (*kitmān*), and why *amīrs*, *mulūk*, and *sulṭāns* tend to model their conduct on that of Imams even though they have not been properly elected. After all, election is only a device (*wasīla*), according to Ibāḍi doctrine, and authority (*wilāya*) ultimately stems from 'mutual satisfaction and acceptance between the leader and his followers'. So if a local ruler more or less conforms to the norms of 'just government' then he is unlikely to receive much opposition either from the tribesmen or from the *ʿulamāʾ*.

By extension, the Ibāḍi theory of the Imamate also serves as the vehicle through which a latent sense of Omani 'nationalism' finds expression. This is why opposition to outside influence in the region is nearly always couched in religious terms and in attempts to rally the tribes under the leadership of an Imam who can legally wage *jihād* against the impious (i.e. non-Ibāḍis).

Another point of importance is that Ibāḍi doctrine recognizes no divorce between 'church' and 'state'. Nowhere can this be more clearly demonstrated than in the theory of military power. The Ibāḍi approach is simple. Because the just Imam and his community are indissolubly bound by a divine contract to support one another, it is the duty of the Muslim to obey his leader in the call to arms. Since the military potential of the community is always at the Imam's disposal he has no need of a standing army; indeed, he is not permitted to have one, for that way lies the slippery path to despotic power (*salṭana*; *jabbāra*).

One practical effect of applying this theory is that physical force remains vested in the hands of the tribal shaikhs; the moment they think their position is threatened they withdraw support from the Imam on the grounds that his actions are innovatory (*bidʿa*) and not within the terms of the established principles of the *sharīʿa* (what is termed in the Imam's election *al-maʿrūf*). In this way the Imam is deprived of any real independence in his conduct of government, and is automatically precluded from imposing any structural changes in the organization of society. Yet even though Ibāḍi government is fettered by the very rigidity of its basic doctrine, and the power of the Imam and the *ʿulamāʾ* is essentially moral and their institutions religious, the Imamate may still flourish (*ẓuhūr*) so long as the community itself stays 'worthy'; once, however, the benefits which derive from political unity begin to feed back into the political system and wealth and power become unevenly distributed, the central authority of the Imam is eroded and the state simply falls apart into its constituent 'tribal' parts.

Thus the Imamate is really no more than a supra-tribal state. The Ibāḍi ethic arose out of tribalism (albeit modified by commercialism), and its practices have been developed to preserve the tribal system. Even the status of the Imam is largely modelled on that of the *tamīma* (paramount shaikh, cf. Chapter VIII) 'selected' to carry out certain prescribed duties for his tribal followers. Like him, the Imam must at all times be accessible to his people, he must consult with their leaders, and he enjoys no more privileged a position than any other Muslim. Nor is he the supreme arbitrator in interpretation of the law: that is a matter for the consensus (*ijmāʿ*) of the leading *ʿulamāʾ* (*ʿulamāʾ al-kibār*). The Imam is no more than a *primus inter pares*.

Here is part of the explanation of why the tribal system of social organization which the Arabs brought with them to Oman was perpetuated as they settled. What exactly is meant by this term 'tribal' will be developed in the following chapters, but that it is a system which is basically ill-adapted to the needs of an agricultural economy based on *falaj* irrigation may be provisionally subsumed.

UNIFICATION OF VILLAGE AND ARAB SOCIETY

One of the great tasks facing the first major line of Imams in the ninth century was to restore the country's economy after the upheavals of the preceding period. Maritime trade soon recovered, and indeed reached new levels of prosperity, once the bases at the entrance to the Gulf of the piratical '*bawārij* of Hind' were destroyed (*Tuḥfa* i. 123; *Kashf* edn. Klein, note 2), but organizing the Omani marine was a relatively easy task compared with tackling the country's internal economy.

The early Imams were faced with a particularly difficult problem, for it was essential that a new system of village organization be introduced if agriculture was not finally to collapse. This was a matter of urgency, for ever since the Sasānid regime had given way to the rule of a people who had little experience in the ways of village life, the yield of the land must have been declining. True, the kind of terms the Arabs had first agreed with the *dhimmis* in the Gulf, by which the villagers paid half the produce of their land to the Arabs (Balādhuri *Futūḥ*, p. 78 et seq.), probably imposed no larger a burden on the peasant class than that which they were accustomed to paying their former Persian overlords: but the reciprocal security the villagers originally enjoyed was lost, once the Islamic regime guaranteed by the Madinese-appointed governors collapsed. By the latter part of the Julandā period, virtually all influences restraining tribal exploitation were removed. Not only was this Arab regime rapacious in its demands on the yield of the land, it was also parasitic in that it failed even to provide basic administration capable of maintaining the irrigation systems on which the livelihood of Arab and non-Arab alike ultimately depended.

As we have seen, this situation was initially rectified by the new Ibāḍi government, organizing the *dhimmis* into properly protected groups (*raᶜāyā*) in accordance with the principles developed in early Islamic times. In return for the right to retain non-Muslim status and occupation of land the villagers paid the *jizya* poll tax (this removed some of the discrepancies of the early *ad hoc* treaty terms); but now they really did enjoy the security and other rights to which they were entitled as second-class citizens of the Muslim state. Once basic order had been established, however, the processes of sedentarization began to modify the relationships between the Arab Muslims and the Persianized non-Muslim population whilst the conversion of the '*majūs*' was probably actively encouraged, even though it would have meant a loss of income to the state as the *jizya* was replaced by the much less onerous *ᶜushr* (tithe) taxation system to which Muslims were subject (see pp. 145-8).

Also helping to break down some of the old barriers that existed between the Arab tribesmen and the Persianized villagers were certain egalitarian principles inherent in the Ibāḍi system of government. Thus, even though the Ibāḍis did not go so far as some of the more extreme Khawārij groups in selecting an Imam, the head of the community could come from a relatively humble back-ground, and it is worth noting that the first full Imam of Oman, al-Wārith b. al-Kaᶜb al-Kharūṣi al-Yaḥmadi, appears to have originated from a family of small farmers even though he was a tribesman of impeccable descent (*Tuḥfa* i. 115). Again, while we know nothing of his personal background, his successor, the Imām Ghassān b. ᶜAbdullāh al-Yaḥmadi, certainly showed a real awareness of village problems (cf. *Tuḥfa* i. 125-8), and it was during his Imamate that the first, and one of the most fundamental rulings concerning *falaj* organization, is recorded.[6]

So with their own Imams taking a close interest in the land, the general attitude of the tribesmen towards agricultural work must also have started to change. Certainly the names of the *khabūras* shown in Table 10 (which as explained in Chapter V probably preserve in them elements of the land-tenure system in Izki about this time) indicate that even though the Arab clans and the indigenous groups were then still living quite separately, the former had begun to own their own land, and this incorporation into village life is also reflected in an increasing use of village rather than tribal *nisbas* (surnames) during the First Imamate. In turn these shifts in attitude would have speeded up the merging of the Arab and non-Arab populations.

Integration of the villagers and tribesmen into a single social structure is in fact one of the most remarkable features of present-day village organization in Oman. In other parts of the Middle East and North Africa such homogeneity is rare, and studies like Bujra's (1971) on Ḥurayḍa in Ḥaḍramawt, or Champault's (1969) on Tabelbala in the North-West Sahara, clearly shows that class structure has often been deliberately preserved through the exclusive social organization of immigrant groups. It is particularly interesting to contrast the attitudes displayed elsewhere towards those who do the actual work on the land with those prevailing in Oman (cf. the role of the *bayādīr* in Oman, the *ḥirthān* of Ḥaḍramawt, and the *harratīn* of Tabelbala). This subject of assimilation has already been studied by the writer in some detail (Wilkinson 1974): the conclusions may be summarized as follows:

1. There are elements in Omani society, notably the numerically important *bayāsira*, which the Arabs have continued to reject and who still only enjoy client (*mawlā*) status. These groups probably represent the descendants of some of the earliest inhabitants of the Arabian Peninsula enslaved by Persian and Semitic migrants; even the influence of Ibāḍism has been unable to break down the prejudices against such people who are considered to have no *aṣl* (racial origin).

2. By contrast the *ahl al-bilād*, the subject peasantry of Persian times, were gradually assimilated into the Arab tribal structure and in central Oman, where the influence of Ibāḍism is particularly strong, the term *bīdār* is now merely an occupational classification, whereas in northern Oman, where new Arab groups have entered the region since the collapse of the original Ibāḍi Imamate, it retains many of the overtones associated with the word *mawlā*. In both areas, however, the work organization of the *bayādīr* shows vestiges of the old pre-Islamic order (cf. Section III in Chapter V).

3. The Arabs themselves became cultivators, and as they did so, the old prejudices against working the land disappeared.[7] This is what 'ᶜAyyūb b. Kirriba' (cited Quatremère 1835; cf. also Nöldeke 1871) meant when he said that whereas the 'Nabateans' (i.e. sedentary population) of 'Baḥrayn' became Arabs (nomads), the Arabs of Oman became Nabateans. ᶜAyyūb's remark is

nevertheless very misleading, for, whilst it is true that 'Nabatean' indicates sedentary, it also implies non-tribal (cf. Ibn Khaldūn *Prologomena*, chap. II, §9), and this by no means describes the situation in Oman, where the Arabs as they settled introduced their *ʿarab* (bedu) system of social organization into village life, and assimilated the Nabatean (sedentary) population as equals into it.

THE PERPETUATION OF THE ORIGINAL SETTLEMENT PATTERN

So Ibāḍi government helped close the gap that originally existed between the Arabs and the inhabitants of the land to which they had fallen heir with the coming of Islam, and in doing so put a stop to the economic decline of the Julandā period. But in the process it more or less froze the economic and social life of the country, through fixing its settlement pattern around the new structure of society it created.

The pre-existing population centres were maintained, and, as will be shown in later chapters, a new form of tribal organization grew up around this fixed settlement pattern. Concomitantly economic and administrative functions remained decentralized, so no urban development occurred in the interior. The Imam as head of state did have a fixed residence (perforce in the tribal interior in direct contact with his followers[8]), but since he had no formal advisory body, no standing army, and no court society, none of the institutions normally associated with a 'capital' really emerged at Nizwā or Rustāq[9] (any more than they did at Bahlā, where the Nabāhina maintained an equally decentralized system of government during the longest period of non-Imamate rule in the country's history). How the seat of government might have developed had the Ibāḍi-tribal system broken down is indicated by the way Nizwā grew during Muhannā b. Jayfar's Imamate (A.D. 841-51). He, it is recorded (*Tuḥfa* i. 150-1), maintained 10,000 troops along with 8,000 or 9,000 riding beasts in his capital; in addition he had living in his service in the quarter of Suʿāl below his fort no less than 14,000 subject peoples (*raʿāyā*). In other words, Nizwā had a population at least three times larger than 'normal'. (It was incidentally to prevent a recurrence of such centralized power that the *ʿulamāʾ* finally formalized certain interpretations of the constitutional powers of the Imam, and disbanded the early *shurāt* organization described at the beginning of this chapter.)

Ibāḍi influence also emphasized the dichotomy inherent between coastal and interior Oman and more or less isolated the latter into a self-supporting cultural and political unit. True, some measure of trade always continued between the two, but for the outward-looking cosmopolitan society of the main port, hinterland commerce was normally of relatively little significance and often organized quite separately from the entrepôt trade (cf. Muscat and Maṭraḥ; Qalhāt and Sūr, Ṣuḥār and Dibā, at various periods of history). Only when Oman was unified did this level of economic interchange tend to rise; but, as explained in Chapter VI, the intrusion of wealth into the interior in the form of capital investment automatically triggered off reaction in the tribal system, so that the new linkages between coast and interior were destroyed. So while Ibāḍi government did at various times become involved in maritime commerce and even occasionally support a powerful fleet, its attempts to bridge the two Omans were inevitably doomed, and the interior always finally closed in on itself. Its villages were never really affected by the changing fortunes of maritime trade, and commercial organization in the interior hardly ever rose above the level of the periodic market.

Thus Ibāḍism not only helped maintain the tribal system, it also perpetuated a settlement pattern associated with it.

THE IMPACT OF THE SHARĪʿA[19]

To complete this survey of the influence of Ibāḍism on settlement organization in Oman it remains to discuss the specific impact of certain *sharīʿa* rulings. These will be considered first as regards laws that apply generally throughout the Islamic world, and then as regards rulings specific to the Ibāḍi system of government.

Inheritance Laws

If it is true, as the writer has suggested earlier, that the Ibāḍi *madhhab* really does differ little from the Sunni *madhhabs* at the personal level, then there should be little that is special about the Omani situation. That this is not altogether the case therefore suggests that either the hypothesis is incorrect or some of the presumptions underlying commonly accepted thinking about the relationship of Islam and the land need questioning. One particularly important case in point concerns Islamic inheritance laws, which are often invoked to explain parcellation of land holdings and hence agricultural inefficiency: this thesis would certainly also appear to apply to Oman, if Fig. 24, which shows how one particular water right in the Falaj Malki has been subdivided over a period of roughly fifty years, is to be taken at face-value.

Yet if these inheritance laws are examined carefully it will be seen that they contain nothing to indicate that the land is treated more unfavourably than other elements of economic production: rights of succession are just as liable to break up a merchant's business or a nomad's herd as they are a piece of cultivated land, should the heirs fail to co-operate. And herein surely lies the original main purpose of the laws; to ensure that while each member of the family, male and female, is provided for, family entity is reinforced by having to work together to maintain the viability of a heritage. Thus if each heir takes his inheritance in kind and insists that the holding is physically divided, then all members of the family lose; if, on the other hand, the heirs regard their inheritance as a share in a joint holding, then family ties are strengthened and economic linkages reinforce the social ones. There is however one pre-condition for expecting such co-operation; that is, that members of a family should marry endogamously (amongst themselves). Once members of the

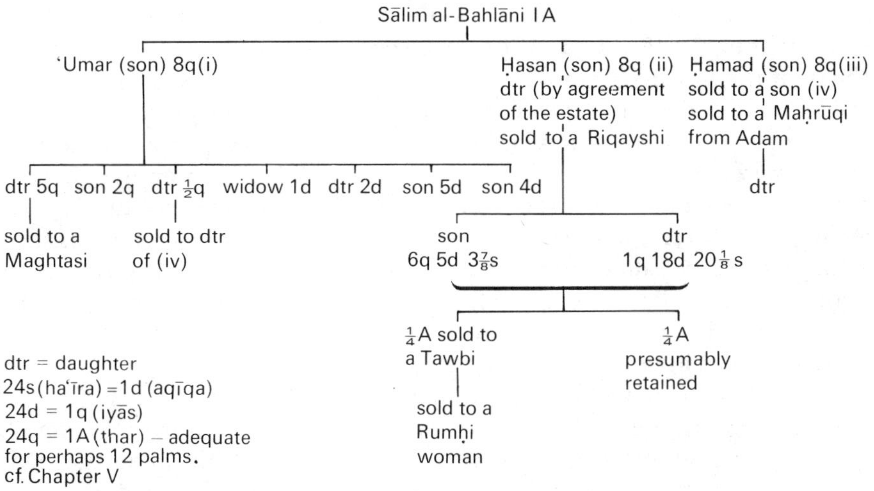

Fig. 24. Changes in ownership of a water holding (taken from the Malki Falaj book).

family marry outside the self-supporting social isolate, then rights to capital have to be realized, transference of property becomes necessary, and land-holdings are physically split up. It is unfortunate, therefore, that in many areas of the world Muslim inheritance laws have been applied to societies for which they were not originally designed and consequently do play a role in fragmenting land-holdings. But in Oman, where village society is largely made up of family-groups practising parallel-cousin marriage (cf. Chapter VIII) physical fragmentation of property does not appear to be a major problem. For example, while it is true that the specific evidence provided by the *Falaj Malki* book does show that inheritance laws keep holdings fairly small, it also shows that these are frequently operated as a joint family concern: thus when a shareholder dies, his (or her) rights are notionally split amongst the heirs as prescribed by the *sharīʿa* (as shown in Fig. 24), but the holdings are immediately reshuffled so that in the end the total number of operational units in the village changes little (even if there is an increase in total population). From the point of view of the way land is held, therefore, the writer believes that the inheritance laws, *per se*, are not detrimental to the efficient organization of the agricultural settlements of Oman: on the contrary, they are socially helpful, because they tend to maintain a reasonable distribution of wealth amongst the inhabitants and strengthen certain co-operative systems in the villages. Conversely, of course, they also play a role in perpetuating the clan system which underlies the social organization that is labelled 'tribal' (these points are further discussed in Chapters VIII and X).

Taxation

The second aspect of the application of the *sharīʿa* rulings to land organization in Oman that requires examination is specific to the Ibāḍi system of government organization, and concerns the strict adherence to the tax laws and the permitted forms of state expenditure.

While it is convenient to refer to the financial impositions prescribed by the *sharīʿa* as 'tax', it should be remembered that the original purpose of levying what is variously termed as *zakāt, ṣadaqa,* and *ʿushr*, was to ensure that the more affluent members of the community fulfilled the social duty of supporting its poorer members. Although such a view of Islamic taxation might be considered somewhat hypothetical even for an Ibāḍi government seeking to live up to the ideals of early Islam, the fact remains that the *sharīʿa* did introduce quite new concepts, both of the way money was to be raised from the land, and of how it was to be spent.

In pre-Islamic times there appear to have been two main systems of taxing crops operating in the western part of the Sasānid Empire: the one a proportional levy amounting to between a half and a sixth of the yield according to the nature of the cultivation and the facilities provided, the other a payment fixed on the basis of the area under cultivation. The latter system, introduced in the fifth century by Kawādh, required proper cadastral surveys and was probably designed for regions of extensive grain cultivation like the Sawād of Iraq (cf. Ṭabari i. 960-3; Māwardi, pp. 256-7; Løkkegaard 1950, pp. 109-10). For this reason alone it is highly unlikely that it was in use anywhere in Oman. There is however, some positive evidence that proportional levies were imposed in Oman: this is the reference to the *khirāṣ* and *mikyal* that occurs in a letter supposedly written by the Prophet to two of the Arab tribes living in northern Mazūn (Ibn Saʿd I. ii. 35); if this source is genuine then it also indicates that the tax liability was assessed before the crop was harvested,[11] a manifest unfairness which was automatically rectified in the Islamic code whereby crops are taxed in kind, quality for quality, after harvesting.

The *sharīʿa* system however, went much further than just rectifying such relatively minor injustices of the old system: it entirely revolutionized the basic concept of taxation (at least for Muslims in the *ʿushr* lands). Instead of trying to extract as much money as it could from the yield of the land it started from the standpoint of the individual and assessed him according to his means.

So under Islamic laws as they apply in Oman, *zakāt* is only due on six kinds of agricultural produce: *barr, shaʿīr, dharra, sult, zabīb,* and *tamar* (Jannāwuni pp. 476-505). The first four classes cover various grain crops, the fifth refers to dried fruits like raisins and figs, and the sixth to dried dates. In certain Sunni *madhhabs* there is a tendency to move away from the concept of only taxing durable produce, but the Ibāḍis adhere to it rigidly. All fresh fruits, legumes, green fodder, grasses, and pulses[12] are exempt, as also are freshly picked dates (*ruṭab* and *bisr*; cf. Sālimi *Jawhar*, pp. 117-19 for discussion of the principal, and *Tuḥfa* i. 190 for ruling during the First Imamate).

It is obvious from the foregoing list that the *sharīʿa* rules were evolved to suit agricultural economies typical of the Arabian Peninsula. This in turn once again illustrates that problems only arise when the early Islamic guidelines are literally applied outside the context of the region for which they were developed. Thus the exemption from taxation of green crops is obviously not aimed at exonerating wealthy farmers who specialize in growing these crops, but at freeing the poor man, laboriously scratching a living on the fringe of the desert, from liability to pay the tithe on his little plot of vegetables and animal-feed. Similarly, because fishermen and donkey-breeders are nearly always poor people in a place like Oman, they too are classed as *miskīn* in *sharīʿa* law and exempted from taxation, unlike camel- and small-livestock-herders, who may be relatively rich (*Tuḥfa* i. 89; Saʿīd b. Khalfān al-Khalīlī *Laṭāʾif*). Nor is the *sharīʿa* concerned with taxing perishable produce such as milk, vegetables, or dates when they first ripen, for in the traditional economies of the Peninsula these are not major items of trade and only have temporary value. On the other hand what it is interested in is taking something of durable value from the rich to give to the poor; and so it imposes a form of annual capital tax on the wealthier members of society. In a largely non-monetized economy this is taken in kind, from the merchants so much gold and silver, from the herdsman so many head of livestock, and from the cultivator a certain proportion of the non-perishable produce that represents a potential increment to his capital. To ensure that the small man does not suffer from these rough-and-ready methods of tax assessment, holdings below a certain size (the *niṣāb*) are exempted.

Two rates of taxation apply to cultivation, and the only criterion followed for selecting one or the other is the amount of physical labour employed. So where cultivation involves little or no manual labour for watering the crop, as for example in the cases of dry-land farming (*baʿl*), or where irrigation channels flow directly from the water source to the gardens, then the full tithe (*ʿushr*) is due; if it involves drawing water by manual labour (with or without the assistance of animals), or the water has to be transported physically to the place of use, then the tax is half this rate (i.e. 5 per cent). The special case of *qanāt*, usually referred to by the jurists as *kaẓāʾim*, are subject to the higher tax rate because the water flows without the use of labour, and so they belong to the class of irrigation system which also includes rivers and is generically referred to as *anhār* (cf. Qudāma, p. 37; Khuwārazmī, p. 71; Māwardī, pp. 258-9; *Lisān al-ʿArab*, art. *QNA*). In Oman therefore, the people of the Batina Coast pay 5 per cent on most of their dates because they are irrigated by a well system involving considerable manual work,[13] but in the villages of the interior the rate is normally 10 per cent. Both rates are obviously very low when compared to the amounts that the villagers must have paid to the Persians in pre-Islamic times or to the Arabs immediately after the conquest: but it does seem reasonable that the people of the Batina should pay less in view of the fact that they must work harder to gain their living. At least, so it would appear, until it is realized that the villagers of the interior pay the same tax on their produce whether the water supply is from a simple *ghayl falaj* or a costly *qanāt*.

THE PERPETUATION OF ARAB ATTITUDES TOWARDS THE LAND

So far in this discussion the writer has been maintaining that the laws of the *sharīʿa* are beneficial to the individual cultivator because they appear to have been designed for just the type of society and environment that exists in Oman. But once we begin to look at these laws from the point of view of the agricultural economy as a whole the picture changes considerably for, amongst other failings, they take absolutely no account of the capital factor in production. Whether Muḥammad really was still as ignorant of agricultural practices at the time when his every word was being accepted as divine, as not even to know how palm trees were fertilized (cf. Yaḥyā b. Adam text, pp. 79-80) is perhaps debatable ground, but that his experience was pretty limited is obvious; and in so far as he did make recommendations about cultivation, they were largely based on second-hand gleanings from Companions who knew little more than he. So to apply reported sayings that were at best appropriate only to the simpler forms of irrigation techniques then in use in Western Arabia to the capital-intensive irrigation system which the Arabs inherited from the Persians in Oman was, to say the least, unfortunate. True, the *ʿulamāʾ* have interpreted some of these guidelines as liberally as possible (cf. for example the rulings dealing with methods of distributing water discussed in Chapter V), but their rigid adherence to the principles of taxation and other matters involving state organization has inevitably had the effect of perpetuating many of the old Arab attitudes towards the land. To treat *qanāt* as though they were the same as a *ghayl* or river water simply reflects the kind of ignorance which led the Arabs to attribute the Omani irrigation system to the supernatural powers of Sulaymān b. Dawūd. And if the jurists classify all these irrigation systems as *anhār*, is it any wonder that the ordinary Arab in Oman consider them as *aflāj*, God-given gifts to be 'shared'?

Such unrealistic attitudes towards the economic infrastructure of community organization are also manifest in the low priority which Ibāḍi law accords to investment in the land. This will be illustrated by a brief study of the Imamate budget.

The State Budget

Zakāt is the only tax levied on Muslims, and so it makes up by far and away the largest part of the state's regular income.[14] Other local sources of income and capital are unreliable and often only of historical interest. Thus when the Imamate has control of the coast it derives some income from foreign non-Muslim merchants (notably 'Banians'), but while as '*ḥarbis*' their taxation rates may be higher than those applying to Muslims in fact they rarely pay more (cf. the reasons given in Chapter I). Originally *jizya* payments from resident non-Muslims must have been of considerable importance, but the receipts would have rapidly decreased once the *majūs* converted to Islam, for the *kharāj* rules (which made the land rather than the owner liable to tax) never applied in Oman.

The right to a fifth of the booty (*khums al-ghanīma*) certainly provided income at the height of the great Imamates (e.g. the Yaʿāriba were able to carry out many of their works with the plunder from the Portuguese at home and abroad),[15] but when the Imamate is confined to the interior it is of no significance. In this connection it should be noted that Muslim enemies of the state may not be plundered or enslaved (cf. Qalhāti, 198[r]), so that confiscating the property of local rulers overthrown by a restored Imamate government is considered highly dubious legal procedure, and when indulged in has inevitably led to serious repercussions.[16] Finally, the state does acquire some '*ṣawāfi*'[17] property by regular processes, through inability to trace owners, and from bequests and rights of reverter under the inheritance laws (*mawārith ḥashrīya*);[18] but the total is not great, and this source of income may be considered of little importance (on the Izki *falaj*, for example, the total *bayt al-māl* holdings from all sources in 1825 only represented about 8 per cent of the shares).

It can be seen that outside the exceptional periods of the First and Yaʿāriba Imamates, state income has been more or less limited to the *zakāt*. Since this imposes very low rates of tax (none of which go above 10 per cent) this means that the state budget is small. Furthermore, there is nothing government can do to supplement it or to alter the taxation system. Once again the Ibāḍis find themselves shackled by the rigidity of their principles, principles which were in reality developed in a period when Oman was a powerful maritime state and earning large sums of money from its non-Muslim population.

Rigid principles also govern the way this money can be disbursed. Thus the Quranic rulings (*Ṣūra* ix. 58-60) are quite clear about the principle of how *zakāt* is to be spent: it is to be distributed to the needy and deserving. Unfortunately it is less precise about exactly who receives what, for while it designates eight classes of recipients, four general and four special, it also adds that *zakāt* may be used *li sabīl Allāh* (for God's purpose). Now there are no less than five guidances affecting the interpretation of this clause (cf. the discussion in the work of the Maghribi Ibāḍi jurist Jannāwuni, pp. 515 ff.), but while all *madhhabs* agree that 'God's purpose' includes *jihād*,[19] the Ibāḍis refuse to accept the 'let-out' interpretation that it means the general requirements of the Imam (*ḥājāt al-Imām*), for that may lead to a devaluation of the true puposes of *zakāt* and encourage tyranny (Sālimi *Jawhar*, pp. 122-3). So the interpretation that generally seems to have obtained in Oman from the time of the First Imamate onwards is that one-third of the taxes collected should be distributed to the poor in the area where they are collected (cf. the letter of appointment of the *wāli* of Rustāq quoted in *Tuḥfa* i. 190-2): this third represents the apportionment to the four easily identifiable Quranic classes (the *fuqarāʾ*, *masākīn*, *ghārimūn*, and *ruqqāb*). The other two-thirds corresponds to the four obscure special classes along with the *li sabīl Allāh* purpose, and so goes into the communal *bayt al-māl* fund administered directly by the Imam; in cases of extreme emergency, however, some maintain that the needs of the Imamate may take precedence over the disbursement to the poor (*Ṣāʾighi bāb al-imāma*, pp. 131 ff.).

So it is from these two-thirds of the *zakāt* plus any other *ṣawāfī* revenues (the capital it should be noted is, in principle, held mortmain)[20] that the Imam has to administer the state. The first call on his funds are the stipends of state employees and military and security expenses; it is only when these have been met that income may then be expended on such public works as irrigation, roads, and the like (Ṣāʾighi *loc. cit.*). The state may not normally borrow for the latter purposes, because indebtedness is only permitted for military and security needs (cf. *Tuḥfa*, i. 125 for *qarḍ al-difāʿ*).

Thus by the time *zakāt* is collected in kind and converted into cash and subventions given to the shaikhs (which in effect is what military and security expenses mean), little remains for expenditure on capital projects.

AN EXAMPLE OF IBĀḌI LAND ADMINISTRATION

Despite this shortage of funds, the Imamate does sometimes succeed in spending some money on development, as the following account of the administration of Abu Zayd ʿAbdullāh b. Muḥammad al-Riyāmi, who, for thirty years, was *wāli* (governor) at Bahlā on behalf of both the twentieth-century Imams, will show. This account, presented as a summary of his biography as given in the *Nahḍa* (pp. 420 ff.), will also help to give the reader some general feel of the kind of 'just' government that we have been discussing.

The first feature of the *wāli* that the biographer stresses is his simplicity and piety. This is exemplified by describing how he personally used to help the garrison of the Bahlā castle collect firewood, and how he removed with his own hand the water-moss from the irrigation channels belonging to the *bayt al-māl*. He lived most frugally, and half a *raṭl* of dates from the *bayt al-māl* sufficed for the needs of his household. He absolutely refused all presents from those whom he governed, even to the extent of a drink of water at a man's house. His *majlis* was simple, and he kept a very close personal eye on affairs in Bahlā, going out by day and night to inspect his district. As well as being a man of action, renowned for his courage, he was a scholar of no mean ability. He had studied under ʿAbdullāh b. Ḥumayd al-Sālimi, and wrote a book on grammar as well as pious and legal works. Before his appointment as *wāli* he had instructed in the Masjid al-Ḥawāri in Izki, his adopted home, and the famous *ʿālim*, Muḥammad b. Sālim al-Riqayshi numbered amongst his pupils.

The biography then continues with a list of some of the works he carried out as *wāli*. He paid particular attention to the defences of his region, repairing the forts at Jabrīn and Bahlā and ensuring that their needs were properly furnished. He purchased considerable quantities of weapons over which he kept personal control, and spent 70,000 Omani *qirsh* (Maria Theresa dollars: i.e. then *c.* £20,000) on maintaining the great outer wall which defends the lands of Bahlā. Roads were repaired and thirty wells dug to provide for time of drought; he also appointed an agent to supervise the proper upkeep of the wells in the desert. His major work of development however, consisted of restoring the al-Maḥyūl branch of the Falaj al-Jizyayn[21] at a cost of over £22,000 (N.B. this at between-world-war values): by decree of the Imam the water was shared between the peoples of Upper and Lower Bahlā. He also carried out repair work on the Falaj al-Maytā (var. al-Mēthi), cementing all its branches from the Khaḍr quarter to the walls of lower Bahlā, and made unspecified repairs to the Maḥdith *falaj*. (This meant that in fact he carried out major improvements on three of Bahlā's five *aflāj*; the other two are Maqīl and ᶜAyn Lāmih.)

The author of the *Nahḍa* also states that the *wāli* paid considerable attention to making sure that *bayt al-māl* and *waqf* property was well invested: he cites as examples the fact that Abu Zayd planted over 7,000 palms for the *bayt al-māl*, of which 500 were of the valuable *khalāṣ* variety, and that he also tried to re-establish sugar growing: such investments meant that in summer no less than 430 *mabkhūr* ([sic], *makhbūr*?, shares, presumably *athar*s, half-hour periods, cf. Chapter V) of water a day had to be rented.

However, all these achievements of the worthy Abu Zayd must not blind us to the basic fact that the financial resources of the Imamate are extremely limited, and development takes low priority in the way funds are spent. The only really important sums spent on the country's economic infrastructure in the past have always derived from Oman's overseas activities. Whenever Omani government has been denied the wealth of her maritime trade, the agricultural heritage has been neglected. So it was not until the seventeenth century (when the Yaᶜāriba, for the first time since the collapse of the First Imamate in the ninth century, carved out a powerful mercantile empire and filled the state coffers with the booty of the Portuguese) that active steps were taken to repair the ravages that the country's irrigation system had suffered since the First Imamate broke up in civil war eight centuries before. But the great works of investment carried out by the Yaᶜāriba (cf. Chapter VI) signalled a move away from the law and spirit of the primitive Ibāḍi Imamate. The succession became dynastic, the Imams failed to make proper payments for development, they favoured certain tribes at the cost of others, they encouraged capitalist land finance, and much of their personal property should have belonged to the *bayt al-māl*. Eventually revolt broke out, central government collapsed, property was destroyed, and tribal rule once again held sway. The concomitant was a renewed decline in the agricultural prosperity of the country.

Summary

Such is the penalty that has had to be paid for the admirable democratic principles of the Imamate and for maintaining tribal concepts of personal freedom. Under the Sasānid organization the peasant had to pay heavily for use of the land, and in those days the idea that a third of the product of the land should be paid in tax, a third used for the maintenance of the tillage, and only the remaining third retained by the tax-payer for the nourishment of his family seems to have been considered a fair principle (cf. Løkkegaard 1950, p. 110). While this is obviously too facile a generalization to accept at face-value, it does at least reflect something of the realities of developing and maintaining a sound agricultural economy in an insecure human and physical environment. Certainly the capital and maintenance costs of *qanāt* are high and can only leave a comparatively small return for the farmer. Beckett and Gordon (1966) conclude from their study of *qanāt* in the Kirmān district, 'In order to yield only a reasonable return on the considerable sum of money invested in a *qanāt* the land-owner's share of the crops irrigated is about 70 per cent of the yield which leaves the peasant cultivator little incentive to increase his crop by more painstaking husbandry', while Sir John Malcolm (1815, ii. 472) was of the opinion that the Persian taxation system on Crown Lands, by which the peasant paid 50 per cent, rising in places to 75 per cent of his produce to the King, was very favourable to the peasant if the land was properly administered. Whether we concur with Sir John's opinion or not, the fact remains that where marginal land has been developed by an expensive irrigation system like *qanāt* it is certainly necessary that the farmer pays a considerable proportion of his yield to those who provide him with the facilities and the security which allow him to grow and harvest his crops in peace.

The paradox of Islamic law lies in the fact that in the conquered land the Muslims were able to recognize such economic realities: the *fay*ʾ irrigated by *qanāt* in Persia, for example, was taxed more lightly than that watered by other means because the profit was less (Lambton 1953, chap. 2). But in their homelands the Muslims had to introduce tax régimes that were only appropriate for a tribal society living on the fringe of the settled land and designed to perpetuate the structure of that society. Hence the anomaly of Oman. Although Ibāḍism did away with many of the injustices of the past, spread the wealth inherited from the old régime amongst all the inhabitants, and gave the villagers a new dignity, it utterly failed to produce a system of organization which even maintained the yield of the land, let alone increase it. Based on an ethos that was opposed to capitalist tenure, Arab government in Oman not only did little to encourage private investment in the land, it also failed to provide the alternative of an efficient state organization of the economy. Precluded from intervening in the affairs of individual communities, each village was left to look after its own piece of land. In some measure, as shown in Chapter V, the villagers did succeed in organizing themselves to meet this challenge, and are able to finance the normal maintenance of their *qanāt*: but in the event of major disaster, whether the work of nature or, as has all too frequently been the case, that of man, there has been no outside organization to help them and so more and more settlement has been abandoned. Even more serious, perhaps, is the fact that there has been no financial organization set up to ensure that the long-term maintenance of the irrigation system is carried out: the villagers themselves rarely recognize the causes which imperceptibly, but inexorably, diminish the flow of their water supplies, and they have evolved no methods for amassing a fund to finance the major overhauls which are periodically needed.

These are some of the reasons why the area under cultivation in Oman is today but a shadow of the 'land abounding in fields and groves' that the Persians created. The penalty paid for some of the more admirable social concepts that the Ibāḍi state has brought to Oman has been the inability of the tribesmen fully to adapt to the requirements of an agricultural community. It speaks volumes for the work of the Persians that the *qanāt* irrigation system they bequeathed the Arabs has survived in any way at all some 1,200 years of exploitation by such a turbulent people.

NOTES TO CHAPTER VII

[1] *Shurāt*, the military activists, those who 'buy' their salvation in the afterlife by selling their lives for the faith in this world: as Abu Isḥāq Ibrāhīm b. Qays al-Hamdāni, eleventh-century leader of the Ḥaḍrami Ibāḍis, says in his *Dīwān* (p. 119), 'I am the *shārī* man who has made a contract for his soul; he wakes in the morning hoping for death in the fight [for the good] after the model of Mirdās [Abu Bilāl Mirdās b. ʿUdayya].'

[2] This account of the organization of the Ibāḍi *shurāt* is taken from the *sīra* of one of the original Basran-trained Ibāḍi missionaries, Munīr b. Nayr al-Riyāmi (quoted *Tuḥfa* i. 89 92). It specifically applies to the short-lived Imamate of al-Julandā b. Masʿūd (mid-eighth century) but it is clear from later references to the *shurāt* that some similar sort of organization of religious warriors continued at least for the early part of the First Imamate.

[3] The following account of the Ibāḍi movement is mainly drawn from primary Omani and Maghribi Ibāḍi sources, and is too compressed for detailed references to be given. The most important source used for the outline of the theory of the Imamate is the *bāb al-imāma*. (81r 99r) in Ṣāʾighi's *Kanz al-adīb*: a fuller treatment of this subject will be found in Wilkinson B.S.O.A.S. (in press).

[4] Although the Ibāḍis take their name from a figure of an earlier period, ʿAbdullāh Ibn Ibāḍ, he was a very shadowy and unimportant personage in the history of the movement: indeed, many Ibāḍi sources when discussing their sect omit all mention of him.

[5] In Oman there is no inherited religious status. Indeed the only family with a claim to a Qurashi relationship, the Āl Raḥīl, was one of the most active proponents of this Ibāḍi system which recognized no family claim to lead the Imamate.

[6] This was the all-important principle that a *qanāt* community has access to the headwaters of its irrigation supply even if this lies in the territory of another group. For the story of how this Imam came to reorganize his officials because of a decline in the agricultural yield of the land, see p. 100.

[7] Rössler (1898, fn p. 72) remarks 'Sclaven werden in ʿOmān hauptsächlich zur Bedienung im Hause verwendet. Feldarbeit wird von Freien, Arabern, gethan . . .'

[8] This is why the great cosmopolitan port of Ṣuḥār, although the seat of government in both the Sasānid and early Islamic period, was not chosen when the Imamate was established. It is also one of the reasons why the Āl Bu Saʿīd dynasty failed to maintain political control in Oman once they shifted their capital from the interior first to Muscat, and subsequently to Zanzibar and Salāla (in Dhofar); this was a mistake the Yaʿāriba Imams never made, even though their interests, like those of the Āl Bu Saʿīd, were increasingly orientated towards their maritime empire.

[9] Nizwā was chosen as capital of the First Imamate, partly because of the tribal balance existing there (cf. Wilkinson 1972). It has always been considered the 'correct' seat for the Imam but Rustāq has also been used, notably by the Yaʿāriba.

[10] The specifically Ibāḍi practices mentioned in the following discussion are based on a number of works. For the system of taxation, (the Maghribi Ibāḍi, fl. end second century A.H.) Jannāwuni's section on *zakāt* is most comprehensive, and may be compared to a standard treatment in an Omani source such as the eighteenth-century Maḥrūqi; al-Sālimi's *Jawhar* and *Talqīn al-Ṣubayān* and Saʿīd b. Khalfān al-Khalīli's special work on the taxation of livestock are also of passing interest. Inheritance laws are dealt with fully by al-Ḥasan al-Bisyāni and have been translated into German by Sachau (1894); the work of his eleventh-century master Ibn Baraka is also interesting. The *Tuḥfa* has much of value for the general organization of the First Imamate, notably direct quotations from Munīr b. Nayr al-Riyāmi's *Sīra* (cf. *Tuḥfa* i. 89 92), the letter of appointment of the Wali of Rustāq (ibid. pp. 184 93) and the instructions of the Imam al-Ṣalt b. Mālik al-Kharūṣi for the Socotra expedition (ibid., pp. 168 83): the *Nahḍa* has correspondingly useful information in connection with the twentieth-century Imamate.

[11] Similar taxation systems were still being used on the Persian side of the Gulf until recent times (cf. Fraser 1825, pp. 74-5).

[12] There is a disparity over precisely what the term *quṭāni* is meant to cover, but in any case the types of crop involved are of minor importance in Oman.

[13] The date-palms growing unirrigated on the shore would, however, belong within the *baʿl* classification and therefore pay 10 per cent (cf. Yaḥyā b. Adam text, p. 86, read with Māwardi, pp. 258-9).

[14] The Ibāḍi state is absolutely rigid in adhering to the prescribed taxes both on Muslims and non-Muslims. Even in the early Islamic state various traditional taxes such as custom's tax and agricultural impositions, usually referred to euphemistically as *ʿushūr* or more openly as *maks* (pl. *mukūs*), were collected despite Islamic injunctions to the contrary (cf. Forand 1966 and Gibb (1955) Rescript of ʿUmar II, clause XIV). An example of such customary taxations in modern times is provided by the tax imposed until recently in the Abu Dhabi villages of the Buraimi oasis by the Āl Bu Falāḥ in order to provide for the upkeep of the *Amīr*'s horses quartered there: on each five *suds* of water there was a tax obligation of one basket (*jarāb*) of *ḥashaf* dates, that is dates which fail to mature; if *ḥashaf* dates could not be supplied, then the unfortunate land-owner had to make up his commitment with mature dates. Such taxes are not found in Ibāḍi Oman, and there are numerous examples of how illegal or even questionable impositions were removed by Imams after a period of corrupt rule. The greatest temptation must have been to impose supplementary taxes on the rich merchant classes in the ports. That they could afford to pay is evidenced by the enormous fortunes merchants made in Ṣuḥār in the tenth and eleventh centuries, despite the imposition of *mukūs*. When the Būyids were eventually evicted from Ṣuḥār by an Omani Imām in the middle of the eleventh century, Ibn Khaldūn (*ʿIbar* iv. 490) states specifically that with the restoration of the ascetic life (dressing in wool!) justice prevailed, the *mukūs* was dropped, and the only tax collected on the merchants was the statutory $2\frac{1}{2}$ per cent wealth tax (quarter *ʿushr*) which is all that the *sharīʿa* permits.

[15] For example, the great fort at Nizwā (ʿAqr quarter of Lower Nizwā) which took over twelve years to build was reputedly paid for by the booty the Yaʿrabi Imam Sulṭān b. Sayf b. Mālik acquired in plundering the Portuguese at Diu. This new fort incorporated part of the earlier one built at the end of the First Imamate by al-Ṣalt b. Mālik al-Kharūṣi (237/851-272/886), which had been recently repaired (*c.* 1626) by the first Yaʿrabi Imam, Nāṣir b. Murshid: (*Tuḥfa* i. 107, 116, 120, 125-7; ii. 4-5, 55).

[16] There are three interesting examples of the restored Imamate confiscating the property of the old régime: in each the action was against the advice of the moderates, and did, indeed, prove in the end to be a two-edged weapon (for the case of confiscating the property of 'Sultan' Muẓaffar b. Sulaymān al-Nabhāni and the Bani Ruwāḥa in 1482, see *Tuḥfa* i. 371-5, 379-82; the introduction to the *Dīwān Sulaymān b. Sulaymān al-Nabhāni*, and *Nahḍa*, p. 326: for the case of ʿAzzān b. Qay's Imamate (1868 71) see *Tuḥfa* ii. 256-8; and for that of Sālim b. Rāshid al-Kharūṣi (1913-20) see *Nahḍa*, p. 224; these last two cases are also well documented in the relevant India Office records).

[17] *Ṣawāfi* in Oman has tended to become a general term for all land to which the state is entitled.

[18] Whilst the principle that property not claimed by those designated as inheritors by the *sharīʿa* (N.B. only one-third of a person's property may be beqeathed at the will of the testator) escheats to the *bayt al-māl* applies in Oman (*Tuḥfa* i. 242, fn.; cf. Khairallah 1941, p. 5 for similar Ḥanafi practice), al-Sālimi (*Jawhar* pp. 472-4) shows that some consider it should be distributed amongst the poor or become *waqf* (cf. also Lambton 1953, p. 203, fn. on early Shīʿi practice). In principle property acquired under these rules should be treated by the *bayt al-māl* in the same way as *zakāt*.

[19] *Jihād* it should be remembered has two aspects, one defensive, the other agressive. This is reflected in the two types of Imam which feature in Omāni history, *shāri* and *dāfiʿi* Imams. While it is the duty of both to expand the Muslim state if the enemy do not outnumber the Muslims two to one, an Imam may be specifically elected a *shāri* Imam with this duty if the *ʿulamāʾ* consider the time propitious (Ṣāʾighi *bāb al-imāma*). On the other hand it is a fundamental duty of an Imam to defend the community (cf. the phrase *ʿalā ʾl-jihād fī sabīl al-difāʿ* in the oath to Rāshid b. al-Walīd as quoted by the fifth-/eleventh-century Abu Saʿīd al-Kudami cf. *Tuḥfa* i. 281 and *Kashf* MS. 478).

[20] The statement that *ṣawāfi* and *bayt al-māl* property is, in principle, mortmain needs some qualification, because there is a danger in applying terms of English law, in which concepts of property derive from a feudal system, to the *sharīʿa*, where they do not. If we follow the definition of mortmain in Earl Jowitt's *Dictionary of English Law* as 'such a state of possession as makes it inalienable; whence it is said to be in a dead hand — in a hand that cannot shift away the property' we do have a concept that is of some value in describing *waqf* and *bayt al-māl*; but only so long as it is realized that this ignores the historical evolution upon which actual administrative practices are based.

[21] That is the *falaj* of the two branches. This *falaj* is mentioned at the beginning of the seventeenth century when it is recorded that the Nabhāni *mālik* built a fort to protect it when he was attacked by the ʿUmayri *mālik* of Sumāyil and his Bani Hinā allies (*Kashf* tr. Ross, p. 147). Bahlā was the centre of incessant fighting in the later Nabhāni period, and it is probable that a great deal of damage occurred to its irrigation systems at that time.

CHAPTER VIII

Formalized Social Structure

THE TRIBE AS A CLAN

In attempting to isolate the influence of Ibāḍism on the system of land organization in Oman, it has become increasingly clear that all forms of central government are so closely bound up with the tribal system that it is frequently impossible to specify what is to be attributed to Ibāḍi influence and what to tribalism. The only influences the writer has analysed as specifically Ibāḍi are those that stem from the principles of 'just' government enshrined in religious laws, principles to which the Omanis as Ibāḍi Muslims always attempt to adhere, even when the Imamate itself is in abeyance.

The question now follows of what exactly the word 'tribal' means in the Oman context. More specifically, we need to ask what precisely are the functions of the tribal system, how far does it represent a social organization imported by the Arabs, to what extent is it adapted to the Omani village environment, and what influence does it have on the organization of the land?

In this chapter, the local notions of tribal structure and of the way the formalized hierarchy has been determined in terms of 'biological' proximity will be discussed. In Chapter IX we will examine how locational interests in reality modify this aspatial model of the tribe as a clan, once a tribe begins to settle and establish itself in the Omani agricultural environment. Finally in Chapter X the relationships between the social and the land organization will be examined, and the basic aim of the tribal system elucidated.

GROUP RELATIONSHIPS PERCEIVED IN CLAN TERMS

Though the Omani tribal system in fact regulates how sub-groups of Omani society organize their territorial, economic, and family relationships, the tribesmen themselves tend to view the tribe as integrated by just one factor, clan organization. This extremely important notion that the tribe and the clan are synonymous underlies many misconceptions about tribal organization, by Omanis and foreigners alike.

Since a clan (*āl* or *yāl*) is essentially a group of people who consider themselves to be bound to each other by obligations deriving from their common descent, perhaps the best way to describe the basic principles which are deemed to govern the organization of the tribe is to define certain local notions about 'family' (cf. Fig. 26).

1. *The legal family*. The fundamental idea of the legal family is that it forms a group which shares blood-guilt and is obliged to seek revenge (*istiqaṣṣ*, *akhadh thāra*) for the killing of one of its members. In tribal law this group consists of the victim's or malefactor's ʿ*ayāl*, that is all those who are agnatically related to him through patrilineal descent from his grandfather (*jadd*). Such a group is in effect treated as a legal person.

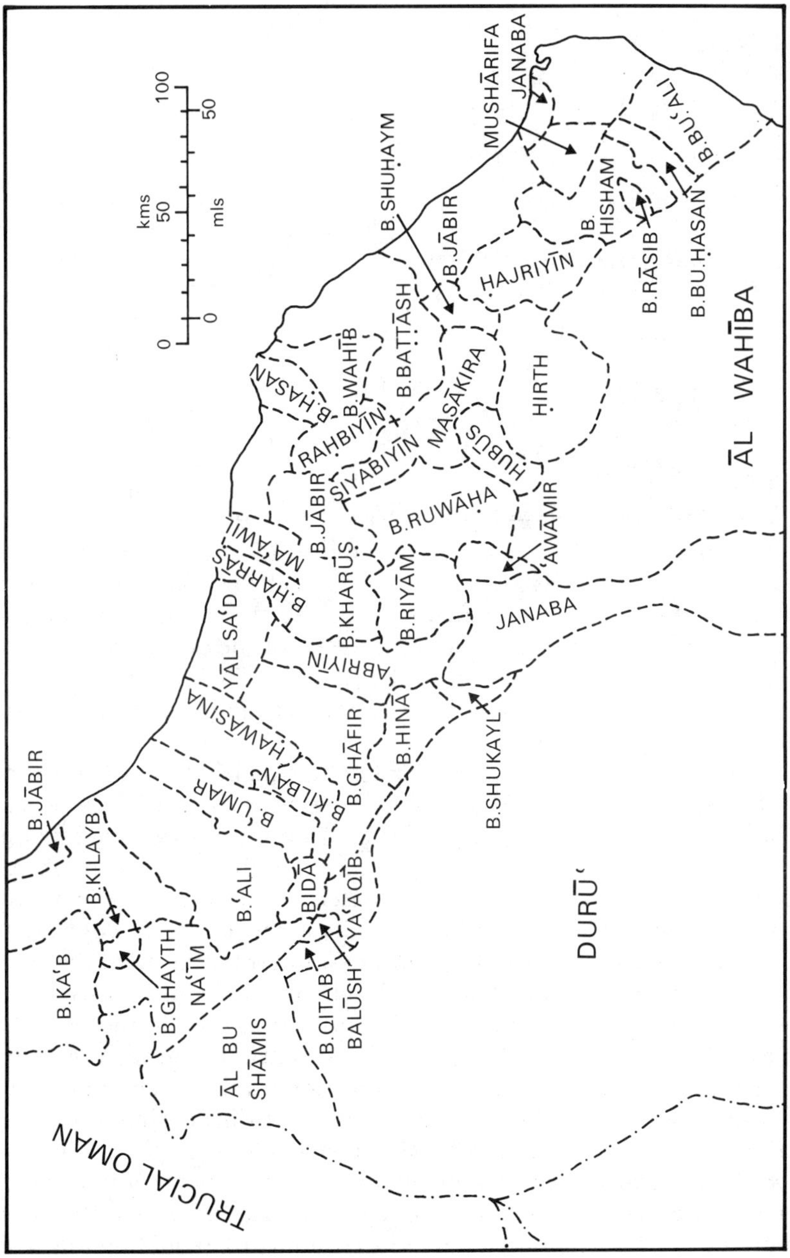

Fig. 25. The main tribal groupings of the Sultanate (after a map prepared for the Government by Petroleum Development (Oman) Ltd. *c.* 1962.

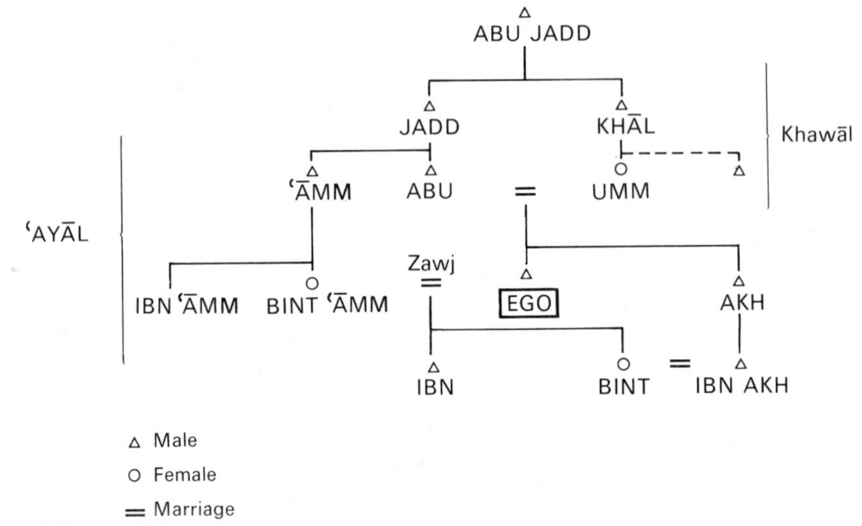

Fig. 26. EGO's principal relatives in parallel-cousin (FaBrDa) marriage pattern.

2. *The immediate family*. The ultimate decision about whether blood-wit (*dīya*) is to be accepted as alternative settlement for a killing is, however, less the affair of the whole legal family than it is of the immediate family, that is the sons, brothers, father, and paternal uncles of the deceased. This, it should be noticed, is not the same thing as the *conjugal family*, which is a residence group and not a legal kin-group (except in so far as *bayt*, house, is both a residence and a kinship term).

3. *The extended family*. In the legal definition of the *ʿayāl* as given above, it will be seen that it is the individual who acts as the reference-point for the composition of the family-group. If such a definition were rigidly observed, then it follows that the *ʿayāl* is unique to each individual (or, more correctly, to each set of brothers): thus a man's descent would automatically break up into different legally obligated family units with the passage of time (cf. Fig. 27). On the other hand should a man's descendants feel that they continue to form a family-group, and deliberately choose, for the purposes of mutual support, to disregard their exact relationships one with another, then they must abandon such an Ego-(or generation-) centred approach to defining the composition of the *ʿayāl*. This they do by nominating a common ancestor as their legal *jadd*: and in this way there can be no diminution of corporate responsibility by reason of remoteness of ancestry. Membership of the group is indicated by assuming the name of the *jadd* as an eponym and attaching it in *nisba* form (adjectival from of a name, e.g. Rāshid *nisba* Rāshidi) to the personal names of each individual. The corollary of extending the *ʿayāl* obligations to a family-unit larger than that which is legally obligatory is that it is unthinkable for a member to kill another. Should such a misfortune occur, then the blood-debt must be settled in such a way that no individual inherits a

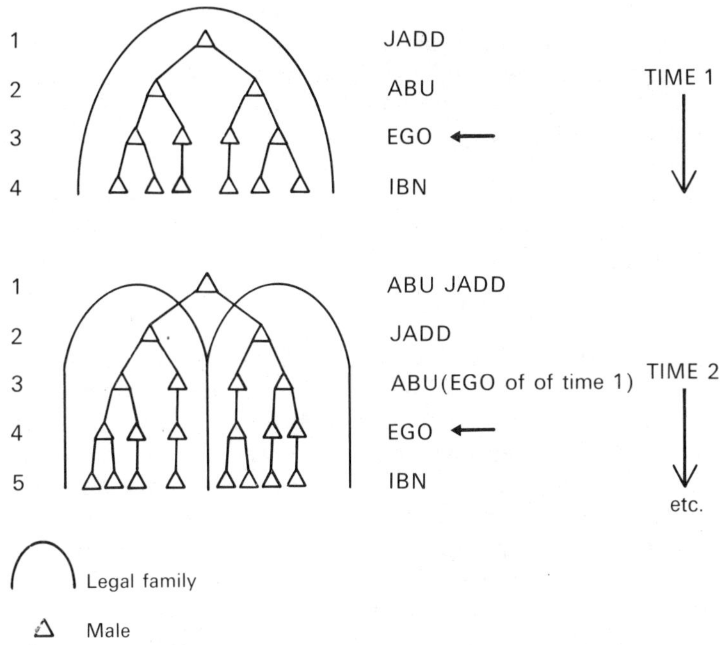

Fig. 27. Changes in legal family units through generations.

legacy of revenge: if this proves impossible, then the unity of the extended family-group is automatically destroyed, and it will tend to break back down into its true legal family units.

4. *The descent group*. So the descendants in male line of the ancestor who is termed a *jadd*, form a distinctive group whose first obligations in matters of revenge and defence are to each other. Such a group from now on will be designated as a descent group, and its sense of unity will be referred to as *ʿaṣabīya*.

In the particular type of society under consideration such a group is theoretically endogamous and forms a self-perpetuating social 'isolate', because unlike most non-'Middle-Eastern' tribal societies its members practise parallel-(i.e. not cross-) cousin marriage (Murphy and Kasdan 1959). Since it is this marriage pattern which basically explains certain peculiarities of Arab tribal structure this rather bald statement requires some development.

5. *Marriage pattern*. In the ideal marriage pattern a man marries his father's brother's daughter (*bint ʿamm*, cf. Fig. 26), and to this end he is considered to have particular rights over her. However, the number of such marriages that can in fact take place is severely limited for demographic reasons, and so frequently a man has to marry a more remote cousin. The preference nevertheless remains for marriage at as low a level of segmentation as possible. This is confirmed by statistical studies of real situations (Randolph and Coult 1968; Ayoub 1959; and literature cited therein): these show that

even though only some 10 per cent of marriages are of the father's brother's daughter type, some two-thirds are within the clan and over half of these are within the agnatic descent group (that is a patrilateral parallel-cousin marriage of one degree or another). Of the non-kin marriages a high percentage tend to be between clans which have a close association with each other.

It can be seen, therefore, that marriages within the kin-group really do represent a high proportion of the alliances made, although we might note at the same time that the external marriages are of greater importance for the political and demographic survival of the group than their numbers might suggest.

Because there really is a high incidence of parallel-cousin marriage, of some kind or other, within a clan, and because this represents the preferred type of marriage, there is a strong tendency to presume that all marriages have actually been contracted according to the ideal pattern. One result of this is that the distinction which legally differentiates a man's obligations to his *khawāl*, that is male relatives through the female side, from those to his *ʿayāl* tend to be ignored: consequently, when a man marries outside the group, his *ʿayāl* normally extend protection to the male relatives of his wife, *a fortiori* once a son is born of the union. Marriage therefore forms an extremely important means for effecting group reconciliation, and members of shaikhly families make particular use of the rights of limited polygamy accorded by Islam, not for the purpose of sexual gratification, as is often supposed, but as a means to extend their influence through the bonds of family obligations.

6. *Lineages*. Another notion that arises from the presumption that the marriage pattern is of the ideal type is that it is only necessary for a man to quote his lineage for a limited number of generations in order to arrive at the ancestor common to his own self-perpetuating family-unit. The minimum number of generations quoted is two, because from his grandfather stems not only his immediate family (see No. 2, above) but also his wife, that is, the mother-to-be of his own descent; and it is doubtless because this group is so intimately linked that the legal definition of the family-unit (see No. 1, above) has arisen. Frequently, however, a man will give his ancestry back to his great-grandfather (*abu jadd*) because by so doing he is identifying the forebear common to both his father's and his mother's family and so effectively affirming that he has renounced his legal right to differentiate between the two. This lineage is quoted in the form of an ascending list of ancestors linked by the word *ibn* (son of, or '*bin*' written in the form *b*. for grammatical reasons), e.g. Rāshid b. Saʿīd b. Muḥammad.

However, we should also notice that while a man normally only quotes as forming an integral part of his own name those direct forebears who form his minimal lineage, this by no means implies that he considers himself as detached from the rest of his (extended) family-group (see No. 3, above); indeed these names of themselves indicate in various ways his incorporation into the larger unit. First, the quoted names merely represent a compressed version of the complete lineage which implicitly goes back to the eponymous ancestor with whose *nisba* the individual completes his name. Second, the idea that the individual forms part of a continuing descent group is emphasized by referring to him in his youth, not by his given name X, but as *Ibn* (son of) Y, where Y is the name of his father, and then as *Abu* (father of) Z where Z is the name of one of his sons (often, but by no means always, his eldest). Thirdly, there is the fact that the actual names of X, Y, and Z are normally those of earlier forebears, and that these derive from a set of names which together are peculiar to the descent group (the conventions about which particular names are used are complex and far from rigid). By drawing on this name-set, the living members of a descent group not only honour and perpetuate the identity of their ancestors but indicate the continuing association of the individual family-units through cross-reference to common forebears. This point may be illustrated by the case of the present head of one of the most famous families in Oman: his lineage, as given over thirty-eight generations, features eighteen different names, but of these three occur no less than nineteen times (i.e. they make up 50 per cent of the names of his direct forebears). This example also brings out another important point about lineages: unless a family-group produces a sufficient number of distinguished individuals for their names to be properly recorded (as with the above case of the Nabāhina), the names of a man's more remote forebears not only become meaningless as individual identities are forgotten, but will also rapidly become confused. Here, then, is another reason why a man only quotes two or three generations of his ancestry before jumping to the name of the next significant forebear, his descent-group *jadd*.

THE 'TRIBE' AS A DESCENT GROUP

We can now start to consider the idea that the 'tribe is made up of clans, which rightly or wrongly, acknowledge some kind of kinship' (cf. Rodinson 1971, p. 13). In the descent-group model of the tribe, the basic premise is that all members acknowledge the man whose *nisba* they bear to be their *jadd*, and so feel bound to each other by the kinds of obligations which unite the legal family. The fact that there may be internal divisions within the group and that individual units may be on bad terms with others is in no way the concern of non-members, for it is a 'family' matter and as such the conflict is limited and governed by rules which do not apply when dealing with outsiders. When threatened by non-members, all the sections are united and their internal relationships in no way diminish their corporate responsibility to act together in defence and revenge.

From the point of view of the outsider, therefore, the clan organization of the tribe is analogous with the structure of the legal family: that is the tribal forebear (*jadd*) acts as the reference-point for defining those with *ʿayāl* relationships, while the position of the father as the reference-figure for defining an individual's immediate family-group corresponds to the *fakhdh* or section forebear. If, therefore, the legal family may be described as a minimal descent group, the tribe may be described as a maximal descent group, because it comprises the offspring of the highest ancestor in the attributed lineage whose name can evoke the same sense of corporate responsibility (*ᶜaṣabīya*) which the *jadd* produces for the legal family. The main expressions of this 'family' unity are as follows: first, the tribe tries to placate any internal disruption caused by a killing, whereas it 'enjoys' a feud with another tribal group (a feud here being used as a set of relationships between two groups characterized by hostility whenever their members meet, which can only be terminated by the intervention of an outsider: cf. Peters 1967); second, the tribe makes offensive and defensive war together; third, it recognizes the authority of one of its members as a leader (shaikh — correctly *shaykh*); fourth, it controls a piece of territory (usually called a *dār* in Oman).

The idea that such a group is 'bonded together' as a family is inherent in the term most commonly used to designate it amongst the settled tribesmen of Oman, *jumāᶜa* (cf. also *rubāᶜa*), and amongst the bedu tribes of the region *ṭāyifa* (correctly *ṭāʾifa*). And it is because such groupings form the quasi-permanent social units which determine the enduring alliances and enmities between the peoples of the country, that the most significant question two strangers seeking to establish their relationships will ask of each other, is of the pattern *min ay ṭāyifa(t) ent?* from what 'tribe' or 'bonding' are you?

Case-study of the Maᶜāwil (cf. Fig. 28)

Perhaps the best way to understand how the tribe is regarded as being made up of a number of clans who descend from a single ancestor is to take a specific example. Discussion will therefore be initiated by following Abu Sulaymān Muḥammad (b. ᶜĀmir, var. b. Rāshid, b. Saᶜīd b. ᶜAbdullāh) al-ᶜAdawi al-Maᶜwali's description of his own tribe, the Maᶜāwil and its eighty or so sections (*fakhdh*, pl. *afkhādh* or *fukhūdh*), as he describes it in the *Nubdha fi ansāb al-Maᶜāwil* (abbreviated *Nubdhat al-Maᶜāwil*).[1]

This work, written in the second half of the eighteenth century by a well-known Omani *ᶜālim*, is partly based on his own knowledge of his tribe and partly on the description given in the remnants of an ancient manuscript which he had discovered in Manḥ. The value of his account is enhanced by the fact that there also exists, somewhat fortuitously, a detailed first-hand account of a tribal war between the Maᶜāwil and the inhabitants of nearby Nakhl recorded in Rössler's dialect study *Nachal und Wād il Maᶜāwil* (Rössler 1898). Together, these two documents provide considerable insight on the ideas of tribal structure amongst the settled peoples of central Oman.

The author of the *Nubdhat al-Maᶜāwil* starts his account of the tribe with a sketch of its genealogy as derived from the Manḥ manuscript. He says that the eponymous ancestor was a man called Maᶜwila whose descent from Adam he traces through thrity-nine ascendants (*abā*). In enumerating these he some-

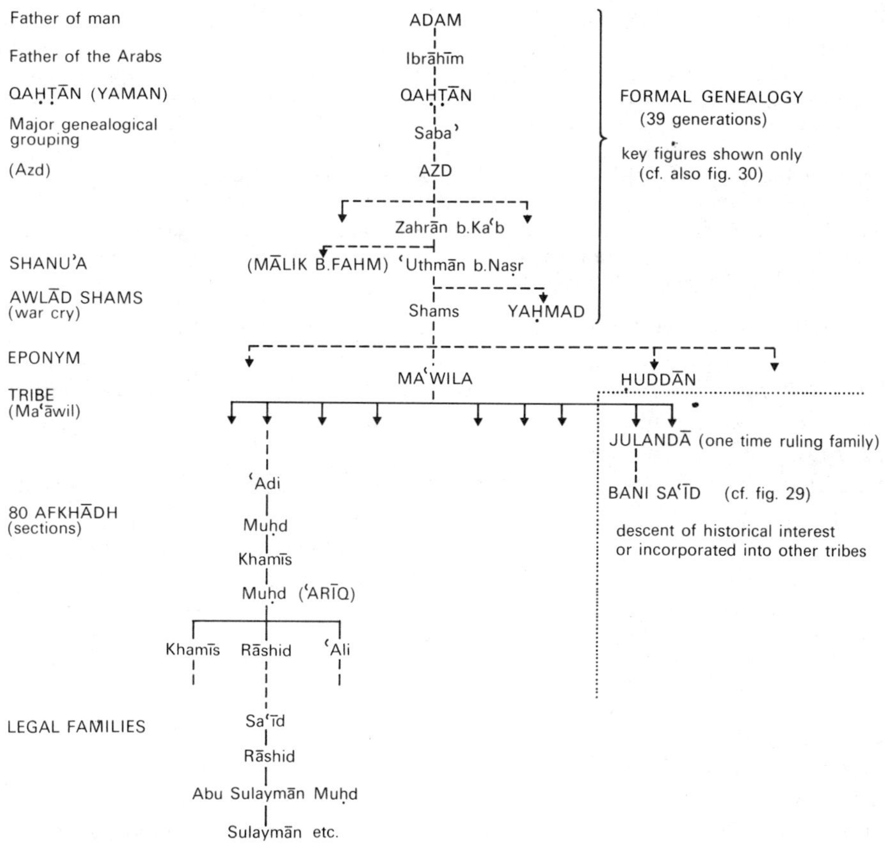

Fig. 28. The Maʿāwil.

times adds details about them as, for example, that Hunāʾa b. Mālik b. Fahm (the eponym of the Bani Hinā) and Maʿwila both descend from Zahrān b. Kaʿb (respectively at the seventh- and sixth- named forebears: cf. Fig. 30). The significance of these remote tribal forebears will be dealt with at a later stage (cf. the section on Formal Descent Groups).

In his introduction Abu Sulaymān also states that the Bani ʿAdi, his own section of the Maʿāwil, are now named the Awlād bin ʿArīq, and that some of them live in Maṭlaʿ (Upper) Ifi and some in Muslimāt which they share with the Awlād Bin Qabīl and Awlād Hadāla (spelling uncertain), a grouping which is related to another important section of the Maʿāwil, the Bani Bu Ghassān; both these places are villages in the tribe's main territory (*dār*), the Wadi Bani Maʿāwil, but at this stage of analysis the geographical aspects do not concern us.

The author then moves on to a detailed account of the different sections which make up the tribe, and describes his own in the following terms:

our section (*fakhdh*) is Awlād ᶜAdi (the male descent of ᶜAdi) who is our forebear (*jaddnā*) and its *nisba* is al-ᶜArīqi. ᶜArīq is our forebear (*jaddnā*) Muḥammad b. Khamīs b. Muḥammad b. ᶜAdi who was known as al-ᶜArīq as a boy. Al-ᶜArīq in classical Arabic means 'to do with horses and Arabs' for, as a poet has said, 'Our forebear did not take his name from a diminutive: ᶜAriq is not spelt with a *ḍamma* but with a *fatḥa*' [i.e. it is not the diminutive of rad. ᶜRQ ᶜUrayq, but the specific form ᶜArīq]: ᶜArīq is the *qawm* and its horses and it is honourable to take one's *nisba* from ᶜRQ. Now this Muḥammad died as a young man and of his two names the declared *nisba* (*mashhūr al-nasab*) derives from ᶜArīq but the declared relationship (*mashhūr al-intisāb*) from Muḥammad. Muḥammad had three sons Rāshid b. Muḥammad, Khamīs b. Muḥammad and ᶜAli b. Muḥammad, so it is from him that the line of descent branches out. Rāshid is our (particular) forebear (*jadd*).

A preliminary analysis of this description immediately brings out several points of importance for understanding the internal descent-group structure of the Maᶜāwil. The first is that every member belongs to a group called a *fakhdh* in which the individual's identity is submerged (it will be noticed Abu Sulaymān does not say 'my *jadd*' but 'our *jadd* is Muḥammad b. Khamīs b. Muḥammad b. ᶜAdi'). The members of this particular *fakhdh* are the male descent (*Awlād*: cf. also the terms *Wuld* and *Bani*) of Adi (the first-named forebear of their lineage), and this they acknowledge by adding to their personal lineage names the *nisba* which derives either from ᶜAdi, or the nick-name of his great-grandson (Muḥammad) ᶜArīq: as such they are bound to each other by ᶜ*aṣaba*/ᶜ*aṣabīya* (although this is not spelt out in this particular case, it is in the descriptions of a number of the other *fukhūdh*).

But while ᶜAdi is the earliest-named forebear of this group, its status (*karam*) derives not from him, but from Muḥammad, that is the man who was also called ᶜArīq. And, as the anonymous poet has stated, this attributed name is honourable for it is associated with the fighting unit (*qawm*) of the ᶜ*arab* (true Arabs, bedu tribes) and their noble steeds, horses (*khayl*); perish the thought that Muḥammad may have been a vulgar donkey-herder whom his associates called 'the little sweaty one' (ᶜ*Urayq*)! So it is that Muḥammad was the founder of a noble line, and, as our author reminds his group on more than one occasion, it is as his unified descent alone that they enjoy their standing.

The next point to notice is that this group does not exist in isolation. It forms a *fakhdh* (a limb or branch) of the Maᶜāwil, a group which is made up of all the *fukhūdh* listed in the *Nubdhat al-Maᶜāwil*. A man therefore bears two *nisbas*, that of his *fakhdh jadd* showing to which section he belongs, and that of his tribal *jadd*; since the former is of interest only to other members of the tribe, it is the latter he will use when dealing with outsiders.

The third point concerns the gaps in the genealogy. It may be noticed that while we know our author's own minimal lineage, he makes no attempt to link his family back to his declared *jadd* genealogically. All that he says is that his lineage descends from Rāshid, one of the three named sons of Muḥammad ᶜArīq. By contrast Muḥammad's genealogy is spelt out back to a great-grandfather ᶜAdi. Then again comes a genealogical blank, and the next-named forebear is Maᶜwila himself. Maᶜwila's own genealogy is then given, apparently in full, back to Adam, with special comments on two of his ancestors.

SEGMENTATION

In his description of his *fakhdh*, Abu Sulaymān's treatment of the group ancestor is somewhat confused. This, at first sight, is surprising, because, if the unity of the group is based on the theory that they all descend from a single progenitor, we would expect to find this man unequivocally named as *jadd*. In fact there are no less than five man labelled in this way (ᶜAdi, his great-grandson Muḥammad, and the latter's three sons, Rāshid, Khamīs, and ᶜAli) and two of these give rise to clan *nisbas*. So we find that even though Muḥammad, from whom the ᶜArīq *nisba* derives, clearly forms the key-figure in the ancestry of the group (in bedu tribal terminology he would be referred to as the *rukn*, i.e. cornerstone or pivot), its members do not declare themselves as forming his descent, but that of his great-grandfather (*abu jadd*) ᶜAdi: they are therefore called the Awlād (or Bani) ᶜAdi and this they show by using another *nisba* ᶜAdawi. In addition to this, it would seem that all members also recognize that they descend from one of the three named sons of Muḥammad, and Abu Sulaymān actually uses the word *jadd* to designate Rāshid b. Muḥammad as his own sub-group's forebear.

The real reason why there is such a profusion of *jadds* and *nisbas* is that the group is losing its sense of family unity. It has now divided into three sub-sections and these are beginning to refuse the obligations imposed by declaring themselves the direct descent of Muḥammad; instead they will only acknowledge that they are vaguely related through an ancestor four generations back from their own particular *jadds*. Whether the rest of the Maᶜāwil actually designated these three sub-groups as respectively the *Awlād* (cf. *Bayt* amongst certain bedu groups) Rāshid, Khamīs, or ᶜAli is not clear, but it is worth noting that Abu Sulaymān appears to do so when describing other *fukhūdh* in a similar state of fragmentation. It is also significant that he admits that the group is no longer known as the Awlād ᶜArīq but as the Awlād Bin ᶜArīq (the descent of the sons of ᶜArīq). While therefore the actual *nisba* ᶜArīqi is still used by members of the *fakhdh*, this attributed name (cf. French *surnom*) conveniently glosses over the problem of specifically having to identify Muḥammad as the *jadd*; and this is why Abu Sulaymān has to remind his fellow-clansmen that ᶜArīq is none other than Muḥammad and it is through him alone that they have any group status. Be that as it may, Muḥammad's personal name is fast losing significance, and as it does so it will gradually be dropped from verbal accounts of the clan's genealogy: when it is no longer mentioned at all it will mean that the original sense of family obligation has finally disappeared among his descent.

This kind of ambivalence over naming the group forebear is indicative of change in the group's political structure. So too is the number of generations quoted in the descent from the person reputed to be the common ancestor. This is because when a group interposes an ancestor in its lineage, it is in effect declaring that it forms a distinctive sub-unit within the family, and hence a potential rival to the rest of the members. It is precisely at points where genealogical information is given in most detail that we must suspect that the cohesiveness of the group breaks down; conversely, only when there is an absence of lineage names may political unity be presumed. As Peters (1967) has pointed out 'split . . . occurs where relationships are most intense'.

What then causes segmentation to occur inside a clan? To answer this question, it is first of all necessary to realize that segmentation has virtually nothing to do with the natural process of genealogical branching with the passage of time. In the model of the tribe as a descent-group genealogies are telescoped so as to record details at two specific points only, that where the tribe divides from others, and that which affects its *fakhdh* sub-groupings; conversely, from the point of view of its real component family-units, no attempt is made to show the genealogical train leading back to the *fakhdh* eponym, or of the latter to the tribal eponym. Ideally the forebears of the sections are presumed to be the 'sons' of the tribe's eponymous ancestor, for then there can be no 'degree' in their relationships. Any other genealogical details recorded represent modifications of this principle, and indicate the historical evolution of the internal relationships within the group. Thus, in the case of the particular Maᶜwili clan under consideration, it is as much a mistake to presume that ᶜAdi was really Muḥammad ᶜArīq's great-grandfather as it is to believe that only thirty-nine generations separated Maᶜwila from Adam! This, of course, is not to say that the names of sectional and tribal eponyms are purely fictitious: rather, that they record the identities of certain personalities who, at some time or other, gave a group its sense of constituting an individual social entity.

So the idea that the members of a tribal unit actually descend from an eponymous ancestor is no more than a genealogical rationalization of all the factors — spatial, economic, political, as well as kinship — which give rise to differential organization within the larger social grouping. These aspects of the subject will be treated more fully later and it is sufficient here to make three general points in connection with segmentation. The first is that the number of people within a group who are actually related by blood is inversely proportional to the size of its population. The second is that the closer-knit the locational interests of a group, the more likely it is that the names of its sub-divisions really do indicate differences in family organization. In the case of the Maᶜāwil, for example, there are nothing like eighty 'political' subdivisions within the tribe, and a study of its *afkhādh* shows that the majority of them are made up of no more than relatively small lineage-units: indeed, on one or two occasions Abu Sulaymān points out that a *fakhdh* only has a couple or so members. Conversely, the more dispersed the members of a tribal group, the greater the political significance of its formal internal divisions, and the more suspect the genealogical relationships. The third point is that a clan group must be of a certain minimal size to be independent. This is not just for economic and defensive reasons, but also because a biologically isolated population (which is theoretically what the Arab clan unit is) does not become demographically stable until it has a membership of between three and five hundred (Sauvy 1969, p. 30).

GENEALOGICAL ASSIMILATION

Just as organizational division within a tribe finds expression in genealogical subdivision, so does the opposite process of assimilation (or recruitment) demand rationalization through lineage unification. In reality, of course, it will rarely be found that a collection of people who share an area of common locational organization actually derives from the same forebear, for even in the smallest *falaj* settlement or bedu encampment in Oman there will almost inevitably be found elements who have a different origin from the dominant group: on the other hand, because these people have to live together in a measure of harmony some, if not all, may try and play down the symbol which separates them from their neighbours, that is their clan *nisba*, by fusing the ancestry of their eponymous *jadd*s.

At first sight it might be thought that this would then fix the relationship of the groups in perpetuity. In reality the situation is much more fluid for, as Peters (1960) has shown, the process of slipping and inverting generations presents no difficulties where lineage names are repetitious. If therefore, the sense of unity between the two groups continues to develop, the genealogical relationship can be adjusted accordingly.

Assimilation is, nevertheless, an essentially reciprocal process, and assumes not only that two groups wish to fuse, but that both are prepared to forget their own ancestry in order to identify with each other. Genealogical detail may, therefore, reflect the stages in the drawing together of tribal units as well as the reverse process of segmentation. In the case of the Maᶜwali genealogy for example, the Bani Dawla (who in reality are the indigenous peoples of Lower Ifi that have been assimilated into the Arab tribal structure) are simply shown as descendants of Maᶜwila himself, because this establishes that they are the equals of the other clans (and not *mawālī*), but have no special relationships with any of them, whereas in the case of the politically active part of the tribe the genealogical relationships are complex, for the descent from Maᶜwila is unquestioned and the genealogy is concerned with rationalizing the evolution of group associations within his descent.

In concluding this discussion of the internal divisions of an Omani tribe as represented by its genealogy, it must be emphasized that the lineage structure performs two functions. First, it rationalizes group relationships in terms of family obligations which arise through postulating a common ancestor and ordering his descent in a genealogical hierarchy; second, it distinguishes between those clans which, in the eyes of the tribesmen themselves, form the genuine, and those which form the attributed, descent of this eponymous ancestor. Genealogical interpretation is therefore exceedingly complex.

TRIBES OF SIMPLE AND COMPLEX GENEALOGY

For all the people of Oman, the descent group, so long as it is living together, is a very real unit of social organization. And, in the normal course of events, the members of such a group do tend to live together; by *bayt*s (houses) within the *farīq*s (quarters) of the various *ḥilla*s (settlements) that constitute the *dār* (tribal homeland); words, it will be noticed, that have a tribal as well as a locational connotation. So, from the point of view of the individual, *Fulān* (EGO) is surrounded by his kin: around his own house, in which he lives with his conjugal family, are concentrated the houses of the rest of his immediate family and other close relations; beyond come the dwellings of his more distant relatives and the rest of his section (i.e. members of the family about whose exact relationship he is somewhat vague), and their settlements in turn merge into those of the other members of his tribe (i.e. the descent group). Of course all *Fulān*'s relatives do not live in quite such an orderly way. Some may have moved further afield into rather more distant settlements, while others may even have abandoned the home area to live right outside the area of 'family' influence. Despite these perturbations to the pattern of kin settlement, the fact remains that a certain order in the normal spatial distribution of *Fulān*'s relatives does exist (a correlation between spatial proximity and kinship proximity), and *Fulān* himself is not only aware of this, but is actually liable to presume that this is the normal arrangement of things. He thus believes that many of his neighbours must be his relatives, precisely for the reason that 'our families have always lived together'.

So we can see how the ground is prepared for the individual to subscribe to the view that those who share his geographic, economic, and political interests form his kin, and why he is ready to accept an explanation of the ordering of the relationship between the groups of people with whom he associates in terms of family branching. Such an explanation is satisfactory to him because not only does it rationalize the order he perceives in terms with which he is familiar, but at the same time it provides him with a code which ordains how he is to behave towards others, and which allows him, in turn, to anticipate how he will be treated by them.

It is obvious, therefore, that the longer a group of people has been living together as a coherent entity, the more the tribesmen are going to believe that they are genuinely descended from a common ancestor. In the case of the Maʿāwil, whose presence in the area called the Wadi Bani Maʿāwil may be traced back some fifteen hundred years to the time when they originally migrated into Oman (cf. Chapter IX), there is not the slightest doubt, either amongst themselves, or in the eyes of other tribesmen, that their dominant clans really do descend from the eponymous Maʿwila. True, there are a few elements in the tribe which are vaguely recognized as perhaps being of a different descent, and there are other groups like the Bani Dawla whose artificial assimilation is subconsciously realized: but these elements play a very small part in the tribe's internal affairs and are most unlikely to precipitate the kind of situation in which the whole group has to respond as a single unit. Furthermore, since many of these assimilated groups are not ᶜ*arab* in origin, the forebears of their eponymous ancestors have no formal significance for the social structure into which they have been incorporated, and so their assimilation poses no particular problems in genealogical terms (cf. the section on Formal Descent groups, below). So we find the Maᶜāwil are welded together as a single descent group in such a way that it is almost impossible to pick holes in the clan-rationalization of their tribal identity other than by *a priori* argument.

By contrast, we may take the case of the Ḥawāsina, the tribal group which controls the main passage through the mountains linking the Sirr and the Batina Coast which is now known by their name, the Wadi al-Ḥawāsina (cf. Figs. 4 and 25). The story of the evolution of this tribe only really starts in the Yaᶜāriba period, some 250 years ago, when a small group called the Ḥawāsina, then living on the western side of the *najd* (pass) between the westward draining Wadi al-Kabīr and the eastward draining Wadi al-Ḥawāsina, made common cause with the old-established group of this strategic valley, the Bani Saᶜīd, to evict the Bani Lām (a group which had probably intruded in late Nabāhina times) from its two main villages, Ghayzayn (now the Ḥawsāni capital) and Hajari.[2] Thus united, the Ḥawāsina and the Bani Saᶜīd (whose common interests rapidly led them to identify themselves as of common descent) were in a position to demand the right to act as carriers between ᶜIbri and the Batina, and this in turn eventually gave them control of Khābūra, the regional port for the Sirr. As their power grew, so other small groups of the area increasingly became drawn into their political organization. But unlike the Bani Saᶜīd, these groups did not fully integrate into the Ḥawāsina clan structure, and the Sunaynāt, Maqābīl, Ḥawāmid, Makhāmira, and the Yāl Bu Qurayn were described to the writer as *tabaᶜ al-Ḥawāsina*, that is, 'followers of the Ḥawāsina'.

This brief sketch of the evolution of the Ḥawāsina as a tribe shows that the group's identity has arisen, not from any atavistic sense of belonging to a common descent group, but from the need to remain united so as to maintain control of a wadi whose strategic siting brings economic benefit, and to defend this 'locational' interest against would-be usurpers (notably the neighbouring Bani ᶜUmar). Since, therefore, the group has come into existence in what, by Omani standards, are recent times, we may expect to find that its descent-group structure has not yet been perfected, and that its genealogies will show signs of artificial manipulation.

This indeed proves to be the case, for, in contrast to the Maᶜāwil who now present a flawless descent from a single eponymous ancestor, the Ḥawāsina still divide into three main components, each of which has its own vestigial genealogy. Most important numerically are the Bani Saᶜīd, who almost certainly represent the descendants of the first main Arab group to dominate the Wadi al-Ḥawāsina. Long established in their valley, they, like the Maᶜāwil, have fully assimilated the earlier settlers into their clan structure, albeit the name of at least one of their sections, the ᶜUlayy (= ᶜ*Ulayj*, diminutive form of ᶜ*ilj* pl. ᶜ*ulūj*), indicates that this particular section, at least, is of non-Arab origin (cf. the Bani Dawla in the Maᶜāwil). The Bani Saᶜīd's eponymous ancestor according to Siyābi (p. 109), is Saᶜīd b. ᶜAbbād al-Julandi, a member of the original Arab ruling family in Oman (incidentally of Maᶜwali extraction) who lived at the end of the seventh century;[3] other members of his attributed descent are also to be found amongst the Ḥawāsina's neighbouring allies, the Bani Kilbān, while a few exist as far afield as the Sharqīya (amongst the Ḥubūs and the Masākira). Welded into this majority group are the true descent of Ḥawsan, reputedly the nickname of a man of Ṭayy lineage; it is from this clan that the shaikhly family of the tribe, the Sawālim, derives (Siyābi, p. 153).

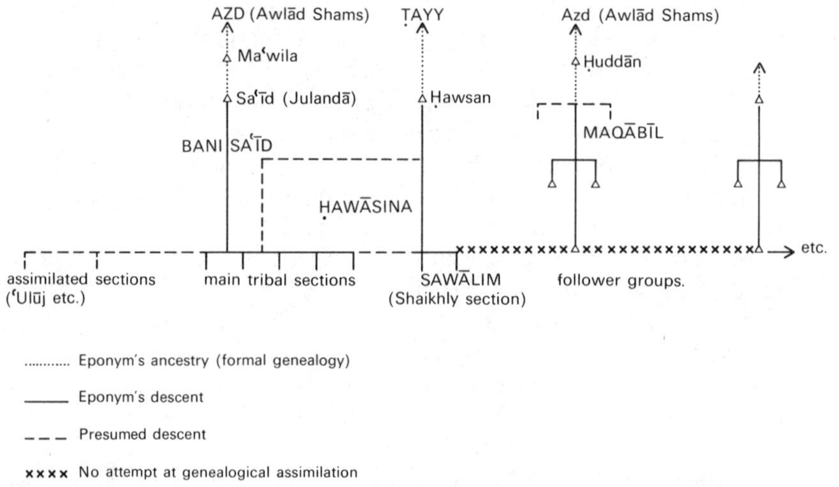

Fig. 29. The Ḥawāsina.

The identification of the two groups has been achieved as follows (Fig. 29). The Ḥawāsina consider themselves to be a section of the Bani Saᶜīd, but use their own *nisba* at all times, whereas the other sections of the Bani Saᶜīd normally use the name of their own eponymous ancestor except when dealing with outsiders, when they presume that Saᶜīd descends from Ḥawsan: and by so declaring themselves as Ḥawāsina, they of course disregard the fact that Saᶜīd al-Julandi is of Azd and not Ṭayy extraction.

The third element in the tribe are the 'followers', that is those groups which share certain interests with the dominant clans and recognize, in some measure, the authority of the Ḥawsani shaikhs. In their case no attempt has been made to integrate them genealogically, either into Ḥawsan's or Saʿid's descent, for they still retain their own clan identity and some of their members live in the territory of rival tribes. The support of follower-groups for a particular tribe, therefore, is tempered by the fact they recognize that they have their own clan obligations, and it is only when their locality interests are directly threatened that they show full solidarity (*ʿaṣabīya*) with the dominant groups of the *dār* in which they live (cf. Chapter X).

Fig. 29 of the descent-group structure of the Ḥawāsina shows just how complex it is when compared with that of the Maʿāwil (Fig. 28).

FORMAL DESCENT GROUPS

Now clearly the main stumbling-block that faces the Ḥawāsinas' desire to identify themselves as a single clan is their eponymous ancestors' own ascent, that is the genealogical superstructure which has been referred to as 'formal genealogy'. If, for example, Saʿīd and Ḥawsan had no predecessors of any significance, there would be no major difficulty in the two groups assimilating in terms of common descent. Unfortunately for them, memories are long in Oman, and even though the Ḥawāsina and the Bani Saʿīd might themselves choose to forget that they do not really stem from a common forebear, others are not prepared to do so. Certainly amongst the tribes of central Oman such manipulation would not even be attempted, for amongst them, the ancestry of tribal *jadds* has considerable significance, and formal genealogy is most certainly not to be cast aside at will. There, the descent group is one thing, and the tribe another, and it is only when the tribesmen themselves genuinely believe that the political unit called a tribe is made up of such a kin-group that the two are identified.

As a result a clear distinction has to be made between the following five types of group, all of which tend to be labelled somewhat loosely as 'tribal':

1. a descent group, e.g. the Bani Fulān (*fulān* = so-and-so).
2. a formal descent group, that is, a descent group whose eponymous ancestor features in 'formal genealogy', e.g. the Bani Fulān b. . . . Adam.
3. a descent group living together as a tribe (a tribe here being defined as a quasi-autonomous political unit exhibiting the characteristics described on p. 162, above), e.g. the Āl Bu Shāmis.
4. a formal descent group living together as a tribe (e.g. the Maʿāwil).
5. a tribe which has no genealogical expression of its unity (e.g. the Sharqīya Hināwis).

These distinctions will be more clearly understood once we have examind the nature and role of formal genealogy.

The basis of formal Arab genealogy goes right back to early Islamic times and may, in part, be viewed as a symbol of Arab unity in the face of the inner pressures of party strife and the external pressures of non-Arabs seeking Arab status. The genealogical structure may thus be considered as an attempt to

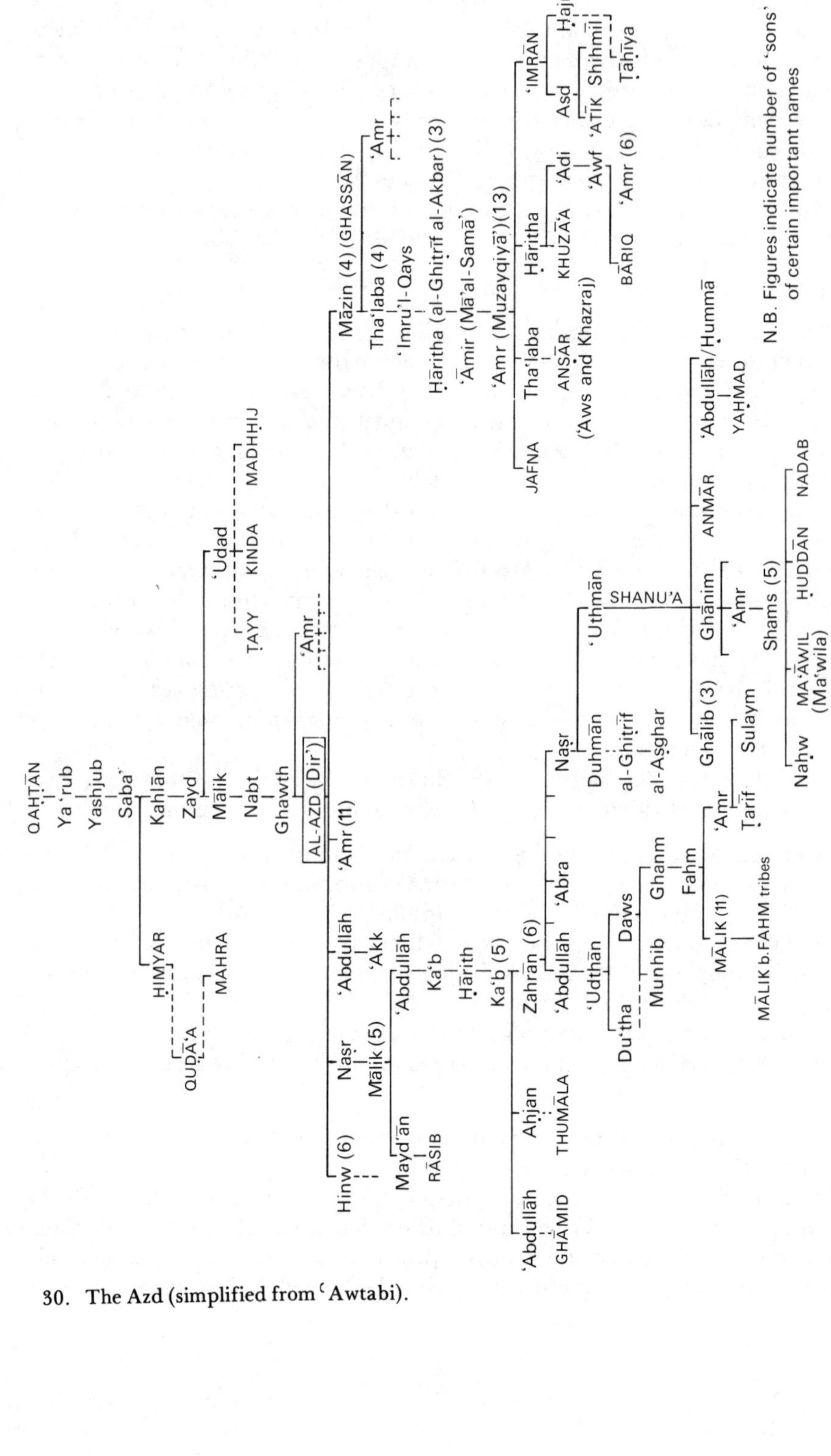

30. The Azd (simplified from ʿAwtabi).

rationalize the degree of solidarity existing between groups at the time it was developed, whilst simultaneously trying to show that these groupings were but the internal divisions of a single people. The resulting scheme was presented in its final form in the famous genealogical book of Hishām b. Muḥammad al-Kalbi (Ibn al-Kalbi), called the *Jamharat al-nasab*. In this work all the eponymous ancestors of the Arab tribal groups are shown as originally descending from either ᶜAdnān or Qaḥṭān, but the fact that the relationship of these two to the original progenitor of the Arab race, Ibrāhīm (Abraham), is left somewhat obscure is probably due either to an inherent, or to a politically fostered, belief that the Arab nation divided into two quite distinct parts (the Northern and the Southern Arabs). Since under this genealogical arrangement each branch (*rahṭ*) of the Arab tribal family-tree unites to form increasingly bigger units, the genealogists proposed the following sixfold ascending classification of the resulting clan groupings (their own examples from the ᶜAbbāsid genealogy are given in brackets): *faṣīla* (ᶜAbbās), *fakhdh* (Hāshim), *baṭn* (Quṣayy), *ᶜamāra* (Quraysh), *qabīla* (Kināna), *shaᶜb* (Muḍar); there was debate about this last classification because some maintained that groups like Muḍar, Rabīᶜa, Ḥimyar, and Kahlān, cited by Ibn al-Kalbi as examples of a *shaᶜb*, should be considered as *qabāʾil*, and that the term *shaᶜb* be retained for an even higher grouping such as Yaman.

The composition of these groupings is a subject that still requires considerable research, even though some important preliminary ideas have been propounded by W. Caskel and G. Strenziok in their introduction to the *Ǧamharat an-Nasab. Das genealogische Werk des Hišām Ibn Muḥammad al-Kalbī* (Leiden 1966). What we should note here is that in some measure Ibn al-Kalbi's genealogy must have represented what the Arab tribes believed to be the evolution of their relationships at the time he was writing, and that the legerdemain by which the higher genealogical levels have been manipulated for political purposes did fit in with pre-existing notions and transmitted history, otherwise the *Jamhara* would not have continued to be used as the basis for all subsequent works of this nature. There are, nevertheless, certain important differences in the relationships between some of the groups as revealed in these later works; for a study of the broad genealogical relationships of the Omani tribes Ibn Durayd's *Ishtiqāq* should always be consulted.[4]

Formal Arab genealogical works continued to enjoy a certain popularity as a literary form in the century or so following Ibn al-Kalbi's basic study (partly because their structure provided a useful framework for displaying a mass of miscellaneous information), but as the importance of tribal organization decreased in the politics of the Islamic world, they eventually went out of vogue. In Oman, where the isolation from the outside world and a fixed settlement pattern continued to preserve something of the early social organization (cf. Chapter IX), *Ansāb* continued to be produced, and along with other written documents they help record the evolution of tribal relationships.[5]

Apart from these written sources, which retain for the Omanis something of the history of their eponymous ancestors, the names of forebears also feature in tribal organization in two other ways, the call to arms (*ṣāyiḥ*), and the *nisbas* carried by certain families.

Most significant is the call to arms because it is the real test of tribal unity, the appeal to make war (aggressive or defensive) together. It is therefore naturally couched in the imperative terms of kinship obligations, and is usually of the form 'oh clan so-and-so' (*yā āl fulān*). Moreover, amongst the older tribes of central Oman, this rallying cry is often expressed as an appeal to a remote forebear. So, for example, we find in the nineteenth century the sections of the Maʿāwil rallying under their *bawāriq* and *barāghīm* (fanions and war-horns) to form the *qawm* (the military unit of the tribe), not as the descent of Maʿwila, but as the Awlād Shams (Rössler 1898). This, despite the fact that the union of the Awlād Shams (Maʿāwil, Ḥuddān, Nadab, and Naḥw: cf. Figs. 28 and 30) had ceased to exist for at least a thousand years, and that the appeal had not the slightest genealogical significance for the tribe which actually came to their help, the Bani Ruwāḥa.

Yet this archaic war-cry did serve some purpose. It reminded both the Maʿāwil and others of who they were. It recalled, amongst other things, the times when their clan had led the major Shanuʾa Azd migration into the Persian heartland of Oman, and how their shaikhs (the Julandā) became masters of all the tribes of Oman. Similarly, it was not without significance that their enemies, the miscellaneous tribal groups of Nakhl, in turn rallied themselves under the names of one of their local heroes, Shādhān (b. al-Imām Ṣalt b. Mālik al-Kharūṣi al-Yaḥmadi), for, by evoking the great line of Yaḥmad Imams who dominated the history of the First Imamate, they reminded the Maʿāwil that their power belonged to the old order of the 'days of ignorance' and that it was one of the Nakhl families who brought the true Imamate state to the people (cf. Wilkinson, in *J. Omani Studies*, in press).

The second use is in the acknowledged right of particular families to employ the eponym of a remote ancestor, even where there are others who are recognized as being of the same descent. So, for example, back in ʿAwtabi's time (eleventh century), it was recognized that, while all members of the Bani Ṣāmit (a tribal grouping of the period living in the Jabal Minqāl behind Qalhāt) were entitled to bear the *nisba* of the eponymous ancestor, the shaikhly family, and they alone, could use the *nisba* of Salīma (ibn Mālik b. Fahm), Ṣāmit's famous 'father' (cf. Fig. 31). The significance was that this family were the sole members of the tribe who could evoke wider clan obligations through appeal to others who carried the Salīma *nisba*: since these included the shaikhly clans of a number of other important groupings (including the Julandā b. Karkar family, then rulers of Huzw on the south-west Persian coast), this gave them considerable potential political power.

Such rights are still jealously guarded by the descendants of these once probably 'noble' (*sharīf*) families, and may even now give them a degree of pre-eminence within certain tribal groups. The following quotation from the biography of Abu Zayd (cf. p. 150) as given in the *Naḥda* (p. 420) may serve as an example:

he was from the Awlād Rāshid b. Sālim b. Maṣʿab b. Riyām, one of the senior *fukhūdh* of the Bani Riyām and numerically important: if there appears in a document *Fulān b. Fulān* (so-and-so) al-Riyāmi, then he is from the Awlād Rāshid in recognized uninterrupted succession. Other members of the Bani Riyām, without exception, give their *nisba* according to the *fakhdh* to which they genealogically belong and do not give their *nisba* as Riyāmi, except in the context that they belong to the grouping generally designated as Riyām.

In other words, Abu Zayd was from the clan that gave the Bani Riyām their name and has, since time immemorial, provided its shaikhs. Often such groups probably represent the only genuine descent of the eponymous ancestor in a tribe (cf. the Ḥawsan descent in the Ḥawāsina).

So the preservation in Oman of formal genealogy in clan nomenclature, tribal war-cries, and the *nisbas* of certain 'shaikhly' families represents the survival of an earlier organization in present tribal structure; the roots of this organization lie in the history of Arab migration and settlement in Oman.

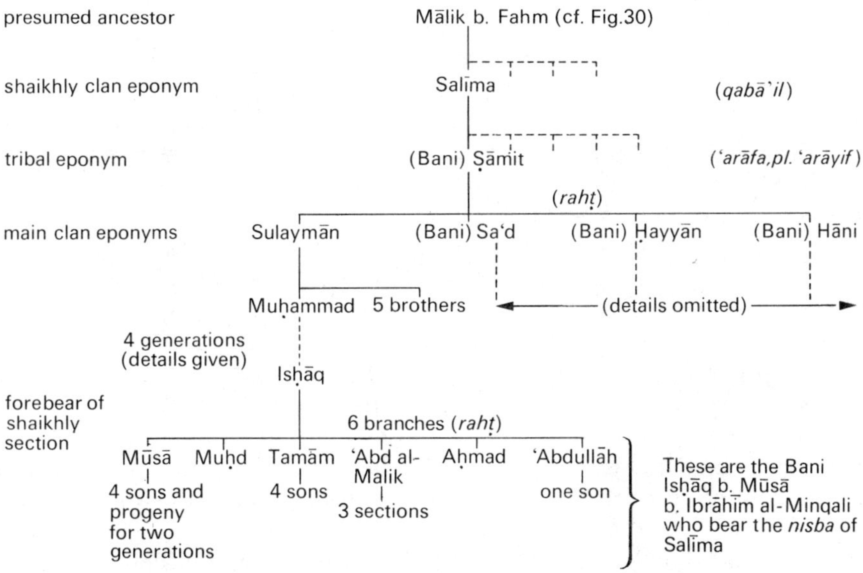

N.B. This tribe is the only Salīma tribe to remain in Oman. Its *dār* was in the Jabal Minqāl (S.E.Oman) where its capital was at Ḥasā (sp.?): there was also a secondary concentratration of Salīmā shaikhs living on the Batina coast, mostly from the Bani Sa'd (it was from this clan that A. Ḥamza Mukhtār b.'Awf, the mid-8th century Ibāḍi general came).

31. The Bani Ṣāmit b. Salīma at about the middle of the eleventh century A.D. (adapted from ʿAwtabi who gives many more details).

The Influence of the Original Tribal Pattern on Formal Genealogy (cf. Fig. 33, p. 244)

Study of the available evidence for the early history of Arab colonization of Oman (discussed further in Chapter IX) shows that the way the tribesmen moved into the country tended to conform to a pattern of migration that has characterized certain kinds of colonizing movements throughout history. In this a pioneer group leaves the home area where, for any number of reasons, living conditions are in decline, and by its success in establishing itself in a more attractive place initiates further waves of migration from the old area of settlement into the new. People from neighbouring regions then tend to move into the more or less abandoned area of original settlement and either assimilate into their social organization those inhabitants who remain, or cause them to move away; should the latter happen in association with some of the incoming elements, a further series of migrations may be set off, and so the process of depopulating the depressed homeland area is prolonged and extended over a greater area. In the new lands, too, the arrival of each migrating wave sets up population reactions as the newcomers either assimilate with their predecessors, or start a move towards new 'frontiers of settlement'.

In the case of the Arab migrations into Oman each of these changes found a counterpart in tribal reorganization, which in turn had to be accommodated into the rationalizing pattern of descent hierarchies. Particularly important were the relationships that developed between the earliest settlers, who for the most part had colonized the western bajada zone and the mountains at either end of the range, and the Shanuʾa Azd and their followers who occupied the central mountain zone in a later major wave of pre-Islamic migration.

The focal point of this new tribal organization was an alliance between the various Azd groups (cf. Fig. 30) by which the Bani Hinā (shaikhs of the main Omani Mālik b. Fahm and associated Quḍāʿa tribes, and heads of a confederation which included their 'brother' tribe, the Bani Salīma of south-east Oman and south-west Persia, and the ʿImrān Azd of northern Oman) accorded pre-eminence to the shaikhly family from the Maʿāwil of the Shanuʾa Azd which effectively made the latter leaders of all the Arab tribes of Oman, a position subsequently reinforced by their appointment as *julandā* by the Persians (cf. Chapter VI). And it is because of the importance of this particular merging of interests that Hinā (Hunāʾa) and Maʿwila have been genealogically linked at the closest point possible within the bounds of credibility, and that Abu Sulaymān al-Maʿwali emphasizes their relationship in his introduction to the *Nubdhat al-Maʿāwil*. However, the idea that all three Azd confederations (Shanuʾa, ʿImrān, and Mālik b. Fahm) were related to each other and to a number of other groups outside the region through a remote ancestor Dirʾ (called al-Azd) does, in part at least, seem to reflect certain very much older associations connected with the semi-legendary history of the dispersal of the Azd. But whether or not such possible earlier alliances played a part in the development of the Azd bloc in Oman, the fact remains that the form that union took there led to some major manipulations of Azd genealogical structure (just as it did for a number of the other major genealogical groupings in the country).

Of course, such translations of political change into descent-group terms took time, for even though Arab genealogy had not then been fossilized, the framework of clan relationships deriving from past history which Ibn al-Kalbi was later to fix did already exist in embryonic form and could not simply be discarded at will to fit changing circumstances. And since such modifications to the genealogical forms normally took much longer to achieve than the political changes they represented, the kind of major upheavals in political organization that periods of intense migration brought about inevitably led to some dissociation between the formalized descent-group structure and the actual tribal groupings. Even so, by the time Arab genealogy began to take on its final shape in the eighth century, it incorporated many of the changed tribal associations that had developed and so really did indicate important political relationships in the early Arab settlement pattern of Oman. These relationships more or less dominated tribal politics until the civil war which brought to a close the period of the First Imamate: from that time onwards the largest confederations finally began to break up, so that many of their names (Azd, Kinda, Sāma, ʿAbd al-Qays etc.) disappeared from the tribal scene. But because by then tribal descent had been formalized, it was no longer possible to manipulate this now rigid structure to rationalize the new confederations as they emerged. From the tenth century onwards, therefore, the divorce between formal descent-group and tribal-group structure accelerates.

If this is so, the question that now arises is, why should the names of these old groupings have been retained in central Oman, when elsewhere in the country, as indeed throughout most of the Arab tribal world, formal genealogy has long since been abandoned and present-day relationships rationalized in terms of an eponymous ancestry that is rarely more than fictionally related to the remote past?

Fundamentally the answer to this question lies in the fact that in central Oman little new inward migration has occurred and so the modern tribal groupings simply represent the reorganization of still-recognizable units from the old order into a new political hierarchy. By contrast, in the desert borderlands and mountain regions around the central core this is not so (cf. Chapter IX), and there virtually all sense of continuity with the tribal past has been lost: indeed, amongst the bedu, formal genealogy is almost meaningless and group-names frequently do not even refer to a person but to a symbol.[6] Since, therefore, their eponymous ancestors have themselves no forebears of any historical significance, their genealogy is fluid and may be adapted to embrace the largest and loosest political organizations. And this is why the distinctive fourfold clan hierarchy which anthropologists have recognized in similar societies elsewhere, the hierarchy which leads Peters (1960) to suggest a division of tribal descent into primary, secondary, tertiary, and within-tertiary sections in the case of the camel-herding bedu of Cyrenaica, and Evans-Pritchard (1940) into maximal, major, minor, and minimal lineages for the Nuer, may also be identified in the tribal structures of the frontier regions of Oman. In central Oman, on the other hand, this is not possible because, even though the higher levels of the ancient tribal organization corresponding to the primary section or maximal lineages have long since disappeared, many of the sub-groupings still exist as real socio-political units. So the formalized genealogical structure still continues to perform two functions: first, it helps rationalize group relations at the lower levels of tribal hierarchy;[7] second, it gives members of these formal descent groups a sense of 'belonging' to a country and a 'nation', a sense of having roots in a land and in a history.[8]

Formal Descent Groups and the Tribe

It is obvious that in much of Oman a very real distinction has to be drawn between formal descent groups on the one hand, and tribal groups on the other (except in those cases where the two are genuinely to be equated in the eyes of the tribesmen themselves), and this is quite clearly laid down in the law books. Thus in ʿIsā b. Ṣāliḥ al-Ḥārithi's *Khulāṣat al-wasāʾil* (ii. 24–5) there is a section entitled 'it is not correct for a man to relate himself to other than his clan', in which it is stated that no group may genealogically assimilate itself to another regardless of the circumstances of amalgamation; this ruling is backed up with relevant *ḥadīth* and the comments and judgement of other Omani *ʿulamaʾ*.

Unfortunately these ground-rules are not always rigidly adhered to in practice for two main reasons. First, because major political groupings do exist amongst the tribes, these require labelling, and it is frequently convenient to give them the name of the dominant clan (cf. the remarks on the Bani Riyām quoted on p. 175, above). Second, there is no cut-and-dried boundary which divides those tribes that basically adhere to the rules of formal genealogy, and those which do not. Consequently there can be a confusion in tribal nomenclature even in central Oman, and this confusion in turn can lead to the following kind of determinist reasoning in European writing (Aramco 1952, p. 83): 'The fragmentation of the social structure in Oman may be clearly seen in the fact that the number of tribes owing allegiance in whole or in part to the Imamate falls not far short of a hundred' (200 in United Nations 1963). The authors then try to explain this phenomenon: 'in the wide regions of the Hasa, where the landscape is devoid of the rugged mountains and deep walled-in valleys common to Oman and the life of the people is less disrupted by divisive factors, there are hardly more than ten tribes'. The implication is clear: the physical characteristics of the mountain landscape has led to the fragmentation of Omani society, whereas the homogeneity of the desert plain has somehow caused the inhabitants to draw together into major tribal grouping. Yet, a few lines later, the same report notes that there are only eighteen important tribes connected with the Imamate. No explanation of this equally remarkable phenomenon, however, is proferred: indeed, the authors completely fail to point out that these eighteen or so tribes represent amalgamations of elements from the hundred 'tribes' (i.e. descent groups) identified earlier, and they make no mention of the fact that some of them have populations of between twenty and twenty-five thousand (according to Lorimer), figures which compare with the size of the Ḥasawi tribes.

This kind of confused description of tribal organization in Oman (which is all too often found in the reports of British officials also) really stems from two factors: first, a failure to identify the differences between formal descent groups, descent groups that are politically organized as tribes, and tribes that are not rationalized in descent-group terms; and second, a failure to understand what the Omanis mean by the term *shaff*.

SHAFF

Shaff (variant *ṣaff*) is really no more than a notion the Omani tribesmen have evolved in order to circumvent the problems posed by a rigid genealogy when trying to rationalize the higher levels of tribal association. When, for example, they describe the Maᶜāwil and the Bani Ruwāḥa as forming *shaff wāḥid* (Rössler 1898), what they mean is that even though the two groups form distinctive 'clans' by reason of their different ancestry, they behave towards each other as though their eponymous ancestors were in fact 'brothers': members of the one group will thus be welcomed and protected when in the territory of the other, they will help each other when attacked by outsiders, and in some circumstances both will recognize the authority of some paramount leader. The obligations of *shaff*, therefore, are similar to those imposed by postulating a common descent, and the function in tribal organization is identical, i.e. rationalizing and ordering group relationships in 'family' terms and thereby giving them an enduring quality. Since *shaff* has the advantage that it may be used without any of the constraints involved in manipulating genealogy (formal or fictional), it can be used for all levels of tribal association, even to the level of the ultimate polarizations of tribal interests in Oman, the so-called Hināwi and Ghāfiri *shaff*s. And as we shall see in Chapter X, these 'moiety' divisions are described in *shaff* terms precisely because they are related to modern tribal groupings, whereas in earlier times the alliances were labelled according to the formal genealogy which divides the Arabs into two major descent groupings, Nizār and Yaman, a notion that was already largely inappropriate to the tribal structure of Oman even at the time of the first great civil war at the end of the ninth century A.D.

LEADERSHIP

So there are two notions involved in explaining tribal group formation,

ʿ*aṣabīya*, which rationalizes mutual obligations in terms of common descent, and *shaff*, which provides an alternative explanation of group relations when kinship cannot be invoked because of the problems posed by formal genealogy. Of themselves, however, these 'clan' linkages remain somewhat inert unless appeal to 'family' obligations is invoked through the 'head of the family'.

It has been observed of 'Arab Bedouin society [that it] is characterized by the potentiality for massive aggregation of its agnatic units, on the one hand, and atomistic individualism, on the other. Cohesive relations between and within sections do not have an enduring, continuing quality, but are situational and opportunistic' (Murphy and Kasdan 1959). While this statement loses a little of its force when applied to the settled Arab tribes of Oman (where the fact of being fixed in a permanent settlement pattern produces a rather more predictable situational pattern than in the desert), it still remains true that the larger the socio-political unit in Oman, the greater its inherent instability. In other words, once the appeal to family obligations begins to become notional and the rationalizing genealogical order obviously artificial, it is the obligations of loyalty and obedience to particular members of the tribe which maintain its functioning as a clan unit. On what base, therefore, do notions of loyalty and obedience to these particular members rest?

The three essential features upon which shaikhly leadership depends were succinctly described over two hundred years ago by a young Swedish scholar, when he observed of the Egyptian bedu 'they collect by families . . . and elect a *scheik*, or chief, whose job it is to settle the differences that may arise between them, and to lead them when they have a war to wage against their enemies' (translated from F. Hasselquist, French edn., Paris, 1769, i. 108).

The first feature is that the shaikh (*shaykh*) is elected in conclave by the family-groups who make up the tribe. Such elections are still reputed to occur amongst the bedu of Oman, but amongst the settled tribes open conclave appears to be unusual and selection tends to be on the basis of consultation. The authority of the shaikh, none the less, still derives from the basic fact that he is generally accepted by his followers and that they remain satisfied with the way he carries out his duties. This is why the paramount leader of a large tribal unit in Oman is sometimes referred to as a *tamīma*, one who has been 'confirmed' by his followers (a notion also inherent to the Ibāḍi system of government; cf. Chapter VIII).

But what Hasselquist fails to note, although doubtless he was aware of the point, is that the shaikh is not jut selected from any part of the tribe, but from a particular family. This does not mean that his position is fully hereditary, but that the person chosen to succeed is normally one of the deceased leader's fairly close male relatives. Yet precisely because there is no fixed hierarchy of succession, and the sole theoretical criterion for choosing a man is his suitability and acceptibility for the duties he has to carry out, it is quite frequent for the position to switch between 'legal families', even though it is very rare for it to pass right out of the 'extended family'. There are, therefore, two stages in selecting a leader who has the full support of the tribe: the first, and often the most difficult one, is for the shaikhly family itself to agree on which of its members it is to select for pre-eminence; the second, and marginally less difficult stage, is to ensure that the rest of the sections agree on the choice. Failure to reach agreement at either stage will result in weak and divided leadership, and thus accentuate the fissiparous tendencies inherent in the clan system.

The second and third features in Hasselquist's description concern the two duties for which the leader has been selected, that of settling internal disputes and that of leading the tribe in war. In the view of many writers, the latter is considered the more important, because war is the one obvious situation in which the tribe acts together. The present writer is not convinced that this really is so; he believes that the military duty becomes increasingly subordinated the larger the tribal unit and the more complex its structure. Furthermore, these responsibilities can be split between two different people in Oman, and when this happens it is inevitably the shaikh that holds the power of arbitrating within the group who is the senior. This can be seen even amongst the bedu tribes, where it is not unusual for an ageing shaikh to delegate military responsibility to a younger member of his family (who may thus prove himself as a worthy potential successor), and the writer even knows of a case (the Bani Yās) where the leader (*ʿaqīd*) of the *qawm*[9] came from a quite different clan from that which provided the tribe's paramount leader (in this case referred to in the plural as *al-shuyūkh*). Certainly, amongst the settled tribes of the region, such division of authority can occur at quite a low level of group association, and may be considered 'normal' amongst larger tribes held together by *shaff*, rather than by *ʿaṣabīya*, bonds. It is also worth noting in this context that in the parallel Ibāḍi theory of the *imāma*, it is only in the special case of a *shārī* Imam (who conducts aggressive *jihād*) that it is specified in the election that the head of the community must himself lead the Muslim army in the field (Ṣāʾighi, *bāb al-imāma*).[10]

In a major tribal grouping, the problem of finding a leader from one of its own members who has both the ability and authority to arbitrate between the numerous sections is often extremely difficult. If the Bani Ruwāḥa is taken as an example, this leader is hardly likely to come from the Bani Hishām, who, from the eleventh century at least, have provided the shaikhs of the true Ruwayḥi clans (who live in the strategically important villages that control the upper end of the eastward-draining Wadi Sumāyil and the westward-draining headstream of the Wadi ʿAndām called the Wadi Maḥram cf. Figs. 3 and 25). True, they have from time to time produced strong men, but as often as not they have been divided in the sort of way which in 1954 led to an outbreak of fighting in the mosque of the tribal capital at al-Janā (once known as Ḥamamat) and the death of fourteen tribesmen: this particular leadership crisis would undoubtedly have led to a feuding situation and the final break-up of the tribe, had it not been for the firm intervention of the Khalīlis (see below).

If, then, the Bani Hishām are incapable even of holding together the elements of the tribe which consider themselves to be bonded by *ʿaṣabīya* obligations (perceived true kinship), how much less are they able to keep control of the *tabaʿīn* (follower-groups) or of their *shaff* allies? If the cohesiveness of this tribe is to have any degree of permanency clearly it must look outside its own groups to find a leader who is capable of judging impartially between the interests of some 20,000 souls belonging to over seventy different descent groups! From where do such leaders come?

Elitist families

The simple answer is, from a few élite families. At this point it will be useful to look at a particular case-study, to obtain some idea of the origin of such families and how they obtain their tribal position. To maintain a degree of continuity in the examples cited, the case of the major Bani Ruwāḥa tribal confederation (that is the tribe to which the Maʿāwil are bound by *shaff* alliance) will be pursued, and the background to the Khalīli position in it examined.[11]

The Khalīlis are a lineage of the Bani Kharūṣ, a group still existing as a tribe in the Ghadaf (cf. Fig. 25) and one which earlier formed part of the great Yaḥmad confederation within the Shanuʾa Azd (cf. Fig. 30). Genealogically the origins of the family can certainly be traced back at least to the First Imamate and possibly into the remote period when the Shanuʾa were still migrating through central Arabia. It is clear from a study of this ancient history that their original power was rooted in the early tribal organization and that it was as a (the?) shaikhly family of Yaḥmad that they first became involved as leaders of the Imamate. But once the First Imamate collapsed and brought down in its wake the unity of the Yaḥmad tribal grouping, the leading Kharūṣi families made use of their old alliances with the ʿAtīk of the northern Jawf to ingratiate themselves with the new holders of political power, the Nabāhina (an ʿAtaki family), and eventually settled at their capital Bahlā.[12] Their first direct relations with the Bani Ruwāḥa were far from friendly. After a temporary success in ejecting the Nabhāni *mālik* from Bahlā and restoring the Imamate in the Jawf during the sixteenth century, the new Kharūṣi-backed Ibāḍi regime gave orders for Bani Ruwāḥa property to be confiscated because of their continued support for Sulaymān b. Sulaymān b. Muẓaffar al-Nabhāni. Retribution quickly followed: the Bani Ruwāḥa re-established the dispossessed Nabhāni *mālik* and drove the Kharūṣi families first out of Bahlā and then, when they tried to settle there, from Izki.[13] Thereupon all returned to the tribal fold except the Khalīlis, who found sanctuary in a small village in the foothills at the extreme southern end of the Batina coast called al-Bawshar. And it was while living there that the relationship with their erstwhile enemies began to change as the result (according to local stories) of two members of the family being rescued from the clutches of the Bani Jābir of Lower Sumāyil by Ruwayḥi tribesmen.

But whatever role this particular incident may or may not have played in preparing the way for a *rapprochement*, the first real shift in the relationship between the Khalīlis and the Ruwāḥa stemmed from deliberate planning by Saʿīd b. Khalfān al-Khalīli (1812?–71: *éminence grise* behind ʿAzzān b. Qays, Imam 1868–71, and grandfather of the Imam-to-be Muḥammad b. ʿAbdullāh al-Khalīli, Imam 1920–54). Moving to the property his family had acquired in the Ruwāḥa-aligned settlement of Upper Sumāyil, Saʿīd expressly exploited the discontent of the Hināwi tribes of the region so as to win them over to the Imamate cause. And when the temporary Imamate of ʿAzzān b. Qays was overthrown and the Ghāfiri alliances revenged themselves on Saʿīd's Hināwi supporters, his son ʿAbdullāh (*c.* 1862–1914) had no difficulty in exploiting the murder of his father to rally opposition to the Sultans of Muscat and thereby consolidate his family's position as protectors of the Ruwayḥi confederation. Thus his son, the Imam-to-be Muḥammed b. ʿAbdullāh al-Khalīli, eventually fell heir not only to a considerable fortune but also to the main fort in the Sumāyil Gap and the leadership of one of the most powerful tribes of central Oman.

The first thing to note from this particular case is that leadership of the great tribal confederations emerges from families that have traditionally been closely associated with 'state' politics, families that are themselves of impeccable descent but which have severed their tribal ties with their own clan. Thus it will be noted that the Khalīlis have for long been dissociated from Kharūṣi tribal politics, and that tribe itself now actually 'follows' the Bani Ruwāḥa's main rivals, the Bani Riyām. And who leads the Bani Riyām? None other than the Nabāhina, the ʿAtaki family which for five hundred years held the position of *mulūk* of Oman, and which once led the Bāni Ruwāḥa!

Obviously, therefore, such marriages between élite families and great tribal groupings stem in part from the mutual benefits to be derived from the association. This once again emphasizes the extraordinarily close relations that exist between tribal and government organizations in the interior of the country. Yet of themselves these reciprocal benefits do not adequately explain the basis of elitist authority, nor precisely how these families are able to intervene in the affairs of a 'clan' organization to which they do not belong by right of actual or assumed descent.

To explain 'elitism' in the Omani context is a complex task, but it may be simplified by considering authority as arising from two sources, temporal power (*imāra*: cf. *Amīr* or Emir) and religious authority (*ʿilm*: cf. *ʿālim*, pl. *ʿulāmaʾ*). The former embraces such matters as inherited family status, possession of land and wealth, command of strategic sites, and force of arms, and it is this form of power that the Nabāhina have tended to foster in their long history as *mulūk* of Oman; similarly their influence with the Riyām has tended to be based on coercion rather than persuasion. Leaders like the

Khalīlis, on the other hand, have tended to depend less on temporal power than on their ability to settle differences between clans through moral influence. Their authority, like the *wilāya* of an Imam, depends on the degree to which tribesmen are prepared to accord them the right to judge in their disputes and to accept their decisions, and this in turn depends on their *ʿilm* qualifications.

ʿIlm is an acquired personal quality which cannot be transmitted by birth. Although a family which regularly produces *ʿulamāʾ* does gain a general respect, its members do not enjoy group charisma: this is why in Oman, unlike, say, the Ḥaḍramawt, there are no families who hold inherited religious positions as guardians of sanctuaries, or who enjoy the special status normally accorded to descendants of the Prophet, or who hold fully dynastic positions in the Imamate. A leader who has *ʿilm* therefore has something which is individual to him, a quality which sets him above his fellows. This in turn means that his authority is not undermined by the kind of family rivalry which beset *amīrs* or shaikhs. However, the quality of impartiality that makes an *ʿālim* acceptable as an arbitrator by all does depend on his cultivating detachment from the internal politics of individual groups, and this automatically weakens certain other aspects of his tribal authority. So it is that pure *ʿilm*, which may be viewed as universal authority without the power to enforce it, is of limited value without *imāra*. It is only by cultivating both together that a leader can succeed in overcoming the fissiparous tendencies inherent in all large tribal blocs and in this way ensure that continuing support of a major tribal unit which is a prerequisite for success in Omani 'state' politics.

So elitist authority in Oman derives fundamentally from possession of temporal power and from personal 'religious' qualifications. But because it does not essentially depend on hereditary position, its perpetuation in a particular family depends on its members regularly replenishing vitality at the twin founts of *imāra* and *ʿilm*. This is why the influence of such families within tribal groups is ephemeral, and why the Bani Ruwāḥa, whose component tribal groups have normally drawn their shaikhly leaders from the same clan since time immemorial, have found their paramount leaders from no less than three outside families over the last four or so hundred years — the Nabāhina, the Yaʿāriba, and the Khalīlis.

Yet it should not be thought that in conservative Oman the influence of an élite family collapses in a night, any more than it is built up in a day. A study of Omani history will quickly convince the reader that certain lineages have developed a remarkable resistance to the political environment and, like some plants of the desert, revive with the first passing showers. The Nabāhina, for example, who first began to emerge from the ʿAtīk Azd as an important political family towards the end of the twelfth century (cf. the *Dīwāns* of Ibn al-Naẓar and Sitāli; *Tuḥfa* i. 336-7, 354-8) and dominate the course of what little we know of the next five hundred years of Omani history, reappear within a century and a half of the overthrow of the last of their *mulūk*, first as paramount leaders of the powerful Bani Riyām (which is the most influential tribe in the Ghāfiri 'moiety'), then, in the twentieth century, in the new role of Imam-makers and, finally, aspiring to be independent 'Kings of the Green Mountain' (the Jabal Akhdhar).

This is how, in a country where the principles of social and religious organization are rooted in the theoretically democratic principles of clan organization and Ibāḍi Islam, political power is in reality dominated by family. Indeed, much of Oman's political history may be described as a repetitious account of the mutual searching for partnership between a handful of élite families on the one hand and the few select 'descent groups' who control the country's principal strategic sites on the other.

SUMMARY

In this chapter analysis of the tribe has deliberately been concentrated on the notional concepts which underlie the social organization, and *ʿaṣabīya, shaff,* and shaikhly power have been analysed in a way that would allow the role of 'family' in tribal formation to emerge and the clan-model of social organization to be appreciated.

Geographical features affecting the functioning of the tribes have deliberately been ignored, because in the model of the tribe as a clan the spatial dimension finds no place: it has been suppressed through the false syllogism that a clan lives together, therefore people who live together form a clan. This is not to say that tribesmen are themselves unaware of the importance of territory in explaining group relationships: rather, that it constitutes a passive feature which of itself has no role in determining what by definition is a kinship organization. So the logic of tribal functioning is sought in its rationalizing descent-group hierarchy. Nowhere has this been more fully developed than amongst the nomadic tribes which inhabit the desert borderlands of Oman: for them genealogy has no fixed point of reference, and eponymous ancestors may be 'invented'. But amongst the settled tribes of central Oman where the evolution of political groupings has been recorded more or less historically, the relationship of tribal ancestors became fixed at an early stage, in the framework of formal Arab genealogy, and this flexibility was thereby lost.

Consequently, a substitute rationalization of tribal behaviour had to be found, and this was developed in the notion of *shaff*: concomitantly certain purely kinship terms used to describe the higher levels of tribal associations were dropped, and words like *ṭāyifa* and *jumāʿa* substituted. Thus the pure clan-model has broken down in that region and the tribesmen are themselves subconsciously aware that some dimension other than that of clan is necessary to explain tribal loyalties. Hence the somewhat confusing explanations that tribesmen will offer for defining *shaff* once kin relationships have been exhausted: for most Omanis *shaff* is simply something that exists. Its objectives are none the less quite clear: mutual support based on the same rules which govern the descent group. The social code in Oman therefore differs little from that of the desert. The behavioural pattern, on the other hand, does differ, for, as one more-educated tribesman put it, there are two elements involved in tribal political behaviour: *qabāyil* (clans) and *jughrafīya* (geography). It is to the second element that we now turn, to see how locational connectivity and territorial identity affect the intensity of social interaction between clans, and how the group-solidarity called *ᶜaṣabīya* or *shaff* is conditioned by geographical factors.

NOTES TO CHAPTER VIII

1 In his biography, as given in Ibn Ruzayq's *al-Ṣaḥīfa al-Qaḥṭānīya* (fols. 261ᵛ et seq.), the author is named as Abu Sulaymān Muḥammad b. Rāshid b. Saᶜīd b. ᶜAbdullāh al-Maᶜwali, and it is stated that he died a few years after the Imam Aḥmad b. Saᶜīd (1783). The *Nubdhat (fī ansāb) al-Maᶜāwil* forms the last few pages (420 et seq.)of Damascus MS. Taʾrīkh 385 (the rest of which is made up of a copy of the *Qaṣīda al-Ḥimyarīya* and Maᶜwali's history of Oman entitled *Qiṣaṣ wa akhbār jarat bi ᶜUmān*; all three works are copies made for a Maᶜwali shaikh living in Izki in 1896). Much of the context of the *Nubdhat al-Maᶜāwil* is also to be found included under the author's bibliography in the *Saḥīfa al-Qaḥṭānīya*.

2 They claim to have acquired the latter village by purchase: be that as it may, their title to both villages was subsequently confirmed by one of the Yaᶜāriba Imams (according to one of the Ḥawsani shaikhs).

3 Saᶜīd and his brother Sulaymān jointly succeeded their father ᶜAbbād who ruled during the Caliphates of ᶜUthmān and ᶜAli and was killed (*c.* A.D. 690) in an uprising that provided the opportunity for the Bani Ḥanīfa of Yamāma to extend their *Khāriji* state to Oman. The brothers, who were away collecting taxes in the coastal district at the time of the invasion, returned, killed the *Khāriji* governor, and restored Julandā rule. They had to flee the country (reputedly to Zanj, East Africa) when al-Ḥajjāj b. Yūsuf brought Oman back under central-government control (Balādhuri *Ansāb* XI. 125-47; Yāqūt art. Maskin; *Tuḥfa* i. 67, 74-8; *Kashf* edn. Klein, pp. 11-15.).

4 Ibn Durayd (Abu Bakr Muḥammad b. al-Ḥasan b. Durayd), the famous ninth-century grammarian and philologist, was himself an Omani, from one of the Mālik b. Fahm clans. He would seem to have belonged to one of the Omani merchant families which was partly based in Basra and partly in Oman itself; in his youth he travelled extensively between the Gulf emporia. During the Zanj uprising Ibn Durayd lost his property in Basra and then spent a considerable time in Oman: although he seems to have left the country before the deposing of the Imam al-Ṣalt b. Mālik al-Kharūṣi in A.D. 886 he nevertheless became heavily embroiled in the events which eventually led to civil war there (Wilkinson *Arabian Studies iii*, in press).

5 The most important is Salma b. Musallim al-ᶜAwtabi's *Kitāb ansāb al-ᶜArab* (for MS. details see bibliography). This work, probably written in the fifth/eleventh century by a member of a distinguished Ṣuḥāri family, belongs to the extended literary form of *Ansāb* and since it deals with a wide range of Arab tribes (perhaps all in the original version), much of its content is quite unrelated to Oman. It does, however, contain some extremely valuable local material and this, when read in conjunction with other near-contemporary sources (cf. Wilkinson in *Arabian Studies* iii, in press), allows us to make a partial reconstruction of the tribal picture in Oman just at the time when it began to change drastically during the country's 'Dark Ages'.

Also of some interest for Omani tribal studies are Ibn Ruzayq's massive *al-Ṣaḥīfa al-Qaḥṭānīya* (Rhodes House, Oxford MS. Afr. S.3, of 478 folios dated 1852) and its twin *al-*

Ṣaḥīfa al-ʿAdnānīya (British Museum Or. 6569, 477 folios dated 1843), a work which should be used in conjunction with his immense commentary to *al-Qaṣīda al-qudsīya al-Qurānīya fi manāqib al-ʿAdnānīya* (vol. II only is in the British Museum: Or. 6565). Ibn Ruzayq's value, however, is as a plagiarist: his own contributions are frequently highly misleading.

The *Isʿāf al-aʿyān fi ansāb ahl ʿUmān* (Beirut 1384/1965) of Sālim b. Ḥumūd al-Siyābi is also worthy of mention because, even though this living Omani author has sometimes stretched the evidence in the classical and local sources (incidentally he would never appear himself to have seen a copy of ʿAwtabi), much of his work is based on his own intimate knowledge of the tribes and what they themselves believe to be their genealogy. It is, therefore, a useful guide for tracing something of the way in which the modern tribes have evolved from the older groupings.

6 In studying assimilation patterns amongst bedu groups in South-East Arabia the use of *wasms*, i.e. ownership markings on livestock (and some other possessions, hawks, wells, etc.), is probably a more important indicator than genealogy. The points that particularly need examining are the circumstances under which a group will adopt a new *wasm*, and at what levels of organization distinguishing marks (*ʿazili*) are used.

7 As, for example, the explanation proferred for the two main feuds of the Ghāfiri tribal alliance in the central Sumāyil Gap. The first of these is primarily maintained between the Bani Jābir and the Bani Ruwāḥa, and here the proferred explanation goes right back to the famous pre-Islamic story of why their forebears ʿAbs and Dhibyān quarrelled! The explanation of the second is more recent in origin. In this case the stories relate (*Dīwān of* Rāshid b. Khamīs al-Ḥabsi 1v-2v; Ibn Ruzayq *al-Qaṣīda al-Qudsīya* 132; *Tuḥfa* ii. 86-90; Siyābi 40 et seq.) that the Āl Musīb (Siyābiyīn) and the Ḥabs (Ḥubūs) were two brother tribes, 'sons' of Shihāb b. Nuwayra (of Taghlib origin), who originally settled alongside each other in al-Rawḍa, a village in the northern Sharqīya. Relations between the two subsequently deteriorated until finally, some time in the Nabāhina period, the Ḥabs, with the help of some of the other Sharqīya tribes, drove the Āl Musīb out of the village. The latter thereupon settled at Nafʿa (to the various parts of which they gave the same names as their old settlement in al-Rawḍa), a village which lies near the exit of the Wadi al-ʿAqq on the main route between the Sharqīya and the Wadi al-Sumāyil; from there, with the help of their new neighbours (whom they in turn assisted in their political objectives), they did everything they could to harass the Sharqīya tribes and impede them from linking up with the Hināwi *shaff* tribes in the Ghadaf (for the kind of results, cf. *Tuḥfa* ii. 253 et seq.). So we can see how the behaviour of a tribal confederation which basically owes its existence to the fact that it controls the cross-roads between the western and eastern Sumāyil Gap, and the Ghadaf and the Sharqīya, has been accounted for in terms of clan feuds: on the other hand, forr al geneology has prevented both the Sumāyil Ghāfiris and the Sharqīya Hināwis from rationalizing their alliances in descent-group terms, even though each forms a more united 'tribal' group than does, for example, the amorphous Bani Yās (i.e. the 'descent' of Yās) of Trucial Oman.

8 At first sight this statement might appear paradoxical, for the tribal system would seem to be what keeps Oman divided. While this may be true of the 'state', it is not true of the 'nation', because to the Omanis the tribal groupings represent the internal divisions of their community, a community made up of Arabs that have long-established rights to their homeland, and one which has, in their eyes, tried to conduct its affairs according to the true precepts of Islam. The clan system is essential to the ordering of this community for two reasons. First, it is through the tribe that the individual exercises his 'democratic' right to have a say in the way his 'nation' is governed and to discharge his military obligations towards it. Second, it safeguards the 'republican' nature of the regime (cf. the comments of Aucher-Eloy quoted in Chapter I) because as tribesmen the Omanis accord no hereditary rights to any particular group to rule them. So long, therefore, as tribal *ʿaṣabīya* is directed towards upholding the Imamate, there is no conflict between the loyalties of the individual to his clan and his loyalties to his 'nation'.

[9] The *qawm* (in Abu Dhabi dialect *gōm*, pl. *gīmān*) is the military unit of the tribe, a meaning that is sometimes lost by the classical Arab authors who use it as just another word for clan. The proper use of the word is retained by the Omani tribes, as also by many bedu tribes of the Peninsula (cf. Dickson 1949, p. 117, and Raunkiaer, English 1969 edn., p. 75); amongst the Rwala, on the other hand, it appears to mean the actual state of enmity existing between two groups (cf. Musil 1928, pp. 505-6).

[10] In this connection too it is interesting to note that in Julandā times the rule was often split between two members of the family, ʿAbd and Jayfar, Sulaymān and Saʿīd, Rāshid and Muḥammad (cf. Wilkinson in *J. Omani Studies*, in press).

[11] For Khalīlī family history see in particular: *Naḥda*, pp. 323-32 *et passim*; Siyābi, pp. 34 et seq.; *Dīwān al-Sitālī*; *Dīwān Sulaymān b. Sulaymān al-Nabhānī*. For its origins and the Yaḥmad's internal relationships see Wilkinson in *J. Omani Studies* (in press).

[12] Bahlā was the capital of the ʿAtīk (Asad b. ʿImrān Azd) and is often referred to as ʿAtīk in the early sources. The close relationship with the Kharūṣ in part came from a shared interest in the direct passage across the Jabal Akhdhar via the Wadi Bani Kharūṣ.

[13] It was from two other of these families that there descended the real founder of the Ibāḍi renaissance movement in Oman, Abu Nabhān Jāʿid b. Khamīs al-Kharūṣi (*c.* 1734-1822), and one of its Imams Sālim b. Rāshid al-Kharūṣi (Imam 1913-20).

CHAPTER IX

Sedentarization

FROM BEDU TO HADHAR

Before embarking on any account of the role common interests in locality play in tribal organization in the mountain heartland of Oman, it is desirable first to explain certain basic changes which occur to any tribal group as it begins to fix itself in the land. These changes have affected all the Arab groups of Oman at some time or other, but it is amongst the peoples of the desert borderlands that the initial effects are best observed today.

For convenience, words such as bedu and hadhar, settled and nomad, will be used in this chapter, but, as Johnson (1969) has pointed out in his useful compilation on nomadism, there are so many variables involved in the way of life of the people who inhabit the fringes of the desert that it is of limited value to classify their mode of life under such simple terms: the fact that people may not move around to gain a living does not, *ipso facto*, make them 'settled' any more than livestock-herding makes them 'nomads'. So, for example, an Egyptian villager would probably tend to describe all Omanis as 'bedu', even though they may have been living in villages for centuries, because their social organization remains 'tribal' and their attitude towards the land continues to exhibit somewhat *ʿarab* characteristics. To the Omanis themselves, on the other hand, there is a marked distinction between what they call bedu and hadhar, and in local legal works the former are still specifically designated under the term *ʿarab*. In this study such words must simply be considered as general labels that contrast two differing life-styles within the context of the region.

ACQUISITION OF A STAKE IN THE LAND

One of the themes developed in Chapter III was that life in the desert is so poor that the drive for the bedu to improve their economic lot is paramount. Even Wilfred Thesiger, the greatest proponent of the desert mystique in South-East Arabia, is too honest not to point this out.

> Bedu love money: even to handle it seems to give them a thrill. They talk of it incessantly. They will discuss the price of a headcloth or a cartridge belt intermittently for days . . . I chided them for their avarice, and they answered: 'It is all very well for you; you have plenty; but for us a few *riyals* may make all the difference between starving and not starving.'
>
> (*Arabian Sands*, p. 81.)

So it is that the nomads of South-East Arabia will do work that is despised or even considered the job of slaves among other Arabs (Dostal 1967); they will fish, go pearling, make charcoal, and even hew salt in order to supplement their basic living from livestock-herding. More important is the fact that this desire for a better living manifests itself in a push towards the richer pastoral lands of the bajada zone where water and grazing are relatively abundant and varied.

Once a bedu group succeeds in establishing itself in this area, its way of life is liable to be changed in varying degrees by the following factors. First, the range of seasonal and daily displacement is reduced; second, camel-herding may now be supplemented by the keeping of small livestock; third, the stock-rearing basis of their economy may be extended to include agriculture; fourth, there is an increased contact with the settled peoples of Oman. And each of these factors plays a role in the process of what, for convenience sake, may be called 'sedentarization'. However, of these four factors, the one that produces the most fundamental transformation is the diversifying of the economy to include agriculture. So before starting on specific case-studies, it will be useful first to examine the various possibilities open to the bedu for acquiring a stake in the cultivated land of Oman.

One method is to develop abandoned *qanāt* settlement. There is unfortunately no shortage of this. Some *qanāt* have been destroyed in wars and tribal fighting or deserted in times of general insecurity and economic decline; others have failed through lack of maintenance, drought, and other physical factors (see Chapter IV). But revitalization of 'dead' (*mawāt*) land tends to represent a more advanced stage in the process of settling and usually comes after the initial step of acquiring an already 'going' concern.

Such acquisition by peaceful means is not easy, for, as was made clear in Chapter III, the opportunities that a bedu group have to obtain ascendancy over the hadhar is limited by the demographic equilibrium that exists between the inhabitants of the various zones of land-use. It is therefore chiefly in periods of political instability that ownership of land is most likely to pass into the hands of the nomads. This may be illustrated from the documented example of the now defunct *falaj* at al-Bizayli (in dialect Libzayli; near Ḍank) said originally to have been the most prolific of the great Dawūdi *qanāt* in Oman. Having fallen into bad repair in the 'Dark Ages', it was restored, along with several other important *qanāt*, by the Yaʿrabi Imam, Sayf b. Sulṭān b. Sayf (d. 1711)[1] and passed into the personal possession of his family: and it was from here that the last of the Yaʿāriba Imams sought to regain power in the middle of the eighteenth century (Ibn Ruzayq *Imams*, pp. 131 and 166). As a result of events associated with this turbulent period the *qanāt* was abandoned by its original owners and the bedu moved in.[2]

In this particular case the result was disastrous, for by the beginning of the present century it had fallen into such a bad state that it merely supported some forty houses of the bedu Āl Bu Shāmis,[3] while today no one lives there at all and it is difficult even to trace the line of the *qanāt* itself, let alone the area it once irrigated. But as we shall see, such a decline is by no means inevitable. The important point is that it was during a period of general political upheaval that the Āl Bu Shāmis gained control over al-Bizayli, and it was probably in this same period that they also acquired their present principal settlements in the Dhahira, al-Sunayna, and nearby al-Rayḥāni.

Unfortunately, such periods of turmoil are by no means rare in the history of Oman, and so outlying settlements frequently change hands. Just how frequently may be illustrated by another documented example, Tanᶜam, which, according to its recorded history alone, first belonged to the Persians, then to a clan of the ᶜAtīk (ᶜImrān Azd) and their Yaḥmad allies, then to an odd grouping of what were probably refugee elements from well-known tribes living right outside the region (who probably gained control of the main Sirr centres in the unsettled period after the collapse of the First Imamate; cf. notes to Fig. 33); and when once again the record may be traced in the seventeenth and eighteenth centuries it belonged successively to the Ṣawāwifa (a powerful group of the desert borderlands in Nabāhina times allied to the Bani Hinā), the Manādhira (a local group of the ᶜIbri region), the Bani Zufayt (a bedu group now more-or-less assimilated into the Bani Qitab, but once an important independent tribe that controlled the carrying trade between ᶜIbri and the Batina before the Ḥawāsina), and finally it present owners the Durūᶜ (Ibn Durayd *Ishtiqāq*, p. 137; ᶜAwtabi Paris MS. fol. 270r; *Naḥda*, p. 372; *Kashf* MS. 516 (but not *Kashf* tr. Ross); Ibn Ruzayq *Imams*, p. 157; Ross 1873).

But while it is often in periods of political instability that the bedu gain possession of *qanāt* settlement, the means by which they do so are not necessarily belligerent. In the case of al-Bizayli probably little force was used, and the bedu simply filled a 'land vacuum'. Nor does a change in ownership of itself imply the eviction of the previous inhabitants: frequently the poorer elements remain in the village and are simply absorbed into the social structure of the new land-owners. And such absorption, whether into *mawlā* (client) status or by genealogical assimilation, is obviously one of the factors which affect the organization of the tribe and its rationalizing clan structure.

A third method by which bedu acquire settled land is by purchase. In the case of the Durūᶜ (see below) it is almost certain that this is how they obtained their holdings in ᶜIbri, and it is interesting to note in this context that acquiring cultivated land is still one of the chief investments the Omani bedu make with the new wealth they have acquired through oil-company activities in their tribal territories (1955 onwards).

But by whatever means the bedu obtain agricultural holdings, it may be assumed that acquisition of hadhar territory is normally a slow process, and so sedentarization itself tends to proceed by subtle changes rather than dramatic leaps. Consequently a number of stages in the process of settling may be recognized, each of which brings about a corresponding change in tribal organization and attitudes towards the land. It is in an effort to describe these that the following case-studies are presented.

THE EARLY STAGE OF SEDENTARIZATION (THE DURŪᶜ)

A good example of a tribe in the earliest stages of settling is provided by the

Durūʿ. Its relatively recent entry into Oman is borne out by the fact this tribe is the last of those to be discussed to feature in the local chronicles; it is not until the end of the eighteenth century that their name appears, at which time they are described as a nomadic group raiding in the Sirr (Ibn Ruzayq *Imams*, p. 229).[4] Although it is true that since then they have established territorial rights in the bajada zone, their seasonal displacement is still considerable; they take their flocks right out into the lower courses of the Wadis (al-Ṣifā, Ṣōmaḥāl/Sawmaḥān, al-ʿAyn, al-Aswad, al-ʿUmayri, and al-Rifāsh) in search of grazing, and they visit such remote spots as the Umm al-Samīm, Qārat al-Kabrīt, and Qārat al-Milḥ in order to collect salt and sulphur. The sheer size of the Durūʿ tribal territory is itself indicative of the poverty of the land they have acquired and illustrates the general rule that the areal extent of a bedu *dār* tends to be in inverse proportion to the wealth and influence of the tribe to which it belongs. It is only because Durūʿ territory happens to cover the oilfields of Oman that this axiom no longer applies: this is why Siyābi (p. 78) rather bitterly says of them 'whereas formerly they were a few odd sections (*buṭūn*) now they have become a major tribal unit (*qabīla*) independent in its affairs, whether in war or peace.'

ʿIbri is the main market town for the Durūʿ, and it is there that they exchange their livestock and associated produce, along with some salt, charcoal, and woven goods, for their essential requirements and those little luxuries which make life in the desert bearable. They also carry goods between ʿIbri and some of the other principal settlements of the bajada zone, and are not averse to putting their military resources to the service of the highest bidder in the village. Through this settlement, too, the Durūʿ are drawn into a wider set of relationships both with the settled tribes and central government, for ʿIbri is not only the market centre of the Sirr but also a fortified administrative centre with a *wāli* (regional governor) and a *qāḍi al-quḍāʾ* (chief judge). In the same way, albeit of less importance for the tribe as a whole, the strategic isolated settlement of Adam acts as a local centre for the Durūʿ groups living in the south-eastern part of the *dār*.

The relationship of the Durūʿ with the hadhar, however, is by no means limited to such trading and administrative contracts with certain *qanāt* towns of the bajada zone. True, the few direct contacts the poorer groups living in the outlying parts of the *dār* have with the settled peoples do tend to arise from occasional visits to such settlements, but the wealthier members of the tribe spend much of the year in close proximity to them. Not only do they move onto the wells of the inner bajada zone in summer, but some even camp in *ʿarīsh* (palm-frond) huts within the actual bounds of ʿIbri, Adam, and some smaller villages. Here too they have acquired land and water rights: in Adam they completely own one of the four *qanāt*, while in ʿIbri it is said (in 1965) that they own over a third of the date palms; if this is true, it means they have a holding larger than any of the tribal groups who actually inhabit the village. As well as their holdings in these two large centres, the tribe also more-or-less own a number of small settlements in the outlying districts of the Jawf (Kubāra, Ma^{c}mūr, and Falaj al-Ḥarrān) and one of some size, Tan^{c}am, a few kilometers downstream from ^{c}Ibri; since most of this latter village belongs to members of the shaikhly clan (Āl Maḥāmīd) it is regarded as the tribal ^{c}*āṣima* (capital). Such ownership of cultivated land does not necessarily bring about any direct major changes in the nomadic way of life of a bedu tribe. The Durū^{c} neither live in the permanent buildings of the villages where they own property, nor do they themselves cultivate their holdings; in ^{c}Ibri that is left to the *bayādīr* who are responsible to the Mundhiri agent that looks after all Durū^{c} business interests in the town. On the other hand it does affect their way of life in other ways. Politically, it results in a loss of independence, for ownership of a long-term capital investment in the land makes them vulnerable to the authority of central government. This is brought out time and time again in Omani history. For example, in the civil wars of the early eighteenth century when the bedu 'had so infested all the roads of 'Omán, plundering and murdering, that people could only travel in large parties', a determined Omani leader was quickly able to bring the Wahība, the main offenders, under control partly by collecting their flocks together so they could not be grazed, and partly by destroying their main settlement at al-Sudayra; he similarly brought the ^{c}Azīz bedu (i.e. the Bani Qitab; see below) to heel through striking at their settlements in the lower Dhahira (*Kashf* tr. Ross, pp. 180–1). Again in a more modern context, the Imam Muḥammad b. ^{c}Abdullāh al-Khalīli was able to prevent the shaikh of the Janaba from allowing the oil companies into his territory through threatening the Achilles heel of his capital at ^{c}Izz, while a few years later, and despite changing circumstances, his successor was nearly successful in similarly deterring the Durū^{c} by threatening to destroy Tan^{c}am.

So possession of agricultural property alters the balance of political power between the settled peoples and the nomadic tribes: it also affects the internal relationships of the settling tribe, notably in changing the role of the shaikhly section and in the opening up of the gap between rich and poor sections. But it does not bring about any real psychological change in the outlook of a nomadic group towards the land. This only comes about when the village becomes the focus of tribal organization and not just an incident in their annual cycle of movement. What happens then can be illustrated by the example of the Bani Qitab who live in the small collection of *qanāt* villages in the Dhahira now known as the Aflāj Bani Qitab (Fig. 4).

THE SECOND STAGE IN SETTLING (THE BANI QITAB)

The Bani Qitab today fall into two quite distinct groups, those who still live an essentially nomadic life similar to that of the Durū^{c} in a part of the eastern sand desert of Trucial Oman (where their tribal *dār* now makes up a large tract of the inland territories of Sharja and Ras al-Khaima, i.e. the original Jowāsim state), and the southern group who appear to have moved into the lower Dhahira some time before the early eighteenth century. There they made particular allies of the then dominant group of the region, the ʿAzīz (or ʿAzāzina), themselves a relatively late migrant group to Oman (they were still bedu in the eleventh century at least) that had more-or-less settled with their capital in one of the quarters of Ḍank and with sections living in the Aflāj and also in Buraimi. At first the new arrivals began to acquire holdings in the outlying Aflāj by purchase, but when the power of the ʿAzīz was broken in the upheavals of the mid-eighteenth century the Bani Qitab appear to have taken over full possession of the Aflāj, assimilating such of their erstwhile allies who remained into their clan structure.[5]

But, unlike their neighbours the Āl Bu Shāmis, who also appear to have acquired their main settlements about the same time, and the Durūʿ, who acquired theirs somewhat later, the Bani Qitab eventually began to live all the year round in the permanent buildings of the *buldān* and took to cultivating the land themselves. Although they continue to graze livestock, their range of movement has become restricted to the territory around the villages, and the pulsatory pattern of seasonal tribal movement has been more or less abandoned. Living in permanent houses, and as much cultivators as pastoralists, their way of life contrasts markedly with that of their nomadic kinsmen to the north, even though the latter have acquired rights in agricultural settlements (notably part of Dhayḍ which they share with the Jowāsim).

As a result, the whole structure of the southern Bani Qitab has changed. Today their alliances are almost entirely dictated by the interests of the locality in which they live, their internal clan structure has been radically altered by the assimilation of outside lineages, while their relationship with their northern clansmen is now pretty well of historical interest only. At the same time their outlook has begun to change into that of a hadhar group, so that they, like their ʿAzīz predecessors, are now liable to be pushed out of their village, or assimilated into the tribal structure of new bedu arrivals. Should this happen, then they in turn will become but another 'descent group' and only their *nisba* might indicate that they once belonged to a tribal group that included the Bani Qitab of northern Oman.

THE THIRD STAGE OF SETTLING (THE ĀL BU GHUFAYLA)

Yet a further advance in the process of settling may be recognized when a bedu group not only takes to living in a village, but actually attempts to recreate a settlement by restoring one of the many abandoned *qanāt* of the bajada and mountain zones. An interesting example is provided by the story of how one of the Wahība clans deliberately set about creating an independent settlement for political reasons.

This highly segmented tribe, which is made up of many descent groups covering a wide range in the bedu hadhar spectrum, has certainly owned at least one *qanāt* settlement for a long time, for al-Sudayra is cited as being their capital (*ʿāṣima*) as far back as the beginning of the eighteenth century.

More recently they gained control of Sinaw and Burzamān. The former, which in the ninth century was important enough to boast the *wālī* responsible for all the desert borderlands of south-eastern Oman and Mahra-land beyond (*Tuḥfa* i. 153), could still support a population estimated at 3,500 with 18,000 palms at the beginning of the present century (Lorimer ii. 1628), at which time too the tribal groups living there were still independent of the local bedu. Subsequently this settlement, like Burzamān, was more-or-less abandoned due to a decrease in its water supply (probably initiated by the droughts of the 1920s which caused the abandonment of so much settlement in the Sharqīya), and it was then that it passed into the hands of the Wahība who assimilated such of the original population as remained in the village into their tribal structure. Associated with these changes came a shift in the tribe's leadership, and the Āl Bu Ghufayla section now openly began to challenge the authority of the Jaḥāḥīf as the shaikhly clan. But before they could attempt to usurp their power it was first necessary for them to develop a quite independent settlement, and this they achieved through redeveloping an abandoned shallow *falaj* (which they simply named al-Falaj).[6]

The means by which they did so was to enter into a shareholding agreement with some of the old *ahl al-bilād* groups of the area (the Ghulūb),[7] under the terms of which the former provided the capital and the latter the skill to carry out the work: this took less than a year to complete.[8] Hired unskilled labour was paid in cash and not by allocating shares in the *falaj* water rights.

This work of the Āl Bu Ghufayla, although a relatively simple undertaking, clearly represented an important psychological advance in the process of sedentarization. The building of an irrigation system, the laying-out of gardens, the planting of palms which take several years to bear fruit, and the construction of buildings all require deliberate planning and inculcate values which are largely absent in the mentality of the bedu, whose way of life rarely demands taking long term thought for the future.

The Āl Bu Ghufayla have therefore proceeded a step further than the other Wahība sections along the road of becoming a fully settled group. And this differentiation is reflected in a shift in their political role in the tribal group. At present it has given them an advantage *vis-à-vis* their old rivals the Jaḥāḥīf, but in due course such rivalry could split the tribe and perhaps even lead to the final collapse of the Wahība as a political unit. So it can be seen that differential rates of settling also lead to dislocation within the original tribal organization, and this in turn requires developing a new spectrum of group relationships in order to restore political equilibrium. These points will become rather clearer when we consider the case of the ʿAwāmir, for here the process of sedentarization may be seen operating in a much larger group over a much greater period of time and over a much wider area.

THE FINAL STAGE OF SETTLING (THE ʿAWĀMIR FALAJ EXPERTS)

The numerous clans of ʿĀmir Rabīʿa and other supposed descendants of

ʿĀmir b. Ṣaʿṣaʿ who came to Oman represent the last wave of major Arab migration to settle in the country and, as with so many other migrants, they arrived there from central Arabia via 'Baḥrayn'. Compared with the other major genealogical groupings of the region their arrival is of relatively recent date, for they do not feature in the politics of 'Baḥrayn' until the ninth century, and it took another four centuries before they finally displaced the ʿAbd al-Qays as the dominant group there; but from the end of the thirteenth century onwards their dynasties controlled much of eastern Arabia, and this position they more-or-less maintained until the House of Saʿūd established control in al-Ḥasā in the eighteenth century and broke the power of the Bani Khālid. Bedu groups of the ʿĀmir first encroach into the Omani scene towards the end of the twelfth century (*Tuḥfa* i. 342), and in the disordered centuries that followed they began to play an increasingly prominent role in the country's affairs. It is probably then that the Naʿīm-Āl Bu Shāmis, Bani Kaʿb, and other tribes of reputedly ʿĀmir Rabīʿa descent began to move into northern Oman and break up and eventually absorb the confederations of the earlier settlers (notably clans of the Azd, Kinda, and Bani Sāma in the settled lands, and ʿAbd al-Qays and Wāʾil in the desert foreland cf. Fig. 33). Some ʿĀmir elements also began to penetrate central Oman, but it was not until the Jubūr[9] (known to the Portuguese as the Benjabar) developed power in the fifteenth century that their tribes really began to threaten the long-established inhabitants of the isolated core around the Jabal Akhdhar. At first the Jābiri threat was contained by paying them the tithe (de Barros *Asia* Decade II. 3. ii), but once the final remnants of ordered government in central Oman collapsed (as the Nabāhina *mulūk* and rival Imams fought each other after an unsuccessful attempt to restore the Imamate) it was the Jubūr (who had by this time been dispossessed of 'Baḥrayn' by the Portuguese) and other shaikhs of mainly bedu ʿAwāmir tribes[10] who ended up in possession of most of the forts on the desert side of the mountain zone (Buraimi and Lawā in the north, Maqūnīyāt, Yanqul, and Bāt in the Sirr, Manḥ in the Jawf, Samad al-Shān[11] and Ibrā in the Sharqīya).[12] And it was this crisis on their landward frontier, coupled to the occupation of their coastal 'frontier' by the Portuguese in an attempt to maintain some sort of hold over the Gulf, that eventually forced the Omanis to swallow their differences and unite under the leadership of Nāṣir b. Murshid, the first of the Yaʿāriba Imams, to drive out or subjugate the usurpers.

So it can be seen that the history of the ʿAwāmir migration into Oman covers roughly half a millenium, and it is for this reason that its sub-groups are widely dispersed and range from one of the wildest bedu groups who inhabit the outer sand desert of the Dhahira but have as yet not established an exclusive *dār* there, to the *falaj* experts who inhabit the collection of villages between the Jawf and Sharqīya called the Buldān ʿAwāmir.[13]

It is these latter who may be considered as a bedu group that has achieved the final stage of transforming into a hadhar 'tribe'. And since it is they who are also considered the greatest experts in the irrigation systems of Oman it is perhaps appropriate to conclude these case studies with an inquiry into how it is that one of the latest Arab groups to settle should have rediscovered the secrets of the ancient *qanāt* system.

Originally the villages that this particular ᶜAwāmir clan occupied appear to have formed part of a fairly well integrated cultivated area that was largely destroyed in the aftermath of the civil war that brought to a close the First Imamate; only around Izki did a small part of the irrigation system survive, and the rest of this once-fertile district was virtually abandoned (cf. Chapter X). Local tradition records that in the course of time these outlying remnants of abandoned settlement passed into the possession of the ĀlᶜUmayr, a group that controlled much of the Sumāyil Gap area in the sixteenth century and who seemed to have been allied with local ᶜĀmir groups (they themselves may even have been of ᶜĀmiri origin). But whether or not it was through this connection that the ᶜAwāmir obtained their settlements, the fact remains that they were fully established in their *Buldān* at least by the beginning of the eighteenth century (*Kashf* MS., p. 517).

Their first successes in restoring the ruined *aflāj* were probably achieved in much the same way that the Āl Bu Ghufayla developed al-Falaǰ, that is by associating with local hadhar groups to reservice the abandoned irrigation system. But whereas in the case of al-Falaǰ this simply involved restoring a small 'cut and cover' *falaj*, the abandoned irrigation systems of the Buldān al-ᶜAwāmir were full Dawūdi *qanāt* (cf. Fig. 16) so that re-servicing them must have given the ᶜAwāmir considerable experience in the old methods of Persian land development. With this expertise they then began not only to recolonize abandoned settlements elsewhere in the country (notably at the lower end of the Batina coast), but also to create new settlements in virgin land by building simple *qanāt* (e.g. that which they built for one of the Āl Bu Saᶜīd Sultans at Bayt al-Falaj, just outside Muscat). And this is the explanation of the seemingly anomalous situation by which a 'bedu' tribe have become the *falaj* experts of Oman. But the point to note is that it was not the true ᶜAwāmir descent groups, but their hadhar associates, that is, the descendants of the old *ahl al-bilād* families that had become grafted into the tribal structure of the politically dominant group in what was originally an economic partnership, who earned this reputation. Furthermore, it must also be emphasized that their expertise is in no way similar to that of the *muqanni* corps of *qanāt* builders in Persia. There is no record of the ᶜAwāmir constructing a major new *qanāt*, and whilst they can tunnel and work the headwaters of the existing *aflāj*, their constructional techniques (in so far as the writer has been able to ascertain) are largely confined to building 'cut and cover' and other shallow *qanāt*.

CONCENTRATION AND DISPERSAL OF FORMAL DESCENT GROUPS

From this study of the different stages in sedentarization of bedu groups perhaps the most important point to emerge from the point of view of understanding changes in tribal attitudes and organization, is that, as a migrant tribe settles in Oman, concentrating and dispersing there according to the opportunities offered by the new environment, its individual groups develop new relationships with the peoples of the area to which they become attached; at the same time the links with their former clansmen, from whom they are now separated, are loosened. These changes in social, political, and economic organization are also eventually reflected in formalized clan structure. So even if a tribe does continue for a while to preserve something of its outward form as the *Bani Fulān*, it has, in fact, become a pseudomorph, and its composition bears little relationship to the original nomadic group that entered the country. And as parts of the tribe continue to root themselves in the settled lands and the attitudes of some of the members towards village and agricultural life change, and as other elements move on to find new grazing grounds, and perhaps settle elsewhere, the last traces of the old *ʿaṣabīya* disappear until finally the clan-name carries no tribal significance. In other words the *Bani Fulān* has simply become the name of a descent group, and the identity of the forebear is liable to be transferred into the genealogy of the new groups into which the now-scattered descent have become assimilated.

For this reason the bajada zone of Oman may be compared to a tribal shore on which waves of migration break. Each wave modifies the shape of the human settlement pattern, adding new groups and picking up others to lay them down elsewhere. And because the groups of this area are always seeking a new political equilibrium and their economic and social pattern is forever changing, it is pointless to categorize the frontier tribes under such simple terms as nomadic, semi-nomadic, semi-sedentary, sedentary, etc. Some elements are shifting towards the settled end of the bedu-hadhar spectrum and some may even be moving in the opposite direction: but whichever way they are going the fact remains that no tribe is made up entirely of people from a single socio-economic grouping, any more than it is of a single descent.

SETTLEMENT IN THE MOUNTAINS

Up to now we have been speaking in terms of the bajada zone as the place where sedentarization processes are initiated: this is because ever since the establishment of Arab power in Oman no major migration has been successful in directly invading the central core of the country. But in earlier times, when migration appears to have been on a larger scale, certain of the tribal waves carried further into the mountains before they broke, and in the pre-Islamic period the same processes would have been observable in the mountains as well as the desert borderlands of the country. So as the Arabs were channelled into the heart of the settled lands through the lines of weaknesses in the mountain barrier, the surges, backwash, and eddies of their movements across the bajada zone into the mountains and out onto the Batina plain beyond tended to mix the formal descent groups into the most complex patterns.

Yet once the storm-surge which carried these Arab migrants into the heart of settled Oman began to die away, the deposited human material began to consolidate into a more stable pattern. Since it is this pattern that has, above all, determined the way the interests of clan and locality have interacted in Omani tribal society the present chapter will conclude with a study of how formal descent groups have clustered and dispersed as they settled in the mountain core of the region, and with a preliminary discussion of how far the old *'aṣabīya* linkages may still operate between members of a descent group in its final settlement pattern.[14]

THE PRIMARY SETTLEMENT PATTERN OF THE EARLY TRIBAL SETTLERS

Since the origin of the tribal settlement pattern is bound up with the history of Arab migration to Oman, it is extremely difficult to interpret with any degree of certainty. Even so, some general outline can be established from the local records, thanks largely to the detailed accounts of certain tribes given by ʿAwtabi. An attempt has been made to map this in Fig. 33 (pp. 243-8): the notes accompanying it supplement the account given here.

The early tribal picture is least clear in the areas surrounding the mountain core of the country, that is, in the desert borderlands and in the settled areas at either end of the range. There are two reasons why this is so. The first is that these are the areas where early settlement has been most disturbed by subsequent population changes: in particular is this true of northern Oman where, after the collapse of the early Ibāḍi state, the original settlers were in no position to resist the incursion of tribal groups either from 'Baḥrayn' (notably the ʿĀmir and Wāʾil groups), or from the Persian mainland (e.g. Balūsh and Riyāyisa/Awlād Rāʾis).[15] The second is that since these were the first areas to be colonized by the Arabs, they were occupied by tribes who for long retained an essentially nomadic way of life; their political groupings consequently remained far more fluid than was the case with the later settlers, who quickly fixed themselves in clearly defined territories within the mountain zone.

Even so, the present-day distribution of formal descent groups in these borderland districts does still bear some traces of the early colonizing stage and indicates that the areas of original tribal concentration were strongly influenced first, by whether the migrants entered Oman via the northern or southern edge of the Empty Quarter, and second, by the order in which the groups arrived. So we find established early on in the villages of the bajada and foothill zones in the northern part of the country the first tribes to come to Oman from 'Baḥrayn' by the 'Tuʾām gateway' (Buraimi area), that is the ʿImrān Azd (the pioneers of this route) and their successors the Bani Sāma b. Luʾay. In occupation of the next zone of economic land-use (the rich pastures of the inner desert near the mountains) were the mixed-herding tribes made up mainly of ʿAbd al-Qays moving away from this grouping's principal areas of concentration in 'Baḥrayn'. Finally, in the Līwā and the outer sand desert lived the most easterly nomadic elements of the Bani Saʿd (Tamīm). Also found throughout this region were groups from the Mālik b. Fahm tribes, whose onward progression from south-eastern Oman along the western bajada zone towards 'Baḥrayn' had even further extended the already widespread settlement pattern of the first tribes to come to Oman.

Now this southern 'Mālik b. Fahm' migration was, in reality, perhaps the most complex of the Arab movements into Oman. Indeed it is a mistake to think of it as a homogenous affair at all, for the passage of its tribesmen along routes established at different periods by a number of pioneer groups can be traced over some four or five centuries, and it is only due to the personalized and semi-legendary stories about Mālik b. Fahm's struggles with the Persians (cf. Chapter VI), and to the artificial creation of an Azd-Quḍāʿa genealogical link (cf. Fig. 30), that both the time-scale and the tribal relationships of these southern migrants have been telescoped. This is why we find forced into the descent of Quḍāʿa a number of tribal groupings which had nothing to do with each other in their homeland, notably tribes of the Qamr-Riyām confederation, some of whom had early settled in the desert borderlands of southern Arabia, the home of the Mahra nomads (whence the genealogical assimilation of these two groups), and the Bani Rāsib. Similarly fitted into Mālik b. Fahm's own descent are the tribes of the distinctive Bani Salīma group, the majority of which moved away from their initial area of settlement in south-eastern Oman into the Gulf borderlands of south-west Persia (from whom came the Julandā b. Karkar family).

Much clearer than this early settlement pattern in the peripheries of Oman is that in the mountains, where the aforementioned tribes appear to have penetrated (on any scale) only the valleys at either end of the range (cf. in particular on Fig. 33 the Bani al-Ḥārith b. Mālik b. Fahm of the Dibā area in the north, and in the south-east the Bani Salīma in the mountains behind Qalhāt, and the possible Riyām concentration in the Ṣūr area). Until the fifth century A.D., however, the indications are that there had been no extensive Arab settlement in the central mountains, although it is probable that there had been a steady infiltration of 'proto-Arab' groups into this area since time immemorial (some of the *shawāwi* groups subsequently assimilated by the Arabs?), and that the plateau of the Jabal Akhdhar might have already been partially colonized before this date by elements of the Riyām and other so-called Quḍāʿa groups.

Part of the reason why this area had been avoided doubtless lies in the fact that it was situated in the main zone of Persian occupation, but part of the explanation may also be found in the possibility that the early Arab migrants came from the desert borderlands of south-western Arabia, and so were attracted to those parts of Oman which offered a similar environment. Certainly the main Arab colonizing movement into the central mountain areas appears to have been instigated by tribes from a similar setting, for the driving force in the second major series of tribal migrations into Oman were the ʿUthmān b. Naṣr branch of the so-called Shanuʾa Azd (cf. Fig. 30) who originated from the heights of the Ḥijāz. Their onward migration into Oman from 'Baḥrayn' appears to have been initiated by one particular group, because it would seem that it was not until after the Ḥuddān had successfully established themselves in the mountains of the Sirr, probably during the period of weak Persian rule in the later part of the fifth century, that the main migratory wave, which included the rest of their 'brother' tribes of the Awlād Shams (the Maʿāwil, part of the Nadab, and possibly part of the Naḥw) and their 'cousins' the Yaḥmad (in reality a huge tribal confederation), invaded Oman and moved right into the mountain heartland to settle in the valleys of the Ghadaf (at that time still largely undeveloped by *aflāj*; cf. Chapter VI). Also probably related to this Shanuʾa migration was the arrival of certain Kinda clans[16] who settled to the north of the Ḥuddān in the mountains behind Tuʾām.

So with the settling of this second major series of tribal immigrants, all of whom entered Oman by the northern route, and of the Ṭayy, who came by the southern route, the colonization of the mountain zone by the Arabs was more-or-less complete. From north to south, the mountains were divided into major tribal areas, each of which in early Islamic times carried the name of a major genealogical grouping (cf. the Jabal Kinda, the Jabal Ḥuddān, the Jabal Yaḥmad, the Jabal Riyām and the Jabal Ṭayyīn on Fig. 33), while the individual valleys acquired the names of smaller sub-units (e.g. the Wadi Bani Kharūṣ, the Wadi al-Maʿāwil, the Wadi Saḥtan, all in the Shanuʾa settlement area in the Ghadaf). And it is in these same areas today that the majority of the descendants of these old tribal groupings still live.

DISPERSAL

The original areas of concentration in which these groups settled may today be compared to an archaeological site. While the ruins do in places still provide some form of habitation, and while whole blocks may have been incorporated into new tribal buildings, the original edifice itself no longer serves the purpose for which it was constructed; its form may only be traced by piecing together the distribution of clans and their original relationships as recorded in historical documents. But even though it requires considerable skill and imagination to reconstruct the complete settlement pattern of an entire tribal grouping like the Yaḥmad or the Kinda, some of the smaller units may be relatively easily restored and so provide a general picture of the processes by which the early tribes tended to concentrate and disperse as they settled. One such group whose settlement pattern may be so 'restored' with a fair degree of accuracy are our old friends the Maʿāwil, thanks again to the wealth of detail preserved in Abu Sulaymān al-Maʿwali's *Nubdhat al-Maʿāwil*.

As already shown in Chapter VIII, the Maʿāwil formed part of the main Shanuʾa migratory wave whose primary region of settlement was in the valleys that drain eastward from the Jabal Akhdhar, that is the region sometimes called the Ghadaf. Within this area the Maʿāwil themselves concentrated at the point where one of these wadis breaks through the foothills to debouch onto the Batina plan near Nakhl (cf. Figs. 3 and 25). Here, in the 'Wadi Bani Maʿāwil', they eventually began to settle in the *qanāt* villages (the most important of which are Ifi the tribal capital or *ʿāṣima*, Muslimāt, and Ḥibrā) to become hadhar. According to Abu Sulaymān's account, there was some mixing of the clans within the settlements, but in most cases the *fakhdh* members tended to live together; the smaller quarters (*ḥāra* pl. *ḥārāt*) usually held one or two such groups, but in the fortified quarter of Ifi called the *Ḥujrat al-Shaykh*[17] there were found some eight or nine *afkhādh*, two of which had their own distinctive sub-quarters (often referred to as *maḥārāt* in central Oman terminology).

Settled nearby in the principal settlements of this region, although not actually living within the area that may be considered as the tribe's exclusive *dār*, were other members of Maʿwila's attributed descent. So in Rustāq, the capital of the Ghadaf, and in Barkā, its local port, were found (in Abu Sulaymān's time) quite important Maʿwali quarters; some also lived in Nakhl, the main fortress-town near the Wadi Bani Maʿāwil, but these were probably breakaway groups, for there was a standing feud between the peoples of the two places.

In addition there were minor elements of the tribe living further afield in the mountain borderlands of the Ghadaf, in the Wadi Saḥtan and Ṭaww, and further up the Batina coast, at Ṣuḥār and al-Rumays. Some had spread 'round the corner' into the lower part of the Wadi Sumāyil, where they made up the dominant group of a part of Fanjā called al-Ḥafitayn, and a few even lived in Sumāyil itself.

This distribution clearly shows that all these groups belonged to a dispersal of the tribe in its main area of settlement, and that its members may be divided into the three following sub-categories. First, those Maʿāwil that lived in the tribe's exclusive *dār*; second, those that lived together in sufficient numbers to occupy an exclusive *ḥāra* in the main settlements of the region; third, those that had gone to live in places where their numbers were not sufficiently great to form a significant part of the population. These groups in a generalized model could be labelled Ia, b, c, where I represents the area of main settlement, and the sub-classification the dispersal of the group within this area (cf. the AI group in Table 12).

The ability of these sub-groups to act together as a tribe (exhibit *ʿaṣabīya*), depends on three things. First, their desire to do so (the reasons why a group has separated from its followers are therefore important), second what proportion of the population they form in the place where they live, and third, the nature of the spatial barriers separating them. For category Ia, that is the primary concentration, there would be no difficulty in the individuals acting together as a quasi-autonomous political unit, for the descent live together in

Table 12 *Classification of Geographical Distribution of Formal Descent Groups*

	I. *Main concentration*	II. *Subsidiary concentration far from I*
A. Formal Descent Group which settled as a tribe in Oman	(a) the exclusive *dār*; this group dominates the area of settlement and enjoys a degree of autonomy.	(a) primary settlement: occupy exclusive *ḥāra,* but have limited autonomy in the locality and do not form the major group in the area ofsettlement. (Some of the characteristics of Ib).
	(b) secondary dispersal: group occupies exclusive *ḥāras* of the large centres near (a) above.	(b) and (c) a dispersal pattern from (a) may develop as in I, but the numbers in each locality tend to be even smaller and at best will only occupy a *maḥāra* (part of a *ḥāra*).
	(c) tertiary dispersal: small groups living further afield and representing a very small proportion of the population of the place in which they live (usually only a *bayt* or two).	
B. Formal Descent Group that never settled as a tribe.	Liable to be more dispersed than in Group A. Group may have associated with more than one protector tribe as it settled and so more than one primary concentration may exist. No exclusive *dār*, but may own individual settlements. Each of these concentrations may give rise to a dispersal pattern as in A above.	

virtually exclusive occupation of a sizeable settlement area and they recognize the authority of one of their own members as their shaikh. By contrast, the ability of members of group Ib, (i.e. the secondary dispersal) to show solidarity with the rest of the tribe is tempered by the fact that they share locational interests with non-members of the clan and consequently have, in some measure, to recognize the authority of outside leaders. Even so, their own survival within their settlement area is partly safeguarded by their geographical proximity to group Ia. For the small scattered groups of class Ic, that is the tertiary dispersal, the links with the rest of their fellow tribesmen are very much attenuated by reason of their separation from the main groups and the fact that they form a very minor part of the population of the places they inhabit. Nevertheless, their clan identity is still partly safeguarded through their tendency to associate with the more powerful groups of the region which form part of the tribal *shaff* (those Maᶜāwil living in the Wadi al-Sumāyil, for example, would probably have tended to place themselves either under the protection of the Bani Ruwāḥa or of their then paramount leaders). All three groups therefore still retain a degree of active relationship with each other and thus may be considered to form part of the tribe in its main area of settlement organization.

Quite different are the relationships of the groups which form the subsidiary concentration of the original tribe, that is, in the case of the Maᶜāwil, those members that lived on the other side of the Jabal Akhdhar in the confines of the Jawf and Sharqīya (cf. group AII in Table 12). The history of how these groups came to settle there is very uncertain, for it is possible that some formed a breakaway group at the time of the original migration whilst others came from the Ghadaf. There is, however, absolutely no reason to presume that the two groupings were on bad terms with each other for, as already shown, there are innumberable causes why a tribe begins to disperse once it starts to settle.

The main centre of this subsidiary Maᶜāwil concentration appears to have been Manḥ, and for some time they were the leaders of the so-called Yamani *shaff* in what was originally a mainly Nizāri[18] settlement (today there are no identifiable Maᶜwali groups in the village and it is not even clear to what extent they may have existed as an identifiable clan in Abu Sulaymān's time). In addition, there was a small concentration living in Ibrā (they may have settled there via Manḥ, or may have come direct from their original home at Muslimāt), while elsewhere in the Sharqīya were a number of small scattered elements (in Ḥabāt and Damā — N.B. not the Batina Damā; at Maᶜṣā in the Wadi al-ᶜAndām; at Bald Sawt in the Wadi al-Ṭayyīn: the map also shows a place called al-Maᶜāwil, at the foot of the Jabal Kawr).

At first sight this dispersal in the subsidiary area of settlement (cf. group AII in Table 12) is analagous with that already described in the area of primary concentration (group AI), and thus suggests a parallel sub-classification into IIa, b, c. However, an essential difference between class I and class II arises from the fact that throughout the subsidiary area of settlement the dispersed groups cannot maintain the same kind of tribal unity which exists in the main settlement area, for the simple reason that nowhere do they form a sizeable population. Even class IIa is not as independent in its settlement as is class Ib, because the members live too far away from group Ia to count on their support; so clan survival depends not on *ᶜaṣabīya* linkages, but on success in creating *shaff* alliances (e.g. the Maᶜāwil group in Manḥ only retained coherence for as long as it did through linking itself to local elements of the Yaman *shaff*: cf. section on moieties in Chapter X). Tribal identity is therefore weakly developed throughout the subsidiary area of settlement and is liable to disappear over the course of time.

By contrast with this Maᶜāwil model, in which the migrant group originally settled as a tribe and still survives in control of an exclusive *dār* today, is a much more dispersed settlement pattern in which descent groups appear to exist in small random clusters (class B in Table 12). Such, for example, were the ᶜAbriyīn who, before they started to re-form and create a new tribal *dār* centred on al-Ḥamra, existed in little colonies in a number of places in the Sirr, in the Shimālīya tract, in the Wadi Nakhr (on the Jawf side of the Jabal Akhdhar), and in Wadi Saḥtan and ᶜAwābi in the Ghadaf.[19] Yet there was order in this settlement pattern, for when the historical associations of the clan are investigated it becomes clear that even though the ᶜAbriyīn did not originally concentrate in an exclusive *dār*, they did settle alongside particular clans of the Shanuʾa Azd, the majority with the Ḥuddān who pioneered the Shanuʾa settlement in interior Oman, the rest with members of the main Shanuʾa migration who settled in the Ghadaf.

So it can be seen that in order to understand the distribution of a formal descent group of type B, it is necessary first to identify the parent tribe or tribes with whom its members were originally associated in their migration to Oman, and then to trace the pattern of dispersal from each area of initial concentration. Only in this way can some order be discovered in a complex distribution pattern, a pattern which somewhat resembles the scattered erratics left by a glacier when the ice melts: now the individual units of the original descent group form quite distinct, albeit isolated features in the tribal landscape; but their distribution cannot be explained without reconstructing the past tribal climate.

Obviously ᶜ*aṣabīya* is much less strongly developed between members of the group B settlement pattern than it is amongst members of group A. But because their *shaff* alliances are often to a 'related' tribal grouping, the resultant apparently unified behavioural pattern may be rationalized through direct reference to their own eponymous ancestor. Furthermore, a vestigial sense of the original descent-group unity can survive even a long history of geographical separation, and so instigate them to reform as a tribal unit when the opportunity occurs (as happened in the above cited example of the ᶜAbriyīn).

NOTES TO CHAPTER IX

1 *Nubdhat al-Maᶜāwil*, p. 431 and Maᶜwali, p. 371: this *qanāt* does not figure in the list quoted by al-Sālimi in *Tuḥfa* ii. 100, albeit in most other respects his list is similar to that of Maᶜwali.

[2] It was in the possession of the bedu by the time Maʿwali was writing (second half of the eighteenth century).

[3] Lorimer (1908) presumably deriving from (later Sir) Percy Cox's journey in 1902, cf. *British Memorial* Annex B, No. 40.

[4] This is the first mention the writer has been able to trace of the Durūʿ; all the other major bedu groups of Oman have featured in Oman history by the beginning of the eighteenth century, if not earlier. Nothing much is known of the origins of the Durūʿ: Siyābi (p. 78) says they are Labīd of Bani Ṣulaym stock, whilst EI_2 (Matthews, C. D., art *al-Durūʿ*) reports a popular tradition that they are related to the Manāhīl who live in the desert borderlands of South Arabia.

[5] The ʿAzīz who owned one of the quarters of Ḍank similarly became absorbed into the tribal structure of the Naʿīm (or Nuʿaym) who first appear as bedu in northern Oman sometime in the 'Dark Ages'.

[6] The property was *mawāt* (dead land), and no-one seemed to know to whom the settlement had formerly belonged.

[7] The very name Ghulūb indicates that they originated from the old subject peoples (*raʿāyā*), the *ahl al-bilād*.

[8] *Adwan ʿan ḥōl* was the phrase used by the Wahībi informant: N.B. (1) the use of the elative of *dūn* in a temporal phrase to mean 'less than'; (2) ʿ*an* instead of *min* after the elative; and (3) *ḥōl* (*ḥawl*), a year. This last word is used throughout Oman to mean a solar year: for discussion of it see Serjeant 1954, p. 122, fn. 9.

[9] For the background history of the Jubūr see (in addition to the standard Omani sources) Alboquerque (1875 edn.) i. 66, 75, 83–4, 87, 91-2; Philby 1955, pp. 10-12; al-Nabhāni, pp. 108 et seq.; Caskel 1949.

[10] Notably the Hilāl, Qutn b. Qutn, Āl ʿUmayr(?), al-Aghbira and Muḥammad b. Jayfar groups of the Omani histories.

[11] Samad in the Sharqīya, known as Samad al-Shān (Shaʾn, affair) because it was the scene of the final battle which ended the 'First Imamate', should not be confused with Samad of Upper (ʿAlāya) Nizwā. In early histories the former is sometimes called Samad al-Jahāḍim (Mālik b. Fahm group) to contrast with the Nizwā Samad al-Ḳindi.

[12] Ibn Ruzaqy's list in *Imams*, p. 54 is more or less the same as the one he gives in the *Ṣaḥīfa al-Qaḥṭānīya*, p. 421. Its accuracy is confirmed by details of Nāṣir b. Murshid al-Yaʿrabi's campaigns as reported in the *Tuḥfa*.

[13] See also Headley, R. L., in EI_2 art. *al-ʿAwāmir*; Miles 1875; Thesiger 1950; Aramco 1952; Dostal 1967. Although there is some conflict in the evidence presented by these sources they all tend to confirm the commonly held belief that the settled ʿAwāmir are related to the bedu.

[14] Although we will be concentrating on the settled tribes of the mountain zone, a few words must be said about the bedu of the hills, the *shawāwi*. Ethnically they are probably of diverse origin (Arabs, 'proto-Arabs' and 'indigenous' peoples), whilst their membership has been recruited both from groups who have always lived as herders in the mountains and from ex-settled groups who for any number of reasons have lost their property or who have reverted to pastoralism. Like the bedu they have a number of direct ties with the villages, and play an important role as transporters between the settled communities. Although they herd outside the village boundaries they sometimes hold a little agricultural property, and in summer often move on to the village land, where each family has its own tree (called *al-barīza*) around which it camps and where guests are received. In theory the *shawāwi* are the social equals of the village tribesmen but in practice they tend to lead their own simple lives (with certain customs that may be extremely old) and marry amongst themselves: they also have their own *rashīds* (clan headmen). On the other hand, they form an integral part of the settled groups' tribal organization, and recognize the authority of their paramount shaikhs. It is their grazing grounds which fill in the gaps between the villages to give the settled tribes an appearance of owning a continuous tribal *dār* (as shown on Fig. 25), and as a result

grazing conflicts do sometimes involve their settled fellows in tribal war (as too do the acts of individuals involved in the carrying trade).

[15] These Balūch (Balūsh in Arabic) are not the same as the mercenary soldiers used by the Āl Bu Saʿid Sultans as garrison forces, or the miscellaneous peoples originating from Makrān who live in coastal Oman and who, at least as far back as the tenth century, are often generically referred to as Balūch. They belong to a quite distinct group whose present main settlement area is in the southern Dhāhira (where they have an exclusive *dār* centred around their capital at Māzam): although accepted as virtual equals by the Arabs of that area, their claim to be of Qaḥṭāni descent is not taken very seriously (in this claim, however, there may be the idea that they originate from the mixed Arab-Persian population of pre-Islamic 'Kirmān'). They are organized on Arab tribal lines, speak Arabic and not Balūch, are Sunnis (mostly Hanbalite), and have played a very active role in the politics of the Dhahira during the last hundred years (cf. *inter alia* Miles 1910; Cox, quoted *British Memorial* II, p. 113; Aramco 1952, pp. 123, 129 et seq.).

Although Miles reckons they entered Oman about 1720, the present writer believes that their association with the country is to be traced in the history of the Riyāyisa, or Awlād Raʾīs, who, as Thomas (1931, p. 193) reports, are 'Balūch' by origin. These Awlād Raʾīs first feature in Omani history as far back as the thirteenth century, when we read of them, along with their allies from the Jabal Ḥuddān, attacking Nizwā (*Kashf* MS. 484): subsequently they formed part of the northern alliance which supported the later Nabāhina *mulūk*. The writer is inclined to believe that the Awlād Raʾīs were the shaikhly element in a migration of peoples from the Makrān coast which moved into northern Oman in the disturbed conditions of the 'Dark Ages' (that is in the same period as the major ʿĀmir and other tribal migrations from 'Baḥrayn') and for the most part settled there. Some did settle further into the country, perhaps under the aegis of the Nabāhina (with whom the Awlād Raʾīs intermarried), for elements are to be found living as distinctive groups in the Sumāyil Gap today (cf. Chapter X, n. 12).

[16] The Kinda migration to Oman probably dates to the collapse of the Kinda kingdom with which the Shanuʾa groups may have been associated when migrating through central Arabia. Certainly there were close associations between the two groups in Oman in the early days (the mother of one of the early Julandā was from the Sakūn Kinda); the Omani Kinda settled in the Azd *khums* in Basra, and Kinda *ʿulamāʾ* were active in propagating Ibāḍism in Oman.

[17] A *ḥujra* is a fully fortified *ḥāra*.

[18] Dominated by the shaikhly Bani Ḍabba section of the subsidiary Bani Sāma concentration which also controlled Nizār in Izki up to the end of the First Imamate (cf. Chapter X).

[19] The history of how the ʿAbriyīn (ʿAbra b. Zahrān b. Kaʿb cf. Fig. 30) first began to reform in 1656 and then to create a major *dār*, thus making them one of the most influential tribes of central Oman may be traced in the *Nahḍa*, pp. 97-9, 185-6, 375-9, 385-92, 405-10).

CHAPTER X

Settlement and Tribal Organization

In the same way that principles governing the organization of the theoretically self-perpetuating 'legal family' virtually support the whole elaborate structure of clan hierarchies, so the largely self-sufficient nuclei of irrigated settlement represent the minimal units of economic organization upon which a hierarchy of geographical interests has evolved in Oman. The following analysis of the relationships between tribal and settlement organization in Oman will therefore concentrate on the situation which prevails in the *qanāt* village.

The village of Izki is a particularly appropriate case-study for two main reasons. First, just as the *Nubdhat al-Maʿāwil* provides almost unique documentary evidence for studying the clan structure of a tribe, so the record of the water holdings given in the *Malki Falaj Book* (when studied in conjunction with relevant material in the Omani written records and the results of field investigation) gives a remarkable insight into the social organization of a *qanāt* community in the heart of Oman. Secondly, because events in Izki's two main settlements, (al-)Nizār and (al-)Yaman, have more than once lit the fuse which exploded the whole powder-keg of Omani tribal rivalry, a study of the clan organization there provides an excellent starting-point for an investigation of how the 'moiety' system of Oman works.

IZKI

In popular tradition (*Nahḍa*, p. 181) Izki is held to be the oldest village in (central) Oman,[1] and originally to have formed part of an area of almost continuous settlement that extended right out into the plain of the Jawf. Located on a small alluvial plain formed by the Wadi al-Ḥalfayn at the point where it starts to discharge into the bajada zone after its precipitous descent from the eastern flanks of the Jabal Akhdhar to the Najd (watershed, pass) al-Maghbarīya, the village is well situated for control of the south-west link in the wadi complex that provides the main passage through the mountains of central Oman, the so-called Sumāyil Gap (cf. Figs. 3 and 5). Yet despite its size and dominant position, Izki never appears to have developed as a major fortified centre like Nizwā, Sumāyil, Rustāq, or Bahlā.

Part of the explanation may lie in certain siting details. The village plays no central regional role: it lies outside the Sharqīya, it is peripheral to the Jawf (where Nizwā, the seat of the Imamate, has developed as the main market- and fortress-town for most of that region), and it is remote from the main settled area of the Gap (of which Sumāyil is the main centre). Nor does it completely dominate any major line of communication. Movement along the western foot of the mountains by-passes the village, while the whole Wadi al-Ḥalfayn section of the Sumāyil Gap can be avoided by a number of routes from the Sharqīya, notably the Wadi al-ʿAqq (cf. Fig. 5). Furthermore, even within this section Izki is less well sited for physical control of movement than are the villages of the upper Wadi Sumāyil (belonging to the Bani Ruwāḥa) that command the constriction in the pass to the north-east of the Najd al-Maghbarīya. But the fundamental reason why Izki's undoubtedly advantageous location has never been fully exploited is that political power in the village is very delicately balanced between the Nizāris and the Yamanis, and any disturbance of the *modus vivendi* is liable to spark off war between two of the largest tribal groups in Oman, the Bani Riyām and the Bani Ruwāḥa. Before examining the nature of this political split it is necessary to see in what ways the inhabitants do in fact form a single 'village' community and in what ways they do identify themselves as Izkāwis.

The Hydraulic Community

By far and away the most important feature uniting Izki is its unified irrigation system, for it is this which provides the basic livelihood of the villagers, and finances most of the communal institutions (market, mosque, *waqf* trusts for education, hospitality, the poor, etc.) in which the various *ḥārāt* (quarters) shown in Fig. 32 participate.

The communal irrigation system once extended much further than it does now, for the small downstream hamlets of al-Zikayt and al-Ḥabūb and the upstream villages of Upper and Lower Qārūt and Muṭi (correctly Imṭi) originally formed part of an integrated irrigation unit developed to exploit the water resources of the upper Wadi al-Ḥalfayn. Most of this system has been destroyed or abandoned, so that the surviving settlements now form two distinctive knots, that of Izki linked by the Falaj Malki, and the Qarūt-Muṭi cluster formed by a still partially interweaving *falaj* system (the Upper Qārūt *falaj* runs through Muṭi and the Lower Qārūt *falaj* passes through Upper Qārūt which it supplies with drinking water from its *sharīʿa*). Yet even now these two knots are not entirely separate entities, for the feeders to one of the surviving branches of the Falaj Malki take their rise in Lower Qārūt land (where they unite at the Qurn al-Manzif), and this of itself creates a special relationship between the inhabitants of Qārūt and Nizār. (What happens when the Ruwāḥa of Qārūt try to exploit this potential geographical advantage over the Riyām of Izki has already been related in Chap. V p. 98). Since, however, the inhabitants of the Qārūt-Muṭi knot do not regard themselves as Izkāwis, our study will concentrate on the area shown in Fig. 32.

Today the cultivated area of Izki is sadly reduced, and all that survives of the Falaj Malki and its reputed 120 feeders and supplementary *aflāj* (*Tuḥfa* i. 262) are the two headstreams of the Falaj Malki proper and a half-dozen or so minor *aflāj*. Even so, these two headstreams (one of which draws regular base flow at considerable depth in the fan of the Wadi Masdūd, a small side wadi whose two branches cleave into the flank of the Jabal Akhdhar, while the other taps the less reliable flow in the gravels of the main Wadi al-Ḥalfayn near Lower Qārūt) still irrigate virtually all the lands of Nizār (about 1,000 houses)

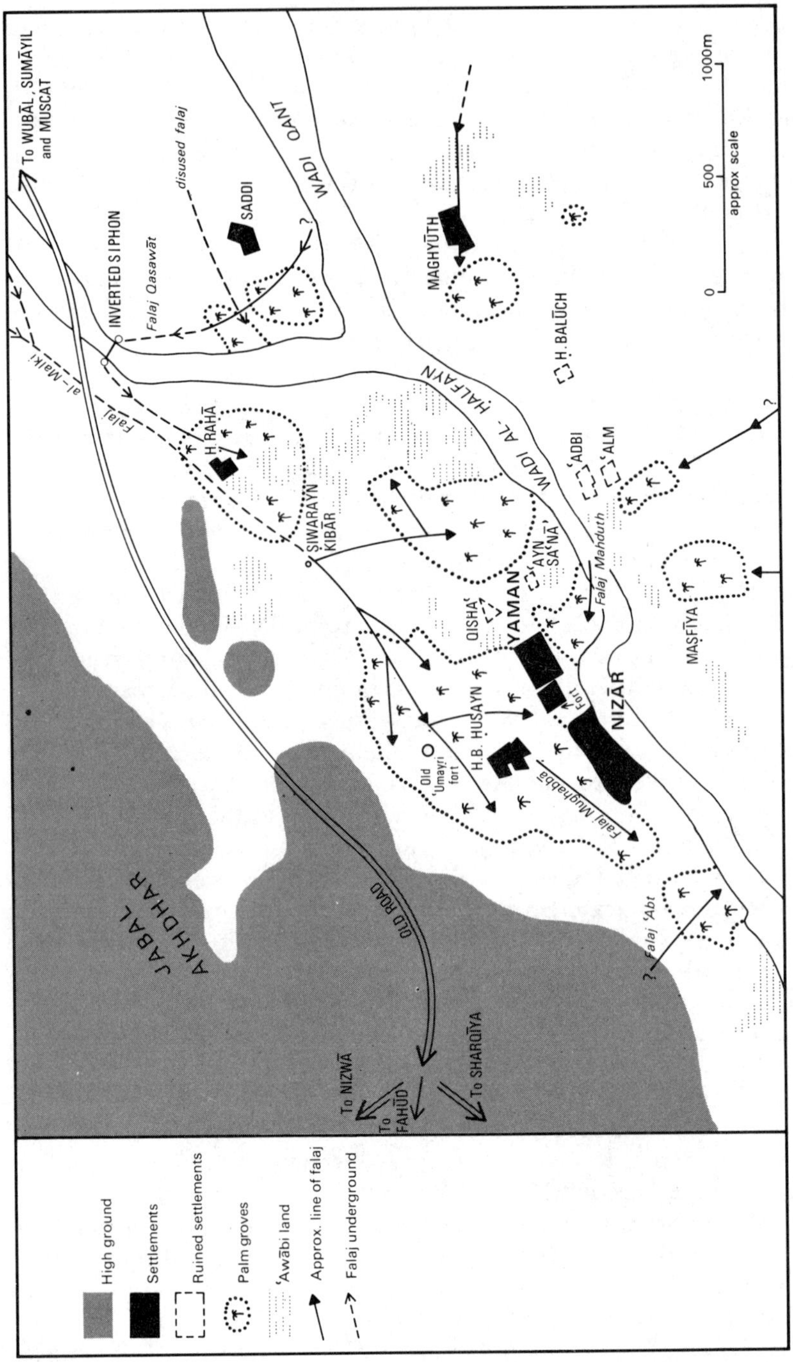
To WUBĀL, SUMĀYIL and MUSCAT
INVERTED SIPHON
Falaj Qasawāt
disused falaj
SADDI
WADI QANT
MAGHYŪTH
H. BALŪCH
H. RAHĀ
Falaj al-Malki
ṢIWARAYN KIBĀR
WADI AL-ḤALFAYN
'ADBI
'ALM
'AYN SA'NĀ'
QISHA'
YAMAN
Fort
NIZĀR
Falaj Mahduth
MAṢFĪYA
H.B. HUSAYN
Old 'Umayri fort
Falaj Mughabba
Falaj 'Abt
JABAL AKHDHAR
OLD ROAD
To NIZWĀ
To FAHŪD
To SHARQĪYA
0
500
1000m
approx scale
High ground
Settlements
Ruined settlements
Palm groves
'Awābi land
Approx. line of falaj
Falaj underground

Fig. 32. Izki.

and its associated settlement Ḥārat Bani Ḥusayn (a walled settlement of 100 houses), as well as the gardens of Nizār's great rival, Yaman (today only about 125 houses).[2] Whereas the lands of Yaman and Nizār are on two different branches of the *falaj*'s distributory network (cf. Fig. 21A), the *bilād* themselves are juxtaposed so that the inhabitants glower at each other from behind the walls of their *ḥujras* (a fully fortified settlement): a constant reminder for the Yamanis of the traditional dominance of the larger settlement are the old guns trained on them from the now-ruined fort which Muḥammad b. Nāṣir al-Jabri built in the early part of the last century to dominate Yaman (this fort was dismantled by the Sultan's army about 1958).

As may be seen from Fig. 32, two smaller *aflāj* extend this irrigation system, the Falaj ʿAbt which prolongs the Nizār branch, and the *ghayl* Falaj al-Maḥdūth which belongs to Yaman and draws its water from near by in the Wadi al-Ḥalfayn. In addition there is the interesting al-Mughabbā, a pool of artesian water which rises within Ḥārat Bani Ḥusayn itself, and by means of a *manzifa* pump (now mechanized) irrigates some 7,000 palms integrated into Nizār and Ḥārat Bani Ḥusayn land. Beyond this Malki land lie a number of virtually ruined minor settlements, each with a tiny vestigial *falaj* watering its palm groves; their owners for the most part live in the main *ḥārāt*. Also partly integrated into the Malki irrigated area proper are the settlements of Saddi and Ḥārat al-Raḥā, watered by the Qasawāt Falaj (the land of Saddi lies outside the Malki area, but that of al-Raḥā is contiguous with it; furthermore the Malki *falaj* itself runs through the *bilād* and supplies it with drinking water). This *falaj*, according to local informants, was built (or more probably completely reconstructed) by Ḥimyar b. Munīr al-Nabhāni, a native of Izki who held high office in the early eighteenth century under the Yaʿāriba.[2a] The story of the Qasawāt *falaj* is a good illustration of the point made about land investment and the Imamate cycle in Chapter VII (p. 151). Thus we find that while Ḥimyar's investment increased the economic prosperity of his home village, it also introduced a system of land tenure which disregarded the tribal tradition of small *mulk* ownership. So it is not surprising to find that when Yaʿāriba power began to collapse, Ḥimyar's two new settlements were plundered and his sugar factories and residence burnt (Ibn Ruzayq, *Imams*, pp. 103, 106, 144). His *falaj*, on the other hand, survived, for even though the main channel leading to al-Raḥā has been buried underground and crosses the wadi which separates it from Saddi by an inverted siphon (*gharrāq fallāḥ*), its source lies at no great depth in the Wadi Qant and it is therefore of fairly simple construction and difficult to destroy completely. But when it was repaired and its two dependent settlements once more reconstructed, the water rights passed into the hands of the inhabitants and the water-sharing agreement was modified to give Saddi a fairer division (by extending the *dawrān* and allocating the extra shares to Saddi: cf. Chapter V). So the water of the Qasawāt Falaj, which must originally have been, more or less, the personal property of a single man, is now owned by many: the many, on the other hand, could never have organized themselves to build the *falaj*.

The history of the Qasawāt *falaj* is a microcosm of that of the whole Falaj Malki system. Thus, much of the extraordinary investment by the original *hanāqira* (landlords), which led the Arabs to call Jurnān by the name of Izki or Ziki (the Prosperous),[3] was destroyed in the Nizār-Yaman fighting which precipitated civil war at the end of the ninth century, while further devastation took place in the Yaʿāriba civil war of the early eighteenth century. On the other hand, at other times the village vendetta has merely simmered, for the necessity of preserving the surviving Persian heritage has tended to counterbalance the tribal propensity for self-destructiveness.

Some aspects of the organization of the irrigation and water-tenure system which helps maintain this relative peace have been described in Chapter V, in which the principles and methods of *falaj* organization were examined. From that description two main points emerge. First, the whole structure of share-holding is rooted in a unified system, and it is only through the *falaj* administration that the individual receives his water. Second, under the peculiarities of the Izki system, co-operation between shareholders is further reinforced by the fact that water can be drawn anywhere: thus instead of the land being divided into *khabūra* blocs belonging to individual tribal units, as tends to be the case on the standard *dawrān*, holdings are dispersed and there is a continuous and active trading in water shares, both between individual members of the community and through the *falaj* organization itself. But this integration is only partial, for while the holdings on each of the two primary branches of the irrigation network are intimately entwined the *shilla* division of the water clearly separates the gardens of Yaman from those of Nizār.

Other features that tend to unity a *falaj* community arise from the Islamic inheritance laws and the principles of Ibāḍism discussed in Chapter VII. These tend to militate against capitalist or feudal tenure and to encourage small *mulk* holdings, with the result that not only does land tend to be fairly well distributed amongst the inhabitants (see below), but also systems of joint ownership (*māl mushāʿ* or *mushtarak*) have often to be operated if the penalties of parcelling are to be avoided: this in turn encourages a degree of good-neighbourliness. Just how closely land holdings may be interwoven, even on a *falaj* system not organized on the Izki system, can be judged from the following extract from a report on land purchased by the oil company when building the road through the Sumāyil Gap:

> In Biyāq the total amount paid for a strip 9 metres wide and approximately 770 metres long was MT $9,195. This figure includes payment for palm trees and other cultivation. This transaction involved 34 separate pieces of land owned by 15 single land owners and 4 groups of joint owners of the land on which they stood, 3 cases of other property and crops owned by persons other than the owners of the land concerned, and 6 cases where an agent acted for an absentee or a group of minors. In total 23 individuals and an unnumbered group known as 'the children of Nasir b. Majid' were involved in this purchase. 48 palms were specified in the deeds.

Quite obviously the basic systems of land and water organization in the *falaj* community call for a high degree of co-operation between the land-owners and impose certain restraints on any particular group wishing to 'go it alone'. It is only when we examine the actual ownership of water rights in Izki that we begin to realize how widely based the communal interest in the *falaj* in fact is.

Distribution of Falaj Shares

Analysis of the actual shareholding in the Falaj Malki (based on the situation in 1825 as shown in the *falaj* record) reveals that the thirty or thirty-two *bādas* which made up the *dawrān* (Table 10) were held in four classes of ownership: two or four *bādas* belonged to the *falaj* itself, five and a quarter were *waqf*, about two and a quarter were *bayt al-māl*, while approximately seventeen were held by the *aṣḥāb al-uṣūl* (registered *mulk* holders of the *khabūra* shares: cf. Chapter V). Because of lacunae in the *falaj* book it is not possible to trace who owned the other three and a half *bādas*, but there is some reason to suppose that much of it was *waqf* or *bayt al-māl*.

The first notable feature to emerge from this preliminary breakdown of shareholding is that an appreciable quantity of the *falaj* water belonged to institutional organizations. On the assumption that the *wakīls* administered their trusts honestly, the benefits of these holdings were distributed as follows. All the money raised from the *falaj* share was spent in the village, either on the upkeep of the *falaj* or on such communal charges as education, paying for guests, helping the poor (cf. section on the *qaʿāda* in Chapter V). Of the *bayt al-māl*, one-third was devoted to the poor and needy of the village, while the rest went into central state funds (cf. Chapter VII).[4] *Waqf* holdings were devoted to the specific purposes for which they were given, and here it is fortunate that the *falaj* book[5] provides enough information to give some idea of who the principal beneficiaries were.

In Oman *waqf* is classified, somewhat loosely, into *waqf li sabīl Allāh, waqf masjid*, and *dhurrīya*: this last comprises family bequests and is not specifically identified as *waqf* in the *falaj* book, so need not be dealt with here. Of the bequests mentioned in the book the *waqf masjid* class (inalienable donations given to a mosque) was the major beneficiary, and no less than sixteen mosques feature there.[6] All of these were in the village, mostly in the three large *ḥārāt* (some belonged to specific tribal groups living there), but one or two were in the peripheral hamlets. All the other bequests, including, one supposes, that of a belligerent female who left two *athars* of water to the '*Ḥujras* of Nizār and Ḥārat Bani Ḥusayn for the purchase of gunpowder (*shūra*), saltpetre, and shot', presumably belong to the general *li sabīl Allāh* class, and were mostly given over to the poor and orphans of the village (purchase of food was the commonest purpose specified, but there was also provision for clothing and for aromatics for burying their dead). Some of these gifts were made to particular groups — to the poor of *maḥārat* so-and-so (these are the small clan sub-quarters in the main settlements), to the poor of a specific tribal group, or to the poor dependants of a nominated mosque (in such cases the exact usage is often specified, e.g. to provide rice, ordinary dried dates, or higher-quality *farḍ* dates). Educational bequests also occur, usually for teaching the *Qurān* in designated *madrasas* – one gift was made specifically for the provision of a blackboard (*mus(h)akhbūṭa*)! Another fairly common bequest, from women in particular, was to pay someone to visit the deceased's grave and to fast for her in the month of *Rajab*. Some gifts were made for more general purposes, such as the equipping and upkeep of particular wells with buckets and ropes, and the provision of help in time of such natural disasters as drought and gales (alternative uses also specified); there were also some gifts to the *falaj* itself. Certain of the *waqf* holdings were simply described as *li-sabīl Allāh*; there is reason to suppose that some of these were gifts for which the original purposes no longer applied.

The important thing is that all *waqf* bequests were for the benefit of the inhabitants of Izki and it was the poor of the village who were the principal beneficiaries of the institutional holdings which made up at least a quarter of all the *falaj* shares.

An examination of the privately held *mulk* shares (Table 14 in appendix, p. 234) shows that virtually all these were owned by the villagers themselves; indeed, cases in which outsiders owned water were so uncommon that the *falaj* book usually made some special indication of the fact.[7] The main reason for this retention of property within the village community is, of course, the endogamous marriage pattern discussed in Chapter VIII; but even in those cases where external marriage did occur, so that the heritage subsequently fell to an outsider, the evidence in the *falaj* book indicates that such holdings were normally sold straight back into the community.[8] Also of considerable social importance is the fact that, despite the distorting effect of the Dallāl family holding (in 1825 they owned nearly one-third of the *mulk* water, most of which should have belonged to the people of Ḥārat al-Yaman, as is proved by the *fatwā*s which later redistributed this political holding),[9] and despite the fact that at this time Ibāḍi influences in Oman were particularly weak, the number of shareholders in the *falaj* was quite large and the rights were spread surprisingly evenly amongst them. True, there were eight families (not lineages and excluding the Dallāl) who held half the *mulk*, but the average holding amongst the seventy-five or so members was only about twice that of the average holding amongst the next seventy-five (the latter held an average 1·4 *athars* – enough base flow, the writer estimates, to grow roughly 18 palms). The remaining fifty of the 200 or so *aṣḥāb al-uṣūl* (owners of the basic *khabūra* shares) owned less than one *qiyās*, that is, less than the estimated quantity of water needed to irrigate one palm, and must have operated their holdings jointly with others (*māl mushāᶜ*); this, however, by no means implies that such joint shareholding arrangements were of necessity confined to families within this group.

The most striking feature to emerge from the over-all picture of land and water tenure in Izki (when allowance is made for the fact that the Dallāl water holdings subsequently passed back into the hands of the Yamanis) is that virtually all the benefits of the Falaj Malki were confined to the village, and that they were remarkably well distributed amongst its inhabitants. The poor benefited from the considerable amount of water held in mortmain, while the *bayādīr*, as a class, were automatically guaranteed at least 10 per cent of the produce of the land through the system of organization of agricultural labour described in Chapter V. Considerable quantities of water could also be rented on an annual basis by those who had not the capital to buy *khabūra* shares, while of the shareholders proper there was only one who was disproportionately wealthy, and even he only owned one *bāda* of water (i.e. about one-thirtieth of the total water available to the village). Analysis of the water holdings by lineages (cf. Table 14 in appendix) also shows that the water was reasonably well shared from a clan point of view (particularly after the Dallāl holding had been redistributed), though a possible exception occurs in the case of the ʿUzūr (see below).

Although it has not been possible to make a quantitative analysis of present-day water holdings in Izki, inquiries there tend to confirm that this earlier pattern is still generally valid and that it is also characteristic of the other main villages throughout Ibāḍi Oman (but not of northern Oman, where much of the land belongs to shaikhly clans and the villagers often farm it on a share-cropping basis, nor, of course, of the Batina, where the tenure system based on well-irrigation is quite different).

Thus, in central Oman, at least, members of a village are vitally concerned in the prosperity of their *falaj* system, not just because it provides them with a living, but also because it belongs to them, and to them alone. The leading families, naturally enough, have the greatest interest in it, but, because share-cropping and tenant farming are atypical of the tenure system in Ibāḍi Oman, there are many smallholders who benefit directly from the wealth of the *falaj*. Many of the village institutions are run on income that derives from the *falaj*, and the poor and destitute are also supported from its revenues. Since it is this *falaj* system which is the *raison d'être* of the village, and probably gives rise directly to nine-tenths of the inhabitants' regular income, the communal *falaj* organization normally cuts across individual loyalties to clan and party, and so the administration of the irrigation system tends to be placed in the hands of certain families who are traditionally regarded as the most competent to safeguard this source of communal wealth. The *ʿarīf* and his *bayādīr*, who look after the day-to-day running or the *falaj*, often come from old *ahl al-bilād* families, that is, the original villagers assimilated into the Arab tribal structure, while the *wakīl* and other functionaries who control the financing of the *falaj* (and such other communal institutions as *waqf*, mosques, education, and the auctions through which virtually all trade is conducted)[10] are drawn from the *ahl al-ʿilm*, that is, from the same grouping from which the Imamate draws its officials, men whose understanding is supposed to rise above tribal passions.

The Tribal Split

Working against this community of interest in the village institutions is the clan system. According to the Izki village tradition, as kindly recorded for the present writer by his former colleague in Oman, Mr Hugh Massy,

> The ʿUzūr and the Awlād Mufarrij were originally the only tribes in Izki. After the usual quarrel between them, the ʿUzūr called in the Bani Tawba and the ʿUmūr to help them and the Awlād Mufarrij called in the Awlād Bahlāni; and that was the beginning of infiltration of other tribes into the area. The Awlād Bahlāni resided in old al-Yaman before the Bani Ruwāḥa rebuilt it. The Awlād Mufarrij are now extinct except for one family, but one source said that they were the original stock of the Awlād Rāshid . . . they had a famous ancestor [*jadd*] called Abu Zayd.

These oral traditions accord well with the evidence from the written sources, which shows that the ʿUzūr were the shaikhly clan of the Bani Sāma (a genealogical grouping of the Nizār moiety), while the Mufarrij, to whom Abu Zayd (in fact ʿAbdullāh b. Muḥammad, the Wāli discussed in Chapter VII) belonged, were a lineage of the Awlād Rāshid, that is, the dominant clan of the Bani Riyām (a group of the Yaman moiety). They confirm too that Bani Sāma clans were associated with Izki right back in pre-Imamate times and that at that time they more or less controlled the villages downstream as far as Manḥ, while the Riyām were the dominant tribe on the Jabal Akhdhar and in the villages which guarded access to it.[11] Thus the tribal polarity towards the two quasi-independent settlements of Nizār (originally Bani Samā) and Yaman (originally Bani Riyām) has existed in the village since the beginnings of Arab settlement, and it is the enmity between them that has been directly responsible for the reduced prosperity of the village.

As already mentioned, this rivalry was fully unleashed in the civil wars which brought to a close the two greatest periods of prosperity Oman has known in Islamic times. In the first war, a vast part of the Falaj Malki irrigation system was destroyed and the power of the Nizāris broken. In the eighteenth-century outburst it was the turn of Yaman to suffer and many of its inhabitants fled the village, never to return. Many of the ruins to be seen in the village today are the result of the events of that period (cf. Fig. 32): the Ḥiṣn al-ʿUmayri, at that time the main fort, was destroyed, as too were the whole of Ḥārat al-Yaman and numerous small settlements dependent on it; Saddi and al-Raḥā were also ravaged. Although these larger settlements were rebuilt, some of the smaller ones were permanently abandoned; these include al-Qishaʿ (which belonged to the Awlād Bahlāni), ʿAdbi (which belonged to the Darāmika, hence its old name Maḥall al-Darāmika), ʿAyn Ṣanʿāʾ (which belonged to the Umbu ʿAli), and Ḥārat al-Balūsh.[12] Since this time the fortunes of the Yamanis have fluctuāted, but never really recovered. Under the rule of the Āl Bu Saʿīdi Imam, Aḥmad b. Saʿīd (ruled *c.* 1749-83), the Yamanis were once more in favour and Ḥārat al-Yaman was reconstructed: indeed, they even held the upper hand in the village for a short while at the end of the eighteenth century (Ibn Ruzayq *Imams*, p. 193 et seq.), but by the second quarter of the nineteenth century the 'Nizāris' had regained their traditional hold (N.B. this is the period of the analysis of holdings discussed in the previous section), thanks largely to the famous 'Ghāriri' leader Muḥammad b. Nāṣir al-Jabri who built the fort which overlooks Yaman and who more or less made Yamani-Hināwi land in the Sumāyil Gap a family fief, 'extorting seventy *ṣā*ᶜ for each thirty harvested until the people were forced to abandon their land' (*Tuḥfa* ii. 198-9). The 'Yamani' rights were once again restored under the Imam ᶜAzzān b. Qays (1868-71; *Tuḥfa* ii. 257), and the evidence from the *falaj* book indicates that it was at this time that a great deal of the property of the Dallāls was redistributed amongst them. After that the affairs of Izki feature as a particularly sensitive point of rivalry between the Bani Ruwāḥa, whose paramount leaders, the Khalīlis of Sumāyil, supported the 'Yamanis', and the Bani Riyām, led by the Nabāhina based in Tanūf and Birkat al-Mawz, who sponsored the 'Nizāris'.

This brief sketch of the Nizār-Yaman feud in Izki shows that the quarrels in the village, far from being localized, formed part of a much broader picture of tribal struggles in Oman. To understand how villagers, whose very existence depends on a community of interest in the *falaj*, can be divided by tribal schisms that have twice virtually annihilated their settlement and on many other occasions seriously endangered it, requires a detailed knowledge of the clan relationships in the village. For this purpose a survey of the 'descent' groups of the Izki region is given in an appendix to the chapter; this should be studied in conjunction with the accompanying Table 14 which shows the water holdings of the various clan-lineage groups as at 1825, and provides details of certain minor groups not discussed in the appendix text. A summary of this information is given in Table 13 opposite.

Polarization of the Descent Groups

From this survey it might appear that the whole population of the village is 'tribal'. Such an impression is in part deceptive. In the first place, the numerically important *bayāsira* are only clients of the tribesmen, while many of the *bayādīr* and other assimilated groups lack the mental outlook of tribesmen, even though they may have assumed clan *nisbas*: they are first and foremost villagers, and their behaviour is almost entirely activated by events within the locality in which they live. But the same is also true of many of the groups of undisputed Arab tribal descent. To understand how far and under what circumstances ᶜ*aṣabīya* linkages outside the village do in fact operate and affect relationships within the locality, it is necessary to analyse the history of settlement in Izki from the point of view of clan concentration and dispersal along the lines suggested at the end of Chapter IX.

The story of Arab settlement in Izki starts with two clans taking possession of the village, the Awlād Rāshid and the ᶜUzūr; and it was the names of the old 'moieties' to which they belonged that led their respective settlements also to be called Yaman and Nizār (for discussion of moiety groupings, see below).

Table 13 *Summary of Principal Clan Distribution in Izki (see Appendix I for details)*

I *NIZĀR*

AWLAD RĀSHID (Riyām)

Bani Tawba and miscellaneous other true Riyāmi descent groups.

ʿUmūr (ʿAbd al-Qays)
ʿUzūr (Sāma)

Āl ʿUmayr (ʿĀmir)
Barūmiyīn (North Africa)
Ruwājiḥ
Bani Baḥri (Azd)
Ramāḥ

Awlād Bahlāni (ʿAbs)
Fuzāriyīn (Dhibyān)
B. Hinā (Mālik b. Fahm)
Ḥirth (Azd?)
Maḥārīq (Tamīm?)
Naʿb (Quḍāʿa)

YAMAN

DARĀMIKA (Kinda)

Maghtasiyīn (Riyam)
Ṣuqur (Riyam)

Fuzāriyīn (Dhibyān)
Naḥwiym (Shanuʾa Azd)
Umbu ʿAli (Ṭayy)
Awlad Bahlāni (ʿAbs?)

ḤARAT BANI ḤUSAYN

RIQAYSH (Kinda)

ʿUzur (Sama)
ʿAdāwina
Bani Tawba (Riyām)

II *ḤARAT al-RAḤĀ*

AWLAD RĀSHID (Riyām)

Maḥarīq (Tamim?)
ʿAbriyīn (Azd)

SADDI
MANĀDHIRA
Qurūn (Bani Hinā)
Awlād Shams (Wā'il)

III *MAGHYŪTH*

BANI TAWBA (Riyām)

Manādhira
Awlad Ḥusayn (Ṭayy?)
Zakāwina

QĀRŪT (UPPER)

BANI RUWĀHA proper

Bani ʿAwf (Wāʾil)
ʿUmūr (ʿAbd al-Qays)
Wurūd (Yaḥmad)

IV *ZIKAYT*

BANI TAWBA (Riyām)

QĀRŪT (LOWER)

BANI TAWBA (Riyām)
Bani Salīma (Mālik b. Fahm)
Bani ʿAwf (Wāʾil)
Wurūd (Yaḥmad)
ʿUmūr (ʿAbd al-Qays)
Bani Ruwāḥa proper

MUṬI .

BANI SALIMA (Mālik b. Fahm)
Bani Tawba (Riyām)
Bani ʿAwf (Wāʾil)
Wurūd (Yaḥmad)

N.B. 1. The dominant clan in each *ḥāra* is shown in capitals.

2. The 'formal' descent of the clans is tentative and is indicated in brackets.

But while the ʿUzūr belonged to the powerful Bani Sāma tribal grouping, those elements that had settled in the Lower Jawf were living outside the main tribal area (cf. Table 12, class AII), whereas the Awlād Rāshid *ḥāra* formed part of the Bani Riyām's main settlement area (cf. class AIa). When, therefore, the so-called Nizār-Yaman civil war broke out, the weaker tribal group was evicted from its property, and its leaders had to seek refuge with their fellow tribesmen in northern Oman. Eventually their land passed into the control of the Riyām, and those Sāmi groups who remained came, willy-nilly, to recognize the paramount authority of the increasingly powerful Awlād Rāshid.[13] A further important change occurred in the tribal relationships of the village when the Awlād Bahlāni (a breakaway Ruwayḥi group (?) who originally came in as allies of the Awlād Rāshid) gained possession of Yaman. Whether it was because of the means by which they did so or for some other reason, the fact remains that they inherited the locality feud with Nizār (from now on the centre of Riyāmi power in Izki), and consequently emerged as the leaders of all those who opposed the Awlād Rāshid hegemony in the village. When, therefore, the next major civil war broke out (the so-called Hināwi-Ghāfiri war of the eighteenth century), it was again the weaker group that was defeated, and the settlements of the Awlād Bahlāni and their Yamani allies were largely destroyed. Although, as a result, Bahlāni influence was perpermanently broken, some of the other groups did return to rebuild Yaman; but their relations with the Riyām remained very strained, and outbreaks of fighting were frequent. They were able to survive only by allying with the shaikhly Hawāshim of the Bani Ruwāḥa (cf. Chapter VIII), the sworn enemies of the Awlād Rāshid.

Thus throughout its Arab history there has been a major, but unequal, tribal split in Izki. At present this is reflected in Nizār, Ḥārat Bani Ḥusayn, and al-Raḥā being strongly aligned towards the true descent groups of the Riyām, while Yaman and Saddi represent the foothold of Ruwayḥi influence in this predominantly Riyāmi village. A similar tribal polarity occurs in the upstream knot of settlements (Qārūt and Muṭi), but east of the Najd al-Maghbarīya it is Ruwāḥa influence which predominates.

Now the Riyāmis have an advantage over the other clans living in Izki precisely because their settlements form part of the tribe's primary *dār*. Even those groups who inhabit Yamani *ḥārāt* (as do the Ṣuqūr) enjoy a degree of independence in their dealings with the rest of the people with whom they live, because they can rely on the support of their powerful kinsmen. Conversely, groups like the Maghtasiyīn of Yaman, who have moved into Yamani villages because of quarrels with their own clansmen, cannot defy the rest of their tribe with the same degree of impunity that would have been possible had they moved right outside the area of Riyāmi influence. So all the true Riyāmi groups of Izki are deeply concerned in the relationships between members of their clan, whether or not they are living in the village.

By contrast, all the other descent groups of Izki are less motivated by obligations to clans living outside the village. This has not always been so. As a key settlement in central Oman, Izki early attracted to it elements from certain Ṭayy, Azd, and non-Riyāmi Quḍāʿa tribes that had created *dār*s for themselves in the neighbouring regions. The position of the Izki members of these tribes must originally have been analagous to that of those elements of the Maʿāwil which spread out from the exclusive *dār* into neighbouring centres (Table 12, AIb): they would still have formed an integral part of the tribe in its territorial organization. But in the course of time, the political coherence of these tribes weakened (unlike that of the Maʿāwil), so that today any sense of clan identity is virtually confined to the localities in which members of the descent have concentrated, and the *ʿaṣabīya* linkages rarely bridge the geographical barriers which separate the individual groups. Such barriers, it should be remembered, exist not only between knots of settlement but also within them: thus members of the same clan living in different *ḥārāt* in the Izki area frequently have little contact with each other.

The above remarks apply with even more force to small groups living in a tribe's secondary area of concentration (e.g. small class II groups in Table 12): amongst such examples in Izki are a number of families which bear the *nisba*s of Kinda, Sāma, and Azd tribes whose main settlement areas were in northern Oman.[14] From the very start the survival of these groups depended on building alliances with non-related groups in the centre in which they settled: those which were less successful were soon assimilated into more powerful clans, and, like the Maʿāwil of Manḥ, eventually lost even the identity of their formal descent. The more successful preserved it and, indeed, on occasion may represent the only group of the original tribe that today live together as a clan (e.g. the Bani Salīma of Muṭi).

Also represented in Izki are elements of descent groups that probably never had an independent *dār*, and from the start lived dispersed under the protection of more powerful neighbours (cf. Table 12, group B). Such, for example, are the Manādhira, who probably originally came to the Jawf under the aegis of one of the Sirr tribes. Once their subordinate position began to disappear with the break-up of the old tribal organization, the Manādhira started to emerge as a distinctive group in this particular locality. But clan relationships with other members of their descent group remain non-existent, and their 'tribal' role is confined solely to the place in which they live.

Quite distinct from all these groups are the small elements which may be classified as belonging to a tribe's tertiary dispersal, that is, groups which have completely cut themselves off from the rest of their kinsmen (deliberately or not does not matter) and are themselves too small to play any clan role in the place in which they live (cf. Table 12, group A class IIc, and to a lesser extent class Ic; also the group B sub-classes). Such are the ʿAbriyīn inhabiting the Riyāmi-controlled settlement of al-Raḥā; not only have they separated themselves completely from the main ʿAbriyīn groups of Oman, but they actually live in a settlement dominated by their traditional tribal enemies. So, even though they bear the *nisba* of one of the most important present-day political groupings in Oman, they are of no account in the general tribal equation. Furthermore, even within the locality in which they live, they have little influence, because their numbers are small and they occupy only isolated *bayts* (houses) there. In this they differ from some of the groups already discussed, which, because they occupy a discrete *maḥāra* (tribal sub-quarter of a settlement), are able to retain a degree of clan identity and play an active role within their own settlement (though remaining too few to influence the wider course of events in the village).

To sum up, it can be seen that all the descent groups of Izki live in what might be considered a tribal-locality continuum. 'Tribal' characteristics are most marked amongst the descent of Riyām, for their 'clan' organization extends far beyond the village; by contrast the descendants of the old *ahl al-bilād* families, now assimilated into Arab tribal structure, represent groups whose interests are almost entirely dictated by the locality in which they live. Somewhere between the two come all the other 'formal' descent groups: it may be generally said of them that the larger the proportion of the population they form in their settlement area, the more 'tribal' their attitudes are liable to be.

Leadership in the Village

These tribal-locality relationships are also reflected in Izki's leadership syndrome. Dominant in the tribal scene are the shaikhs of the Awlād Rāshid, the leaders of all the true Riyāmi clans and masters of Nizār, their 'capital'. Their claim to authority over the whole village, however, is challenged by many, not least by sections of their own tribe, notably those that have taken sanctuary in one of the rival 'Yamani' settlements (e.g. the first Bani Tawba to settle in the village, or the present-day Maghtasiyīn of Yaman whose political importance is quite disproportionate to their numbers because of their 'nuisance' value to the Awlād Rāshid both within the village itself and generally throughout the tribe). Awlād Rāshid authority is also weak among those Riyāmis who inhabit 'Yamani' villages (e.g. the Ṣuqūr of Yaman) even when there is no particular quarrel between them, because in these places their 'clan' authority is partly neutralized by the influence of the 'locality' leaders. Conversely, the authority of the Awlād Rāshid is by no means absolute in their own settlements because living there are descent groups of some size which are not of Riyāmi origin and therefore do not accord them 'clan' authority; such, for example, are the ʿUzūr of Nizār who, despite living in the Riyāmi capital, have their own clan *rashīds*.[15]

But the main challenge to the Awlād Rāshid hegemony comes from the Darāmika, because, as leaders in the main non-Riyāmi *ḥujra*, they automatically have considerable influence with all the other Yaman-aligned settlements, as also with the minority groups who live in the Riyāmi-dominated settlements (particularly where the Riyāmi group is not in an overwhelming numerical majority, e.g. in Maghyūth). On the other hand, because the majority of the Yamanis have few politically meaningful associations with their clansmen living outside the village, Darmaki power is localized. So even in Yaman itself their authority is somewhat less than that enjoyed by the Awlād Rāshid in Nizār, and their decisions may be openly flouted on occasion by the two groups which do have outside clan support, the Ṣuqūr and the Maghtasiyīn; their influence in the village is also challenged by the Manādhira of Saddi, who in turn are bitterly resented by the Qurūn. Thus in order to counteract the strong 'tribal' power of the Awlād Rāshid and to strengthen their own hold over the Yamani faction, the Darāmika shaikhs have tended to 'follow' the powerful non-Izkāwi Hawāshim, the shaikhly clan of the true Bani Ruwāḥa descent groups, and hereditary enemies of the Riyām. Even so, the power of the Darāmika still remains weaker than that of the Awlād Rāshid, because the Yamani party is smaller and is only allied with the Ruwāḥa through *shaff* bonds, whereas the 'Nizāris' are integrated into Riyāmi tribal structure by both *shaff* and *ᶜaṣabīya* obligations. In other words, while the Awlād Rāshid shaikhs command both locality and clan allegiance, the Darāmika command only the former.

The third group to play a major role in the leadership of the village is the (Bil) Riqaysh. This family exhibits many of the characteristics of 'elitism' discussed in Chapter VIII. In addition to its wealth and other *imāra* attibutes (notably control of the Bani Ḥusayn *ḥāra*), it has produced several distinguished *ᶜulamāʾ*, most famous of whom was Muḥammad b. Sālim al-Riqayshi, the formidable *wāli* who subdued and governed ᶜIbri for twelve years on behalf of the Imām Muḥammad b. ᶜAbdullāh al-Khalīli and who, throughout his long career, regularly stymied the Nabhāni shaikhs (paramount leaders of the Riyām) in their political aspirations (cf. *Nahḍa* pp. 368 et seq. and Thesiger 1959, pp. 145 and 289-9). Learning (*ᶜilm*) has given its shaikhs a reputation for fairness, and their acceptability as arbiters in village affairs is enhanced by the fact that their clan neither lives in Nizār, nor acknowledges descent from Riyām, even though they have close links with both. Their role in locality affairs, therefore, is analogous to the tribal role of the Khalīlis (cf. p. 182, above), and in so far as Izki can be regarded as a single community, the shaikhs of the Riqaysh tend to act as its leaders.

All these remarks about the various groups who command authority in the village are, of course, generalizations. To understand the influence of a particular leader at any given moment, personal and situational factors must also be taken into consideration, as too must the influence of outsiders, notably the paramount leaders of the major tribal confederations in the region (the Nabāhina of the Bani Riyām, the Khalīlis of the Bani Ruwāḥa, and the Ḥirth of the Sharqīya Hināwis), and of the official government appointments in the village (the *wāli, qāḍi*, and tax collector).[16]

TRIBAL POLARITY

The foregoing analysis of clan and locality linkages in Izki has shown that the people of the village, despite their communal interest in the *falaj* system and a number of lesser institutions, are fundamentally divided in their settlement pattern and have been drawn into the political orbit of one or other of the two major tribal organizations of the area in order to safeguard their interests in the place in which they live. In the case of the Riyām polarity, both clan and locality interests are involved. By contrast the Ruwāḥa polarity is hardly, if at all, dictated by clan linkages, and arises almost entirely from the need of the weaker non-Riyāmi descent groups to find a power capable of counteracting the influence of the Riyām in the village. The Bani Ruwāḥa shaikhs willingly respond to this appeal because this maintains their tribal bridgehead to the west of the Najd al-Maghbarīya.

Now, this pattern of tribal polarization occurs wherever sizeable elements from different descent groups share a common economic resource in Oman, and functions through the same mechanisms in the larger units of communal locational organization as it does at the level of the village. A detailed discussion of the nature of these other locational interests is not appropriate here, but analysis of spatial linkages certainly reveals some grouping of settlement interests into a geographical hierarchy. Thus in the mountain zone where *falaj* settlements are often constructed in valleys cut off from each other by high divides, the inhabitants have to reach some form of understanding over such matters as access, defence, water supply, and transport of goods: this is why they are often referred to by outsiders as the *ahl wādi fulān*, the people of such-and-such a wadi, even though they themselves may think of their loyalties in terms of membership of particular clans and villages. Loose regional associations have also developed, and it is no coincidence that names like the Jawf, Ghadaf, Sharqīya, Jaʿlān, Sirr, Tuʾām (cf. Fig. 2) are as old as Omani history itself. Certain of these regions in turn are drawn into geographical proximity through the accessibility linkages shown on Fig. 5, and this has given rise to the use of rather vague geographical terms like Oman Proper, Northern Oman, and so on. Finally, because the advantages of Oman's maritime siting can only be exploited by the people of the area when they are sufficiently united to resist outside powers, this too helped to encourage the people of the interior from time to time to subordinate their individual group interests to the loose organization of the Imamate state.

At each level in this geographical hierarchy a degree of political equilibrium is achieved through polarization towards ever-larger tribal groupings. Thus, if the direct alliances which equalize the power of the two tribes that themselves maintain political equilibrium in Izki are examined, it will be found that these include groups from the Jawf, the Sharqīya proper, the Jabal Akhdhar, the Sumāyil Gap, and the Lower Batina coast: it is no coincidence that these five geographical regions make up the heartland of the Omani Imamate. And if all the feuds and alliances directly involving the tribes inhabiting this core region are then analysed, it will be found that these embrace all the tribes of the Sirr, the northern Batina, and much of the rest of south-east Oman: the fact that these districts constitute the marchlands of the Imamate and, along with central Oman, make up the territory of the present-day Sultanate of Oman is also not fortuitous. If in turn we examine the relationships of the tribes of the northern marchland with their neighbours, we will find that their political equilibrium involves not only their neighbours in the core area, but also the tribes of the Dhahira and Trucial Oman, while those of the south-eastern marchlands extend the direct alliances to the desert borderlands as far as Dhofar. In other words, political balance in the marchlands of the Imamate involves not only the tribes of the core area, but also those living in the outer frontier zone.

So, despite the fact that the *dār*s of the tribes inhabiting the outer part of the region are not contiguous with those of central Oman, and that the inhabitants of the former area have for long ceased to subscribe to the Ibāḍi system of government which, over the course of time, has become identified with a sense of political community amongst the latter, both remain linked by direct *shaff* alliances: thus a full-scale war between the tribes of the Sirr would also involve tribes from the core area and the northern frontier area, while a similar situation in, say, the Badīya would engage the tribes of the core area with those of the Jaʿlān and their bedu neighbours. On the other hand, those tribes which live beyond these districts have no direct links with the inhabitants of central Oman, and so they neither consider themselves to be Omanis nor belong to the tribal alliances which emanate from this region.

The Moiety Groupings (Hināwi and Ghāfiri: Nizār and Yaman)

It has now been shown that the geographical uniqueness of 'Oman' finds its counterpart in an exclusive tribal organization which polarizes the loyalties of groups in their clan and neighbourhood units into two self-balancing halves or moieties: since these are more or less perceived in terms of descent-group alliances (*shaff*), they each bear a tribal label, Hināwi and Ghāfiri. At an earlier period these moieties were called Nizār and Yaman (that is, the same names that are retained in the two principal settlements in Izki).

The basic difference between these two sets of labels lies in the degree to which the locational or the clan element predominated in tribal structure at the time when the crises occurred which caused the moiety groupings to crystallize.

In the earlier moiety organization, those clan linkages which originally bonded the tribes at the time of their migration to Oman were still very significant, even though they had already been modified by locational interests arising from the process of settling: so when civil war broke out in the core of the Imamate at the end of the ninth century, conflict did not just spread from the point of original confrontation, as was more or less the case in the Hināwi-Ghāfiri war, but flashed across the geographic barriers through the powerful mechanisms of the *ʿaṣabīya* obligations which still activated clans in their dispersal. Moreover, this war involved people from a much wider area than that which marked the collapse of the Yaʿāriba Imamate some eight hundred years later. There are three main reasons why this was so. First: the Ibāḍi state, with its claim to universality, still represented an ideological challenge to the Caliphate, and did, in practice, command the loyalties of the people of a large part of southern Arabia. Second: at that time the Omanis controlled much of the rapidly expanding maritime trade of the central Islamic empire through their military and commercial fleets. Third: the deep and complex differences that had split the Arabo-Islamic world into the two opposing camps which rallied under the tribal names of Nizār and Yaman were still of relatively recent creation: the memory of the part the Azd-dominated Omani groups had played in past confrontations between the two factions was therefore fresh, and could arouse passions amongst tribesmen from as far afield as Khurāsān, Iraq, and Syria. So it was that when the Bani Sāma (of Nizār genealogy) and their allies were defeated by the Azd (of Yaman genealogy) of central Oman, and their rival Imamate overthrown, the surviving Sāmi leaders fled to the Caliph's governor in 'Baḥrayn' and deliberately distorted the issues in Oman as a Nizār-Yaman tribal war. The Caliph, only too willing to crush the Ibāḍi state and gain possession of the coveted ports of Oman, responded to their appeal and was easily able to raise an army from the Azd's tribal enemies for invading the country.

Yet in reality the original differences between the two parties was only partially 'tribal', for the seeds of the conflict lay in territorial interests which cut across the formal alliances; to wit, an attempt by the dominant group of central Oman (then under the political leadership of the Yaḥmad Azd and the military leadership of the Bani Hinā Azd) to dominate the Imamate and exclude the northern tribes from any benefit from, or say in the government of, the wealthiest part of the country. So, even though the latter were dominated by the Nizāri Bani Sāma (one of whose shaikhs was traditionally chief elector of the Imam), they were strongly supported by their Yamani neighbours, and it was from the Ḥuddān of the Sirr (i.e. a 'brother' tribe of the Yaḥmad of central Oman) that the northerners selected their rival Imam.[17] Even so, the real foundering of the old alliances did not occur until after the Caliphate forces, aided by the more extreme elements of the northern confederation, had savagely pillaged and destroyed the settlements of central Oman; and as they remained in occupation of the coast, aided by the Bani Sāma who now started to propagate Sunni doctrine, and as the Ḥuddān began to ally with the Qarāmiṭa of 'Baḥrayn' the tribes began to realign themselves along 'national' and 'religious' lines and the breach between northern and central Oman grew. Thus from the tenth century A.D. onwards the names of the higher levels in the old tribal hierarchy rapidly disappeared and in the ensuing 'Dark Ages', clan fragmentation was accelerated as locality interests grew until by the fifteenth century de Barros (*Asia* Dec. II, 3. ii) was able to describe (with a reasonable degree of accuracy) the political situation in central Oman entirely in terms of rivalries between places, without any mention at all of tribal groupings. As a result, Omani territory became so fragmented, and its people so weakened by the rivalry between the *mulūk* (princes) of the various districts, that it finally fell prey to outsiders. And as already related, it was the resulting occupation of the bajada zone by ʿĀmir tribes from 'Baḥrayn', coupled to an extension of Portuguese control over the coastal areas, that eventually produced the reaction which led the original Arab settlers in central Oman to reunite under the banner of a properly elected Imam to evict the foreigner.

The successes of the first Yaʿāriba Imams can largely be attributed to the way they exploited the vestigial *ʿaṣabīya* of the early Arab tribal settlers in the interests of the state. Dispossessed groups were encouraged to drive out the usurpers and establish their own *dār*s, while new alliances were manipulated so that they might combat those groups unwilling to submit. And so it was during this period that the present tribal pattern of Oman really took form. But despite the fact that these new groupings were partly based on the revival of old clan loyalties, so cutting across the purely regional groupings which had been tending to develop in the late Nabāhina period, they still bore little resemblance to the tribal structures of the earlier Yaman-Nizār moieties (the retention of the old clan names to label these new groupings is a feature that must be interpreted with great circumspection). When therefore a political crisis, not dissimilar to that which destroyed the First Imamate, split the country at the end of Yaʿāriba times, the moiety divisions which crystallized were quite different from those of the earlier period. Unfortunately, the fact that the names of these two parties derived from the tribal followers of two early protagonists, the Bani Hināʾ (a pseudomorph of the ancient Yamani Bani Hinā that had played such an important role in the earlier civil war) and the Bani Ghāfir (who share the same ancestry as the Nizāri Bani Sāma), has led many Omanis, as well as Europeans, into the trap of believing that the Hināwi-Ghāfiri divisions are to be identified with those of a thousand years before. In reality the *shaff* names were purely symbolic, red rose and white rose, and the outward spread of fighting from the core of the state was caused by individual groups in each locality seizing the chance to further their own ends as the last vestiges of central government broke down.

THE TRIBAL SYSTEM

Thus all tribal organization in Oman, from the level of the *fakhdh* to that of the complete moiety, may be viewed as a mechanism for balancing power between clans within localities. If, for example, the Awlād Rāshid of Nizār in Izki try and take the lands of Yaman, they know that they will have to reckon not only with its inhabitants but also with the Hawāshim. Once a full Hawāshim-Awlād Rāshid confrontation occurs, then automatically the groups in direct *shaff* alliance with the Ruwāḥa and the Riyām would become involved: at this point the paramount leaders of the former would try and enlist the support of the Ḥirth-led Sharqīya Hināwis, and this would immediately involve the Ghāfiri confederation (Bani Jābir, Siyābiyīn, Nadābiyīn of the Lower Wādi Sumāyil): then the bedu would be enlisted (the Durūʿ and Janaba with the Ghāfiris, the Wahība with the Hināwis), and so the conflict would continue to grow.

That it does not always do so is due to the fact that the tribal linkages are increasingly complex and situational the greater the number of people involved. The whole system does not immediately react to change in one of the component entities, and this lag allows time for tempers to cool and for community leaders to try and resolve problems peacefully. But once the slack in the system begins to be taken up, and the mollifying influence of moderate men to be overruled by leaders seeking to profit from rising passions, then conflict spreads until eventually all the tribes of Oman become involved. This is what happened in the civil wars which brought to an end the country's two greatest periods of history. But on no other occasions has the complete moiety organization been brought into play.

The main barriers to the spread of fighting as revealed by an examination of all the so-called Hināwi-Ghāfiri conflicts since the end of Yaʿāriba times are primarily geographical. For example, it is very rare to find that events in the Sumāyil Gap involve the people of the Sirr, or that tribes in the Sharqīya go to the help of the Hināwis in the northern Jawf. True, clan *ʿaṣabīya* does play an important part in the initial spread of fighting, but it is the boundaries which delimit the major sub-regions of Oman that also tend to determine the situations from which *shaff* alliances arise: hostilities do not spread at a steady rate, but tend to escalate by spurts as the containing forces which determine each level of the tribal-cum-geographical hierarchy are breached.

So even though the tribal system of Oman is perceived in terms of kinship, and is in theory spatially unconfined, it is clear that the situations which provoke conflict arise from territorial interests, and that in reality the tribal system is designed to maintain political equilibrium in localities. In this respect it might be said that Omani social structure has adapted to its environment. But having admitted that, the fact remains that its basic conception is fundamentally unsuited to the needs of settlement organization in Oman. At best it may be described as a primitive solution to the problem of bringing order into a world where every man is for himself: it prevents the strong from continually attacking the weak, it permits a degree of economic exchange to be carried out between rival communities, and it has certain ideals which might be described as vaguely 'democratic'. But its methods are based on placing groups in opposition to one another rather than on uniting them, and so are extremely wasteful of both human and natural resources: just how wasteful may be seen by anyone who cares to read Omani history with an eye to its record of *qanāt* destruction and abandonment of settlement.

It is, of course, true that the worst excesses are normally avoided by the conventions of tribal warfare, but once the situation escalates to involve people who are not permanent neighbours these conventions tend increasingly to be ignored and wilful destruction occurs. In a bedu society this matters relatively little, for there wealth is not held in long-term investments in the land. But in a society which depends on a delicate irrigation system for its survival the results are disastrous.

Even worse than such outbursts of violence are the long-term effects of the 'democratic' principles involved in Omani tribalism and the Ibāḍi government system, for while these have been successful in opposing feudalism, capitalist land-tenure, and *dirigiste* bureaucracy, they have militated against any real development of co-operative systems between communities. Only at the level of the individual *falaj* settlement does any central institution exist for maintaining the irrigation network, and this, as we have seen in the case of Izki, is despite, rather than because of, tribal organization.

The tribal system is therefore fundamentally unsuited to the needs of the land. It speaks volumes for the skill of the early settlers who developed the *falaj* system that, despite thirteen hundred years of destruction and negligence, some of their work still survives to provide a livelihood for the present inhabitants of Oman. But whether the villagers' lot was better under the Persian regime than under the Arabs is quite a different matter.

APPENDIX TO CHAPTER X

The Clans of the Izki Region

I THE THREE SETTLEMENTS OF THE FALAJ MALKI

If all the villagers were present today the population would probably be between 3,000 and 4,000; at the beginning of the century it was perhaps nearer 5,000 souls.

A. Nizār

Unfortunately it has not been possible to obtain a detailed breakdown of the Nizār population because of the highly charged political atmosphere which surrounded Izki in general and Nizār in particular at the time when the present writer was carrying out his investigations. Nevertheless, with the information collected with the considerable help of Mr Massy, plus the *falaj* book and other written sources, it is possible to reconstruct an outline of its clan structure.

Nizār is the real centre of Riyāmi power in Izki, and its leaders are from lineages of the **Awlād Rāshid**, the only group entitled to utilize the *nisba* Riyāmi in written documents: amongst these are the **Munīr**, the now virtually extinct shaikhly group of the **Awlād Mufarrij**, and the **Masārīr**.

According to Mr Massy there are three other 'true' descent groups of the Bani Riyām (that is, groups recognized as of direct descent from the eponymous Riyām), the **Bani Tawba**, the **Fuhūd**, and the **Āl Ṣuqūr**. All but the Fuhūd feature in the *falaj* book, and in principle may be assumed to live in Nizār. However, this is an assumption that must be treated with reserve, for at the present day the most influential Ṣaqri group of Izki lives in Yaman (q.v.) while the Bani Tawba are widely dispersed through nearly all the Riyām villages of the Izki area.[1] Elements from this last group have long been settled in Nizār, but despite this they are still considered 'a little wild' by the rest of the tribe, probably because the majority still live as *shawāwi* on the Jabal (Akhdhar); certainly some of the groups have only recently started to lead a sedentary life and their main footing in the Izki area may be due to re-developing the little Falaj ᶜAbt which waters the far end of Nizār lands (cf. Fig. 32).

The following groups featuring in the *falaj* book are not of Riyāmi descent, but live in Nizār and perforce recognize, in varying degrees, the authority of its leaders:

The ᶜ**Umūr**. A great problem arises in distinguishing between the groups whose names derive from the root ᶜMR, of which there are no less than five living in and around Izki or amongst the Bani Riyām; they are the ᶜUmūr (ᶜAmri or ᶜUmūri), the Ālᶜ Umayr (ᶜUmayri), the Awlād ᶜUwaymir (ᶜUwaymiri), the Muᶜammara (Muᶜammari), and the ᶜAwāmir (ᶜAmiri). Unfortunately the correct *nisbas* (given in the brackets) are not always followed in speech or in a crudely written document like the *falaj* book; disentangling these groups is further complicated by the fact that there are other ᶜMR groups in Oman including the important Bani ᶜUmar (*nisba* Maᶜmari). However, it would appear that the main group in the Izki area are the ᶜUmūr, who derive their name, according to Siyābi (pp. 68-9), from an ᶜAbd al-Qays clan of that name that have merged into the Bani Riyām. An ᶜAmri is at present (1965) *wakīl* of the Falaj Malki. Scattered throughout the area are the **Āl ᶜUmayr**, formerly an important clan who dominated the Sumāyil Gap area in Late Nabāhina times (second half of the sixteenth century) and who gave their name to a now ruined fort in Izki, the Ḥiṣn al-ᶜUmayri.

The other important group in Nizār are the **ᶜUzūr**, who number about 150 individuals. As mentioned elsewhere, these are descendants of the original Sāmi clan who settled in the village and eventually lost their position to their Riyāmi rivals. Other elements assimilated into the Riyām as a result of living in Nizār include the **Barūmiyīn** (said to take their name from an Algerian who settled in Izki), the **Ruwājiḥ**, the **Bani Baḥri**, a descent group of either Yaḥmad (Azd Shanuʾa) or Bani Hinā (Mālik b. Fahm Azd) stock (cf. Siyābi, p. 122; in the *falaj* book a Baḥri ᶜ*ālim* appears to have been responsible for the *fatwā*s concerning redistribution of property after ᶜAzzān b. Qays, Imam 1868-71, took Izki). Also of some interest are the **Ramāḥ**, (*nisba* Rumḥi), who since time immemorial have provided the chief ᶜ*arīf* of the Falaj Malki: it is fairly certain that this clan, who are also found in the Ghadaf, are one of the more important groups of non-Arab origin in central Oman.[2]

In addition there is some reason to believe that there are a few **Awlād Bahlāni** and **Fuzāriyīn** who live in Nizār as well as in Yaman (q.v.), and here too are found odd elements from important Omani tribes such as the **Bani Hinā** (Mālik b. Fahm Azd; one family features in the *falaj* book), the **Ḥirth** (a major Sharqīya tribe), plus some **Maḥāriq** (a Tamīm descent group concentrated in the Adam area), and **Naᶜb** (a Quḍāᶜa clan, here probably closely associated with the Bani Tawba).

B. Yaman

As explained in Chapter X, Yaman once belonged to the **Awlād Bahlāni**, the principal rivals of the Bani Riyām of Nizār (they may be of ᶜAbs descent, that is the same genealogical stock to which the true Bani Ruwāḥa clans belong: cf. Siyābi, p. 33). After it destruction in the civil war at the end of Yaᶜāriba times Yaman was rebuilt by one of its smaller groups, the **Manādhira**, and only a few Bahlāni returned. The Manādhira were soon dispossessed by the **Darāmika** who themselves had lost their own settlement of ᶜAdbi in the upheavals, and most of them settled in Saddi (q.v.): from there they continue to plot against the Darāmika.

Despite their machinations, the Darāmika (whose growing hold over Yaman can be traced in the considerable increase in their *falaj* shares between

1825 and 1875) still hold sway in Yaman and they also own two small cultivated areas on the left bank of the Wadi al-Ḥalfayn, al-Maṣfiya, and al-ᶜAlm (cf. Fig. 32). Genealogically the Darāmika are of Kinda origin, and the tribe is still numerically important in and around the original area of Kinda concentration (the Jabal Kinda on Fig. 33).

Also living in the village are some true Riyāmi descent groups, notably elements of the **Maghtasiyīn** (a lineage of the Awlād Rāshid who formerly lived on the Jabal but took refuge there as the result of a feud), and some **Ṣuqūr** (spelt with a *sīn* in the *falaj* book, but normally spelt with *ṣād*): the main centre of this latter Riyāmi clan is in Birkat al-Mawz (it should be noted that the Ṣuqūr of Izki live in Yaman and not in Nizār; in 1965 one of their members was the village tax-collector). Other groups living in Yaman include some **Fuzāriyīn**, who derive their name from a famous Dhibyān tribe (Siyābi, p. 70), **Naḥwiyīn**, who presumably take their name from Naḥw (one of the brother tribes of the Maᶜāwil and Ḥuddān, Shanuʾa Azd), and **Umbū ᶜAli**,[3] an influential group of Ṭayy stock most of whom live in the Sumāyil area (in Izki they owned ᶜAyn Ṣaᶜnāʾ until it was destroyed).

C. Ḥārat Bani Ḥusayn

The origins of the eponymous Bani Ḥusayn seem to be unknown, but they were probably one of the earliest groups to settle in Izki, for their name is attached to a *khabūra* of the early land-tenure system (see Table 10): it is reported that the last member of the clan died during the present century.

By far the biggest group here are the **Riqaysh** (Bil-Riqaysh). Of Kinda origin, they lived in Ḥamamat (modern al-Janā) and in al-Khaḍrā, two settlements respectively in the so-called Wādi al-Gharbi and the Wādi al-Sharqi which form the heart of Bani Ruwāḥa territory (cf. Chapter VIII), until, as a result of events in the eighteenth century, they quarrelled with their hosts, and the majority came to live in Izki: they seem rapidly to have obtained control of their present settlement, and by 1825 owned more water rights in the Falaj Malki than any native lineage. Also living here are some **ᶜUzūr** (q.v. under Nizār), a few **ᶜAdāwina**[4] and a small group of **Bani Tawba** (q.v. under Nizār). One estimate put the number of houses of these various groups at 70 Riqaysh (including dependants), 15 ᶜUzūr, 5 ᶜAdāwina, and a couple of Bani Tawba.

GROUPS OF CLIENT STATUS

It is important to remember that in all these settlements there also live considerable numbers of **bayāsira**, who are *mawāli* of the more important clans (cf. Chapter VII). There appear to be few signs in a village like Izki of an (ex) slave class (*ᶜabīd*), and it is suspected that imported slaves have never played an important part in village societies in interior Oman. The following Table gives a list of some of the more important *baysari* groups (spellings uncertain) and the clans to which they belong.

Bayāsira Groups

Arab group	*Client Baysari group*
Awlād Bahlāni	al-Khuwayṭiriyīn
Awlād Rāshid	Awlād Ghāwi (about 100 in Izki) and al-Shaʿmal
Awlād Munīr	Awlad al-Mutajaḥḥadal
Bani Tawba	Awlād Qanzāʾil
Bani Riyām (unspecified)	Awlād Rīḥ (originally belonged to the Manādhira)
Awlād Bil-Riqaysh	Awlād Maḥram (N.B. Maḥram is the name of the main centre of the Riqaysh before they came to Izki) and Awlād Alfi (originally clients of the Hawāshim, the shaikhly clan of the true Ruwāḥa descent groups)

For further details see Wilkinson 1974.

II SETTLEMENTS WATERED BY THE QASAWĀT FALAJ

A. Ḥārat al-Raḥā

The land of this settlement runs into that of Nizār, while the Malki *falaj* itself passes through the *bilād*: some of the inhabitants hold water rights on the main *falaj*. The principal group here are the **Awlād Rāshid**. There are also some **ʿAbriyīn** (Azd) and **Maḥārīq** (cf. under Nizār).

B. Saddi

As explained under Yaman, the dominant group are now the **Manādhira**, a clan whose origins have not been traced, but who were once fairly important in the Sirr: they are still the leading group of al-Silayf (near ʿIbri), while their name is also attached to the Falaj al-Manādhira, near Yanqul. The Izki group has a permanent feud with the other important clan of Saddi, the **Qurūn** (Bani Hinā stock?), who came from the outlying hamlet of al-Ḥabūb (between al-Zikayt and the Buldān al-ʿAwāmir) and settled in Saddi after the Manādhira. Miscellaneous groups include a **Shamsi** family (a minor clan of Wāʾil stock (?) whose main centre is in al-Khaḍrā in the Sharqīya).

III AL-MAGHYŪTH

A small settlement in the main Izki area, but with its own independent water supply.

The main group are **Bani Tawba** (q.v. under Nizār). In opposition to them there are three groups, **Manādhira** (q.v. under Saddi), **Awlād Ḥusayn** (Ṭayy stock? nothing to do with the eponym of Ḥārat Bani Ḥusayn), and the

Zakāwina (the main concentration of this group is in Samad in the Sharqīya according to Miles 1919, ii. 438).

IV DOWNSTREAM SETTLEMENTS

Zikayt, a small settlement belonging to the **Bani Tawba**: also some **Āl ᶜUmayr**(?). Between Zikayt and Izki are al-Rasays, al-Ṭaybi, al-ᶜUwayna, and al-Zāhir, four small areas of cultivation each with its own independent water-supply belonging to small **Bani Riyām** groups (who spend most of the year on the *jabal*?).

V UPSTREAM SETTLEMENTS ON THE IZKI SIDE OF THE NAJD AL-MAGHBARĪYA

These are quite separate from Izki itself, but closely involved in the political situation there.

A Al-Qārūt

ᶜAlāya (Upper) and Sifāla (Lower) form two quite distinct parts to the village. They are fed by a number of *aflāj*, but most of these have more or less dried up and the whole water-supply is very precarious and has to be supplemented by wells and *ghayl*. Possession is strongly disputed between the Bani Riyām and the Bani Ruwāḥa.

At present, Upper Qārūt belongs to the **Bani Ruwāḥa** (Bani Hishām and others), while Lower Qārūt, until about thirty years ago, belonged to the **Bani Salīma** (q.v. under Muṭi), at which time its *qanāt* went dry and the palms died. Subsequently a group of **Bani Tawba** purchased the land cheaply from the Bani Salīma and, with elements of the **Bani ᶜAwf**, **ᶜUmūr**, **Wurūd**, and **Ruwāḥa** from Upper Qārūt and some of the original Bani Salīma themselves, succeeded in getting the *falaj* to flow again. They were subsequently joined in their new settlement by elements of the **Bani ᶜAwf** from Muṭi (q.v.) and **ᶜUmūr** (q.v. under Nizār).

B. Muṭi (correctly Imṭi)

A strongly fortified settlement built at the foot of the Jabal guarding the ravine of the Wadi Muṭi. Only two of the original *aflāj* are working: one of these feeds direct from a tunnel within the limestone flanks of the Jabal itself.

The dominant tribe here are the **Bani Salīma** (b. Mālik b. Fahm Azd; cf. Fig. 31). This appears to be the only place in Oman where remnants of this famous tribe of pre-Islamic times are still to be found living as a discrete unit in Oman. There are also elements of a number of other descent groups here, including the **Bani ᶜAwf** (Wāʾil stock, whose main *dār* is in the upper reaches of the wadis draining towards the Ghadaf, notably the Wadi Farᶜ). At the southern end of the village there is a small quarter, containing about a third of Muṭi's population, which is inhabited by **Bani Tawba** and **Wurūd** (Yaḥmad stock; also found in the Ghadaf at Nakhl and the Sharqīya).

Table 14 *Shareholders of Permanent Water Shares (of more than an athar) in the Falaj Malki by Clans c. 1825 (Based on the falaj record)*

Tribal group	*Approx. water holding in athars*	*Notes* (*Supplementary to the main text*)
Dallāl*	105	A special case. These shares almost certainly belonged to groups from Yaman, as is clear from the subsequent (re?) distribution of the water, some of it by order of *fatwās*.
Riqaysh*	42	It would appear that the Riqaysh were well settled in Izki by this time, but their earlier connections with Ruwāḥa territory can be traced through entries like 'estate of Muḥammad b. Khalf b. Jāᶜid, *Ṣāḥib Ḥurayrat al-Khaḍrā*' (i.e. shaikh of Khaḍrā village in W. Maḥram).
Awlād Rāshid*	32 (at least)	22 belong to one family, the descendants of Muḥd b. Khalf al-Riyāmi, 4 belong to an individual of the Awlād Mufarrij, 3 to the Munīr, whilst 3 belong to other Riyāmis, one of whom came from Tanūf. It is suspected that some of the other families whose *nisbas* are not given (see below) are also Awlād Rāshid or associated Riyāmi groups.
Ṣuqūr*	22	
ᶜUmūr*	14	
Darāmika*	13	Subsequently obtained a large amount of the Dallāl holding.
Awlād Bahlāni*	11	
Bārūmi*	8	One individual—*nisba* is Umbārūmi in the book.
Salīma*	7	Indicates presence of at least one family (from their full names the 7 individuals are all probably directly related).
Fuzāra*	5	
B. Tawba*	5	
ᶜAbriyīn*	4	
Ruwājiḥ*	4	
Manādhira*	3	
Zahhābi	3	No information.
Jabri*	3	Son of the powerful Jabri shaikh,

		Muḥammad b. Nāṣir. This is the only direct holding held by this family recorded in the *falaj* book.
Naʿb*	3	Quḍāʿi clan.
Ḥarbi	3	Single individual, possibly of the once famous B. Hinā shaikhly clan, but more probably a member of the Muḥāriba which, according to Siyābi, p. 52, are of Qays ʿAylān stock incorporated into the Wahība.
Ghanīmi	3	Three brothers, no information.
Umbū ʿAli*	2	Two individuals, one the grandson of the author of the *Kashf al-Ghumma* and the other referred to as *Ṣāḥib Firq* (near Nizwā).
al-ʿArīf* (Ramāḥ)	2	Although not given the Rumḥi *nisba*, the succession of names used in the family clearly indicates it is the same family as the present *fālāj ʿarīf*.
Jābiri	2	One individual from the B. Jābir, a tribe in the Sumāyil area and in Eastern Oman (cf. Fig. 25)
Qaṣṣābi	2	Three individuals, two related; no information except that this *nisba* might just possibly refer to their occupation (Izki was once famous for its sugar-cane).
Ṣāḥib Maṣīra	2	Important island off the south coast of Oman.
Maghyūthi	2	i.e. From the neighbouring settlement of Maghyūth (see III above).
Ismāʿīli	1	Individual probably from the group (of Quḍāʿa stock) who now mainly live near Ibrā and form part of the Masākira.
Maḥārīq	1	An important tribal group chiefly in Adam. The indications in the book are that the family involved in Izki had connections with the Darāmika.
Hināʾi*	1	B. Hinā; an individual.

In addition to these holdings are the members of the following families whose *nisbas* are never given in the *falaj* book (some may be of ʿUzūr stock).

Muḥammad b. Saʿīd	20	possibly same family.
Sulaymān b. Saʿīd	5	
Aḥmad b. Mūsā	13	ditto
Muḥammad b. Mūsā	8	
ʿUbayd offspring	9	probably Riyāmi
Muḥammad b. ʿImrān	3	

Four women of non-Izkāwi origin also owned more than 1A (*thar*): one from the B. Kharūṣ (2A), one from the Siyābiyīn (1A), one from Sumāyil (1A) and one with a *nisba Shwayhabīya* (1A).

* discussed in the text.

N.B. The term 'Ṣāḥib' is explained in Chapter X footnote 7.

NOTES TO CHAPTER X

[1] Reference to this tradition and how Izki antedates Nizwā by a 'hundred' years has already been made on p. 130. Incidentally, there are some interesting burial (?) mounds (some of which may be of the first-millennium type) to be seen on the rim rocks above Zikayt.

[2] Lorimer estimates Yaman and Nizār as respectively 350 and 450 houses at the beginning of the century. These figures presumably include the subsidiary settlements polarized towards these two principal *ḥujras*. The present figures were given by a reliable local source, but the writer believes those for Nizār are somewhat on the high side.

[a] I have recently seen copies of a set of judgements concerning this *falaj*. These clearly indicate that Ḥimyar, along with two lesser associates, rebuilt this *falaj*. The *qāḍis'* rulings concerned, *inter alia*, the settlement price for buying out the original shareholders and new arrangements for property which came under the trusteeship of the Imamate authorities (*waqf*, minors etc.).

[3] Jurnān is reputedly the name of the idol worshiped there in pre-Islamic time (*Nahḍa*, p. 181; Jurfān ibid, p. 44 is a typographic error): the site of the blocked-up cavern (*kanīsa*, cf. Reinhardt 1894, $98 '*kanys* – ohne Licht und Luft') in which this idol was supposed to have been kept is located in the cliff (made up of old coarse cemented outwash material into which the present wadi has cut) crowned by Nizār. There is a great deal of superstitition about all this area, and a small irrigation channel which ran through the cavern was closed 'because it was haunted by *jinn*'.

An interesting parallel to the Izki change of name is provided by al-Sumāyil/Sumāʾil, reputedly a contraction of *Ism Allāh* ('the name of Allāh') because it was there that one Māzin b. Ghuḍūba of the Ṭayy was converted by the words of the very idol he was worshipping and so became the first Omani Muslim (ʿAwtabi Paris MS. 118; cf. *Tuḥfa* i. 53 et seq.).

[4] Although the Imam is the ultimate custodian of both *waqf* and *bayt al-māl*, the two are kept rigidly distinct. This is well-brought-out by the acrimonious debate (*Nahḍa*, pp. 388-91) which followed the Imam Sālim b. Rāshid al-Kharūṣi's attempt, at a time of great need in 1913, to appropriate for the *bayt al-māl* such *waqf* as had been bequeathed for the purpose of visiting graves and making readings from the Qurān for the dead; this action he tried to justify on the pretext that the *waqf* purposes were not true Muslim practice, but in the end he was over-ruled.

[5] The details of bequests given here are for the actual water rights, although in some cases there is an associated land bequest: so for example, we find water given for the ʿ*ābīya* (that is land for seasonal crops) called al-ʿAqāq, the *māl* (field) al-Rāfiʿ, the *bustān* (garden) Sahlān, the *jilba* (plot) al-Dakk, etc. Usually the water is left without land, so it is not surprising to find mosques actively exchanging their gifts in order to rationalize their water holdings (as described in Chapter V).

[6] The fact that one of these mosques was called the *bayādīr* mosque is of some interest for understanding the status of this group. The bequest for the Nawrūz festival at one mosque is also of some interest, because it may indicate vestigial practices from pre-Islamic times.

[7] Thus one finds the occasional mention of owners with a place rather than a clan *nisba*, e.g. Maḥram, Ṣūr, Tanūf, Adam: once or twice a person is described as '*Ṣāḥib Makān*'; this means that the individual was the leading personality (occasionally a government appointee) of the place referred to. The holdings of most of these outsiders are usually tiny vestiges of an inheritance, entered simply to keep the mathematics of the holdings straight; normally heritages were sold to true Izkāwis. The history of the individual holdings also nearly always shows that women either retained their inherited water rights under some sort of joint family arrangement or else sold them to their male relatives.

[8] The actual marriage patterns in Izki have not been investigated in detail. The general evidence, however, strongly suggests that the village forms a geographical 'isolate', that is, a population group within which an individual has the likelihood of finding a mate so neither inter- nor intra-clan marriages normally extend beyond the neighbouring areas. In this connection it is also worth noting that there is only a handful of women who can fairly certainly be identified as of non-Izki origin recorded in the *Malki Falaj Book*, and in 1825 only three of these had holdings of any significance (one Kharūṣi woman held two *athar*s, one from the Siyābiyīn held one *athar*, as also did a woman from Sumāyil).

[9] Who this Dallāl family was is something of a puzzle, but that they were not natives of the village is fairly certain. From a number of odd clues, both from within the *falaj* book and from other sources, the writer suspects that they were the agents for the powerful Jabri family who virtually ruled the Sumāyil Gap area in the first half of the nineteenth century; before this they had acted for the later Yaᶜāriba 'Imams' who built up enormous land holdings in the villages of Oman. It is possibly as agents (*dallāl*) that they derived their family *nisba*.

[10] Virtually all small sales of local produce in the villages of Oman are conducted by auction (*munādā*). A common procedure is for the potential clients to gather in a ring around the vendors, who circulate, displaying their goods and shouting the last bid received. The *dallāl* (auctioneer, an official appointment) then records the sale and collects any taxes due. Permanent shops are only found in the bigger centres and traditionally only sell specialized local produce (pottery, textiles, and the work of various kinds of smiths) and imported goods. The present increase in the number of permanent shops is an indication of the changing economic organization of the village (improved transport, an increasing dependence on imported goods, rising purchasing power stimulated by earnings from external sources, etc.). Traditionally, the marketing of local produce destined for export (mainly dates and dried fruit) tended to be controlled by the merchants who resided in the regional ports through a network of agents living in the main market centres of the interior.

[11] The Riyām in fact only really begin to emerge as an independent tribal grouping of major importance in central Oman with the final breakdown of the Yaḥmad confederation in the twelfth century.

[12] These are the Balūsh/Balūch referred to in Chapter IX, n. 15. The descendants of the group ousted from Izki during the eighteenth century are now said to be living in al-Jayla (Legayla), a village in Bani Jābir territory in the eastern part of the Sumāyil Gap.

[13] The former importance of the ᶜUzūr is indicated by the vestigial titles of *bāda*s 7 and 14 (cf. Table 10). The fact that there is no holder identified by the ᶜUzri or Sāmi *nisba* in the *falaj* book should be treated with caution, for while their position in Izki is now relatively insignificant it may well be that one or two of the families recorded without a *nisba* are from this clan.

[14] The presence of ᶜAbd al-Qays and Wāʾil elements in Izki are also not unexpected, for even though they retained their bedu way of life well into Islamic times, they were closely associated with the above-mentioned hadhar clans, and some would have joined them in their dispersal.

[15] A *rashīd* is a leader at the lowest level of tribal organization.

[16] Appointing a local member of the village or the tribe on the principle of 'divide and rule' is, of course, not unknown in Oman; it was in this way that the recently deposed Sultan kept control of Izki.

[17] It is worth noting that this split between the tribes of northern and central Oman has roots at least as far back as the beginning of the Imamate, for the overthrow of Julandā power represented, in part, a defeat of the northern tribes and the passing of power from the Awlād Shams into the hands of their 'cousins' the Yaḥmad of central Oman (Wilkinson in *J. Omani Studies*, in press). The continuing success of the Yaḥmad Imams, therefore, depended on their playing down their own tribal role whilst simultaneously courting the support of the Bani Sāma *ʿulamāʾ*, who thereby effectively became Imam-makers. Once religious and tribal power began to re-identify towards the end of the ninth century this balance was upset, so when eventually the Sāmi *ʿulamāʾ* were ousted from the Jawf by a Yaḥmad tribal army from the Ghadaf they rejoined their fellow tribesmen in the north and attempted to reactivate the old alliances of the late Julandā period by offering the Imamate to the Ḥuddān (a brother tribe of the Julandā, themselves now of no importance). In this they were only partially successful because the Bani Hinā, who had been the principal supporters of the Julandā, remained loyal to the Imamate cause that they had so belatedly accepted. After the defeat of the northern confederation the Bani Sāma abandoned all support of the Imamate principles since they themselves could never be recognized as Imams; it is from this time onwards that northern Oman becomes Sunni and the Ibāḍi ideal becomes more or less confined to central Oman.

NOTES TO APPENDIX TO CHAPTER X

[1] There is only one Tawbi family mentioned in the *falaj* book: they owned some 5 *athar*s of water between them. There is, however, also mention of a father and daughter (owning approximately 3 *athar*s between them) who bear the *nisba* al-Naʿbi al-Matūb, which perhaps indicates that local elements of this once important Quḍāʿa clan (the Naʿb) have been assimilated into the Tawba.

[2] Lorimer reports that the Ramāḥ are an artisan group, specialists in metal work, who live at ʿAyn al-Ramāḥ in the Wadi al-Farʿ, where they number about 1,500 persons.

[3] Amongst the Umbū ʿAli of Izki today are the Sarāḥina, the family to which the reputed author of the *Kashf al-Ghumma*, Sirḥān b. Saʿīd, belonged. Incidentally, the evidence in the *falaj* book (in which his grandson features) confirms this author's provenance, but shows that he came from the Umbū ʿAli, a clan of Ṭayy origin, and not the Bani Bu ʿAli, as suggested by Ross.

[4] The ʿAdāwina are a particularly interesting clan, for they would appear to be one of the earliest refugee groups that came to Oman. Originating from the northernmost part of the Ḥijāz they were forced to flee from the tyranny of Jumāz b. Mālik b. Fahm, the ruler of that area. Initially they placed themselves under the general protection of the Maʿāwil (i.e. of the *Julandā*; the *Nubdhat al-Maʿawil*, p. 423 still records them as a Maʿwali clan), but in ʿAwtabi's time they formed a quite distinctive group within the Azd alliance. A word should be said here about this Jumāz, in connection with whom ʿAwtabi mentions the ʿAdāwina (Johnstone MS. 204). According to him Jumāz was the nickname of Ziyād b. Mālik b. Fahm who once ruled the Arab tribes of the borderlands between Ḥijāz and Shām (*min Bilād al-ʿĀliya* (al-ʿUlā) *ilā jānib Ayla* (Eilat) *min al-Shām*), and it is to his tyrannical behaviour that *Qurān* Ṣūra XVIII, vv. 33-5 is supposed to refer. Now there is no mention of a Jumāz/Ziyād amongst the progeny of Mālik b. Fahm in the standard genealogies (cf. Ibn Kalbi, edn. Caskel, table 211), but he does feature in Ibn Durayd's *Ishtiqāq* (p. 490) under the form Ḥimār (read Jumāz) b. Naṣr b. al-Azd (the 'Jawf' over which he tyrannically ruled was in 'Yaman' according to this author). Here we have yet another example of the Omanis preserving a set of traditions concerning the Azd which differs from the standard ones.

Conclusion

One of the main aims of the foregoing analysis of the nature of tribal organization has been to account for the way settlement itself is organized. This is appropriate because Omani social structure essentially reflects both the way Arab migrants have adapted to the physical requirements of their new homeland and how far they in turn have imposed their own notions of social organization on it. It is precisely because of the intimate man-land relationship which exists in Omani tribal structure that the geographical distinctiveness of the region is reflected in a self-balancing tribal hierarchy peculiar to it (the Hināwi and Ghāfiri moieties).

Regional distinctiveness arises from the way certain features of the area interact with each other; notably its physical geography (whose main characteristics in turn are largely determined by an arid climate, an 'insular' setting, and the way mountain, desert, and sea, are disposed), its settlement pattern (which more or less reflects the way occurrences of fresh water have been exploited), its traditional economy (based on cultivation, livestock-herding, and fishing), its external relationships (largely dictated by its continental isolation and its strategic maritime siting), and its political systems (characterized by a split between the isolationist views of a conservative, self-sufficient tribal society inspired by the Ibāḍi theory of Islamic community on the one hand, and the outward-looking pragmatism of a cosmopolitan maritime trading-society on the other).

The *mise en valeur* of the natural resources of this region was in large measure completed in pre-Islamic times; since then, it is only in the context of maritime trade and overseas expansion that important shifts in the economic structure have tended to occur (before the advent of the oil era). The general pattern of human occupancy in Oman has, then, been fixed since a remote period, and this in turn has imposed certain constraints on the way that the inhabitants of the land have subsequently been free to organize their society.

At one time there was a risk that man's hard-won hold in this harsh land would be lost when, with the coming of Islam, the Arabs of the desert fringes took possession of the settled areas and replaced the old quasi-feudal order of the evicted Persian ruling classes with the law of the nomad and the *sharīʿa*. Fortunately the new rulers gradually adapted to their new environment, so that they in turn became cultivators, and assimilated the population of the villages in which they settled into their social organization. By accepting some of the constraints necessary for preserving the economic basis of life in their new homeland, the Arabs ensured that their descent could continue to live there.

Yet the new social structure evolved by the Arabs was a compromise, for in the order they developed during the ninth century the organization of the

Persian land-heritage was grafted on to a life-style which originated in nomadism, while the 'state' system owed much to the adaptation of the universal precepts of Islamic community to tribal political structure. A 'traditional' pattern of life eventually emerged, which gave rise to the features of social organization that have been investigated in this book, an organization which, although applied to an agricultural economy, still retains something of the independent spirit of the desert and rejects the claims of central government to dictate how its affairs are to be conducted, while simultaneously refusing the servitude of capitalist land-tenure. The cost paid for maintaining some of the 'democratic' principles inherent in tribal society and Ibāḍi ideology has been a dramatic decline in the yield of the land. Only twice in the Arab history of Oman have large-scale investments in the economic infrastructure of the land taken place, and on both occasions they consisted in little more than restoring settlement that had been abandoned or neglected in the preceding centuries; in both cases much of the good work was wilfully destroyed, as primitive tribalism reacted against the growing dynastic and capitalist rule which brought about the economic upsurge.

Today, as a result of altering relationships with the outside world, this whole picture of traditional life in Oman is radically changing. Effective centralized government has been imposed on the inhabitants of the area, thanks to imported technology; the wealth of the country is no longer in its agriculture but in the demand of the developed countries for a hitherto untapped natural resource, oil; while the threats to the region's political independence spring not from the interests of outsiders in its maritime potential, or from the old internal schisms, but from imported ideologies: these have already fanned a rebellion in Dhofar and introduced the risk of it spreading into Oman and the Gulf beyond.

The need for the wasteful tribal mechanisms for maintaining internal political balance is fast disappearing, while the long-established Imamate tradition died with the Imam Muḥammad b. ʿAbdullāh al-Khalīli in 1954 (even though the Imamate cause was actively espoused for another decade or so). It is inconceivable that 'church and state' can ever again be reunited in the original manner, whatever titular forms future governments may adopt. At the same time the embryonic state divisions have taken on a new reality, so that 'Trucial' and 'non-Trucial' Oman have now been finally divorced, and in the latter the seat of power has once again shifted from the interior to the coast; this time, development in the capital-area of Muscat will probably ensure that it stays there.

The investment of oil revenues through the centralized mechanisms of government is also having its impact on the socio-economic structure of the region, all the more so as development policy in the Sultanate is constrained by two major features. The first of these is that the state budget is small, once the relatively large requirements of the military have been met. Since the calls on government finance have been even greater than would have been the case had the previous Sultan permitted some development in the private and public sectors of the economy, investment policy has naturally had to be extremely selective. To date (1973) the emphasis has been placed on providing facilities for external communications (modern seaport at Maṭraḥ, and airport near al-Sīb); government administration facilities (both military and civil); and certain essential social services (sanitary, health, and education): of necessity, the major efforts have been concentrated in the Muscat region. The second feature is that investment in the agricultural economy has been largely left to *ad hoc* private enterprise, with the government's own participation confined to initiating the long-term investigations necessary for planning a new rural economy. The consequence of both these features has been a redistribution of population, with a growing rate of migration from the interior towards the new centres of economic and social development on the coast: the resulting imbalance will become increasingly marked as the size of the population inevitably grows.

Thus the present over-all picture is of a region in which the material lot of nearly all the people is improving, but one in which all aspects of the 'distribution pattern' are becoming increasingly unbalanced. Distribution of oil wealth is unrelated to the formal political units into which geographical Oman has now been divided, so that extravagant expenditure has taken place in the states with least development potential, while little or no investment has occurred in the old populated centres; distribution of income is opening up the gap between rich and poor, to create a new class structure; distribution of economic and social opportunity is causing rural depopulation and a parasitic growth of the coastal settlements around Abu Dhabi, Dubai, and Muscat; distribution of population is leading to regional imbalance. And the whole is leading to a fundamental revolution in the social, economic, demographic, political, and geographic structure of the region.

So it is that the mechanisms which emerged over a thousand years ago to perpetuate the basically unchanging way of life, termed 'traditional', are becoming increasingly irrelevant to the present situation. That 'traditions' may help retard the speed of change may not be altogether a bad thing, but the concomitant risk is that a dual society will be created. Moreover, it must be recognized that even in the improbable event that the external economic and political forces which are initiating change were to weaken, this does not mean that the old *status quo* would be restored. The 'traditional' system has now been irrevocably changed with the implanting of the seed of cultural revolution.

The question therefore arises, 'have any of the traditional institutions in their original form any really constructive part to play in the planning of the future?' The answer must in all truth be 'no'. On the other hand, the answer to the question 'could they profitably be adapted to the new society?' is, it is hoped, 'yes'. The question that inevitably follows, 'how?', is certainly beyond the competence of the present writer to answer, as indeed it probably is of those who are actively concerned in trying to shape the new Oman. Here, however, it is at least encouraging to see that foreigners are a little less sure of their role in the Sultanate than was the case a few years ago. Today we have learnt that regional needs vary, that the experience of an Indian or a Sudani province is not always relevant to the requirements of the Arab Peninsula, and that practices current in the arid lands of the United States are not always applicable to the arid lands of the Middle East. Past failure is now admitted and the reasons for it analysed. So most western and some Arab advisers have at least learnt that planning does not consist of such simple solutions as growing tomatoes instead of palms; some have even discovered the necessity for examining the links between the economic and social aspects of traditional organization, so that change may be introduced in the one with the minimum of dislocation in the other.

Just as it would be a foolish planner, and an arrogant one, who was prepared to dismiss the whole of the traditional land organization of Oman because it was tribal, so it would be a poor Omani who turned his back on the past and considered *aflāj*, palm trees, and camels as nothing more than symbols of 'backwardness' and the sooner forgotten the better. Doubtless if one was building Oman from scratch one would not now attempt to develop it with *qanāt*. Yet surely the fact that enormous inputs of capital, labour, and knowledge worth countless years of oil income have already been invested in the land makes it worth while investigating what can be done with these old irrigation systems. In this connection it is worth pointing out that the experiences of consulting-groups with the long-abandoned *qanāt* of the marginal area of agricultural settlement in the Trucial States should not discourage efforts to study their potential in the Sultanate, where much land has only recently been abandoned and where only a little effort may be sufficient to bring it back under cultivation. True, one cannot expect to restore the *falaj* system to the pristine glories of a millennium and a half ago, but at least an increased yield from the land may be possible at relatively low cost, and this would have the advantage of preserving some of the better aspects of communal village organizations which are now rapidly disappearing in face of the individual forms of capitalist land-tenure that are being introduced with mechanically pumped well-techniques. Furthermore, a policy of *qanāt* improvement, if also coupled to restrictions on the use of pumps, would have the merit of diminishing the risk of upsetting hydrological eqilibrium in the individual drainage basins, and thus allow time for properly planned agricultural schemes to be investigated.

Again, it may be that instead of over-concentrating on the potential offered by introducing exotic crops and livestock, which has frequently been the tendency in development schemes elsewhere, a major study of the possibilities offered by the traditional economy would bring its rewards. Research into finding new uses for dates will at least show whether or not there is any future in upgrading the forms of cultivation understood by the villagers; while in a world where the demand for protein is growing, the development of Oman's pastoral and fishing resources along modern lines must surely bring long-term dividends and provide a new lease of life for a country where supplies of oil are limited but which, unlike some of the other Gulf oil states, has the advantage of considerable land potential. Fortunately, recent reports from Oman suggest that such lines of research are being actively pursued.

While it is true that there must be a rational development of the capital-area, it is equally important that this should not be at the cost of the rest of the country; a major growth pole in the interior must be fostered. In a state which is having to fight a major war for its very survival, and which has only recently been unshackled from the oppressive regime of the late Sultan, such hopes may appear Utopian. Yet it is precisely because the oil reserves of Oman appear to be limited that it is imperative that such funds as are available should be invested with the minimum of wastage, and aimed at creating a structure that is not doomed to collapse once oil revenues begin to run out. The fact that this can only be achieved at the cost of frustrating some of the natural ambitions of the urban Omanis is, of course, a basic political problem. Hence the necessity for the small oil-rich states also to face up to the responsibilities that their fortuitous wealth has brought them, by contributing to Oman's development. It is after all on political stability in the long-established centres of settlement in the Gulf that the survival of these anomalous desert political units depends.

If then the writer has baulked at directly answering questions about the future of Oman, he hopes that he may have contributed something of value by providing a groundwork study for traditional organizations, and thus have thrown some light on one aspect affecting development studies for the region. And even if in this he proves too optimistic, he trusts that at least he has contributed to an understanding of the past of a country which, through its success in safeguarding certain basic principles of personal freedom in the conduct of its affairs, has proved itself worthy to be considered one of the civilized nations of the world.

NOTES TO FIG. 33

The Map attempts to indicate the main settlement pattern around the time of the civil war at the end of the third/ninth century. In fact, evidence from the beginning of the Islamic period down to the thirteenth century A.D. has been used, but no material from later sources has been incorporated and the temptation to argue *ex post facto* has been resisted.

The primary tribal territories are shown in capitals and some of the more important secondary concentrations are also indicated. The five principal groupings which gave their names to the divisions of the mountains are shown in cartouche. Details of this settlement pattern are as follows: AZD (cf. Fig. 30) Continued on page 245.

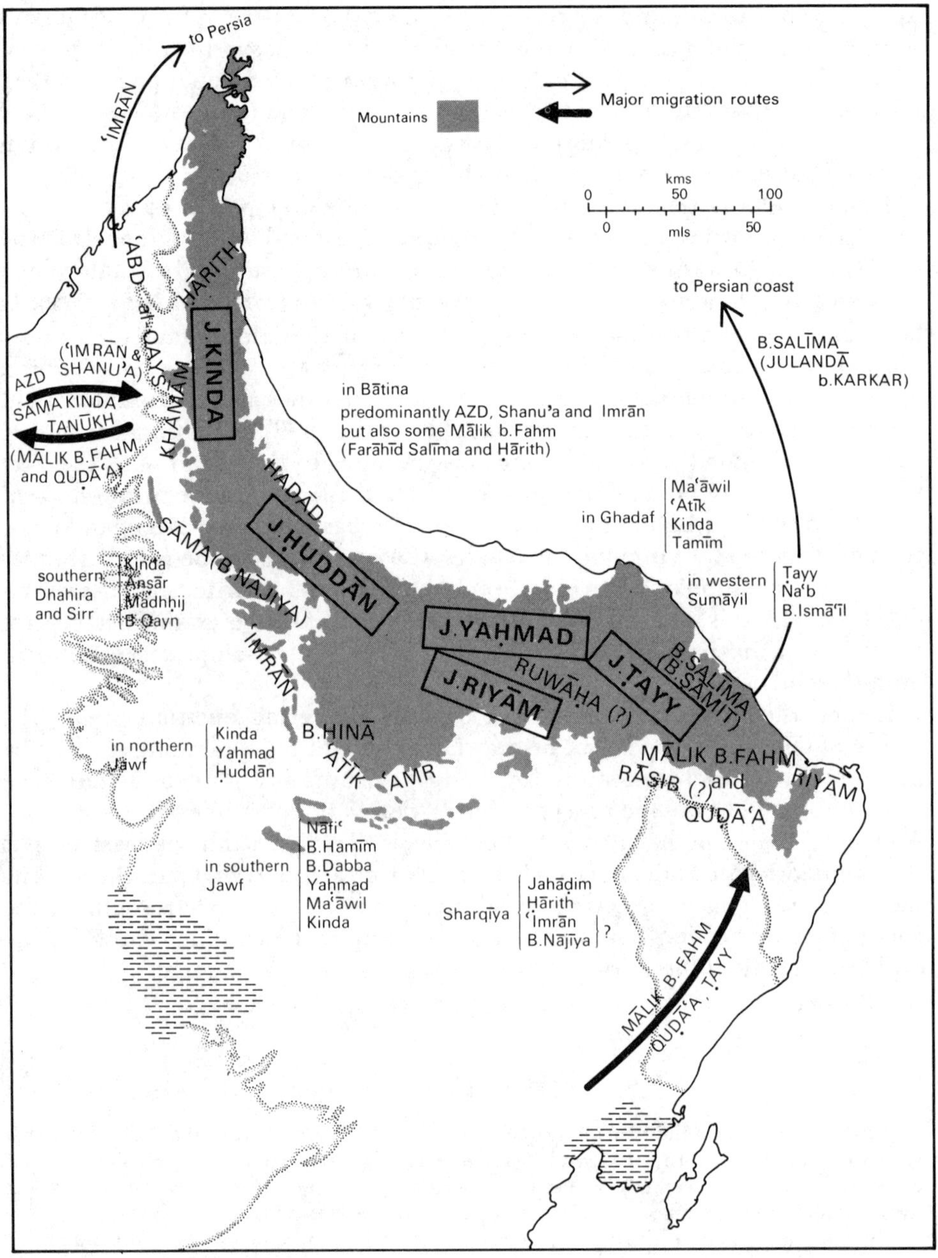

Fig. 33. The early tribal pattern.

1. MĀLIK b. FAHM
Ḥārith. Main concentration behind Dibā (Laqīṭ and ʿUqāt sections). Secondary concentration in Sharqīya with capital at Ibrā. Other elements in Sirr and Batina.
Khamām (Shubāba descent) mainly in Tuʾām. Appear to have been leaders of the northern Mālik b. Fahm.
Farāhīd (Shubāba descent). Main grouping (known as Muwāziʿ) in Badīya; shaikhly sections in Batina.
B. Hinā. Main concentration in northern Jawf and southern Sirr where also elements of *Maʿn* from whom the *B. Hamīm* of Lower Nizwā.
B. ʿAmr elements include *B. Ṣulaym* in northern Jawf and *Washiḥīn* in northern Sirr (Ḍank?). N.B. the main ʿAmr groups lived in Dhofar.
Jahāḍim controlled Samad (al-Shaʾn).
B. Salīma controlled J. Minqāl and Qalhāt (*B. Ṣāmit* section). Majority in coastal Kirmān. Elements of shaikhly group in Batina.

2A SHANUʾA (ʿUthmān b. Naṣr descent)
(a) *Awlād Shams*
Ḥuddān in Jabal Ḥuddān (capital Yanqul?) along with some elements of brother tribes.
Maʿāwil in Ghadaf (W. B. Maʿāwil); also in Jawf (Manḥ).
Nadab in W. Sumāyil?
(b) *Yaḥmad* (= Ḥummā (b?) ʿAbdullāh)
Many sections. Concentrated in Ghadaf, notably W. *Saḥtan* and W. B. *Kharūṣ: Fajḥ* in J. Ḥuddān area? Elements also in Jawf (Bahlā and Firq) and Sirr (Tanʿam).

2B Associated with 2A were elements of 'brother' tribes who had migrated with them to Oman, al-Namir (*Ammār*), *Duhman b. Naṣr* (two groups: the *Rubʿa* from al-Ghiṭrīf al-Aṣghar and the *B. Yashkur*), ʿAbra b. Naṣr (*ʿAbriyīn*).

3. ʿIMRĀN
As the first Azd group on the northern migration route into Oman they were concentrated in the northern part of the country. The Ḥujr descent dominated a confederation known as the *Hadād* (included *B. Ṭāḥiya*, *B. ʿAli* and elements of two tribes from ʿAmr b. 'Awf . . . b. ʿAmr Muzayqiyā, the *Mulādis* and *Rabīʿa*) on the Batina side of the mountains (Ṣuḥār area), while the Asad lived on the western side, notably in Sirr and the northern Jawf. The shaikhly clan of the latter were the *ʿAtīk* (capital Bahlā): from them were to spring two important families of later times, the *Nabāhina* and the *Yaʿāriba*.

A secondary concentration from both genealogical groupings may have existed in the Sharqīya.

4. Miscellaneous Azd
Minor elements of other Azd groups not already mentioned were also to be found in Oman, presumably assimilated into the main Azd confederation. These included elements of
(a) ʿAmr b. al-Azd: two branches *Māwiya* and *ʿIrmān* (*sic*: read ʿImrān?): two other branches, the *Saʿd* and *Ṣayq*, were assimilated into the ʿAbd al-Qays (q.v.);
(b) Hīnw b. al-Azd: the *Khawāla*.
(c,d) Sections of *Ghāmid* and *Thumāla* (latter with the Ḥuddān?).

QUḌĀʿA

Quite distinct in this genealogical hodge-podge are 3 groups in Oman,

1. The *Qamr* – *Riyām* whose early settlement pattern extended from Dhofar (the Jabal Qamr?) to the Jabal Akhdhar plateau. In early times the main centre of the Riyām appears to have been in the Jaʿlān where they controlled a port called Ruḍāʿ (Ṣūr area?). Their political importance in central Oman did not develop until well after the civil war at the end of the third/ninth century when they began to gain control of the settlements at the foot of

this Jabal. Associated with the early history of the Qamr-Riyām migration are the *Mahra* of Southern Arabia and it is probably because of this history that all these groups have been assimilated into the same formal genealogical structure.

2. Also from the descent of Mahra b. Ḥaydān . . . b. al-Ḥāf b. Quḍāʿa are various numerically small groups which emerged as distinctive groups in central Oman at the same time as the B. Riyām, notably the *B. Ismāʿīl* of Sumāyil and the *B. Naʿb*, one section of which became the shaikhly clan of the B. Hinā confederation in the 'Dark Ages'.

3. The *Rāsib*. In the first half of the first century of Islam the Rāsib were clearly an important and distinctive group for they gave their name to one of the five tribal armies recruited from S.E. Arabia. There is a great deal of deliberate blurring of the Rāsib genealogy but they were not in fact from the Maydʿān of Azd but rather were a distinctive grouping amongst the southern tribes genealogically grouped as Quḍā'a. Their early disappearance from the political scene is probably due to shifts in the tribal alliances.

KINDA

Elements of three major groupings in Oman.

1. The *Sakūn* in which the main clan appear to be the Darāmika.

2. The B. *Thābit b. Rafd* from al-Ḥārith al-Akbar who had 5 divisions, *Ghulayb, Hilāl, Kaʿb, Dāhir* and *Sharqī*.

These two groups made up the majority of the settlers in the Kinda primary *dār*, the Jabal Kinda. Their main villages were in the Wadis Ḥaṭṭā, Qawr and Hām from which they controlled the passes between Julfār and the northern Batinā/Shimālīya (cf. Fig. 5).

3. The third grouping were probably later arrivals and belonged to the Kinda clans which provided the royal line, the al-Ḥārith al-Aṣghar. Although their families were to be found in the J. Kinda the majority lived widely dispersed and controlled a number of important centres: notably
(a) the *B. Saʿd b. al-Arqam*, formerly paramount leaders in the Jabal Kinda until displaced by the Thābit b. Rafd. They also seem to have been displaced from Karshā (a now ruined settlement between Nizwā and Manḥ) and Dawt in the W. Ḍank. In ʿAwtabi's time they controlled ʿAyni, a village in Yaḥmad territory near Rustāq, and Sawni (modern ʿAwābi) which commands access from the W. B. Kharūṣ to Rustāq).
(b) The *Mālik b. 'Imru ʾl-Qays* descent controlled Upper Nizwā (Samad Nizwā), Nakhl (Ghadaf), the fortress of Fidā (in the W. Ḍank) but had lost control of Kudam (near al-Ḥamrā) in ʿAwtabi's time.

ṬAYY (correctly *Ṭayiʾ*)

A sizeable but politically unimportant group in early Omani history. All Oman groups descend from Nabhān b. Ghawth and appear to have migrated in association with the southern Azd. Their capitals were Ḥudā and Ṣiyā in the main area of settlement, the W. Ṭayyīn and the Sayḥ Ḥattāt. Individual groups were also to be found in the Sumāyil Gap and at the southern end of the Batina around Damā (modern al-Sīb area).

SĀMA b. LUʾAY

(a) The main confederation was called the B. Najw/Nājīya and controlled much of the Dhahira. Elements may also have settled in the Sharqīya.
(b) A politically important secondary grouping of (shaikhly) clans lived in the Lower Jawf; the B. *Ḍabba* (*ʿUzūr*) in Izki and Manḥ, the B. *Nāfiʿ* (B. Ziyād, from whom the *Umbu Saʿīd* and *Mushāqiṣa* of Lower Nīzwā, a settlement which they shared with the Hamīm, Maʿn Mālik b. Fahm, q.v.).
(c) Quite distinct were the *B. Ghāfir* of the W. Bani Ghāfir who were allied with the

Yaḥmad. Throughout Omani history they have tended to be at feud with their fellow clansmen.

ᶜABD AL-QAYS (*nisba* ᶜAbdi).

The politically dominant group in 'Baḥrayn' of this period; their tribes lived all along the Arabian coast of the Gulf from the borderlands of Iraq to Oman, where they first settled as allies of the Mālik b. Fahm.

The main group in Oman were the *Dīl*, from whom the *B. ᶜAwf*, the major bedu group of the Buraimi area, The other groups belonged to the *Anmār* who in Oman divided into three main political groupings.

1. The B. ᶜĀmir b. al-Ḥārith b. Anmār who formed part of a grouping called the B. *Kharijīya* and lived in W. Trucial Oman.

2. The B. *Jadhīma* b. ᶜAwf b. Anmār who occupied E. Trucial Oman and had settlements in the Khaṭṭ area. They had close links with the *Nukra*, the dominant group of 'Baḥrayn'; elements of the latter were also to be found in Oman.

3. Their rivals the B. al-Ḥārith b. Anmār of the Dhahira led by the *Quwwa* (b. Mālik b. ᶜAmr b. al-Ḥarith) who controlled a confederation called the *Barājim* which included a number of non-ᶜAbdi tribes, notably the *B. Ṣayq* (of ᶜAmr b. al-Azd origin).

Sections of other major ᶜAbdi groups like the B. ᶜIjl (*ᶜUmūr*) were also found in the region.

Some elements of ᶜAbdi tribes had settled outside the main tribal *dārs* (e.g. there was an ᶜAbdi quarter in Ṣuḥār inhabited by an Anmār group called the Ẓafār).

MISCELLANEOUS

1. *ᶜAbs*
Hishām, (the shaikhly group), Bil-Ḥasan Ḥamam, form the true descent groups of the tribe which was to emerge as the *Bani Ruwāḥa* (b. Qaṭīᶜa b. ᶜAbs). No mention in this period of their *Dhibyān* (B. Jābir) rivals.

2. *Tamīm*
A few elements in Oman possibly from Basra: e.g. the Āl Jadhīma b. Khāzim: in the W. Bani Kharūṣ there was a quarter of the capital Hajar (modern al-Hayjar?) belonging to the *Muqāᶜis* which may owe its name to this famous Tamīmi tribe.

3. *Sirr area*
Amongst the tribes here was an interesting collection of what may have been refugee groups (from Syria?) living in Ḍank, Silayf, Tanᶜam, and ᶜIbri. They included *al-Qayn* (Quḍāᶜa from Shām); *al-Ḥārith b. Kaᶜb* (Madhḥij of Bal-Ḥārith); B. Nabīt and B. Quṭn of Anṣār (attributed Azd lineage).

THE BEDU FRINGE

The bedu fringe of Oman for the most part consisted of elements from the following groupings:

1. *Mālik b. Fahm and Quḍāᶜa* (qq.v.)
As associates in the main southern migration into Oman, elements of both genealogical groupings were concentrated in the bajaḍa zone of S.E. Oman. The Mālik b. Fahm, however, had a much wider dispersal than the Quḍāᶜa and so not only were found in central Oman, but also (along with elements of the northern Azd groups) amongst the bedu as far as 'Baḥrayn'.

2. *Rabīᶜa*
The only important group of this enormous genealogical confederation in the region were the *ᶜAbd al-Qays* who, as already discussed, controlled the deserts of what is now Trucial Oman. (Later they were largely displaced by *ᶜĀmir* bedu groups, cf. Chapter IX.)

Elements of other Rabīᶜa groups may, however, have been found in Oman during the period under consideration, for certainly by the end of the 'Dark Ages' there were numerous *Wāʾil* sections and a few *Taghlib* settled in Oman, the former in the northern Jabal Akhdhar bloc, the latter in the Sharqīya. It is possible that during the earlier period they may have been mixed in with the ʿAbd al-Qays bedu.

3. *B. Saʿd* (Tamīm). Elements of this grouping were found in the western desert of Baynūna (the Līwā area).

Bibliography of cited works

A. *ARABIC SOURCES*

* = Omani or Ibāḍi source.

** = an early Omani source (pre-fourteenth century A.D.) discussed in the writer's forthcoming bio-bibliographical study in *Arabian Studies* iii (q.v.). A number of later works shown by * are also discussed in this study.

B.G.A. = *Bibliotheca Geographorum Arabicorum*, ed. M. J. de Goeje (Brill, Leiden).

B.M. = British Museum.

ᶜAbd al-Wahhāb. *Kitāb lamᶜ al-shihāb fi sīrat Muḥammad b. ᶜAbd al-Wahhāb* (B.M. 23, 346). cf. also printed edn. by Aḥmad Muṣṭafā Abu Ḥākima, Beirut 1967.

**Abu Isḥāq (Ibrāhīm b. Qays al-Hamdāni al-Ḥaḍrami), *Dīwān al-sayf al-naqqād.* Kuwait n.d.

ᶜAbd al-Laṭif al-Baghdādi, *Kitāb al-ifāda wa ʾl-iᶜtibār*, text and translation in Zand, K. H., Videan, J. A. and I. E., *The Eastern Key*. Allen and Unwin 1965.

Abu Yūsuf, *Kitāb al-kharāj*, text Būlāq A. H. 1302, translated and annotated by Fagnan, E. as *Le livre de l'impôt foncier.* Paris 1921.

*Anon. Anonymous titleless history of Oman down to 1783. (B.M. Add. 23.343 pt. 2).

**al-ᶜAwtabi (Sal(a)ma b. Muslim (Musallim?)), *Kitab Ansāb al-ᶜArab.* Two MSS.: Bibliotheque Nationale, Paris, MSS. arabes 5019; private possession of Prof. T. M. Johnstone.

al-Bakri: *Muᶜjam mā ʾstaᶜjam*, ed. Wüstenfeld, F., Göttingen and Paris 1876 and 1877.

al-Balādhuri. *Ansāb al-ashrāf*, vol. xi ed. Ahlwardt, W., Leipzig 1883.

——, *Futūḥ al-buldān*, ed. de Goeje, M. J., Leiden 1866.

Balᶜami, *Chronique de Tabari*, trans. Zotenberg, H., 4 vols., Paris 1867-74.

Bozorg b. Chahrayar al-Nākhudhi al-Rāmhurmuzi (falsely attributed to), *Kitāb ᶜajāyib al-Hind* (Livre des Merveilles de l'Inde), Leiden 1883-6.

**Falaj Malki Book* from Izki (described at various points in the text).

*al-Ḥabsi (Rāshid b. Khamis), *Dīwān*, B.M. Or. 6566.

al-Hamdāni, *Ṣifat Jazīrat al-ᶜArab*, ed. Muller, D. H., Leiden 1884-91.

*al-Ḥārithi (ᶜIsā b. Ṣāliḥ b. ᶜAli b. Nāṣir), *Khulāṣat al-wasāʾil fi tartīb al-masāʾil*, 2 vols., Damascus n.d.

**al-Ḥasan al-Bisyāni/Bisyawi, *Mukhtaṣar al-Bisyawi*, printed in Zanzibar 1886 but not seen by the writer who used the German translation of the section on inheritance laws made by Sachau, C. E., in *Sitzungsberichte der Königlich preussischen Akademie der Wissenschaften*, 1894, sec. 8.

Ibn al-Athīr, *Kitāb al-kāmil fi ʾl-taʾrīkh*, ed. Tornberg, C. J., Leiden 1851-76.

**Ibn Baraka (Abu Muḥammad ᶜAbdullāh b. Muḥammad), *Kitāb al-jāmiᶜ* ed. ᶜIsā b. Yaḥyā al-Bārūni, Cairo(?) 1971.

**Ibn Durayd, *al-Ishtiqāq*, ed. ᶜAbd al-Sallām Muḥammed Hārūn, Miṣr 1958.

——, *al-Jamhara*, Hyderabad A. H. 1345.

Ibn al-Faqīh, *Mukhtaṣar kitāb al-buldān*, ed. de Goeje, M. J., Leiden 1885 (B.G.A. 5).

Ibn al-Kalbi, *Jamharat al-nasab*, (a) Book I: B. M. Add. 23, 297. (b) Extracts (?) from the Escorial MS.: B. M. Add. 22.376. (c) Caskel, W. and Strenziok, G., *Ǧamharat an-Nasab. Das genealogische Werk des Hišām Ibn Muḥammad al-Kalbi*, 2 vols., Leiden 1966.

Ibn Khaldūn, *Kitāb al-ᶜibar*, Būlāq A. H. 1284.

——, *Muqaddima*, cf. trans. Rosenthal, F., in 3 vols., London 1958.

Ibn Khordādhbeh (Khurradādhbih), *al-Masālik wa ʾl-mamālik,* ed. de Goeje, M. J., Leiden 1889 (B.G.A. 6).

Ibn Manẓūr, *Lisān al-ᶜArab* (references are given by article).

Ibn al-Mujāwir, *Taʾrīkh al-Mustabṣir*, ed. Löfgren, O., Leiden 1951 and 1954.

**Ibn al-Naẓar (Abu Bakr Aḥmad b. Sulaymān of the Bani al-Naẓar from Sumāʾil). *Dīwān* known as *Daᶜāʾim al-Islām*, quoted copy is B.M. MS. Or. 2434/2915.

Ibn Qutayba, *Kitāb al-maʿārif* (various editions, normally ed. Okacha, T., Cairo 1960 if not stated).
*Ibn Ruzayq (Razīq? Ḥumayd b. Muḥammad), *Imams = History of the Imâms and Seyyids of ʿOmān,* trans. Badger, G. P., Hakluyt Society 1871 (for original, see Cambridge U.L. Add. 2892).
——, *al-Ṣaḥīfa al-Qaḥṭānīya*, Rhodes House, Oxford, MSS. Afr. S. 3.
——, *al-Ṣaḥīfa al-ʿAdnānīya*, B.M. Or. 6569.
——, *al-Qaṣīda al-qudsīya al-nūrānīya fi manāqib al-ʿAdnānīya,* B.M. Or. 6565 (vol. ii only.)
Ibn Saʿd, *Kitāb al-ṭabaqāt al-kabīrāt*, ed. Sachau, H. *et. al.*, Leiden 1905 17.
al-Idrīsi, *Géographie d'Édrisi*, 2 vols., trans. Jaubert, P. A., Paris 1836 and 1840.
al-Iṣṭakhri, *Masālik al-mamālik,* ed. de Goeje, M. J., Leiden 1870 (B.G.A. 1).
*al-Jannāwuni (or al-Janāwani: Abu Zakarayā b. al-Khayr), *Kitāb al-waḍʿ*, with marginal glosses by Muḥammad Abu Sitta al-Qaṣabi, Cairo 1886.
*al-Khalīli, (Muḥammad b. ʿAbdullāh), *al-Fatḥ al-jalīl min ajwibat al-Imām Abi Khalīl,* Damascus 1965.
*al-Khalīli, (Saʿīd b. Khalfān), *Laṭāʾif al-ḥikam fi ʾl-ṣadaqāt al-naʿam*, Bombay A.H. 1309.
al-Khuwārazmi, *Mafātīḥ al-ʿulūm*, ed. van Vloten, G., Leiden 1895.
*al-Maḥalli, *Dīwān Mūsā b. Ḥusayn b. Shawwāl al-Maḥalli*, B.M. Or. 6560.
*al-Maḥrūqi (Darwīsh b. Jumʿa b. ʿUmar al-Maḥrūqi al-Adami), *Kitāb al-dalāʾil*, B. M. Or. 2085 (first 19 *bābs* only).
al-Masʿūdi, *Murūj al-dhahab*, ed. and trans. de Meynard, C. B. and de Courteille, P., Paris 1861-77.
*al-Maʿwali (Abu Sulaymān Muḥammad b. Rāshid), *Qiṣaṣ wa akhbār jarat bi ʿUmān*, Al-Ẓāhirīya, Damascus Taʾrikh 385.
——, *Nubdha fi ansāb al-Maʿāwil*, Taʾrikh 385, bound in with above.
(N.B. The present writer used microfilms of both these MSS. in which the page-numbers are almost illegible. Reference errors may therefore have occurred.)
al-Māwardi, *Kitāb-aḥkām al-sulṭānīya,* ed. Enger, R., Bonn 1853. Cf. trans. Fagnan E. as *Les Statuts gouvernmentaux*, Alger 1915.
*al-Mubarrad, *al-Kāmil fi ʾl-adab*, ed. Wright, W., Leipzig 1864-92.
al-Muqaddasi, *Aḥsan al-taqāsīm fi maʿrifat al-aqālīm*, ed. de Goeje, M.J., Leiden 1906 (B.G.A., 2nd edn.).
al-Nabhāni (Khalīfa b. Ḥamad b. Mūsā al-Nabhāni al-Ṭāʾīy), *al-Tuḥfa al-Nabhānīya fi taʾrīkh al-Jazīra al-ʿArabīya*, 2nd ed., Cairo A.H. 1342.
**al-Qalhāti (Muḥammad b. Saʿīd al-Azdi al-Qalhāti), *Kitāb al-kashf wa ʾl-bayān*, B.M. Or. 2606 (vol. ii only).
Qudāma (b. Jaʿfar), *Kitāb al-kharāj* ed. Ben Shemesh, A., in *Taxation in Islam* vol. ii, Leiden 1965.
*al-Ṣāʾighi (Sālim b. Saʿīd), *Kanz al-adīb wa sulāfat al-labīb*, Cambridge U. L. Add. 2896.
*al-Sālimi (ʿAbdullāh b. Ḥumayd/Ḥumayyid), *Jawhar al-niẓām fi ʿilmay ʾl-adyān wa ʾl-aḥkām,* ed. Abu Isḥāq Ibrāhīm Aṭfayyish, Cairo A.H., 1381 (1961-2).
——, *al-Lumʿa al-murḍīya min ashiʿʿat al-ibāḍīya*, Tunis n.d. (written 1905).
——, *Talqīn al-ṣubayān*, Damascus 1963.
——, *Tuḥfat al-aʿyān bi sīrat ahl ʿUmān,* 2 vols., Cairo 1380/1961 edn.
——, (ed. and commentary). *al-Jāmiʿ al-ṣaḥīḥ, Musnad al-Imām al-Rabīʿ b. Ḥabīb al-Farāhīdi*, pt. 3, Damascus 1963.
*al-Sālimi (Muḥammad b. ʿAbdullāh b. Ḥumayd), *Nahḍat al-aʿyān bi ḥurriyat ʿUmān*, Cairo n.d.
al-Sharīshi, *Sharḥ Maqāmāt al-Ḥarīri*, Cairo 1962-3.
*Sirḥān b. Saʿīd (attributed), *Kashf al-ghumma: al-jāmiʿ li akhbār al-umma.*
1. The manuscript quoted is al-Ẓāhirīya, Damascus Taʾrīkh 346.
2. *Kashf* tr. Ross = the partial translation of the historical chapters made by Ross, E.C.

under the title 'Annals of Oman' in the *Journal of the Asiatic Society of Bengal* 1874, pp. 111 96.
3. *Kashf* ed. Klein = Chapter 33 of the Berlin MS. edited and annotated by Hedwig Klein as a doctoral dissertation, Hamburg 1938.
*al-Sitāli (Abu Bakr Aḥmad b. Saʿīd al-Kharūṣi), *Dīwān,* Damascus 1964.
*al-Siyābi (Sālim b. Ḥumūd), *Isʿāf al- aʿyān fi ansāb ahl ʿUmān*, Beirut 1965.
*Sulaymān b. Sulaymān, *Dīwān al-Sulṭān Sulaymān b. Sulaymān al-Nabhānī*, Damascus 1965.
al-Ṭabari, *Taʾrīkh al-rusul wa ʾl-mulūk,* ed. de Goeje, M. J., Leiden 1879-1901.
Yaḥyā b. Adam, *Kitāb al-kharāj,* ed. Juynboll, Th. W.; cf. also Ben Shemesh, A., *Taxation in Islam* vol. i, Leiden 1958.
al-Yaʿqūbi, *Taʾrīkh,* ed. Houtsma M. Th., Leiden 1883.
Yāqūt, *Muʿjam al-buldān*, Beirut ed. 1955-8. References to Yāqūt are to this work and are given by article unless the *Udabāʾ* is specified.
——, *Udabāʾ = Irshād al-arīb·ilā maʿrifat al-adīb*, ed. Margoliouth, D.S. in E. J. W. Gibb Memorial Series 6, Leiden 1907-26.
al-Zabīdi, *Tāj al-ʿArūs* (references are given by article).

B. *EUROPEAN SOURCES*

Abu Dhabi, Government of (1969). *Statistical Abstract, 1* (July 1969).
Abu Hakima, Ahmad (1965). *History of Eastern Arabia 1750-1800: the Rise and Development of Bahrain and Kuwait*, Beirut.
Adams, R. McC. (1962). 'Agriculture and urban life in early Southwestern Iran', *Science*, cxxxvi. 109-22.
Alboquerque (1875 ed.), *The commentaries of the Great Afonso Dalboquerque*, Hakluyt Society.
Aramco (the Arabian American Oil Company Relations Department, Research Division) (1952). *Oman and the Southern shore of the Persian Gulf*, Cairo. This book was withdrawn on publication and only a few copies passed into private hands.
Asad, T. (1964). 'Seasonal movements of the Kababish Arabs of Northern Kordofan', *Sudan Notes and Records,* xlv. 45-58.
Aucher-Éloy (*sic*). Ed. M. le Comte Jaubert: *Relations de voyage en Orient de 1830-1838*, 2 vols., Paris 1843.
Ayoub, M. R. (1959). 'Parallel cousin marriage and endogamy: a study in sociometry', *Southwestern Journal of Anthropology*, xv. 266 75.
Bagnold, R. A. (1941). *The physics of blown sand and desert dunes*, London.
de Barros, J. (1945 edn.). *Asia*, 6th ed., Lisbon.
Barth, F. (1961). *Nomads of South Persia*, Oslo.
Bathurst, R. D. (1967). 'The Yaʿrubi dynasty of Oman', unpublished D. Phil. thesis, Oxford
Beadnell, H. J. Llewellyn (1909). *An Egyptian oasis*, London.
Bechtel (1966). *Desalination in the Eastern Province of Saudi Arabia*, Report FAO/SAU/6 prepared by Bechtel Corporation for the United Nations.
Beckett, P. H. T. and Gordon, E. D. (1966). 'Land use round Kerman in Southern Iran', *Geographical Journal*, cxxxii. 476-90.
Belgrave, Sir Charles (1960). *Personal column*, London.
Belgrave, James H. D. (1965). *Welcome to Bahrain*, 5th edn., London.
von Bergman, E. (1876). 'Zur muhammedanischen Münzkunde', *Numismatische Zeitschrift*, viii. 28 44.
Bibby, G. (1970). *Looking for Dilmun*, London.
——, (1973). 'The Al-'Ubaid Culture of Eastern Arabia', *Proceedings* [of the 1972] *Seminar for Arabian Studies 1973*, pp. 1-2.
British Memorial. *Arbitration concerning Buraimi and the common frontier between Abu*

Dhabi and Sa'ūdi Arabia, 1955.

Buckingham, J. S. (1830). *Travels in Assyria, Media, and Persia*, 2 vols., London.

Bujra, A. S. (1971). *The Politics of stratification. A study of political change in a South Arabian town*, Oxford.

Butzer, K. W. (1957). 'Late glacial and postglacial climatic variation in the Near East', *Erdkunde*, xi. 21 35.

——, (1961). 'Climatic change in arid regions since the Pliocene', In 'A History of Land Use in Arid Regions', UNESCO, *Arid Zone Research*, xvii. 31 56.

Caetani, L. *Annali dell' Islām*, 10 vols., Milan, 1905-26.

Caponera, D. A. (1954). *Water laws in Moslem countries*, FAO Development Paper *43*, Rome.

Caskel, W. (1949). 'Eine "unbekannte" Dynastie in Arabien', *Oriens*, ii. 66-71.

Caton-Thompson, G. (1931). 'Kharga Oasis', *Antiquity*, v. 221-6.

——, and Gardner, E. W. (1932). 'The prehistoric geography of Kharga Oasis', *Geographical Journal*, lxxx. 369-409.

Champault, F. D. (1969). *Une Oasis du Sahara nord-occidental Tabelbala*, Paris.

Chorley, R. J. (ed.) (1969). *Water, earth, and man. A synthesis of hydrology, geomorphology, and socio-economic geography*, London.

Clark, C. and Haswell, M. (1970). *The economics of subsistence agriculture*, 4th edn., London.

Cooper, H. H. Jr. (1959). 'A hypothesis concerning the dynamic balance of fresh water and salt water in a coastal aquifer', *Journal of Geophysical Research*, lxiv. 461-7.

Cornelius, P. F. S., Falcon, N. L., South, D., Vita Finzi, C. (1973). 'The Musandam Expedition 1971-2 scientific results', *Geographical Journal*, cxxxix. 29-37.

Cressey, G. B. (1958). 'Qanats, karez and foggaras', *Geographical Review*, xlviii. 27 44.

——, (1960). *Crossroads. Land and life in Southwest Asia*, J. B. Lippincott Coy, U.S.A.

Denton, D. A., Goding, J. R., McDonald, I. R., Sabin, R., and Wright, R. D. (1961). 'Adaptation of ruminant animals to variation of salt intake', in 'Salinity Problems in the Arid Zones', UNESCO, *Arid Zone Research*, xiv. 193-8.

Dickson, H. R. P. (1949). *The Arab of the desert*, London.

Djezirei, M. H. (1961). 'Les peuplements d'"avicennia" des côtes sud de l'Iran', in 'Salinity Problems in the Arid Zones', UNESCO *Arid Zone Research*, xiv. 139-40.

Dostal, W. (1967). *Die Beduinen in Südarabiern*, Wiener Beiträge zur Kulturgeschicte und Linguistik, xvi, Vienna.

Dowson, V. H. W. (1921). *Dates and date cultivation of the 'Iraq*, Agricultural Directorate, Ministry of Interior, Mesopotamia, Memoir iii, 3 pts., 1921-3.

——, (1927) Report on visit to Oman in June 1927: India Office file no. R/15/3/11/25.

——, (*et. al.*) (1965?). 'Improvement of date palm growing', Dates/BAG/65/1, draft for FAO Agricultural Study.

——, (1968). 'The present condition of world date culture', *Date Growers Institute Report*, Coachella, California.

Ebert, C. (1965). 'Water resources and land use in the Qatif Oasis of Saudi Arabia', *Geographical Review*, lv. 496-509.

Eldblom, L. (1968). *Structure foncière, organisation et structure sociale. Une étude comparative sur la vie socio-économique dans les trois oasis libyennes de Ghat, Mourzouk et particulièrement Ghadamès*, Lund.

English, P. W. (1968). 'The origin and spread of qanats in the Old World', *Proceedings of the American Philosophical Society*, cxii 170-81.

Evans, G., Schmidt, V., Bush, P., and Nelson, H. (1969). 'Stratigraphy and geologic history of the sabkha, Abu Dhabi, Persian Gulf', *Sedimentology*, xii. 145-59.

Evans-Pritchard, E. E. (1940). *The Nuer*, Oxford.

Evenari, M., Shanan, L. and Tadmor, N. (1971). *The Negev*, Harvard Univ. Press.

FAO (1952). *Report to the Government of Saudi Arabia on date cultivation* (by Abdul-

Jabbar El-Baker).
——, (Dec. 1969). Commodity notes, *Monthly Bulletin of Agricultural Economics.*
Fenelon, K. G. (1973). *The United Arab Emirates. An economic and social survey*, London.
Firmin, R. (1965). 'Forestry trials with high saline or sea-water in Kuwait', In Boyko, H., ed. *Saline Irrigation for agriculture and forestry*, World Academy of Art and Science, iv.
Forand, P. G. (1966). 'Notes on ʿ*ušr* and *maks*,' *Arabica*, xiii. 137-41.
Fraser, J. Baillie (1825). *Narrative of a journey into Khorasān*, London.
Freeman-Grenville, G. S. P. (1963). *The Muslim and Christian calendars being tables for the conversion of Muslim and Christian dates from the hijra to the year A.D. 2000*, London.
Frifelt, K. (1970). 'Jamdat Nasr graves in the Oman', *Kuml. Arbog For Jysk Arkœologisk Selskab*, (Aarhus) pp. 355-83.
Furr, J. F., Ream, C. L., and Ballard, A. L. (1966). 'Growth of young date palms in relation to soil salinity and chloride content of the pinnae', *Date Growers Institute Report*, xliii, Coachella, California.
de Gaury, G. (1957). 'A note on Masira Island', *Geographical Journal*, cxxiii. 499-502.
Gibb, H. A. R. (1955). 'The fiscal rescript of ʿUmar II', *Arabica*, ii. 1-16.
Gibb (1969). *Water resources survey*: interim report to the Government of Abu Dhabi by Sir Alexander Gibb and Partners, April 1969.
Glennie, K. W. (1967). 'Desert sediments of Southeastern Arabia', *Shell Research Report*, no. 1260.
——, (1970). *Desert sedimentary environments*, Developments in Sedimentology, xiv, Elsevier.
——, Boeuf, M. G. A., Hughes Clarke, M. W., Moody-Stuart, M., Pilaar, W. F. H., and Reinhardt, B. M. (1973). 'Late cretaceous nappes in Oman mountains and their geologic evolution', *The American Association of Petroleum Geologists Bulletin*, lvii. 5-27.
de Gobineau, Le Comte A. (1859). *Trois ans en Asie (de 1855-1858)*, Paris.
Goblot, H. (1963). 'Dans l'ancien Iran, les techniques de l'eau et la grande histoire', *Annales Économies Sociétés Civilisations*, xviii. 499-519.
——,(1965). 'Note sur l'interaction des techniques dans leur genèse', *Revue Philosophique de la France et de l'Étranger*, clv. 207-16.
——, (1968). 'Quelques faits nouveaux dans l'histoire des techniques d'acquisition de l'eau: galeries drainantes et barrages-voûtes', *XII Congrès International d'Histoire des Sciences*, Paris, pp. 31-4.
de Goeje, M. J. (1895). 'La fin de l'empire des Carmathes', *Journal Asiatique*, 9th Series, v., 5-30.
Goitein, S. D. (1954). 'Two eye-witness reports on an expedition of the King of Kīsh (Qais) against Aden', *Bulletin of the School of Oriental and African Studies University of London*, xvi. 247 57.
Goudie, A. S., and Wilkinson, J. C. (in press). *The warm desert environment.* Cambridge.
Halcrow. (1969). Trucial States Council: *Report on the water resources of the Trucial States* (excluding Abu Dhabi) to the Trucial States Council by Sir William Halcrow and Partners, 3 vols.
Hamilton, Capt. Alexander (1727). *A new account of the East Indies*, 2 vols., Edinburgh.
Hasselquist, F. (ed. Linnœus, C), *Voyages dans le Levant dans les années 1749, 50, 51 & 52*, trans. from the German, Paris 1769.
Heude, Lt. W. (1819). *A voyage up the Persian Gulf and a journey overland from India to England in 1817*, London.
Issawi; C. (ed.) (1966). *The economic history of the Middle East 1800-1914*, Chicago.
Jayakar, A. S. G. (1889). 'The O'mánee dialect of Arabia', *Journal of the Royal Asiatic Society*, New Series, xxi. 649-87 and 811-89.
Johnson, D. L. (1969). *The nature of nomadism*, Univ. of Chicago, Department of Geography Research Paper cxviii.
Johnstone, T. M. (1967). *Eastern Arabian dialect studies*, London Oriental Series xvii, London.

——, and Wilkinson, J. C. (1960). 'Some geographical aspects of Qaṭar', *Geographical Journal*, cxxvi. 442 50.

Judson, S., Kahane, A., (1963). 'Underground drainage ways in Southern Etruria and Northern Latium', *Papers of the British School at Rome.* New series vi.

Kapel, H. (1967). *Atlas of the stone-age cultures of Qatar*, Jutland Archaeological Society Publications, vi, Aarhus, Denmark.

Kelly, J. B. (1968). *Britain and the Persian Gulf 1795-1880*, Oxford.

Khairallah, I. A. (1941). *The law of inheritance in the Republics of Syria and Lebanon*, Beirut.

Kinsman, D. J. J. and Park, R. K. (1968). 'Studies in recent sedimentology and early diagenesis, Trucial Coast, Arabian Gulf', paper circulated to the *Society of Petroleum Engineers AIME Second Symposium*, Dhahran, Saudi Arabia.

Klaubert, H. (1967). 'Qanats in an area of Bavaria-Bohemia', *Geographical Review*, lvii, 203-12.

Laessøe, J. (1951). 'The irrigation system at Ulḫu, 8th century B.C.', *Journal of Cuneiform Studies*, v. 21-32.

——, (1953). 'Reflexions on modern and ancient oriental water works', *Journal of Cuneiform Studies*, vii. 5-26.

Lamb, H. H. (1968). 'The climatic background to the birth of civilization', *The Advancement of Science*, xxv, 103-20.

Lambton, A. K. S. (1953). *Landlord and peasant in Persia*, London.

Landen, R. G. (1967). *Oman since 1856. Disruptive modernization in a traditional society*, Princeton.

Lane, E. W. *An Arabic English lexicon*, 7 vols., London 1863-81.

La Rosa, G. C. (1953). 'I transmettitori della dottrina Ibāḍita', *Annali Istituto Universitario Orientale di Napoli*, New Series v. 123-39.

Lees, G. M. (1928). 'The physical geography of Southeastern Arabia', *Geographical Journal*, lxxi. 441-70.

Løkkegaard, F. (1950). *Islamic taxation in the classic period*, Copenhagen.

Lorimer, J. G. *Gazeteer of the Persian Gulf, Omān and Central Arabia*, 4 vols., Calcutta, 1908 15.

MacFarlane, W. V. 'Salinity and the Whole Animal', in ed. Talsma, T. and Philip J. R. *Salinity and Water Use*. London 1971.

Maktari, A. M. A. (1971). *Water rights and irrigation practices in Laḥj*, Cambridge.

Malcolm, Sir John (1815). *The history of Persia*, 2 vols., London.

Malloch, A. J. C. (1972). 'Salt-spray deposition on the maritime cliffs of the Lizard Peninsula', *Journal of Ecology*, lx. 103-12.

Massignan, L. (=L. M.) (1908). 'Autour du monde musulman', *Revue du Monde Musulman,* iv. 160-1.

Mazaheri, A. (1973). *La Civilisation des eaux cachées. Traité de l'exploitation des eaux souterraines composé en 1017 A.D. par Karagi* (Mohammad al). Université de Nice Institut d'Études et de Recherches Interethniques et Interculturelles, Études Preliminaires 6.

Meteorological Office (Air Ministry) (1958). Tables of temperature, relative humidity and precipitation for the world, pt. V, *Asia*, H.M.S.O.

Miles, S. B. (1875). 'Some notes on El Bereymi made during my visit to that place in November 1875', in *British Memorial*, Annex B, no. 38 (q.v.).

——, (1910). 'On the border of the Great Desert; a journey in Oman', *Geographical Journal*, xxxvi. 159 79 and 405-25.

——, (1919). *The countries and tribes of the Persian Gulf*, 2 vols., London.

Ministry of Overseas Development (Middle East Development Division, British Embassy, Beirut) (1969). *An economic survey of the Northern Trucial States.*

Mörner, N-A. (1971). 'Eustatic changes during the last 20,000 years and a method of separating the isostatic and eustatic factors in an uplifted area', *Palaeo*, ix. 153-81.

Morton, D. M. (1959). 'The geology of Oman', *Fifth World Petroleum Congress Proceedings*, Section 1, paper 14, pp. 1-14.
Murphy, R. F. and Kasdan, L. (1959). 'The structure of parallel cousin marriage', *American Anthropologist*, lxi. 17-29.
Musil, A. (1928). *The manners and customs of the Rwala Bedouins*, New York.
Naʿimi, A. I. (1965). 'The groundwater of Northeastern Saudi Arabia', *Fifth Arab Petroleum Congress*.
Nicholls, C. S. (1971). *The Swahili Coast. Politics, diplomacy and trade on the East African littoral 1798* 1856, St Antony's Publications no. 2, London.
Niebuhr, C. (1772). *Beschreibung von Arabien*, Kopenhagen. References are to the Swiss 1780 2 vol. edn. entitled *Voyage de M. Niebuhr en Arabie*.
Nixon, F. (1969). *Industrial archaeology of Derbyshire*, Newton Abbot.
Nöldeke, Th. (1871). 'Die Namen der aramäischen Nation und Sprache', *Zeitschrift der Deutschen morgenländischen Gesellschaft*, xxv. 113-31.
Ovington, J. (1696). *A voyage to Suratt in the year 1689*. London.
Pedgley, D. E. (1970). 'The climate of interior Oman', *The Meteorological Magazine*, xcix, 29-37.
Peters, E. L. (1960). 'The proliferation of segments in the lineage of the bedouin of Cyrenaica', *Journal of the Royal Anthropological Institute of Great Britain and Ireland*, xc. 29-53.
——, (1967). 'Some structural aspects of the feud among the camel herding bedouin of Cyrenaica', *Africa*, xxxvii 261-82.
Philby, H. St. J. (1955). *Sa'udi Arabia*. Nations of the Modern World Series, London.
de Planhol, X. (1968). *Les Fondaments géographiques de l'histoire de l'Islam*, Paris.
Popenoe, P. P. (1913). *Date growing in the Old World and the New*, Altadena, California.
Quatremère, M. (1835). 'Mémoire sur les Nabatéens (deuxième section)', *Journal Asiatique*, xv. 97 133.
Randolph, R. R. and Coult, A. D. (1968). 'A computer analysis of bedouin marriage', *Southwest Journal of Anthropology*, xxiv. 83-99.
Raunkiaer, B. (English 1969 edn.). *Through Wahhabiland on camelback*, London.
Reinhardt, C. (1894). *Ein arabischer Dialekt gesprochen in ʿOmān und Zanzibar*, Lehrbücher des Seminars für orientalische Sprachen, xiii, Stuttgart und Berlin.
Rodinson, M. (1971). *Mohammed*, English trans., London.
Ross, E. C. (1873). 'Memorandum on the tribal divisions in the principality of Oman', *Transactions of the Bombay Geographical Society*, xix (1868-73, published 1874).
Rössler, W. (1898). 'Nachal und Wād il Ma'āwil', *Mittheilungen des Seminars für orientalische Sprachen*, vol. i pt. 2, pp. 56-90.
de la Roque, J. (1715). *Voyage de l'Arabie Heureuse ... fait par les François dans les années 1708, 1709 and 1710 ... 1711, 1712, 1713*. Paris.
Rossi, E. (1953). 'Note sull 'irrigazione, l'agricoltura e le stagione nel Yemen', *Oriente Moderno*, xxxiii. 349-61.
Rubinacci, R. (1957). 'La purità rituale secondo gli Ibāḍiti', *Annali Istituto Universitario Orientale di Napoli*, New Series vi. 1-41.
Rumaihi, M. G. (1973). 'Social and political change in Bahrain since the First World War', Doctoral Thesis, Durham.
Sarnthein, M. (1972). 'Sediments and history of the postglacial transgression in the Persian Gulf and Northwest Gulf of Oman', *Marine Geology*, xii. 245-66.
Sauvy, A. (1969). *General theory of population*, London. (English trans. of *Théorie générale de la population*, Presses Universitaires de France, 1966).
Schmidt-Nielsen, K. (1964). *Desert animals: physiological problems of heat and water*, Oxford.
Serjeant, R. B. (1954). 'Hūd and other pre-Islamic prophets of Ḥaḍramawt', *Muséon*, lxvii. 121-79.
——, (1967). 'Société et gouvernement en Arabie du Sud', *Arabica*, xiv. 284-97.

Shell (Petroleum Development (Oman) Ltd.) (1966). Report on water possibilities for the Saih-al-Maleh camp site, Oman (by van der Meer Mohr, H. E. C.), Jan. 1966.

——, (1971). Sib water supply, actual production and expectation (report by Bolliger, W.), Aug. 1971.

Siddiqi, A. (1919). *Studien über die persischen Fremdwörter im klassischen Arabisch*, Göttingen.

Stein, Sir Aurel. (1937). *Archaeological reconnaissances in Northwestern India and South-eastern Īrān*, London.

Stein, L. (1967). *Die Šammar-Ǧerba Beduinen im Übergang von Nomadismus zur Sesshaftigkeit*, Berlin.

Stevens, J. H. (1970). 'Changing agricultural practice in an Arabian oasis', *Geographical Journal*, cxxxvi. 412-18.

Sweet, L. E. (1970). 'Camel raiding of North Arabian bedouin: a mechanism of ecological adaptation', in (ed. ibid.) *Peoples and Cultures of the Middle East*, vol. i, New York.

Taylor, C. R. (1969). 'The eland and the oryx', *Scientific American*, ccxx. 88-95.

Teixeira, P. (1902 edn.). *The travels of Pedro Teixeira*, Hakluyt Society.

Thesiger, W. (1950). 'Desert borderlands of Oman', *Geographical Journal*, cxvi, 137-71.

——, (1959). *Arabian sands*, London.

de Thévenot. (1727 edn.). *Suite du voyage de Mr de Thévenot au Levant*, 3rd edn. Amsterdam, 1727.

Thomas, B. S. (1929). 'The Musandam Peninsula and its people the Shihuh', *Journal of the Central Asian Society*, xvi. 71-86.

——, (1931). *Alarms and excursions in Arabia*, London.

Thornthwaite, C. W., Mather, J. R., and Carter, D. B. (1958). 'Three Water Balance Maps of Southwest Asia', *Laboratory of Climatology*, vol. xi, no. i, Centerton, New Jersey.

Thureau-Dangin, F. (1912). *Une relation de la huitième campagne de Sargon (714 av. J.-C.)*, Paris (Louvre).

Tibbets, G. R. (1971). *Arab navigation in the Indian Ocean before the coming of the Portuguese*, Oriental Translation Fund, xlii, London.

Tiesenhausen, W. (1875). 'Mélanges de numismatique orientale', *Revue Belge de Numismatique*, pp. 329-79.

Tosi, M. (1971). 'Dilmun', *Antiquity*, xlv. 21 5.

Tresse, R. (1929). 'L'irrigation dans la ghouta de Damas', *Revue des Études Islamiques*, iii. 461-574.

Troll, C. (1963). 'Qanat-Bewässerung in der alten und neuen Welt', *Mitteilungen der österreichisen geographischen Gesellschaft*, cv. 313-29.

Trucial States Council (Water Resources Survey). *Hydrological Year Book*, 1965/6 ——.

Tschopp, R. H. (1967). 'The general geology of Oman', *Seventh World Petroleum Congress Proceedings*, v vol. no. 2, pp. 231-42.

Underhill, H. W. (1969). 'Carbonate scale in Roman and modern canals in the Jordan Valley'. *Journal of Hydrology*, vii. 388-403.

United Nations General Assembly. (1963). *Report of the Special Representative of the Secretary-General on his Visit to Oman*, A/5562 of 8 Oct. 1963 (the de Ribbing report).

——, (1965). *Question of Oman*, A/5846 of 22 Jan. 1965 (the Ad Hoc Committee report).

United States Department of Agriculture. (1951). Circular No. 728, *Date culture in the United States*, 1951 edn.

Vita-Finzi, C. (1969). *The Mediterranean valleys*, Cambridge.

Wellsted, Lt. J. R. (1838). *Travels in Arabia*, 2 vols., London.

Weulersse, J. (1946). *Paysans de Syrie et du Proche-Orient*, 2nd edn., Paris.

Wheatley, P. (1959). 'Geographical notes on some commodities involved in Sung maritime trade', *Journal of the Malayan Branch of the Royal Asiatic Society*, xxxii, pt. 2.

The Whitehead Consulting Group. (1972). *Sultanate of Oman economic survey.*

Whitelock, Lt. H. H. (1835). 'An account of Arabs who inhabit the coast . . . called the Pirate Coast', *Transactions of the Bombay Geographical Society*, 1835-6.

Wilkinson, J. C. (1964). 'A sketch of the historical geography of the Trucial Oman down to the beginning of the sixteenth century', *Geographical Journal*, cxxx. 337-49.

—, (1969). 'Arab settlement in Oman: the origins and development of the tribal pattern and its relationship to the Imamate', unpublished D.Phil. thesis, Oxford.

—, (1971). 'The Oman question: the background to the political geography of Southeast Arabia', *Geographical Journal*, cxxxvii. 361-71.

—, (1972). 'The origins of the Omani State', in ed. papers of 1969 S.O.A.S. seminar published as Hopwood, D., *The Arabian Peninsula: society and politics*, London.

—, (1973). 'Arab-Persian land relationships in late Sasānid Oman', *Proceedings* [of the sixth (1972)] *Seminar for Arabian Studies*.

—, (1974). *'Bayāsira* and *bayādīr'*, *Arabian Studies*, i.

(in press). 'The Ibāḍī Imāma', *Bulletin School of Oriental and African Studies*, xxxix.

(in press). 'Bio-bibliographical background to the crisis period in the Ibāḍī Imamate of Oman (end of 9th to end of 14th century)', *Arabian Studies*, iii. 137-64.

(in press). 'The Julandā of Oman', *Journal of Omani Studies*, i.

Wilson, Col. D. (1833). 'Memorandum respecting the pearl fisheries in the Persian Gulf', *Journal of the Royal Geographical Society of London*, iii. 283-6.

Wilson, H. H. (1969). 'Late cretaceous eugeosynclinal sedimentation, gravity tectonics, and ophiolite emplacement in Oman mountains, Southeast Arabia', *The American Association of Petroleum Geologists Bulletin*, liii. 626-71.

Williamson, A. (1973a). 'Hurmuz and the trade of the Gulf in the 14th and 15th centuries A.D.', *Proceedings* [of the sixth (1972)] *Seminar for Arabian Studies*.

—, (1973b). *Sohar and Omani Seafaring in the Indian Ocean*, Muscat.

von Wissmann, H. (1964). 'Ḥimyar, ancient history', *Muséon*, lxxvii. 429-500.

Wright, E. P. (1967?). *Report on the ground water resources of Bahrain*, Institute of Geological Sciences NERC (internal report, n.d. (?1967)).

Wulff, H. E. (1966). *The traditional crafts of Persia*, Cambridge, Massachusets etc.

—, (1968). 'The qanats of Iran', *Scientific American*, ccxviii. 94-105.

von Zambaur, E. (1906). *Kollektion Ernst Prinz zu Windisch-Grätz Beschrieben von Eduard von Zambaur*, vol. i, Orientalische Münzen, Vienna.

APPENDIX

IBĀḌI LAND LAWS

Since this book went to press the writer has had the opportunity, thanks to the kindness of H. E. Sadyi Fayṣal b. ʿAlī, of examining the *fiqh* works in the manuscript collection that is being assembled in the Ministry of National Heritage in Muscat. This material helps expand some of the conclusions reached in the main part of this book, notably in Chapter VII which dealt with the influence of Ibāḍism on land organization in Oman. The following summary of some of the relevant judicial rulings is therefore added to clarify and complement the main text.

The principal sources used are nearly all pre mid-sixth/twelfth century except for the section dealing with abandoned land. Since the nature of these sources is discussed by the present writer in two articles in *Arabian Studies* iii and iv, only a brief list of the main early works relevant to land rulings is presented here:

The *Jāmiʿs* (collected rulings) of Ibn Jaʿfar (A. Jābir Muḥammad b. Jaʿfar of Izki) and A. 'l-Ḥawāri (Muḥammad b. al-Ḥawāri); both authors lived at the end of the third/ninth and in the early fourth/tenth centuries: the *Jāmiʿs* of A. Muḥammad (ʿAbdullāh b. Muḥammad b. Baraka from Bahlā, also known as Ibn Baraka) and of his pupil A. 'l-Ḥasan (ʿAli b. Muḥammad from Bisyā) who date from the end of the fourth/tenth century to the middle of the fifth/eleventh century: the massive legal compendiums of two major authors writing between the end of the fifth/eleventh century to the mid-sixth/twelfth, Muḥammad b. Ibrāhīm al-Kindi's *Bayān al-Sharʿ* (72 volumes) and Aḥmad b. ʿAbdullāh al-Kindi's *K. al-Muṣannaf* (41 volumes). A number of other compilations, notably the anonymous *K. Manthūrat al-Ashyākh* and the *K. Jawhar al-athār* (reputedly by Jumʿa b. ʿAli al-Ṣāʾighi), are based on early Ibāḍi *fiqh* although containing later additions, but the original sources of the rulings are clearly stated. Throughout all these works it is nearly always possible to identify the author of the judgement and this is particularly valuable for dating some of the earliest rulings concerning *aflāj* and land tenure. Other sources will be mentioned where appropriate.

EARLY FALAJ JUDGEMENTS

The problems dealt with in early *falaj* and land judgements not only confirm the thesis that the basic practices of traditional Omani *falaj* organization and terminology were largely determined during the First Imamate but also throw some light on this period of transition. There are two principal aspects dealt with in the rulings: that of regulating the organization of village life within an Islamic framework; and that of ensuring a fair deal for all members of society.

Assimilation

With the earliest *falaj* rulings it is clear from the frequent use of such terms as *fi falaj Islāmi, majūs,* and *dhimmi* that the gap between the two societies in interior Oman was still distinct and that many *aflāj* settlements were in the hands of the non-Muslim population. Joint shareholding between the two communities was not encouraged and it is specifically enjoined that a Muslim should not build on the land of a *dhimmi*. Nevertheless, as shown in the main text of this book, assimilation was taking place, and one of the interesting aspects of this is the extent to which the old organization was absorbed into the new. Amongst the rulings relevant to this subject is the statement that the standard share given by the *hanqari* (landlord) to a worker looking after his property (i.e. the *bīdār*) is one sixth of the produce, although owners may and do give more: this is quite clearly a survival of the pre-Islamic practice (cf. Wilkinson, 1974). Of even greater interest are the forms of agreement between a *falaj* community and what must have been the remnants of the old *muqanni* class. Here the emphasis is always on re-excavating (*ḥafr*) damaged or low-flow *aflāj*: never once is there a hint of constructing new *qanāt*.

The most revealing judgement comes from Saʿīd b. Muḥriz, who was a prominent *ʿālim* from the first half of the third/ninth century. He makes it clear that the standard form of agreement for re-servicing a ruined (*damir*) *falaj* which has been classified as *ramm* (abandoned) or whose limited flow has been determined, is that the *falaj* repairer receives the water rights for ten years. Two practices seem to follow from this. Either the excavator takes over the *falaj* as a going concern for this period 'as did the Majūsi with the Falaj al-Rāḥī' (joint business between the Muslims and non-Muslims with a vengeance!), in which case he is responsible for maintenance; or he hands it over to the community for a stipulated amount (*ʿanā*) in which case it is the community which is responsible for maintenance: should they fail to carry this out properly and the flow declines they are still responsible for the full payment until the ten years are complete. On the other hand, neither party is responsible for a failure of the water supply which cannot be shown to be attributable to negligence.

Another form of contract is to pay for work done, and in a detailed response of A. 'l-Ḥawāri to the people of Muḍaybi (in the Sharqīya) he warns them that the terms must be most carefully stipulated and that they would have no come-back if things did not work out as they hoped. From his communication it would seem that the normal practice was to pay surface work by the day and underground work by the hour: such a basis was necessary because it is not possible to be specific in terms of the volume of soil to be removed. Some maintain that this is possible (as also when digging a well) by classifying the type of soil as solid rock (*ṣafā*), gravel (*ḥashā*), or clay (*madar*), but the general opinion is that excavation is uncertain (*majhūl*) and cannot be made a specification of contract (*thābit*). In the same way such factors affecting the flow of a *falaj* as flooding, blown sand, and collapse are *force majeure* and cannot be held to be the liability of the excavator unless the contract specifically states that he is responsible for the ensuing repairs.

Defining responsibility and limiting potential for dispute

The second set of rulings, those that provide by basic legislation a fair deal for all members of society, may conveniently be divided into two: legislation defining responsibilities and aimed at minimizing disputes over land, and that defining the actual conditions of agreement.

Underlying a mass of *falaj* rulings is the fundamental principle of corporate responsibility: all members of the *falaj* community are responsible for the maintenance and upkeep of the *falaj* as a whole in proportion to their shareholding. The Ḥanbali ruling that upstream members have no responsibility for work downstream of their holdings (Norvelle, M. E. 'Water use and ownership according to the texts of Ḥanbali fiqh', M.A. thesis, McGill Univ., 1974) is never even entertained. Detailed rulings make it clear that this contribution tended to be assessed in terms of manual labour, although doubtless the better-off hired others to do the actual work for them. The same principle, incidentally, is applied to other communal interests, such as the building of defensive walls around a settlement (A. Nabhān Jāᶜid b. Khamīs al-Kharūṣi *c.* 1734-1822, *K. Jawābāt fi Masājid* etc). Conversely decision-making is a communal matter so that, for example, no investment to increase flow or to alter an old-established system of shareholding may be effected without the agreement of all shareholders. Under certain circumstances however, decisions need not be completely unanimous so long as the main shareholders (*jubā*) agree. In the event of a dispute, mechanisms for the appointment of an impartial investigator reporting to the *qāḍi* are laid down; a number of the resulting adjudications are reported in the texts.

Associated with these rulings concerning joint responsibility are safeguards for the interests of minors and missing owners, both of whose property automatically comes under the care of the Imamate authorities. So, for example, whilst an orphan's property is subject to the general provisions obligatory on the community as a whole, some allowance has to be made for his ability to fulfil the obligation and he is not expected to hew hard rock (*ṣafā*), but instead should be put to work cleaning out the silt from a *falaj*.

Another issue that had to be carefully defined in order to avoid inter- and intra-communal disputes was that of the *ḥaram/harīm*, that is the bounding area appertaining to a piece of private or communal property. So the *ḥarīm* of the sea-shore was fixed at 500 *dh(i)raᶜ* (cubit, approximately two-thirds of a metre), access tracks to water at three *dhraᶜ*, four for minor passages in a village, eight for the larger ones between quarters, and forty *dhraᶜ* for roads between centres. This last figure also applied to the *ḥarīm* of a well but for a *falaj* there was a difference of opinion both about the size and its variation once the *falaj* began to subdivide. The general consensus seems to be that 500 *dhraᶜ* applied to the *falaj* before it began to branch, i.e. some 160 m. on either side of the main channel, but around each individual headwater 300 seemed reasonable. In fact these rulings did little more than confirm the practices originally observed when *qanāt* were built, but in the case of *ghayl* flow the rulings were of significance, and there are at least two cases adjudicated on the ground that the points of offtake were too close together (in one the people of the Falaj al-Khawbi claimed that the heaps of spoil excavated from the headwaters of the Falaj Ḍawt, which irrigated Samad Nizwā, were affecting their water supply in the Wadi al-Kalbūh; in the other, the Falaj Dhu Naym, it was clear that the channels of one branch were capturing water from another *falaj*). Associated with these rulings was the principle that access to the headwaters of a *falaj* must not be impeded.

Fair dealings

The material concerning the terms of agreement affecting the land economy is vast and Book xxi of the *Muṣannaf*, for example, includes detailed rulings on contracts between landlords, labour and tenants; as also for weaving, building, inter- and intra-national transportation by land and sea, the hire of boats, mining (these incidentally show that mining was still being carried out both in the Wādi al-Jizzi and near Izki in the early sixth/twelfth century), guards, look-outs, bird-scarers, and shepherds (a ruling of A. 'l-Ḥawāri whereby the owner is liable for the complete month's payment of the *per capita* fee due to the shepherd, even if he sells some of the sheep and goats, shows that in this domain too the traditional practices (see p. 119 are of considerable antiquity). Other business arrangements, notably those dealing with loans, pre-emptions, and options, are equally fully treated in the literature, and, taken in combination with the detailed rulings given for the collection of taxes, illustrate just how carefully the Ibāḍis regulated the socio-economic system and how meticulous they were to see that injustices were avoided.

Only one aspect from this plethora of early legislation on contracts will be touched on, that concerning tenancy agreements (*qaʿādat al-arḍ*).

The early sources confirm that the Ibāḍi ethos was opposed to all forms of profiteering and speculation in land. The extreme case is put by perhaps the greatest of the early jurists, A. Saʿīd al-Kudami (early fifth/eleventh century), who maintains that all renting of land, whether for money, share of produce, or by partnership agreement is immoral and that it should be given free. Such an ideology was of little practical legal value, but it does illustrate the Ibāḍi attitude and shows why the law comes down firmly in favour of the tenants' interests.

So it is held that all tenancy agreements are *majhūl*; this, in effect, means that the risks of cultivation are not specifiable so that extenuating circumstances may be taken into consideration when judging a dispute between landlord and tenant. Both parties must share these risks so that rent may only be taken in the form of a share of the crop (*qaʿādat al-arḍ b'l-ḥabb*), although water (that is, owned water, not in its free state) may be rented for money. Extenuating circumstances affecting the landlord are much less easily invoked: if the water supply diminishes then the landlord must carry out the necessary action to restore the flow; if he fails to supply the fertilizer in a standard agreement then he is in default. The tenant is also protected from sharp practices such as the owner making an agreement for an area of mixed cultivation for one year and then claiming the fruit from the tree crops on the grounds that it was not ripe before the end of the lease. The landlord is also ultimately responsible to the Imamate for the payment of tax on produce from his land.

ABANDONED LAND

It is notable that the early sources have little to say on the subject of *ramm* beyond the principle, already noted, that reviving abandoned *aflāj* is normally payable by ten years of its water rights. The implication perhaps, is that abandoned land was not a particularly important feature in the early Ibāḍi period. In contrast when we come to the period when Ibāḍi rulings start to reappear after the 'Dark Ages' the subject is treated at length, thus confirming that much land was abandoned and the original ownership forgotten during the Nabāhina period. It must be noted however, that the basic principles from which these rules derive, and which would doubtless have applied in the earlier period, did little to encourage reviving old settlements since they make the legal acquisition of ownership rights virtually impossible. It is only with the bending of these laws from the middle of the seventeenth century onwards that major restoration was undertaken.

These basic principles derive from the laws of *uṣūl* (*mulk* ownership rights). Briefly, these state that all land that has been brought under cultivation, or has been built on, has ownership rights (*uṣūl*). New ownership rights may be created by whoever first colonizes barren (*mawāt*) land outside existing settlements. Ownership rights may be inherited, bought, or sold etc., but all such changes should be registered in a properly drawn-up document.

When land goes out of cultivation, the *uṣūl* rights still remain vested in the original owners. In villages the ownership rights to abandoned (*ramm*) land, are generally known, so anyone who wants to bring it back under occupancy may negotiate with the owner. Problems only really arise when the ownership is unknown or imprecisely defined. Three particular cases are of importance: that where the original ownership is known but the heritage not divided over several generations (this particularly applies to abandoned land belonging to a clan group): that where the land has long since been abandoned and the ownership is untraceable: and that where the land has been illegally seized and abandoned, and then falls back under Imamate control.

Two basic solutions apply, but there is dispute over which is the more correct: either the land is deemed to belong to the absent (*ghawāyib*) and so passes under the jurisdiction of the Imam; if the successors cannot be traced the benefits go to the poor (a variant of this is that the land passes into the state property (*ṣawāfi*) and the revenue is used for the general advancement of the community (*ʿizz al-dawla*)): or it is adjudged as belonging to the dead (*ḥashrīya*) and may never be touched unless a true claimant appears to inherit it.

Some particular cases will illustrate how these rules have been applied. The earliest are drawn from the *K. Khizānat al-ʿubbād*, a collection of judgements by Aḥmad b. Maddād b. ʿAbdullāh b. Maddād, the leading *qāḍi* of the middle of the tenth/sixteenth century.

The main case deals with the considerable area of more or less abandoned land in the Bahlā area, notably the huge settlement of Salūt, once the centre from which the Achaemanids colonized the Jawf by means of *qanāt* (cf. Chapter VI), Sayfam, and Jumāḥ (near Jabrīn). These places were illegally seized some time before the end of the fifth/eleventh century because the *Bayān al-Sharʿ* declares them *buldān maghṣūba*; this made it illegal for anyone to eat, buy, or sell produce originating there. In due course this land seems to have been more or less abandoned although a few people appear to have tried to re-cultivate it in the sort of way that is happening today at Salūt. The first recorded attempt to regularize this situation was by a prominent *ʿālim* who lived during the first attempts by the Ibāḍis to evict the Nabāhina and restore their Imamate, Ṣāliḥ b. Waḍḍāḥ al-Manḥi (d. 1471). His ruling was that although the land had originally been illegally seized, none of the legal claimants could be traced and so it fell into the domain of the Imam who might permit cultivation by the poor 'for the duration of their poverty'. This ruling was subsequently reversed by Aḥmad b. Mufarrij who refused permission to someone to cultivate there on the grounds that it was *māl ḥashri*, and so forbidden forever, even for the poor or the benefit of the state. Aḥmad b. Maddād, on the other hand, accepted Ṣāliḥ's original ruling, and at the same time confirmed both his father's and grandfather's lifting of the ban on the produce of this land on the grounds that the situation was far from clear and that some of the present cultivators might well descend from the original holders. Aḥmad made no judgement in the case of another place called Ajrad, because he had been unable to find anything about its legal status in the sources (*athār*).

Aḥmad also upheld Ṣāliḥ's judgement that in a situation where the original ownership of abandoned land is known but the individual rights of the inheritors cannot be traced the land should not be considered as *māl ḥashri*, as some maintained, but that it could be cultivated by the poor, with preference being given to the poor of the clan concerned. In none of these cases, of course, could the cultivators acquire the *uṣūl*.

Finally Aḥmad b. Maddād gives some interesting judgements on when a missing person (*ghāyib*) may be presumed dead: these cases show that this varies from four to eighty years depending on the circumstances and the nature of the testimony concerning the probability of the missing person's decease.

The next major case traced involved regulating the situation over the enormous amount of abandoned land on the Batina coast (see p. 124) once the Imamate was fully restored under Nāṣir b. Murshid al-Yaʿrabi (1034/1624-5 – 1050/1640). The main judgement by Nāṣir's chief elector, Khamīs b. Saʿīd al-Shaqṣi, I found written on a copy (made in 1118/1707 for the then Wāli of Ṣuḥār) of the volume (18?) dealing with land matters in Khamīs's monumental *Minhaj al-Ṭālibīn*. His ruling was that where there are traces of previous occupancy the land belongs to the *ghawāyib* (absent) and so cannot be possessed in *mulk*: it falls within the domain of the Imamate authorities who may deal with it as they see correct. Those who cultivate it pay no other imposition than the normal *zakāt*, which is five per cent when watered by *zijar* (*zigar*, see p. 73) wells and ten per cent when watered by flowing water (*sayḥ*) provided the amount exceeds the tax-free allowance (*niṣāb*). But it is not dead land (*mawāt*) and so its *uṣūl* cannot be acquired. A further clarification is given by the *ʿālim* Masʿūd b. Ramḍān who states that where the boundaries of the abandoned land are not clear or are covered by more recent cultivation then it is a matter for the Imam's local officials to decide with those concerned.

In this judgement from the begining of Yaʿāriba times one is already seeing the start of a shift away from the stricter stances of the earlier period: the abortive ruling that such land is *māl ḥashri* is not even discussed whilst the question of whether the Imamate authorities should use the land for the poor or, alternatively, for the more general needs of the state are not dealt with. Further flexibility of approach must have been provided by a judgement of a chief *qāḍi* of the second half of the seventeenth century, A. ᶜAbdullāh Muḥammad b. ᶜAbdullāh b. Jumᶜa b. ᶜUbaydān concerning an abandoned *falaj* in Suᶜāl Nizwā: that if it cannot be shown that it had come under Muslim organization or belonged to Muslims then it is *mawāt* and belongs to whoever revives it. Since the only proof of such Islamization would be documentary this judgement meant that much abandoned land could now be considered as *mawāt*. In other words the emphasis shifted so that abandoned land was presumed *mawāt* unless contrary evidence could be produced.

So with a pretty flexible set of rules in force and with the Imams increasingly blurring the distinction between their official and dynastic property the way was open for a major re-exploitation of the land by the second half of the seventeenth century. Individual groups could and did recolonize abandoned land but in effect it was the Yaᶜāriba Imams themselves who had the means to do so on a large scale. The Imam Balᶜarab b. Sulṭān developed his palace-fort capital at Jabrīn on land that a couple of centuries earlier Aḥmad b. ᶜAbdullāh had declared was for the benefit of the poor, whilst his brother Sayf b. Sulṭān reputedly held a third of the *uṣūl* in the country, so earning him the title *Qayd al-Arḍ*.

WARFARE AND PROPERTY

One other aspect of Ibāḍi law affecting the land which receives detailed treatment in the sources is the conduct of Ibāḍis in warfare and in subsequent victory or defeat.

The basic rule is absolutely clear, and it is in this that the Ibāḍis radically differ from the extremist Khawārij sects: all Muslims are *ahl al-qibla*. This includes those who apostasize from Ibāḍism as well as those who oppress and do wrong (*jabābira, ahl al-baghi*). It follows therefore, that there is no booty (*ghanīma*) to be taken from their property nor enslavement of their persons: only illegally acquired property (and in effect this usually only affects the official estates of the ruling dynasty) may be taken by the Imam for restitution to the rightful owners (the rules for this are highly complex). Outside the actual war situation, it is absolutely forbidden to burn, ravage, cut down, or otherwise destroy the property of the enemy, or kill them. Even the property of the Omanis who went over to the Qarāmiṭa (Carmathians) was spared once Ibāḍi rule was re-established in interior Oman in the early fourth/tenth century, but in this particular case their houses were burnt if they refused to come back and live in their villages (cf. the letter of A. 'l-Ḥawāri to the Ḥaḍrami Ibādis).

The real problem arises from what is permitted in dealing with a revolt or in expeditions against the enemy. This subject is discussed at considerable length in the so-called *Sīrat al-barrara* in which Aḥmad b. ᶜAbdullāh al-Kindi (the author of the *Muṣannaf*) replies to the accusations made by his old teacher over the way the Imam Muhammad b. A. Ghassān had conducted the siege of ᶜAqr Nizwā (probably at the very beginning of the sixth/twelfth century). In this he says that whilst he agrees with Bashīr b. Muhammad b. Maḥbūb b. al-Raḥīl's exposition (the *K. al-Muḥāriba* written towards the turn of the fourth/tenth century) that killing, burning, laying siege and cutting of supplies of food, water, and materials are an integral part of warfare, such acts should always be carried out with a minimum of violence (e.g. rather than killing one should try and take prisoner). With specific regard to the agricultural domain; the fruit of crops may be removed in order to deprive the enemy of food but actually cutting down palms is a much more extreme action, and may only be justified if it clearly is going to bring a difficult siege to an end. Similarily *aflāj* may be cut but never destroyed.

The final set of rules concern the conduct of Ibāḍis in defeat: they very largely derive from the leading *ʿulamā* who lived at the time when interior Oman was under foreign occupation at the end of the third/ninth century, A. 'l-Muʾthir al-Ṣalt b. Khamis, Ibn Jaʿfar, Bashīr b. Muḥammad al-Raḥīli and A. 'l-Ḥawāri. Conduct should be guided by prudence (*taqīya*), but co-operation should be absolutely minimal and never given when it will lead to injustice against a member of the community.

From the point of view of the land this means that the Ibāḍis may continue to cultivate even if this means that it will bring benefit to the oppressor; but this is to ensure the survival of the community and the individual should never attempt to profit from the situation, *a fortiori* by working on illegally seized land (all dealings in the produce of such land is absolutely forbidden to members of the Muslim community). Where a 'sultan' seizes a proportion of the water rights on a *falaj* rules are given of how to distribute the burden so that it falls fairly on all the shareholders. The problem of recognizing the authority of a 'sultan' through carrying appeals to him is hotly debated, but it seems that Bashīr b. Muḥammad (who was the leading Ibāḍi *qāḍi* in the occupied area of Ṣuḥār) permitted the people of Lawā to do so when their land was seized. For the same reason taxation should not be collected on behalf of the tyrant nor is the individual absolved from *zakāt* as the result of paying such taxes unless these have been correctly assessed and collected as *zakāt* (e.g. the way most native Sultans have collected taxes outside periods of Ibāḍi rule in Oman). Finally, and in this is perhaps to be found the quintessence of Ibāḍism, one should not be dishonest in one's dealings with the *jabābira*.

GLOSSARY

Brief definition of main foreign words used in the text.

aflāj: plural of *falaj* (q.v.).

ʿālim: sing. of *ʿulamāʾ* (q.v.).

ʿarīf: official who supervises the day-to-day running of a *falaj* (q.v.).

ʿaṣabīya: sense of group unity (tribal).

athar: a time share on a *falaj*, approximately half-an-hour.

ʿawābi: seasonally cultivated land.

bāda: the day or night half of the 24-hour day (water distribution).

al-Baḥrayn: old name for the area of Eastern Arabia extending from present-day Kuwait to Qatar including the Ḥasā province of Saudi Arabia.

bajada (pronounced bahāda): zone of coalescing outwash fans at foot of mountains (geographical term).

bayādīr: plural of *bīār* (q.v.).

bayt al-māl: communal property of the Muslim state.

bedu (*badw*): tribal nomads.

bīdār: an agricultural labourer with particular duties.

dār: tribal territory.

dawrān: cycle of water distribution on a *falaj*.

dhimmis: protected non-Muslim population.

falaj: system for distributing a water supply.

fiqh: Islamic jurisprudence.

ghayl: semi-permanent surface or near-surface flow in a wadi (q.v.).

hadhar (*ḥaḍar*): settled peoples.

hanqari (pl. *hanāqira*): a capitalist; important landlord or merchant.

ḥarbi: person originating from a territory which has not submitted to the *dār al-Islām* (the Muslim state).

Ibāḍism: the main *madhhab* (q.v.) of Oman; begins to develop at the end of the first century of Islam. Also survives in a few isolated communities in North Africa, notably in the Wadi Mzàb.

ʿilm: religious learning.

Imam (*Imām*): head of the Islamic / Ibāḍi state.

jabābira: lit. tyrants: collective term for non-constitutional rulers in Ibāḍi law.

jabal: mountain.

jadd: grandfather, tribal forebear.

jihād: Islamic war.

khabūra: the basic units of shareholding on a *falaj* (q.v.).

madhhab: Islamic 'school'.

majlis: assembly room.

majūs: lit. Magians, followers of the 'old' religion in Oman.

mawlā (pl. *mawāli*): person or group in 'client' status.

mulk: Islamic equivalent of freehold.

mulūk (sing. *mālik*): prince, local ruler.

muqanni: *qanāt* (q.v.) builder.
nisba: a surname deriving (usually) from a proper name and indicating relationship to it e.g. Rāshidi from Rāshid (person), Izkāwi from Izki (place).
playa: zone of evaporation in an internal drainage basin.
qāḍi: Islamic judge.
qanāt (sing. or pl.): a horizontal well bringing water from an aquifer (water bearing formation) by means of a tunnelled or 'cut and cover' (cut from the surface and re-covered) gallery.
ramm: abandoned land.
sabkha: salt-flat.
sayḥ (*sēḥ*): gravel plain.
sayl: ephemeral flow in a wadi: flood.
shaikh (*shaykh*): head of a tribe.
sharīʿa: the canonical law of Islam: the point where pure water is drawn on a *falaj* (q.v.).
shawāwi: nomads of the mountain zone.
Sultan (*sulṭān*): a title; normally applied to non-Imam rulers of Oman.
Sunni: 'orthodox' Islam.
tamīma: paramount leader of an important tribal grouping.
ʿulamāʾ: those having *ʿilm* (q.v.), i.e. the religious leaders of the Imamate.
ʿulūj (sing. *ʿilj*): the common (non-Arab) people of the Sasānid lands.
wadi: valley or drainage channel in an arid region (normally dry).
wakīl: Islamic agent.
wāli: local governor.
waqf: inalienable bequest made for charitable purposes; Islamic mortmain.
zakāt: Islamic tax.

INDEX

1. numbers in italics refer to Figure numbers:
2. tribal and family names are normally classified under the main name, not Āl, Awlād, Bani etc; exceptionf Āl Bu, Umbu:
3. individuals are normally classified under the family *nisba* with the exception of Imams and Āl Bu Saʿid Sultans:
4. names of Falajs are to be found under the main name, but Wadi and Jabal names will be found under those entries:
5. Arabic words are normally classified under the singular form:

ʿAbbāsids, 10, 173, 224-5
ʿAbd al-Qays, 177, 196, 199, 237n14, 247, *33*
ʿAbdullah Ibn Ibāḍ, 153n4
ʿAbriyīn, 205, 220-1, *25*
ʿAbs, 187n7, 247
Abu Bilāl Mirdās, 153n1
Abu Dhabi (Ẓabi), 4-6, 23, 26, 34n11, 53-7, 71n3, 72n7, 88, 154n14, 241, *7, 8, 11*
Abu Isḥāq Ībrāhīm b. Qays al-Hamdāni (Ḥaḍrami Imam), 153n1
Abu Zayd — see under Riyāmi
Achaemanids, 76, 85, 122, 126-30, 132
Adam, 51n1, 192, 230, 237n7, *5*
adaptation to desert environment, 58ff
ʿAdāwina, 218, 231, 238n4
aflāj — see under *falaj*
Aflāj Bani Qitab, 193-4, *4, 7*
agriculture, 26-32, 49, 54-6, 58, 92-5, 126, 241-3 — see also under individual crops, livestock-herding, irrigation
Ajman (ʿAjmān), 5-6, *7*
Aḥmad b. Saʿid (Imam), 216
Āl Bu Saʿid, xiv, 2, 50, 107, 154n8, 183, 197, 207n15, 216-7
Āl Bu Shāmis, 70, 171, 190-1, 194, 196, *25*
alfalfa — see under fodder crops
Algeria, 29-30, 230
ʿĀmir Rabiʿa/Ṣaʿṣaʿ, 195-6, 199, 207n15, 225, 247
aquifers, 17, 44, 46-50, 51n1, 57, 71n1, 77ff
Arab migrations into Oman, 10, 65, 88, 116, 126-31, 142, 176-8, 182, 196, 198-205, 224, *33*
archaeology, 86, 129-30, 135n6, 236n1
Arḍ al-Hind, 131
ʿarif, 94, 101, 109-10, 117, 119-20, 215, 230
ʿaṣabiya (tribal cohesiveness), 54, 159, 162, 164, 171, 180-2, 185-6, 187n8, 198-205, 217ff, *23*
assimilation of population groups, 116, 135, 140-3, 149, 167-71, 178, 191, 194-5, 198, 206nn7 & 14, 207n15, 215, 217, 221, 230, 238n1, 258-9
astromony, 106-11
ʿAtīk, 182, 184, 188n12, 191, 245, *33*
attitudes towards the land, 1, 74, 83-4, 93, 101, 122-3, 148, 193-8, 227
auctions, 70, 112-13, 120, 215, 237n10
ʿAwābi (ancient al-Sawni), 121n7, 205, 246, *3, 5*
ʿAwāmir, 120, 122, 195-7, 206n13, 229, *25*
ʿAwf (Bani), 233
ʿAwtabi, Salma b. Muslim, 134n3, 174, 186n5
ʿayāl, 157-62
Azd, 126-31, 134n3, 135n6, 170, 176-7, 184, 196, 199-201, 220, 225, 238n4, *30, 33*
——, ʿImrān, 176, 188n12, 191, 199, 245
——, Mālik b. Fahm, 126-30, 134n3, 135n4, 174, 176, 186n4, 200, 206n11, 207n16, 238n4, 245, 247
——, Shanuʾa, 128, 131, 174, 176, 182, 201-2, 205, 245
ʿAzīz/ʿAzāzina, 193-4, 206n5
ʿAzzān b. Qays (Imam), 155n16, 183, 217, 230

Badīya, 16, 91, 93-4, 99, 108-9, 224, *2*
Bahlā, 100, 143, 150-1, 155n21, 182, 188n12, 208, 245, 258, 262, *3, 5*
Baḥr al-Ṣāfi, 47
Bahrain, xiii, 20, 22, 25, 34n12,
——, meteorological data, 36ff
al-Baḥrayn, xiii, 56-7, 71n1, 127, 142, 196, 199-201, 207n15, 225, 247
Balūch/Balūsh, 8, 199, 207n15, 216, 237n12, *25*
Bandar ʿAbbās, 10
Banians — see under Hindus
Barkā, 202, *5*
Barr al-Ḥikmān, 46, *9*
Basra (al-Baṣra), 93, 134, 137, 153n2, 186n4, 207n16, 247
Bāt, 196, *4*
Batina coast, 8, 15-17, 26-7, 29-31, 35n18, 47-9, 67, 71n3, 73, 83-4, 94, 97-8, 124, 126, 132, 135n8, 147, 169, 191, 197-8, 202, 215, 223, 263, *2, 10, 33*
al-Bawshar, 44, 182
Baynūna, 56, 71n3, 243, *7*
baysari (pl. *bayāsira*), 142, 217, 231-2
Bayt al-Falaj, 197
bayt al-māl, 68-70, 139, 149-51, 155nn18 & 20, 213, 236n4
bedu (*badw*) — see under nomads
bīdār (pl. *bayādīr*), 101, 109-10, 119-20, 121n9, 131, 133, 142, 193, 215, 217, 236n6, 259
Bidbid, 41, *3*
Bilād Sayt, *3*
Birkat al-Mawz, 126, 217, *3*
al-Bizayli (Falaj), 134n2, 190-1
British influence, 5, 10, 34n12, 90, 242